Irredentism in European Politics

Territorial disputes and irredentist disputes are very prone to escalation and very difficult to resolve. Since the end of the Second World War, however, European states have tended to resolve their irredentist disputes peacefully. Markus Kornprobst argues that this pattern has arisen due to the emergence of a territorial status quo norm in the region. A study of all territorial claims made in Europe since 1848 and in the world since 1945 provides the background for detailed examinations of German and Irish irredentism, through which the author traces the development of the territorial status quo norm based on argumentation and compromise. Developing new theoretical and methodological tools to study norm selection, this book will be of interest to scholars and students of international relations, nationalism and European studies.

MARKUS KORNPROBST is Professor of International Relations at the Diplomatic Academy of Vienna.

Irredentism in European Politics

Argumentation, Compromise and Norms

MARKUS KORNPROBST

CAMBRIDGE UNIVERSITY PRESS
Cambridge, New York, Melbourne, Madrid, Cape Town, Singapore, São Paulo, Delhi

Cambridge University Press
The Edinburgh Building, Cambridge CB2 8RU, UK

Published in the United States of America by Cambridge University Press, New York

www.cambridge.org
Information on this title: www.cambridge.org/9780521895583

First published 2008

Printed in the United Kingdom at the University Press, Cambridge

A catalogue record for this publication is available from the British Library

ISBN 978-0-521-89558-3 hardback

Für meine Eltern

Contents

Figures

Maps and tables

Acknowledgements

Doing research may at times resemble the solitary life of a medieval monk who, hidden behind mighty walls and stacks of books, ponders about the world. Research, however, is much more than that. It involves listening, arguing, persuading and becoming persuaded – in short, reflection through the interaction with others. One's research mirrors this interaction in myriad ways. Some of them can be easily acknowledged in a footnote. Others – and these are the most profound influences – go much too deep for a footnote to capture them.

It is the latter and especially precious category that I seek to capture in these acknowledgements. First of all, I want to thank my former fellow graduate students at the University of Toronto for sharing the ups and downs of doing a Ph.D. with me, in particular Corneliu Bjola, Sebastian Dallaire, Marie Desrosiers, Jan Erk, Joshua Hjartarson, Juan Marsiaj, Michele Mastroiani, Anthony Matthew, Vincent Pouliot, Nisha Shah, Reuven Shlozberg, Allona Sund, Anil Varughese and Ruben Zaiotti. Many of the ideas fleshed out in this book developed in discussions with them. Betty, Ray and Sarah Hipworth I wish to thank for all their hospitality – a home away from home in fact – and Sarah, in addition to this, for converting my Bavarico-German English into something intelligible for an English-speaker.

Funding for this research was generously provided by an Ontario Graduate Scholarship, a Joint Initiative in German and European Studies Graduate Award from the Munk Centre for International Studies, University of Toronto, as well as postdoctoral fellowships at the Mershon Center, Ohio State University, and the Department of Politics and International Relations, University of Oxford. There are many teachers and colleagues to whom I am deeply indebted for their comments and criticisms. Lawrence LeDuc convinced me that the really important question about irredentist disputes in Europe is why they are resolved and not why they escalate. Ronald Beiner provided me with insightful comments on the link between epistemes and identity.

Michael Barnett gave me very detailed comments on the theoretical and
empirical sections of this study, which have helped me tremendously to
further elaborate on various aspects of this book. Discussing my work
with Nina Berman, Ted Hopf, Andrew Hurrell, Jennifer Mitzen, Daniel
Nexon and Alexander Wendt has not only always been a true pleasure
but also helped me see my ideas about argumentation and compromise
in a new light. Two anonymous referees and John Haslam provided me
with greatly appreciated and very constructive criticism. Alexander
Volsky's superb research assistance made it possible for me to follow
the leads offered by this criticism. John Haslam was a very helpful editor
who guided me through the process of converting this study from a
manuscript into a book.

Susan Gross Solomon and Janice Gross Stein accompanied this
research from the starting to the finishing line. I wish to thank them in
particular for helping me bundle my diverse research interests into a
manageable and for me very exciting research project, and for encouraging me to dig deeper into a number of crucial theoretical and empirical
issues throughout the years I spent working on this project. There are
also many reasons for me to thank Steven Bernstein. I have learnt a lot
from our frequent discussions throughout my time as a graduate student in Toronto. My earlier study on border disputes in Africa, which
borrowed from his reasoning on norm hierarchies and advocacy, was a
blueprint for this study. He helped me in many ways to make a disserta-
tion out of this blueprint. Perhaps most importantly, I developed my
ideas as to how to link the modes of reasoning and the empirical cases in
numerous discussions with him. Most of all, I want to thank Emanuel
Adler for making me curious, encouraging me to venture out into the
unknown and to draw my own conclusions from these voyages. To the
informed reader, my borrowing from his ideas will be most obvious in
the sections where I write about revolutionary events and the episteme.
Yet our discussions went well beyond this, and dealt in depth with every
major theoretical, methodological and empirical aspect of the topic.

I was very fortunate to have the unequivocal support of my family
and close friends. Ndinodakutenda Sheila nekundibatsira kupedza dis-
sertation; nekundibikira sadza nenyama yehwai zvisingawonike nyore
kuno; nekushingirira kugara neni panguva yandakanga ndisina bet-
sero; nekufadza mweyawangu; nekuva nevimbiso neni; nekundimiri-
ira; asi zvikuru, rudo rwaaindiratidza. Rudo rwako rwakandisimbisa.
Meinen Eltern und Großeltern möchte ich für so vieles danken; ganz

besonders jedoch dafür, dass sie mir immer die Freiheit zugestanden haben, meine Entscheidungen selbst zu treffen, und dass sie mich in ihnen bestärkt haben – selbst dann, als mich diese von einem Kontinent zum nächsten verschlugen. Ich widme dieses Buch meinen Eltern; meiner Mutter, die, viel zu früh verstorben, sich sehr über diese Arbeit gefreut hätte; und meinem Vater, mit dem zusammen mich über dieses Buch zu freuen, mir eine große Freude ist.

Abbreviations

AUD	Aktionsgemeinschaft Unabhängiger Deutscher (Activist Movement of Independent Germans)
BP	Bayernpartei (Bavarian Party)
CDU	Christlich Demokratische Union (Christian Democratic Union)
CnaP	Clann na Poblachta (Family of the Republic)
CPSU	Communist Party of the Soviet Union
CSU	Christlich Soziale Union (Christian Social Union)
DKP	Deutsche Kommunistische Partei (German Communist Party)
DL	Democratic Left
DP	Deutsche Partei (German Party)
DRP	Deutsche Reichspartei (German Empire Party)
EC	European Community
EEC	European Economic Community
EU	European Union
FDP	Freie Demokratische Partei (Liberal-democratic Party)
FF	Fianna Fáil (Soldiers of Destiny)
FG	Fine Gael (Gaelic Nation)
FRG	Federal Republic of Germany (Bundesrepublik Deutschland)
GDR	German Democratic Republic (Deutsche Demokratische Republik)
ICEM	Irish Council of the European Movement
IFF	Independent Fianna Fáil (Soldiers of Destiny)
IMS	Irish Marketing Surveys
IND	Independent Deputy
IRA	Irish Republican Army
KPD	Kommunistische Partei Deutschlands (Communist Party of Germany)
LB	Labour Party
MRBI	Market Research Bureau of Ireland
NATO	North Atlantic Treaty Organisation

NPD	Nationaldemokratische Partei Deutschlands (National-democratic Party of Germany)
PD	Progressive Democrats
SDLP	Social Democratic and Labour Party
SPD	Sozialdemokratische Partei Deutschlands (Social Democratic Party of Germany)
WAV	Wirtschaftliche Wiederaufbauvereinigung (Economic Reconstruction Coalition)
WEU	West European Union
Z	Zentrumspartei (Centre Party)

Introduction

This study is about two pervasive aspects of the social world: argumentation and compromise. We listen to arguments, make arguments and exchange arguments in order to make up our minds about something and in order to persuade others to make up their minds in the same way we do. Some arguments convince us. We are persuaded by the line of reasoning that the argumentation contains. Other arguments, by contrast, are unconvincing. They do not make sense to us. There are different degrees of non-persuasiveness. Some arguments violate our most deeply held beliefs. They upset us, we firmly reject them in their entirety, and we do not even consider abandoning our stance. Others, by contrast, do not violate our most fundamental beliefs and we discard them with less vigour. Since we feel less strongly about our opposition, we are prepared to compromise on our stance if there are incentives to do so.

It is my contention that argumentation and compromise provide a generative mechanism through which nations come to select norms. I depart from the existing literature on norm selection in three important ways. First, my research inquires in depth not only into the international but also the domestic processes through which nation-states select norms. The field of International Relations continues to exhibit a strong tendency to conduct research on the international without the national or to narrow the latter down to elite interactions. Much of the literature on norm selection shares this tendency. Yet the exclusive focus on elites is a convenient but frequently misleading theoretical and analytical shortcut. Domestic processes, involving government elites, civil society actors and the public, are often of key relevance for the explanation of norm selection.

Second, I elaborate on the advocacy literature in several ways. Proposing a sociological theory of agency, I address the neglected question of why actors engage in an advocacy in the first place. Furthermore, I overcome the neglect of world views by including the episteme – i.e. a taken-for-granted lens, comparable to a paradigm, through which

actors look at the world – in my theoretical framework. And, perhaps
most importantly, the literature's insight that successful argumentation
involves the construction of a linkage between already established ideas
and the advocated idea is not the end but merely the starting point of my
inquiry. I distinguish in detail the properties of links that make an
argument persuasive from those that fail to do so.

Third, I do not dichotomise Rationalist and Constructivist selection
mechanisms but propose a synthesis. If a number of conditions are
present, nations come to select norms in three ideal-typical stages: innovative argumentation, persuasive argumentation and compromise. An
innovative normative advocacy, triggered by a change of the environment
in which agents are embedded, persuades large segments of elites and
public by constructing a compelling link between ideas that are already
established and the advocated normative idea, and, finally, recalcitrant
actors bend to the pressure of the newly established majority stance.

The occurrence of these three stages is contingent on a number of
conditions. Much of this book is concerned with identifying these conditions. The environmental change providing the impetus for agents to
engage in innovative argumentation may be constituted by a revolutionary event and/or by a shifting repertoire of commonplaces. The revolutionary event, such as large-scale violence and destruction, makes it
obvious to actors that the old ways of doing things have to change. The
changing repertoire – i.e. the pool of taken-for-granted ideas upon which
agents draw to make the world intelligible to themselves – provides
advocates with novel clues for how the new should look.

Persuasive argumentation requires advocates to construct what is
to their audience a compelling link between the repertoire of commonplaces and the advocated idea. In order to map this construction in detail,
I unpack the repertoire of commonplaces and examine what constitutes
the repertoire, and I also identify what elements of the repertoire as well
as what linkages between these elements and the advocated idea make for
a compelling argument. I contend that the repertoire is constituted by
episteme, identity and already selected norms. Out of this repertoire,
advocates pick those *topoi* (commonplaces) that help them make sense
of the normative idea for which they argue. Advocates link the *topoi* to
the advocated idea in three ways: abstraction (syllogism), comparison
(analogy) and appropriateness (rule-following). Particular linkages
between particular *topoi* and the normative idea are more compelling
to an audience than others.

Finally, even if an advocacy is extraordinarily successful in persuading its audience, it is unlikely that it will convince everybody. Yet the power of an argument is not confined to persuasion. It may sway the unconvinced. A successful advocacy establishes a new majority view. Opposing this dominant stance is costly. This makes recalcitrant actors eager to reach a compromise with the advocates as long as this does not violate their most cherished beliefs. A compromise is impossible if the parties draw upon different ideational pools for making the world intelligible to themselves. If the *topoi* used in the advocates' argumentation are outside of the repertoire of commonplaces held by recalcitrant actors a compromise is impossible.

Pierre Bourdieu cautions that we should refrain from developing 'theoretical theory'. Researchers should not merely talk about concepts but they should try 'making them work' (quoted in Brubaker, 1993: 212). In full agreement with this credo, my theoretical framework seeks to illuminate the dynamics of an important but widely neglected empirical phenomenon: irredentism. In 1648, the Peace of Westphalia institutionalised the sovereign state. Starting with the French Revolution in 1789, Europe's age of revolutions turned the state into the nation-state. A seemingly unshakeable dogma evolved that there ought to be a congruence between the spatial boundaries of the nation and the state. All members of a particular nation ought to live in the same state and this state ought to encompass all of the nation's ancestral homeland. The world, however, is not naturally divided into states and nations. The borders of states and nations are artificially imposed by agents who often disagree about them. More than one nation may call a piece of land part of its homeland. More than one nation may believe that a group of people living in a neighbouring country are co-nationals, and the group identified as co-nationals may or may not share this belief or be divided about the issue itself. These disagreements about what appeared to the protagonists as natural boundaries of the state and the nation gave rise to a plethora of irredentist disputes in Europe from the mid-nineteenth century to the mid-twentieth century. These irredentist disputes proved to be more war-prone and much more difficult to resolve than other forms of territorial conflicts.

Scholarly contributions were not exempt from the spirit of irredentism. Max Boehm wrote his *Europa irredenta* (1923), the last comprehensive study on irredentism in Europe, at a time when the number of irredentist disputes had reached a new peak, the Balkan Wars had demonstrated the volatility of these conflicts, the First World War had shown the destructiveness of modern warfare, and the territorial changes laid down in the Versailles Treaty and the Treaty of Trianon had added new fuel to the already raging irredentist fire in Europe. Boehm was very pessimistic about the future of Europe. He maintained that Europe was flourishing without nationalism but that the contemporary doctrine of nationalism and resulting irredentist conflicts threatened to destroy Europe. Boehm's book, however, did little to prevent this destruction. It was a diatribe against the territorial implications of the Versailles Treaty for Germany and, in some passages, a determined manifesto to fight against them. In this way, his book helped to entrench rather than to overcome irredentist sentiment.

After the end of the Second World War, the nation-state doctrine was exported from Europe all over the globe. This was accompanied by a diffusion of irredentism. Some irredentist disputes, albeit unresolved, have had little impact on world affairs. Swaziland, for example, claims considerable parts of South African territory on the grounds that these areas are Swazi ancestral homeland. This claim never significantly affected Southern African relations. Yet other disputes have been at the core of some of the world's most volatile conflicts, such as Pakistan's claim to the Indian part of Kashmir, Argentina's to the Islas Malvinas (Falkland Islands), Somalia's to the Ogaden, and China's to Taiwan.

Europe, once the exporter of irredentist ideas, however, has somehow succeeded in putting an end to the age of irredentism. In the post-Second World War era, irredentist disputes have become an anomaly in Europe. In the 1950s, almost as many states made irredentist claims as in the inter-war years. Beginning in the late 1960s, however, the overwhelming majority of irredentist disputes have been resolved peacefully by the claimants' recognition of existing borders. Only two disputes – Serbia's claims to territories in Bosnia and Herzegovina as well as Croatia – were settled by force. The aggression of the claimant was rebuked by force. Only one dispute remains. Spain refuses to recognise British sovereignty over Gibraltar. What explains this remarkable development? How have European states, in sharp contrast to Europe's past and other world regions, come to exhibit such a strong tendency to resolve their irredentist disputes peacefully? Why do the peaceful settlements consistently recognise the territorial status quo (and not agree on peaceful territorial change as in previous eras or other world regions)?

I probe the three-stage norm selection mechanism by inquiring into these questions. An examination of argumentation and compromise requires an in-depth analysis. My empirical research focuses on two cases: the irredentist claims by the Federal Republic of Germany (FRG) and the Republic of Ireland. The FRG claimed the entire German Democratic Republic (GDR) and all those territories from Poland and the Soviet Union that had been part of Germany within its 1937 borders, i.e. after the Versailles Treaty and before Hitler's expansionism. It renounced these claims in the early 1970s. The Republic of Ireland claimed Northern Ireland from the United Kingdom and put an end to the claim in 1998. I chose these two cases because they make for an interesting puzzle within the puzzle. While the marked decline of irredentism in post-Second World War Europe poses an important research puzzle, it is particularly puzzling that Bonn renounced its claims almost two decades before Dublin did. Bonn had to reach out across the Iron Curtain. Dublin, by contrast, merely had to come to an agreement with a long-time fellow-member of the European Union.

I argue that the three-stage norm selection mechanism provides a plausible explanation for both cases. First, environmental change, constituted by a shifting repertoire of commonplaces and a revolutionary event, provided the impetus for innovative argumentation. A shocking event – the construction of the Berlin Wall in the German case and the beginning of the Troubles in the Irish case – made it clear to agents that the old ways of doing things had become obsolete, and the new aspects of the repertoire of commonplaces, in particular epistemic and identity change, made it possible for actors to think of alternatives that had previously been inconceivable. An advocacy formed, arguing for the selection of the territorial status quo norm: states ought not to claim territory from other states.

Second, the advocacy resonated with a broad audience. Being persuaded by the argumentation, a growing number of social actors joined the advocacy, and the argumentation increasingly resonated with the public. The successful advocacies in the FRG and the Republic of Ireland linked the advocated normative idea to a number of *topoi* taken from the dominant repertoire of commonplaces by employing abstract, comparative and appropriateness reasoning. The dominant episteme, the Idea of Europe, was a particularly powerful *topos*. In both empirical cases, the taken-for-granted belief in the necessity of overcoming the divisiveness of nation-state borders was the intersubjective foundation for advocacies for – and even against – the territorial status quo norm.

Third, the successful argumentation put pressure on recalcitrant actors to conform. Those who shared the *topoi* invoked by advocates of the territorial status quo norm were eventually prepared to compromise. The advocates failed to convince the most powerful political parties in the FRG and the Republic of Ireland. Yet the Christian Democratic Union (CDU) in the FRG and Fianna Fáil (FF) in the Republic were swayed by the pressure of the newly established majority opinion. Eager to avoid the mounting costs of their recalcitrance, the two parties, who fully shared the *topoi* invoked by the advocates but not the manner in which the advocates linked them to the advocated norm, compromised on their stance.

This book is organised into seven chapters. First, I elaborate on the research puzzle. I list all irredentist disputes between 1848 and 2000 in Europe, and critically review the literature pertaining to irredentism. I criticise in particular the neglect of norms. Second, I develop the three-stage norm selection mechanism. I explain the salience of *topoi* for arguments, conceptualise the reservoir from which they are taken as repertoire of commonplaces, and define the constitutive elements of this repertoire, i.e. episteme, identity and already selected norms. Based on this discussion, I outline the environmental conditions conducive to innovative argumentation, as well as the conditions facilitating persuasive argumentation and compromise. The following two chapters deal with the case of the FRG. The third chapter traces the evolution of the West German repertoire of commonplaces pertaining to the German Question. In chapter 4, I look at how and with what success West German norm entrepreneurs linked elements of the evolving repertoire of commonplaces to the idea of a territorial status quo norm. The fifth and sixth chapters inquire into the evolution of the repertoire of commonplaces on the Irish Question in the Republic of Ireland, and how domestic advocates made use of this evolution for their advocacy for a territorial status quo norm, respectively. Finally, the concluding chapter examines alternative explanations of the two cases, discusses the implications of the findings for the study of irredentism and International Relations theory, and sketches an agenda for further research on argumentation and compromise in world politics.

1 | *Irredentism in Europe*

In 1648, the Peace of Westphalia replaced a system of overlapping authority with a system of clearly demarcated state borders. Two hundred years later and prompted by the French Revolution of 1789, Europe's popular revolutions transformed the state into the nation-state. This added a critical dimension to European affairs. With boundaries between nations having become as significant as borders between states, nations began to strive for the congruence of state and nation boundaries.

The nation-state doctrine gave rise to a new and often deadly kind of international conflict: irredentism. Seeking to reach congruence between the borders of the state and the boundaries of the nation, an unprecedented number of states started to claim territory from other states. Irredentist disputes frequently resulted in full-scale war. When former colonies were finally granted independence, the problem of irredentism started to surface outside Europe as well. The disputes between Pakistan and India over Jammu and Kashmir, Somalia and Ethiopia over the Ogaden, Israel and Syria over the Golan Heights, Argentina and the United Kingdom over the Islas Malvinas (Falkland Islands) are perhaps the best known among a very considerable number of cases.

Since the end of the Second World War, however, and in sharp contrast to Europe's past and other world regions, European states have shown a strong tendency to settle their irredentist disputes peacefully. There is even a consistent pattern of how they are settled peacefully. Almost all irredentist disputes have been resolved by the peaceful *de jure* recognition of the *de facto* existing borders rather than by peaceful territorial change. What explains this remarkable shift? How have European states come to settle their irredentist disputes peacefully in the post-Second World War era? Why have they settled their disputes by the recognition of the territorial status quo?

The purpose of this chapter is to elaborate on this research puzzle and discuss the existing literature pertaining to this puzzle. The chapter is organised into six sections: First, I define irredentism. Second, I examine the importance of studying irredentism for our understanding of world politics. Third, I survey irredentist claims in Europe from 1848 to 2000 and in the world from 1946 to 2000, in order to sharpen the research puzzle. In the final three sections I critically review the literature on irredentism.

Defining irredentism

Amid fears that Europe's post-Cold War future may echo its hyper-nationalistic past, a small literature set on irredentism evolved in the early 1990s. There is a consensus in this literature that irredentism is a particular kind of territorial dispute. Yet there are fundamental disagreements on how exactly to define irredentism. Three contentious issues may be identified: Who is the claimant? What is the motive of the claim? How much of another state's territory is claimed?

First, most scholars use the term irredentism to describe a territorial claim of one state against another (Weiner, 1971; Ben-Israel, 1991; Chazan, 1991; Landau, 1991; Neuberger, 1991; Ambrosio, 2001).[1] Others, however, define irredentism as the attempt of an ethnic minority to be incorporated by the neighbouring 'motherland' (Gutmann, 1991; Reichman and Golan, 1991; Saideman and Ayres, 2000). Donald Horowitz uses both definitions. In his *Ethnic Groups in Conflict* he confines his analysis of irredentism to claims by states (1985: 281–8). Yet similarly to Stefan Wolff (2002), he combines the two definitions in subsequent research (Horowitz, 1991: 10).

Second, among those authors whose definitions identify the state as claimant, there is no consensus on what it is that these states are claiming. Many authors emphasise the ethnic link between a motherland and a minority in a neighbouring country. Irredentist states, according to this definition, seek to retrieve ethnically kindred people and the territory they inhabit from a neighbouring state (Weiner, 1971; Horowitz, 1985, 1991; Reichman and Golan, 1991; Ambrosio, 2001). Some scholars, however, define irredentism literally according to the Italian *terra irredenta*: territory to be redeemed. It is land that is to be

---

[1] David Carment and Patrick James (1995, 1997) are ambiguous on this topic. Their conceptual definition follows Chazan's. Their operational definition partly contradicts the conceptual definition by stating that it is *usually* a state that is the claimant.

retrieved. A government's claim to an ancestral homeland, even if it is not accompanied by the desire to incorporate the people who inhabit it, qualifies – according to this definition – as irredentism (Ben-Israel, 1991; Neuberger, 1991). Finally, there are definitions that include claims to ethnic kin and ancestral homeland (Chazan, 1991; Landau, 1991; Carment and James, 1995).

Third, some definitions of irredentism encompass claims of national unification, i.e. the desire of a state to merge with or annex an entire state (Horowitz, 1985, 1991; Ben-Israel, 1991; Neuberger, 1991). Several definitions, however, rule out claims of national unification by asserting that the claiming state seeks to detach a part of the territory of another state, or tries to retrieve its ethnic kin that constitute a minority in the challenged state (Weiner, 1971; Chazan, 1991; Landau, 1991; Reichman and Golan, 1991; Carment and James, 1995, 1997; Ambrosio, 2001).

For the purposes of this study, I use the following definition: irredentism is a territorial claim by a sovereign state against another sovereign state, aimed at reaching congruence between the boundaries of the nation and the borders of the state. The former are far less tangible than the latter. Whereas state borders are usually more or less unambiguously delimited on maps and even physically demarcated on the ground, national boundaries are imaginations about the spatial limits of the nation. Yet these imaginations appear to the nation as very real. They are persistent and non-selective definitions of a nation's settlement area and ancestral homeland. 'Persistent' means that the imagination of these boundaries rarely changes. It is deeply ingrained in a nation's identity narrative and this does not allow for frequent changes. 'Non-selective' means that this imagination is based on settlement areas of co-nationals and historical regions, and refrains from picking and choosing among these for economic, military or geo-strategic reasons.

This definition of irredentism, along with the definition of the boundaries of the nation, takes the following stances with regard to the above-listed contentious issues on how to define irredentism. First, claims to land and the attempt to retrieve a nation's diaspora qualify as irredentism. Excluding the one at the expense of the other is problematic, because both ancestral homeland and the settlement area of the nation play key roles for imagining a nation's spatial boundaries. Most cases of irredentism are a mixture of both (Carment and James, 1995, 1997). Second, the claimants are states. The dynamics of irredentist claims made by states are very different from those made by non-state actors.

Research on both types of claims is needed, but this study focuses on irredentist claims by states against other states. Finally, the definition includes cases in which a state claims a part of another state's territory as well as cases in which a state claims the entire territory of another state. Excluding the latter is arbitrary. Cases such as North Korea's claim to South Korea (and vice versa), for example, are best classified as irredentist disputes. The central motive of the quest for claiming part of the territory of another state or an entire state is the same: reaching congruence between the borders of the nation and the state. This motive is the defining characteristic of irredentism.

Why study irredentism?

Over a decade ago, Tuomas Forsberg (1995: 9) observed: 'Although territorial disputes are regarded as major diplomatic challenges, knowledge about their nature, occurrence and resolution is weak.' This statement still holds true and applies in particular to irredentist conflicts. Yet is more attention to irredentism actually warranted? What is to be gained from studying irredentism?

There are two principal reasons – one theoretical and the other empirical – that make studying irredentism a very important research enterprise: First, research on irredentism offers an opportunity to scrutinise how and to what extent the international order changes. Current International Relations theory is full of claims that the Westphalian order is not what it used to be. The burgeoning globalisation literature, for instance, makes far-reaching claims about the transformation (Mann, 1997; Wolf, 2001; Prange, 2003; Smelser, 2003) and decline (Cerny, 1995; Brenner, 1999; Lipschutz, 1999; Zürn, *et al.*, 2000; Leggewie, 2001; Robinson, 2003; Walby, 2003) of the nation-state. Yet there is usually very little empirical evidence for these claims. And much of the evidence that is provided focuses on economic and technological processes but neglects to inquire into what the debate is actually about, i.e. the meaning that elites and masses attach to the nation-state (Biswas, 2002; Goldman, 2002).

In a similar vein, the blossoming literature on Europe's evolving regional order puts the meaning that actors attach to borders at the centre of its theoretical assertions. John Ruggie (1998: 173), for example, writes about the possibility of the emergence of the 'first truly postmodern international political form'. Ole Wæver (1995) and

William Wallace (1999) scrutinise the salience of new post-sovereign elements of European order. In the search for analogies for a new order of overlapping authority, Ronald Deibert (1997) and Jörg Friedrichs (2003) suggest the metaphor 'neo-medieval'. Martin Marcussen *et al.* (2001) as well as Thomas Risse (2001) scrutinise the Europeanisation of national identities. Jo Shaw (2001) addresses postnational constitutionalism in the European Union. Jürgen Habermas (1998b) asks the question of whether we are witnessing a transformation to a 'postnational constellation'. Similarly to the globalisation literature, and notwithstanding the fact that these are important arguments dealing with key aspects of Europe's regional order, most authors do not provide empirical evidence for such a reconfiguration of borders in Europe.

Studying irredentism improves on this state of affairs. It provides new insights into the attachment of meaning to the two kinds of borders that have defined much of international and European politics since the Peace of Westphalia in the mid-seventeenth century and the Napoleonic Wars in the early nineteenth century: the borders of the state and the boundaries of the nation. Irredentism is a seismograph that helps us understand what meaning people attach to the borders of the state and the nation. Studying it in detail provides answers to important questions such as the following: How do nations define themselves and distance themselves from others? What significance do nations ascribe to the nation-state? How does the meaning attached to national and state borders change over time?

Yet there is a much more tangible rationale for studying irredentism as well. Irredentism has been a highly destructive force in world politics since the mid-nineteenth century. There is even evidence suggesting that no other issue over which states fight is as war-prone as irredentism (Brecher and Wilkenfeld, 1997a, 1997b; Huth, 1998). A brief and selective overview of some of the most volatile crises from the nineteenth to the twenty-first century illustrates the salience of irredentism. After the dissolution of the Holy Roman Empire in 1806, France annexed Alsace-Lorraine. In 1871, it became part of the newly founded German Empire. In 1919, it returned to France. In between was at least half a century of bitter enmity between France and Germany, fuelled, if not caused, by the dispute over land that they both called their own. Shortly before the outbreak of the Second World War, Nazi Germany provoked the Sudetenland Crisis that was seemingly resolved in the Munich Agreement. Shortly thereafter Hitler invaded Poland – the country that Germany singled out as its arch-enemy after the Versailles Treaty's territorial changes in favour of Poland. Between 1960 and 1990 there were a series of crises between Somalia and Ethiopia over the Somali-inhabited Ogaden in Ethiopia. Full-scale war broke out in 1977. Ethiopia, threatened by Somalia's territorial ambitions, subsequently destabilised Somalia by supporting Somali warlords. In 1982, Argentina invaded the Islas Malvinas (Falkland Islands), which led to war with the United Kingdom.

Four of the most volatile disputes in today's world are about the borders of the state and the boundaries of the nation. Pakistan and India, both nuclear powers, have quarrelled over Jammu and Kashmir since the creation of Pakistan. On several occasions, the dispute threatened to escalate beyond small skirmishes and military posturing. It erupted into war in 1947, 1965 and 1999. Since the creation of Israel, the Arab–Israeli conflict has been fuelled by a plethora of irredentist claims. So far, no fewer than five inter-state wars about territory have been waged (1948, 1967, 1969, 1973, 1982), and although territorial disputes between Jordan and Israel as well as Egypt and Israel have been resolved, a number of explosive issues remain, such as Syria's and Israel's conflict over the Golan Heights. China has been a constant threat to Taiwan, announcing repeatedly that it would invade the island if Taiwan formally declared its independence. Since the Korean War in 1950, North Korea and South Korea remain *de jure* in a state of war with one another. An uneasy truce exists amid North Korea's attempts to acquire nuclear weapons. In short: irredentism has destabilised bilateral relations, regions, and even the entire international system since the advent of the nation-state. Given its significance in world politics, attempting to improve our understanding of irredentist dynamics is surely a warranted research enterprise.

Research puzzle

According to conventional wisdom, the irredentist pattern of destabilising world politics never changes. The same happens over and over again: intractable disputes fuelling, if not causing, enduring rivalries and frequently escalating into war. Much of this conventional wisdom focuses on Europe. In the years immediately following the end of the Cold War, for instance, many authors warned that resurgent nationalism would throw Europe back into the age of irredentism and ethnic conflict of the inter-war years. Newspaper editorials were highly concerned. In the *Wall Street Journal*, Paul Johnson (1988: 1) warned of future irredentist disputes and 'an epidemic of nationalist emotions that threatens to become pandemic'. In the *Star Tribune*, Harold Deutsch (1990: 13) went so far as to argue that Germany might seek another *Anschluss* of Austria and warned of possible border disputes involving Romania, Hungary and the Soviet Union. Jan Urban (1992: 1) argued in a similar vein in the *Washington Post*. Scholars were similarly alarmed (Mearsheimer, 1990; Mayall and Simpson, 1992; Griffiths, 1993; Rotfeld and Karp, 1993). Jervis (1991: 39) put this threat in unequivocal terms:

The resurgent ethnic disputes in Eastern Europe appear much as they were when they were suppressed by Soviet power 45 and 70 years ago. It is almost as if we had simply turned back the clock ... The prospects for international politics in this region are worrisome at best.

Looking closer at the history of irredentism in the world shows, however, how untenable this conventional wisdom is. Patterns of irredentism are not the same across time and space. They vary from era to era and from region to region, and the cycle metaphor does not capture this variance very well. This applies in particular to the settlement of irredentist disputes. Depending on era and region, some settlement patterns are defined by a strong tendency towards peaceful settlement and even towards a certain kind of peaceful settlement such as peaceful recognition of existing boundaries or peaceful territorial change, whereas other settlement patterns exhibit a much more uncompromising propensity of states to pursue irredentist claims.

The following overview of irredentist claims demonstrates this very clearly. Table 1.1 provides an overview of irredentist disputes in Europe from 1848 to 2000. Appendix I explains the coding procedures and lists all cases. Irredentism became a force to be reckoned with in Europe with the popular revolutions in the mid-nineteenth century. Nations in the making began to struggle for a congruence between the boundaries of the nation and the borders of the state. This struggle was highly uncompromising. Between 1848 and 1913, not a single challenging state abandoned its claim by peacefully recognising the sovereignty of the defending state over a disputed territory. There was not even a single challenger revoking an irredentist claim when the defender used force or threatened to use force against the challenger. Four disputes ended by

Table 1.1 *Irredentism in Europe, 1848–2000*

	No settlement	Territorial change by force	Claim revoked by force	Peaceful territorial change	Peaceful recognition
1848–1913	16	3	–	1	–
1919–1938	10	7	2	8	2
1946–2000	1	–	2	0	12

changing state borders in favour of the challenger. In one of these cases, the change was peaceful. In the remaining three, the challenger took the disputed territory by force. Yet the overwhelming number of claims did not end – neither violently nor peacefully. Despite numerous wars and territorial changes, in sixteen cases no settlement was reached.

The inter-war years did not fare much better. Irredentism wrecked Europe and foreshadowed the Second World War. From time to time, there appeared to be some hope for keeping irredentism at bay. Eight claims were settled by peaceful territorial change. For the most part, these were cases in which challenger and defender reached a compromise about competing claims. There were even two disputes that were settled peacefully by the challenger's recognition of the territorial status quo. Yet the dynamics of the remaining cases were very different. Ten disputes remained unresolved, and nine were settled by military might. In seven cases of the latter category, the challenger took the disputed territory by force and in two cases the defender succeeded in forcing the challenger to revoke the irredentist claim.

The post-Second World War pattern, however, is radically different. Between 1946 and 2000, the overall number of irredentist disputes was initially similar to previous eras. Yet at the turn of the millennium only one dispute remained without settlement (Spain versus the United Kingdom over Gibraltar). Only two disputes escalated into war and military defeat in the war made the challenger (Serbia against Croatia and Bosnia-Herzegovina) revoke its irredentist claims. The remaining twelve disputes were peacefully resolved. Equally remarkably, they were resolved in the same way. The challenger recognised the territorial status quo.

These peaceful settlements occurred in three waves. The first wave started with Austria's recognition of the territorial status quo with Italy in 1969. The agreement was modelled after the accord between Sweden and Finland

Table 1.2 *Irredentism in the world, 1946–2000*

	No settlement	Territorial change by force	Claim revoked by force	Peaceful territorial change	Peaceful recognition
Americas	3	–	–	1	–
Central Asia, Far East and Pacific	9	2	–	5	1
Europe	1	–	2	–	12
Near East, Middle East and North Africa	6	3	–	4	–
Sub-Saharan Africa	6	–	–	1	3

over the Åland Islands in 1921. Austria recognised Italy's sovereignty over South Tyrol, and Italy pledged to grant autonomy to the region. This treaty was followed by the FRG's recognition of its borders with the GDR, Poland and the Soviet Union, as well as the GDR's recognition of the status of West Berlin in the early 1970s. Italy and Yugoslavia settled their dispute over Trieste in 1975. The second wave of settlements consisted of Greece's abandonment of its claims to Cyprus and Northern Epirus in Albania in the mid-1980s.[2] Finally, the third wave witnessed the peaceful resolution of irredentist disputes between Estonia and Russia, Latvia and Russia, as well as the Republic of Ireland and the United Kingdom in the latter half of the 1990s. The only case that did not follow the settlement pattern of these three waves was the dispute between Romania and Hungary. Romania was two decades ahead of the first wave when it withdrew its claim to the Hungarian part of Transylvania in 1947.

While this pattern of peaceful settlement through recognition of existing boundaries in post-Second World War Europe marks a sharp break with Europe's past, it is also markedly different from other world regions. Table 1.2 compares the European record with other world

[2] The Cyprus conflict is not an irredentist dispute, as defined in this study. Cyprus is *de facto* divided into two parts since the Turkish-held area proclaimed itself the Turkish Republic of Northern Cyprus. This entity, however, is not internationally recognised (except by Turkey). In accordance with the definition used in this study, only border disputes between two internationally recognised states qualify as irredentist disputes.

regions from 1946 to 2000. In order to ensure comparability with other studies on territorial disputes that take regions seriously (Huth, 1998; Huth and Allee, 2002), the table lists five regions: (a) the Americas; (b) Central Asia, Far East and Pacific; (c) Europe; (d) Near East, Middle East and North Africa; and (e) sub-Saharan Africa.

In the Americas, three irredentist disputes remained unresolved while one was settled through peaceful territorial change. No claim was revoked by force, no territorial change by force occurred and no dispute was peacefully resolved by the challenger's recognition of the territorial status quo. In Central Asia, the Far East and the Pacific, nine disputes remained unresolved, two were settled by military force in favour of the challenger, and none was resolved by the military might of the defender. Peaceful settlement occurred in six cases. In five of these, the parties agreed on peaceful territorial change and in one case the challenger peacefully recognised the territorial status quo. The Near East, Middle East and North Africa exhibit a somewhat similar pattern. Six disputes remained unresolved, three ended with the challenger imposing new borders by force and no dispute was terminated by the defender's (threatened) use of force. Four disputes were peacefully resolved. All of these involved the change of existing borders. No dispute was resolved by the challenger's peaceful recognition of existing borders. Finally, in sub-Saharan Africa, six claims remained without settlement while four were peacefully resolved. Of these four, one was resolved by peaceful territorial change and three by the peaceful recognition of existing borders.

Comparing the post-Second World War patterns of irredentism across regions makes Europe's shift towards peaceful recognition even more puzzling. Not only is the post-war European pattern very different from previous eras but it is also very different from other world regions (only sub-Saharan Africa slightly approximates the European record). In other regions, states are much less prepared to settle their irredentist disputes peacefully. And if they do, they tend to exchange territory peacefully rather than recognise existing borders.

What explains the distinct European pattern? How have European states come to settle their irredentist disputes peacefully since the end of the Second World War? Why do they settle these disputes by the recognition of the territorial status quo rather than by peaceful territorial change? These are the most puzzling questions arising from surveying irredentist claims since they became a force in world politics, and, therefore, this book addresses these questions at length.

Overview of the literature

Research solely focusing on irredentism or touching upon the phenomenon (studies on territorial conflict, nationalism and ethnic conflict) may be distinguished according to its underlying ontological premises.[3] This yields three clusters of literature: material structure explanations, rational choice explanations, and identity explanations.

Material structure explanations contend that material domestic and/or international structures determine the occurrence and dynamics of territorial disputes. According to this scholarly tradition, material structures govern the behaviour of human beings. Motivations, interpretations and practices are determined by these structures. The writings of Vladimir Lenin fall into this category. Building on J. A. Hobson (1938 [1902]) and Rudolf Hilferding (1955 [1910]), Lenin (1975 [1917]) argues that imperialism is the highest stage of capitalism. Capitalist states are in constant need of new markets, and, therefore, are inevitably expansionist and imperialist. The domestic economic structure drives states into territorial conflicts. The argument by Nazli Choucri and Robert North (1979) cannot be entirely subsumed under a Marxist strand of thought, but also locates the cause of territorial conflict in state structure. Lateral pressure, originating in population, technology and resource pressures, intertwined with an increase in material capabilities, causes a state to attempt to expand territorially.

Material structure, defined as the distribution of material capabilities, plays the key role in Realist explanations of territorial conflict. Robert Gilpin (1983) contends that territorial expansion is a function of the distribution of capabilities in the international system. Paul Huth (1998), in a very detailed study of territorial disputes, finds a strong relationship between a challenger's superior military capabilities and the likelihood that the challenger seeks to attain its goal by military means. However, there is no agreement on the impact of the distribution of capabilities. In a study on territorial change, Gary Goertz and Paul Diehl (1992) argue that the distribution of capabilities made no impact during the period studied by Huth (1950–90).[4]

---

[3] This distinction partly coincides with the distinction between physical and mental states by Searle (1983) and the three world images (observational, mental, and institutional facts) outlined by Kratochwil (1989: 21–3).

[4] Goertz and Diehl do contend, however, that the distribution of capabilities matters for the period before the Second World War.

Rational choice frameworks take agency more seriously than material structure explanations. Human beings are not conceived of as mere
puppets of structure, but have autonomy to act according to their
preferences. These preferences are exogenously given. Rational choice
explanations contend that irredentism and internationalised ethnic conflict are a function of rational elite calculations. It is assumed that the
overall goal of leaders is to remain in power. If irredentism helps elites to
stay in power, they play the irredentist card.

Three arguments, modelling different situational variables, are based
on these premises. First, the ethnic ties argument holds that elites are
likely to engage in territorial conflict with the aim of retrieving ethnic kin
from a defending state if their remaining in power in the challenging state
depends on the support of the same ethnic group, and if this support can
be ensured by appealing to the ethno-nationalist sentiment of the group
(Rothschild, 1981; Gagnon, 1994; Saideman, 1997). Second, the demo-
graphics argument postulates that ethnically homogeneous states are
more likely to be irredentist because no ethnic groups are alienated
from a government's pursuit of an irredentist claim. Thus, ethnically
homogeneous states are irredentism-prone whereas ethnically heterogeneous states are not (Kapil, 1966; Horowitz, 1985, 1991; Neuberger,
1991; Carment and James, 1997). Third, Birger Heldt (1999) applies a
slightly modified version of the diversionary theory of war to a sample of
territorial disputes. Elites escalate territorial disputes into war if this
diverts from economic problems, and if the risks and the costs of the
war – including the economic costs – are not too high.

Identity explanations of territorial conflict and irredentism focus on
nationalism or international norms. Those studies that put the nation
into the centre of their inquiry dichotomise nationalisms. A basic distinction is drawn between an ethnic and malign nationalism on the one hand,
and a civic and benign nationalism on the other. Ethnic nationalism is
irredentism-prone, civic nationalism is not (see, for example, Kohn, 1962;
Greenfeld and Chirot, 1994, Rösel, 1995; Shain and Sherman, 1998).[5]

---

[5] Stephen Van Evera (1994) uses another dichotomy. He distinguishes between
diaspora-annexing and diaspora-accepting nationalism. The former claims
territory and uses violence to pursue the claim, the latter refrains from claims and
violence. Instead of a dichotomy, Thomas Ambrosio (2001: 6) deals with levels of
'ethno-territorial nationalism'. If understood as causal arguments – and this is how
the authors present them – these accounts run the risk of being tautological. What

A few scholars assert that identity-constituting norms account for the presence or absence of territorial claims. Linden (2000) contends that democratic norms on the international and the domestic level make irredentism unlikely to occur. Barkin and Cronin (1994) focus on fundamental norms that define the pillars of international order. They contend that irredentism arises whenever national sovereignty dominates state sovereignty as the legitimising principle of sovereignty, as laid down by major powers in a peace agreement concluding a hegemonic war.

Existing explanations and the empirical record

The research puzzle is two-fold: How have European states, in contrast to previous eras and other world regions, come to settle their irredentist disputes peacefully? And why have they done so through the recognition of the territorial status quo? Existing explanations cannot even answer the first part of the puzzle. It remains unclear why irredentist disputes have been peacefully resolved, not to mention why they have been resolved through recognition.

Economic structure explanations cannot explain why capitalist – whether advanced capitalist or not – and non-capitalist states used to make irredentist claims, why some capitalist states made claims and others did not, and why capitalist states in Europe have settled their irredentist disputes peacefully after the Second World War. Capability-based arguments cannot explain why weak and strong states used to engage in irredentism, but have both stopped doing so after 1945.[6]

According to demographics-based rational choice explanations, the post-Second World War qualitative break should never have happened. Most European states are not multi-national states, but ethnically

the authors consider an independent variable (diaspora-annexing and ethno-territorial nationalism, respectively), may not be as independent of the dependent variable (irredentism) as they assume. If understood as constitutive arguments, however, these arguments allude to the importance of national identity – and this is a focus for studying irredentism on which I build. This applies in particular to Ambrosio, who acknowledges the fluctuation of national identity.

[6] Weak states even go to war against strong states in the pursuit of an irredentist claim (Weiner, 1971). This also contradicts King and Melvin (1999) who contend that a state's policies towards an ethnically kindred diaspora are determined by the institutional strength and resources of the diaspora, as well as by the economic resources of the potentially irredentist kin state.

relatively homogeneous. This should make them irredentist-prone across different time periods. Yet they are not. The diversionary argument cannot explain the empirical record either. Independently of economic performance, states have made and renounced irredentist disputes. States such as Italy and Germany claimed territory during times of rapid economic development such as in the late nineteenth and early twentieth centuries as well as during the Great Depression in the inter-war years.

The ethnic ties argument also fails to provide a plausible explanation for the pattern of European irredentism. It is problematic in two ways. First, some irredentist cases have nothing to do with ethnic sentiments. Instead, an irredentist claim may be rooted in beliefs about the borders of the ancestral homeland or in the definition of the spatial boundaries of a civic nation. The latter, for example, was a key motivation for France's irredentist claim to Alsace-Lorraine between 1871 and 1919. France identified the Alsaciens, although then overwhelmingly German-speaking, as part of the French nation not for ethno-national, but for civic-national reasons, i.e. their support for the principles of the French Revolution (Gutmann, 1991). In a similar vein, Yugoslavia's claim to Trieste was independent of ethno-nationalist sentiments. When Belgrade claimed Trieste it did so while the Yugoslav state was trying to overcome ethno-nationalist feelings.

Second, the ethnic ties argument cannot explain the difference of the irredentist patterns before and after the Second World War. If the ethnic ties argument were correct, elites recognised existing borders after the war because they could not strengthen their grip on power any more by stirring ethno-nationalist sentiment. Assuming for the moment that this argument held true, the critical question would then become: Why could elites play the irredentist card to secure their grip on power in the past but cannot do so any more? This question could only be answered by conceptualising ethnicity as evolving identity – a move that rational choice scholars avoid because it undermines the parsimony of their theoretical framework.

The empirical pattern cannot be explained by dichotomising nationalisms either. In the past, nation-states that tended more towards the ideal-type of an ethno-nation and those that tended more towards the ideal-type of a civic nation both made irredentist claims. As alluded to above, not only did Bulgaria, Germany, Hungary, Romania and many other nations that are usually classified as ethnic nations engage in irredentism, but also nations that are considered civic nations such as the French and the Yugoslav in the mid-twentieth century. Since the end of the Second World War, however, European nations have recognised existing boundaries rather than upheld irredentist claims, regardless of whether they tend more towards the ideal-type of an ethno-nation or that of a civic nation.[7]

The democratic norms hypothesis, proposed by Linden (2000), is equally problematic. Democratic and non-democratic states steadfastly refused to forgo irredentism prior to the Second World War, and democratic and non-democratic states have recognised existing boundaries since 1945. Even states in the midst of democratic transitions – there is some evidence suggesting that these pursue more aggressive foreign policies (Mansfield and Snyder, 1995) – have not been an exception to Europe's post-Second World War pattern of peaceful settlement through recognition of existing borders.[8]

Finally, there are two problems with the norm argument presented by Barkin and Cronin (1994). First, the authors cannot account for the time period 1848–1914, when the number of irredentist disputes increased dramatically, although the post-Napoleonic order was founded on the principle of state sovereignty. Second, based on their argument, the authors predict an increase in irredentism because of a renewed shift back to national sovereignty. This shift, however, has not occurred. Irredentism has remained an anomaly even after 1989.

In short, existing explanations, no matter whether they are based on material structure, rational choice or identity, cannot even solve the general aspect of the research puzzle: what accounts for the pattern of peaceful settlement of irredentist disputes in post-Second World War Europe? Needless to say, without a plausible answer to this question,

[7] Apart from this, it is highly dubious whether this simple dichotomisation is an adequate route for addressing the role of nationalism in world politics. For a critical view see Spencer and Wollmann (1998) as well as Brown (1999). See also below.

[8] Linden's argument is also contradicted by the findings of a large-n study on the international repercussions of domestic democratisation processes. Mansfield and Snyder (1995) contend that states are more likely to engage in adventurous foreign policies during democratic transition periods. Note that, if this argument is accepted, the research puzzle of this study becomes even more puzzling. Central and Eastern European states have been in a democratic transition period for more than a decade. Nevertheless, irredentism has remained an exception in European relations.

the more specific second aspect of the puzzle – why peaceful settlement
through recognition? – cannot be answered either.

Episteme, identity and norms

What explains these problems of the existing literature? The bulk of the
literature on border disputes is critically shaped by the positivist quest
for a scientific methodology. Authors focus on material structure and
exogenously given preferences because this allows them to use elegant
methodologies borrowed from the natural sciences. Ideas, by contrast,
are chronically difficult to operationalise and, since they evolve, change
and at times even shift, hardly fit into research designs that are meant to
discover causal effects through variants of the classical controlled
experiment.

In-depth research on nations' attachment of meaning to borders,
especially in the field of political geography (A. Murphy, 1990; Paasi,
1995, 1996; Newman and Paasi, 1997), however, provides plenty of
evidence that examining territorial disputes in general, and irredentism
in particular, cannot do without taking ideational factors very seriously.
More precisely, this research suggests that there are three ideational
building blocks of social reality that a study on irredentism has to
address. I refer to them as episteme, identity and norms.

The episteme – a fruitful conceptualisation of a world view – delineates
what is imaginable for actors.[9] I define it as a set of fundamental and
taken-for-granted beliefs about what is (ontological dimension) and how
what is is causally connected (causal dimension); on the basis of these
beliefs social actors construct the world. Similar to scientists who, according to Thomas Kuhn (1996 [1962]), cannot but look at the world they
study through a particular paradigm, the social actors we study rely on a
lens to make the world intelligible to themselves.

Studies on nationalism have shown that the fundamental ontological
belief that, as Anthony Smith (1979: 2) puts it, 'mankind is "really" and
"naturally" divided into distinct communities of history and culture,
called nations', coupled with the equally deeply internalised causal belief

---

[9] Coined by Foucault (1989a, 1989b), and introduced to the study of world politics
by John Ruggie (1975), a small set of literature on the epistemic dimension of
world politics has developed on which I base my conceptualisation (Adler and
Haas, 1992; Ruggie, 1993; Legro, 2000; Adler and Bernstein, 2005).

that nations have to uphold these divisions in order to preserve their authentic Self, is a key ideational foundation upon which nations build their nationness (Kornprobst, 2005). Such an exclusive episteme makes imagining the nation and the sharp boundaries between nations possible. These imaginations, in turn, harbour the potential for irredentism. Less exclusive epistemes, by contrast, lessen the potential for irredentism. Yet apart from Kratochwil, Rohrlich and Mahajan (1985), who allude to what I refer to as episteme in their study of border disputes, the literature routinely overlooks this important ideational force.

Identity is a narrative category. Identities are constructed through communicative acts and symbols that, by connecting events of past, present as well as desires and expectations about the future, tell stories about Self and its relationship to Other. These narratives are not objectively true or false, but they are intersubjectively plausible or implausible (Somers, 1994; Cruz, 2000). It is obvious that identity matters for the dynamics of irredentist disputes. The identity narrative defines the borders of the nation and its relationship to other nations (Forsberg, 1995). Nevertheless, many positivist scholars shy away from identity in their research on border disputes and irredentism. Goertz and Diehl (1992: 12–21), for example, emphasise the significance of what they call the 'relational' importance of territory (i.e. attachment of people to the land that they call their own). Yet acknowledging that they cannot measure the variable, they omit it from their aggregate-data analysis.

Others mistakenly treat identity, which belongs to the realm of intersubjectivity, as an objective category. Authors such as Carment and James (1995) as well as Huth (1998) use what they regard as objective indicators such as language to infer ethnic kinship. These supposedly objective markers, however, may have nothing to do with the intersubjective ethnic bonds across state borders. After all, neither France nor Germany nor Italy doubt the distinctiveness of Swiss identity, although there are French-speaking, German-speaking and Italian-speaking areas in Switzerland.

Dichotomising nationalisms and inferring a propensity for irredentism from it is problematic for many reasons. As emphasised above, the empirical record simply contradicts the thesis that nations usually classified under civic are never irredentist. Yet there is also again the additional problem of objectifying nationalism. It is misleading to treat national identity as a phenomenon carved into stone. Neither ethnic nor civic nationalism is immutable or entirely path-dependent as

Greenfeld (1992) appears to suggest. National identities may evolve from a predominantly ethnic to a predominantly civic nationalism. Many European nations, albeit not without conflict and contestation, seem to be in the process of such a transformation at the moment.

Finally, norms are interwoven with identity. They constitute identity, as the widely used definition of a norm as a 'standard of appropriate behavior for an actor with a given identity' emphasises (Finnemore and Sikkink, 1998: 891). Norms are important forces shaping irredentist disputes (Kornprobst, 2002). Indeed, irredentism itself is often not merely a policy but an internalised norm that constitutes a nation's identity. The manner in which many nations deal with internal dissent about irredentist claims shows this quite clearly. They brand domestic advocates against irredentism as traitors because these advocates break the nation's taboo against even considering abandoning the vision of reunification with lost lands. Yet there are other identity-constituting norms that may help to resolve irredentist disputes or at least prevent them from escalating into war. The norms of peaceful resolution of disputes and territorial integrity come immediately to mind.[10]

The normative dimension of irredentist disputes, however, remains neglected. The hypotheses proposed by Linden (2000) and Barkin and Cronin (1994) point in the right direction. They acknowledge the salience of norms. Yet in both accounts, norms are made amenable for empirical analysis by treating them as easily measurable independent variables. This is problematic in two respects. First, measuring international norms exclusively by their presence or absence in international treaties is as inadequate as inferring their presence and salience from a particular regime type alone. What really matters for the purpose of analysing irredentism is which norms constitute national identity. The measures used by Linden, and Barkin and Cronin, do not capture this dimension. Second, conceptualising norms as independent variables causing a certain effect conceives of something that is actually a becoming as something that is a being. These authors assume norms to be constant for most of the time. Only rarely, the pendulum swings from democracy to non-democracy or from state to national sovereignty. This conceptualisation leaves no room for tracing what norms usually do, i.e. evolve over time and sometimes shift, even in directions into which they have never changed before.

---

[10] For a detailed study of the territorial integrity norm, see Zacher (2001).

There are two important indications that solving the puzzle of European irredentism is only possible if norms are taken more seriously. First, there is an interesting co-variation between what one may refer to as the territorial status quo norm and the settlement of irredentist disputes in Europe. This norm does not carve state borders into stone for ever – peaceful and consensual change is still possible – but it does call on states to refrain from making *de jure* claims to the territory of other states. There are a number of documents that suggest that Europe may have gone beyond the territorial integrity norm to adopt the territorial status quo norm. In the 1950s, Warsaw Pact states started to push for the recognition of the territorial status quo. In the 1960s, the opposition of NATO states to this proposal waned. In 1975, the Helsinki Final Act included not only a stipulation about territorial integrity (1a/III), but also declared existing frontiers 'inviolable'. States ought to 'refrain from any demand for ... territory of any participating State'. Almost twenty years later, the Badinter Commission of the European Union dealt with the recognition of the former Yugoslav states. It recommended recognition of these states but emphasised that 'respect for the territorial status quo' was a key principle that ought not be violated by them (Radan, 2002: 226). At a meeting in Helsinki in 1999, the European Council decided to add the resolution of territorial disputes to its accession criteria for EU membership.

Second, a similar co-variation holds elsewhere as well. Among world regions, only sub-Saharan Africa somewhat approximates the European pattern of peaceful resolution of irredentist disputes in the post-Second World War era, and parts of this region have also placed a strong normative emphasis on existing borders (Kornprobst, 2002). Initially, this emphasis was highly disputed. During the onset of the decolonisation process, two groups of states and soon-to-be states formed that debated the future of Africa's boundaries. The Casablanca Group distanced itself from colonial borders and advocated the creation of a powerful supranational African polity. The Brazzaville Group, by contrast, advocated state sovereignty and cautioned not to tamper with colonial borders. It was the latter group that won this important contest about the future parameters of African politics. In 1963, the Addis Ababa Conference endorsed the principle of *uti possidetis*. The colonial borders became the borders between African states. Not to alter these borders became a widely endorsed sacrosanct principle of post-colonial Africa. It was a cornerstone of the Charter of the Organisation of African Unity and has assumed an equally important status in the Constitutive Act of the African Union. Some of the divisions originating with the Casablanca and Brazzaville Groups have remained. As a consequence, *uti possidetis* has been somewhat more contested (especially in North Africa and in the Horn of Africa) than the European principle to uphold the territorial status quo. Furthermore, the latter is more absolute than the former. *Uti possidetis* allows for territorial change if it realigns borders with former colonial borders (this is, for instance, why the African Union recognises Western Sahara). Nevertheless, sub-Saharan Africa also exhibits an interesting – although compared to Europe weaker – co-variation between a frequently emphasised principle against changing borders and a relatively high number of irredentist cases settled by the recognition of the territorial status quo.

It is worth inquiring into this co-variation in more detail. Is the European emphasis on the territorial status quo norm more than just empty talk? Is it a norm that is constitutive of the identity of European states? If so, how has this idea evolved into a norm, and is there a mechanism linking this evolution to the pattern of peaceful resolution of irredentist disputes? The next chapter outlines a norm selection mechanism that provides a vantage point from which to study the evolution of innovative normative ideas into identity-constituting norms. It puts under scrutiny the role that episteme, identity and already selected norms play in this evolution, and allows for analysing the impact of this evolution on political outcomes.

2 | *Argumentation and compromise*

In the late 1980s, Friedrich Kratochwil's and Nicholas Onuf's assertion that norms matter in international relations (Kratochwil, 1989; Onuf, 1989) sparked a major controversy. Since the mid-1990s, however, the question has no longer been whether norms matter but how they matter.[1] Constructivist research, following Kratochwil and Onuf, postulates that norms constitute identity. Agents come to adopt and internalise – in short select – norms that define their identity. Rationalist research, by contrast, conceives of norms in a different way. Actors do not select norms. They may adopt them for strategic purposes but do not internalise them. Creating norms and complying with them is assumed to be the outcome of attempts by strategic agents to maximise their benefits.

At first glance, this debate is a contestation between adherents of the logic of appropriateness and proponents of the logic of consequences (March and Olsen, 1989). The one side interprets agency as the following of identity-constituting norms whereas the other understands agency as cost–benefit calculation. Yet a closer look provides a somewhat more nuanced picture. Constructivist research, trying to understand how norms get selected, has gone beyond a more or less static conception of appropriateness. While Constructivists have proposed a number of different processes through which agents come to select norms, the burgeoning literature on advocacy networks has featured most prominently. This literature is underpinned by the logic of argumentation. Hence, much of the recent debate between Constructivists and Rationalists on how norms matter revolves around the contestation

This chapter draws upon material from Markus Kornprobst, 'Argumentation and Compromise: Ireland's Selection of the Territorial Status Quo Norm', *International Organization* 61 (2007): 69–98, © The IO Foundation, published by Cambridge University Press, reprinted with permission.
[1] For the last major debate on this issue, see John Mearsheimer (1994), Robert Keohane and Lisa Martin (1995), John Ruggie (1995) and Alexander Wendt (1995).

between the logic of argumentation – understood more broadly than by Thomas Risse (2000) – and the logic of consequences.[2] This chapter elaborates on the advocacy literature and links these two logics. I contend that, given the presence of a set of conditions, nations come to select norms in three ideal-typical stages: innovative argumentation, persuasive argumentation, and compromise. The logic of argumentation helps to account for what makes actors form an advocacy (innovative argumentation) and what makes this advocacy successful (persuasive argumentation). The logic of consequences explains the process through which actors who remain unconvinced by an argument yield to the pressure of a successful advocacy (compromise).

This chapter is organised into nine sections, which deal with the following four broad issues. First, I review the literature on norm selection. Second, I outline the central tenets of the logic of argumentation and elaborate on the process of reasoning. Third, I develop the ideal-typical three-stage norm selection mechanism and identify the conditions that make this generative mechanism possible. Finally, I discuss the methodology for the empirical chapters of this study.

Building on the existing literature

Two clusters of literature make up the bulk of existing research on how norms matter in international relations. According to the Constructivist advocacy literature, normative ideas matter if they come to constitute the identity of agents. Agents select new identity-constituting norms through communicative encounters. Processes of argumentation culminate in an audience's internalisation of a new norm (Finnemore and Sikkink, 1998; Keck and Sikkink, 1998; Risse, Ropp and Sikkink, 1999; Bernstein, 2000; Khagram, Riker and Sikkink, 2002; Wiener, 2004). The Rationalist compliance literature, by contrast, is based on the assumption of utility-maximising agents. There is no linkage of

---

[2] The bulk of Constructivist literature on norm selection deals with advocacy networks that construct linkages between what is taken for granted and what is advocated. Collective reasoning about these linkages is, as I will show in this chapter, the hallmark of argumentation theory. The logic of appropriateness, at least if not conceptualised so broadly that it subsumes all other logics of action (Müller, 2004), is different. Actors do not reason about linkages between what is already established and what is advocated but simply follow what is established as standards of appropriate action (Sending, 2002).

norms and identity. Persuasive argumentation is assumed to be inconsequential (unless it involves conveying credible incentives or disincentives to an audience). Norms matter if they play a role in agents'
computations of costs and benefits (Downs, Rokke and Barsoom,
1996; Simmons, 2000; Kelemen and Sibbitt, 2004; Langlois and
Langlois, 2004; Dai, 2005).

Both sets of literature have generated a number of important leads for
studying norms. On the one side, the advocacy literature provides
compelling evidence that norms matter when actors have selected
them as identity-constituting norms. A pathway through which this
selection occurs revolves around the construction of an intersubjective
fit between an advocated normative idea and the social context in which
actors are embedded. Advocates, being convinced of this match and
invoking it in their advocacy, persuade the audience through their
argumentation, and not through offering tangible incentives that are
exogenous to the audience's social embeddedness. On the other side,
Rationalists make an equally compelling case that not every norm that
makes a difference in world politics does so because it is an identity-
constituting norm. Even norms that do not constitute identity are of
key importance if they affect the cost–benefit calculations of utility-
maximising agents. Given a particular incentive structure, actors may opt
for abiding by a norm without necessarily internalising it. Thus, the logic of
consequences frequently plays a critical role for the adoption of norms.

What to make of these seemingly contradictory but theoretically and
empirically plausible findings? Rather than being the last word on an
important area of research, these findings provide leads for improving
our understanding about norms in world politics. Important questions
about the mechanisms through which norms shape world politics arise
out of each of these literature sets as well as out of the contestation
between them. These questions point to the need to build on the existing
literature in two ways, namely to investigate the workings of advocacy
in more detail and to examine how the logics of argumentation and
consequences interact.

The advocacy literature has shown that norm selection often involves
argumentation but it falls short of specifying this argumentation process in
sufficient detail. First, it neglects the issue of agency. The advocacy literature
focuses on the question of what makes an advocacy stick with an audience
but it does not address the important question of how advocates come to
reason the way they do. Agents are assumed to believe in their advocacy

(and at times to calculate strategically how best to get their message across). But it is not at all clear how the advocates come to embrace the idea for which they advocate. In short, there is no theory of agency.

Second, the advocacy literature over-emphasises the role of identity narratives and identity-constituting norms at the expense of other ideational forces. This is not at all to dispute that advocates have to construct a fit between the 'extant social structure' (Bernstein, 2000: 465) and the advocated normative idea. Yet the advocacy literature focuses too much on identity narratives and already selected norms. The environment is constituted by other social forces as well. Most importantly, the literature on norm selection neglects world views, although there has been consensus across the Rationalist–Constructivist divide for quite some time that world views matter in international relations (Goldstein and Keohane, 1993; Laffey and Weldes, 1997). Judith Goldstein and Robert Keohane (1993: 8) even argue that world views have a salience unmatched by other ideational forces: 'Ideas have their broadest impact on human action when they take the form of world views.' Norm selection, of course, is one such human action. It is somewhat startling that Constructivists, including students of advocacy networks, widely share the Rationalists' neglect of world views. Much of what is now labelled Constructivism has been inspired by the work of Peter Berger and Thomas Luckmann (1966). The world view (*Weltansicht*) is a key ideational force for Luckmann (1991: 91–3).

Third, the finding that norm selection involves fitting the advocated norm into an already existing social context is an important insight. But precisely because it is such a key finding, it begs the question of how this process of embedding works. Such a detailed inquiry into the process through which advocates succeed or fail to embed the new into the taken-for-granted needs to elaborate on the existing research in two ways: Which already established ideas make for a stronger fit than others? Identity narratives, for example, are a resource for successful argumentation. Yet some aspects of the narrative may make for a more powerful argumentation than others. Furthermore, which ways of linking an advocated idea to internalised ideas are persuasive and which ones are not? Argumentation theory, for instance, has traditionally emphasised the syllogism as a mechanism to link the old and the new. Is this the only way to construct such a fit? Is it an especially persuasive one?

Deepening research on advocacy networks – developing a theory of agency, including world views in the social context, and specifying the properties of a persuasive fit between context and advocated idea – is a prerequisite for improving our understanding of norm selection. Yet it is not sufficient. If we are to take the findings of empirical research on norm selection and compliance seriously, we need to transcend the divide between the logics of argumentation and consequences. The pathways through which norms matter in world politics are hardly ever argumentation all the way down. The cost–benefit calculations of agents play a very important role as well.

There have been two influential attempts to bridge the gap between the logics of argumentation and consequences.[3] Both attempts build – sometimes explicitly, sometimes implicitly – on interpretations of Erving Goffman's path-breaking work on framing (Goffman, 1974). The literature on strategic framing postulates that elites frame issues in a manner that maximises their exogenously given interests. The framing resonates with an audience if it fits the issue into the web of meaning within which the audience is embedded (Barnett, 1999; Acharya, 2004; Cortell and Davis, 2005). Thus, the synthesis is based on a peculiar division of labour. The sender is a *homo oeconomicus*, whereas the receiver is a *homo sociologicus*. The sender freely chooses the frame in order to maximise his or her utility and the receiver is persuaded by the match between the advocated idea and the receiver's social context that the frame constructs. The concept of rhetorical action (Schimmelfennig, 2003) further tilts towards a micro-economic theory of agency. Communicators, framing an issue in a way that serves their exogenously given self-interest, shame recipients into norm compliance. The recipients are rhetorically entrapped and have only two options: either they violate what they publicly stand for or they acquiesce. Since the violation of prior commitments comes at the cost of shame, they acquiesce.

It is dubious to what extent Goffman's work really lends itself to these utilitarian interpretations. Goffman, after all, was a sociologist who was committed to ethnographic research as a means to uncover the deep-seated social forces underpinning people's everyday practices. Independently of this question, however, neither strategic framing nor rhetorical action

---

[3] Additionally, Jeffrey Checkel (1997, 2001) introduces scope conditions. In his view, actors sometimes comply with norms because this offers more benefits than costs to them. Under different circumstances, they comply because they have been persuaded to do so. Yet strictly speaking this is not bridging the gap. Scope conditions do not bridge but keep apart. It is an argument for why the two logics should be kept separate.

provides for a compelling middle path. The former relies on an implausible division of labour. It is just not clear why persuaders are cost–benefit calculators who are disembedded from and unaffected by any social context whereas the persuadees are enmeshed in it. Bridging the gap between sociological and micro-economic approaches requires, in the first instance, a coherent theory of agency. Strategic framing does not offer such coherence. Schimmelfennig (2003) provides a coherent theory of agency but the theory fails to bridge the divide. What makes agents act the way they do are their exogenously given goals and their calculations about the means to achieve these goals. Communicators are cost–benefit calculating actors. And even the recipients act based on utility calculations. They acquiesce because of the costs that shaming inflicts on them. Thus, what Schimmelfennig proposes is a micro-economic theory of agency with a sociological footnote. The findings of the advocacy literature, however, caution that such a footnote is not enough.

The next two sections lay the conceptual groundwork for elaborating on the advocacy literature. Then, the remainder of this chapter develops a norm selection mechanism that fills in the blanks that the advocacy literature has not addressed so far, and bridges the gap between the sociological leanings of the advocacy literature and the micro-economic underpinnings of Rationalist research on compliance.

Argumentation and persuasion

Norm advocacy revolves around argumentation. Argumentation is public reasoning aimed at persuading an audience.[4] This section deals with the latter part of the definition, i.e. persuasion. The following section then clarifies the former part of the definition, i.e. reasoning.

Persuasion as used in this study is not strategic persuasion as defined by the strategic communication paradigm (Seiter and Gass, 2004: 13–29). According to this perspective, persuaders and persuadees are expected utility maximisers. Senders engage in a campaign in order to further their exogenously given interests and the receivers of the message are won over by the incentives and disincentives offered in it by the senders. Trying to capture the full range of incentives and disincentives, this paradigm tends to refrain from limiting the means for winning over an audience.

---

[4] This definition is similar to Cicero's (2003: 8). For the link between argumentation and reasoning, see also Crawford (2002: 14–16).

Definitions of persuasion by authors such as Richard Bostrum (1983: 8) or Erwin Bettinghaus and Michael Cody (1994: 6) allow for the full range of incentives and disincentives, including coercion.

Persuasion through argumentation cuts deeper. There is a twofold difference between how strategic communication scholars and argumentation theorists conceptualise persuasion. First, the process of persuasion works differently. Persuasion through argumentation does not depend on the large shadow of material forces (even to the extent that they coerce) faced by the individual but on the manner in which a message is embedded into a community's system of shared beliefs. This embedding makes it possible for the community to generate agreement or at least a meaningful debate on a line of reasoning. Argumentation theorists and social theorists more generally often refer to this system of shared beliefs as a shared lifeworld (Husserl, 1954 [1937]: 48–56; Schütz, 1974 [1932]; Schütz and Luckmann, 1975; Habermas, 1995a [1981]: 171–293). This lifeworld is inhabited by the participants of a communicative encounter – no matter whether they are persuader or persuadee at a given moment in time. Without such a context, the persuader cannot make an argument that is intelligible to him- or herself, and the persuadee cannot make sense of the persuader's argument. Second, the outcome of persuasion is different. According to the strategic communication paradigm, before the communicative encounter is after the communicative encounter. Communication does not change persuader or persuadee in any way. For most argumentation theorists, by contrast, an idea may become so persuasive and over time seemingly self-evident that it becomes part of the lifeworld. Thus, communication has the potential to change social reality, including the aspects of social reality that constitute an actor's identity.

Argumentation theory traces itself back to Aristotle (Benoit, Hample and Benoit, 1992: 7) and the close connections between lifeworld, reasoning, argumentation and persuasion are the common thread that links research by argumentation scholars together (with the exception of those conceiving of argumentation merely as formal logic). Having said this, however, argumentation theory is anything but a homogeneous body of research. Most importantly, there has always been a tension between empirical and normative approaches to argumentation. Aristotle's work on argumentation, echoed by Cicero (1967; 2003) and Quintilian (1953), already shows this tension. His *Art of Rhetoric* provides many clues for how argumentation works. It gives answers to the empirical question of how an orator can persuade an audience. Yet Aristotle – demarcating himself from the Sophists – sought to balance his explanatory account with normative considerations. He aimed at establishing argumentation as an academic discipline with stringent rules governing the purpose and the methods of argumentation. Only if it followed these principles, he argued, could argumentation contribute to the well-being of the *polis*.

Contemporary argumentation theory still reflects this tension. Habermas (1995a [1981], 1995b [1981]) resolves the tension by focusing on the normative dimension of argumentation. He proposes a consensus theory of truth and postulates an ideal-speech situation that makes sure that everyone has equal access and opportunity to contribute to the development of the consensual truth. Although he deals with empirical aspects of argumentation in some depth, Frans van Eemeren's pragma-dialectical perspective also leans towards the normative end of the research spectrum on argumentation (Eemeren, 1992). Without neglecting normative considerations, Chaïm Perelman and Lucie Olbrechts-Tyteca's path-breaking research puts more emphasis on the simple but important empirical question of which argument persuades and which one does not (Perelman and Olbrechts-Tyteca, 1958). Despite continuing criticism against empirical leanings by more normatively orientated scholars (Johnson, 2000: 270), a sizeable literature has evolved asking the question of what makes argumentation persuasive (Willard, 1989: 16; Benoit, Hample and Benoit, 1992; Blair, 1992: 358).

To some extent, studies of argumentation in International Relations mirror these tensions within argumentation theory. Several normative studies on decision-making in the United Nations, for example, are underpinned by Habermas (Johnstone, 2003; Bjola, 2005). Some scholars sit on the fence. Harald Müller (1994, 1995), Thomas Risse (2000) and Jennifer Mitzen (2005) employ modified versions of Habermas's normative theory of communicative action to explain empirical puzzles of world politics. Finally, a number of studies stand in the tradition of Perelman and Olbrechts-Tyteca's *New Rhetoric* and inquire into how argumentation persuades. This applies to Neta Crawford's seminal research on argumentation (2002) and to the advocacy literature more generally. For the most part, the latter does not proclaim itself part of argumentation theory but it shares its common thread. Agents, being convinced of the normative ideas they advocate, succeed, if certain conditions are met, in persuading others to select these ideas as norms through a message that is anchored in a set of meaning that persuaders and persuadees share (Finnemore and Sikkink, 1998; Keck and Sikkink, 1998; Risse, Ropp and Sikkink, 1999; Crawford, 2002; Wiener, 2004).

Thomas Risse (2000) makes a convincing case that argumentation is a distinct logic of action in International Relations. Yet not only Habermas-inspired research studies the argumentative logic of action. Research in the tradition of Perelman and Olbrechts-Tyteca does as well, because it shares the common thread of argumentation theory, i.e. the linkages between lifeworld, reasoning, argumentation and persuasion. The logic of argumentation, therefore, is broader than often depicted in International Relations. Agents agree on doing something because, through the exchange of arguments, they have come to be persuaded of a line of reasoning that links their shared lifeworld and this doing something. Conceiving of the logic of argumentation more broadly does not make it any less distinct a logic of action. Argumentation does not follow the logic of consequences because actors reason based on the social context in which they are embedded and not based on exogenously given preferences, and because communicative encounters potentially change this social context. Argumentation is not captured by the logic of appropriateness either. The logic of appropriateness is about rule-following and does not allow for collective reasoning about what is already established and what ought to be established. Although under-developed in International Relations, there is also something Georg Wilhelm Friedrich Hegel (1969 [1830]) may refer to as logic of habituation or what Pierre Bourdieu (1990 [1980]) calls the logic of practice. Actors become socialised into a set of practices and, by repeating these practices over and over again, they assume the quality of a second nature. Such a process of habituation is quite different from argumentation. Whereas the latter is about making things explicit through argumentation, the former addresses precisely those forces that shape actors although they do not make them explicit to themselves and others.

Argumentation and reasoning

The previous section repeatedly mentioned the concept of reasoning. Reasoning is part of what makes argumentation a distinct logic of action, and it is – along with the concept of persuasion clarified above – the key component of the definition of argumentation as public reasoning aimed at persuading an audience. Yet what is reasoning? How do actors reason?

This section specifies the process of reasoning by locating *topoi* (commonplaces) in a repertoire of commonplaces, by identifying the three social forces that constitute this repertoire (episteme, identity narrative, identity-constituting norms), and by distinguishing three modes of reasoning (abstraction, comparison, appropriateness).

Some ideas serve as tools that make the world intelligible to actors. They provide them with clues about how the world works. These clues are the firm and unquestioned ground on which actors stand when they reason about the world. I refer to the toolbox (Swidler, 1986) containing the taken-for-granted ideas that actors use to reason about the world as a repertoire of commonplaces. Or, put in Habermasian terms, the repertoire is the shared lifeworld that makes it possible for actors to reason and argue with one another. The repertoire of commonplaces that is dominant in discourse on war and peace in the United States, for example, consists of a plethora of taken-for-granted ideas, many of which are interpretations of historical events. Some of these focus on the Second World War and its aftermath. The Munich analogy cautions never to appease a bellicose dictator again. Having defeated Nazi Germany and having liberated its concentration camps entrenched the idea that waging war is sometimes the only means to fight evil. The US experiences with rebuilding and democratising defeated West Germany and Japan are invoked as lessons that stable democracies can be built on the ruins of a vicious dictatorship.

These examples point to only a small fraction of the repertoire of commonplaces that is dominant in the United States on issues of peace and war. Yet, comprehensive as most repertoires are, they are not infinite. The pool of taken-for-granted ideas has its limits. The ideas within these limits are so familiar to and taken for granted by their adherents that they seem to them to be the natural way of looking at things. Outside these limits are ideas that may well have the potential to make the world intelligible to actors – even more so than the ideas within the limits – but since they do not come to them naturally, they do not use them in their reasoning. There is, for instance, no Hiroshima analogy in the US repertoire of commonplaces. The devastating consequences of air warfare for civilians have been highlighted by the allied attack on Dresden during the Second World War, and, in even more brutal manner, by the US attack on Hiroshima and Nagasaki. Yet, similarly to napalm attacks during the Vietnam War, these chapters of warfare have not made it into the dominant repertoire of commonplaces in the United States. They are not ideas that the majority of Americans accepts as the naturally given starting points for making sense of war and peace.

The advocacy literature does not explicitly conceptualise the pool of ideas upon which actors draw to reason. There is no mention of a repertoire of commonplaces or a similar concept. Yet it is not difficult to extract the forces that, according to this literature set, make the world intelligible to actors. The advocacy literature holds that identity and its constituting norms make up the pool of taken-for-granted ideas in light of which actors make sense of an advocated normative idea. This study partly concurs. Identity and already institutionalised norms are part of the repertoire of commonplaces that help us make sense of an advocated normative idea. Yet, situated at a deeper layer of the ideational fabric, there is an ideational force that the advocacy literature overlooks, i.e. the episteme.

The episteme is a fruitful conceptualisation of a world view. The previous chapter defined the concept and contended that epistemes matter for the dynamics of irredentist disputes. Yet the salience of the episteme goes far beyond that. Similarly to Michel Foucault (1989a, 1989b), who coined the concept, scholarship in International Relations has shown that the episteme is the lens through which actors look at the world. The episteme delineates which constructions of the world are imaginable and which ones are not (Ruggie, 1975, 1993; Adler and Haas, 1992; Legro, 2000; Adler and Bernstein, 2005). It is perhaps no coincidence that the literature on norm selection neglects the episteme. Precisely because the episteme is such a profound ideational force, it is easily overlooked. The episteme constitutes a perspective for looking at the world that is so self-evident to actors, and often also to us as analysts reflecting upon world politics, that it is understood as naturally constituting the world rather than as a social construction that serves as a foundation for inventing and reinventing the world in particular ways.

Neglecting the episteme in studies on norm selection amounts to cutting out the most influential dimension of the tightly interwoven nexus of three important social forces. Episteme, identity narrative and already selected norms are intertwined by mutually constitutive relationships. It is well established that norms, once they are internalised, constitute identity. With the former defining critical aspects of the latter, norms crucially shape the narrative that actors tell about themselves and their relationship to others. Vice versa, identity constitutes norms. Actors imbue norms, even if they are shared with others, with meaning taken from their identity narrative. When states select norms, for instance, they tend to localise them (Acharya, 2004), i.e. adapt them to their identity narratives to various degrees. In a similar vein, identity narrative and already selected norms pull the episteme in their direction. The more powerful constitutive effects, however, run in the opposite direction. The episteme allows for some identity representations and identity-constituting norms to appear natural and self-evident to us but not to others. Comparable to the operating system of a computer that makes it possible to install a certain range of applications, the episteme enables us to conceive of certain identity narratives and identity-constituting norms but blinds us from seeing others.

It is this power of delimiting the imaginable that makes the episteme such an important force for the selection of normative ideas as norms. Revisiting an illustration already used in the previous chapter provides a useful empirical example for this rather abstract claim. Half a century ago, African leaders looked at their continent through two different epistemes. The Casablanca Group took the absence of national boundaries in Africa for granted. Africa, it was assumed, was fundamentally different from the Western world: fragmented into local groupings but unified by an over-arching African culture (ontological dimension of episteme). The super-imposition of the nation-state onto the continent would destroy this unity, breed intra-African conflict, and enable the outside to exploit these con-flicts (causal dimension of episteme). To the Brazzaville Group, by con-trast, the nation-state model seemed self-evident. Like the rest of the world, Africa was presumed to consist of many (partly nascent) nations (ontological dimension of episteme). These nations would have to have the right to rule themselves in order for meaningful liberation to be realised and in order to prevent intra-African conflicts about who should govern the continent (causal dimension of episteme). Eventually, the Brazzaville Group prevailed. This proved crucial for the selection of norms. The norm of *uti possidetis*, for example, became a profound norm shaping intra-African relations. Yet without the taken-for-grantedness of the nation-state lens, the notion that existing colonial boundaries ought to be respected would have been entirely inconceivable.

Thus, it is not only the identity narrative and already selected norms that provide actors with the resources to reason about the selection of a normative idea as a norm. The episteme is also an important part of the repertoire of commonplaces. Yet conceptualising the repertoire is only a first step towards understanding how actors reason. Aristotle (1995) and Cicero (1967, 2003) remind us that agents never use the entire repertoire to reason about a certain issue. They pick those that help them make a particular issue intelligible to themselves.[5] I refer to such an idea that agents take from the repertoire of commonplaces and in light of which they make sense of a particular issue as *topos*.[6] George W. Bush, for example, selected the Munich analogy and a small number of other *topoi* from the US repertoire of commonplaces on peace and war, in order to comprehend the Iraq crisis in 2002 and 2003 (Mutimer, 2007). The lessons of the Second World War remain fresh in the minds of US decision-makers because they are deeply ingrained in the identity narrative. The Munich analogy may not have been particularly apt but it helped the Bush administration to make sense of the supposed Iraqi threat in unequivocal terms. It provided clear guidance because it is an undisputed commonplace – whether plausible or not is a different question – that not appeasing Hitler at the Munich Conference in 1938 could have spared the world a world war. Equating, in more or less unqualified manner, Hitler in 1938 with Saddam Hussein in 2003 forcefully prescribed the military option against Iraq.

Agents connect *topoi* to their advocated ideas in various ways. Borrowing from Neta Crawford (2002: 16–18), this study distinguishes three modes of reasoning: abstraction, comparison and appropriateness. Abstraction is a form of logical reasoning. Inferences are made based on general knowledge about cause–effect relationships. The most thoroughly studied kind of abstract reasoning is the syllogism. In its simplest form, it consists of two premises and a conclusion. The major premise contains a desired goal. The minor premise consists of a cause–effect relationship. The conclusion infers the means to achieve the aim from the cause–effect relationship.[7] The Roman maxim of *qui desiderat pacem praeparet bellum*, for example, is the conclusion of a syllogism.

---

[5] Cicero translates *topos* literally with the Latin *locus*.
[6] *Topos* is usually translated as 'commonplace'. Yet I use the Greek term in order to emphasise that there is a plethora of commonplaces but agents pick only a few of them – here labelled *topoi* – to make a particular issue intelligible to themselves. On reasoning and *topoi*, see also Friedrich Kratochwil (1989: 38), Neta Crawford (2002: 68) and Marco Rühl (2002: 36).
[7] I follow Crawford (2002: 28) in her conceptualisation of the syllogism. By formal logical standards, this syllogism is imperfect. The major premise ought to categorise rather than express a desire. Yet I follow Crawford because I am concerned with practical reasoning and not with how scholars think the actors they study ought to reason. For an overview of syllogistic reasoning, see Günther Öhlschläger (1977).

An actor wants peace (major premise). Only one's own military strength prevents one's opponents from breaking the peace (minor premise). Thus, the actor who wants peace needs to prepare for war (conclusion).

Comparisons equate a phenomenon that is already authoritatively interpreted with something that is new and requires interpretation. The *topos* is – broadly understood and thus including analogy, simile, synechdoche etc. – a metaphor. The *topos* is equated with the advocated idea in more or less qualified form. The Munich analogy, for example, is frequently used in comparative reasoning in world politics. As alluded to above, one of the problems of the use of this analogy (and comparisons in general) is that the less the equation of *topos* and advocated idea is qualified, the more compelling the analogy is but, at the same time, the more the analogy distorts the advocated idea. Put differently, glossing over the differences between *topos* and advocated idea helps our reasoning to reach conclusions but it may make for misleading ones (Kornprobst, 2007).

Appropriateness as reasoning involves relating the advocated idea to existing norms. This may be done in a more or less elaborate manner. Advocates may simply link an idea to an already internalised norm. Additionally, they may also invoke a string of *topoi* that justifies the already institutionalised norm to the advocated idea. Episteme, identity narrative or other established norms may be among these *topoi*. The reasoning underpinning Germany's opposition to invading Iraq, for example, revolved around the *ius ad bellum* as codified in the United Nations Charter. States may go to war only as a last resort and as an act of defence. These norms are embedded in the identity narrative. Germany's breaches of the laws of war in the Second World War, in particular, were invoked as a key lesson not to break norms pertaining to war. Note that the claim that reasoning on the selection of normative ideas involves relating them to already established norms is not tautological. The already selected norms were institutionalised at t_1. This makes it possible for actors to employ these institutionalised norms in efforts to make sense about the selection of another advocated normative idea at t_2.[8]

Figure 2.1 summarises the process of reasoning about normative ideas. Actors employ those *topoi* from the repertoire of commonplaces

---

[8] If the advocated idea gets selected as an idea, it becomes part of the repertoire of commonplaces and advocates may employ the institutionalised norm in a debate on the selection of another normative idea at t_3. For a similar argument on studying ideational change see Walter Carlsnaes (1992).

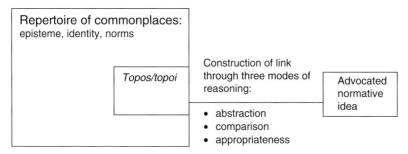

Figure 2.1 Reasoning about normative ideas

that enable them to make sense of a particular issue, and they construct a link between these *topoi* and the advocated idea. The construction of the link proceeds through three modes of reasoning: abstraction, comparison and appropriateness.

Building on this conceptual groundwork, the following three sections develop three ideal-typical stages of norm selection. I contend that the repertoire of commonplaces helps explain why advocacies form (innovative argumentation). Inquiring into the question of what linkages between what *topoi* are persuasive to an audience, I identify the properties of a successful argument (persuasive argumentation). Finally, scrutinising the salience of the repertoire for bargaining processes, I theorise on the conditions under which opponents are swayed by what is to them an unconvincing argument (compromise).

Formation of advocacy: innovative argumentation

What makes actors engage in an advocacy for a normative idea in the first place? I hypothesise that innovative argumentation is made possible by a change of the environment in which agents are embedded. Two aspects of the environment provide the impetus for the formation of an advocacy: a revolutionary event and a changing repertoire of commonplaces.

Theorising on agency requires considerable scholarly restraint. Human creativity eludes the more or less elegant models that, by supposedly uncovering nomothetic laws governing human agency, aim to predict the outcomes of human action. Yet this creativity is made possible by the environment in which human beings are embedded. This allows the student at least to theorise on how a particular environment gives rise to a range of possible practices. For the task at hand, therefore, the

question is the following: What properties make the environment conducive to a new advocacy?

Two aspects of the environment are critical: revolutionary events and
changing repertoires of commonplaces. Revolutionary events may be
appreciated, such as a technological breakthrough, victory in war, or
spectacular economic success. Yet they may also be shocking, such as a
natural disaster, war, ethnic cleansing or genocide. Such an event constitutes a 'cognitive punch' (Adler, 1991: 55). It makes clear that the old
ways of doing things have become obsolete and have to be replaced by
something new (Odell, 1982; Hall, 1986; Toulmin, 1990). A shifting
repertoire – this applies in particular to changes of the episteme but also
to identity narrative and internalised norms – replaces old tools for
making the world intelligible with new ones. Thus, actors come to
reason about the world differently. Revolutionary events and changing
repertoires, therefore, share an important similarity: they turn the world
upside down for agents. This challenges them to abandon old orthodoxies and to search for alternatives.

There are four possible configurations of a revolutionary event and a
changing repertoire. First, if they occur at the same time or follow one
another in a short time sequence, the environment is most conducive to
agents to initiate an advocacy for a new normative idea. In this case, the
revolutionary event challenges actors to embark on new ways of doing
things and the changing repertoire provides them with new clues for
doing so. Second, the propensity of the environment to facilitate the
development of a new argument is medium high if the repertoire
changes but no revolutionary event occurs. The changing repertoire
still enables actors to see the world in a different light, but there is no
'cognitive punch' that makes it obvious to actors that what is established has to change. Third, the propensity for a new argument is
medium low if there is a 'cognitive punch' but no significant change of
the repertoire. Agents may feel the need for change, but the environment
does not give them new clues about the directions of this change.
Finally, the environment is least conducive to change if there is neither
a 'cognitive punch' nor a significant change in the repertoire of commonplaces. Not only are there no novel clues for how to change something; there is not even a trigger that makes change a necessity in the
view of the agents. Table 2.1 provides an overview of the extent to
which different environments facilitate the occurrence of innovative
argumentation.

Table 2.1 *Environments conducive to innovative argumentation*

	Change of repertoire	No change of repertoire
Revolutionary event	High	Medium low
No revolutionary event	Medium high	Low

The hypothesised salience of a significant change of the repertoire of commonplaces for the origins of an advocacy clarifies the use of the terminology 'innovative argumentation' or 'new argument'. The ideas for which advocates argue are rarely ever entirely new. Usually they are recycled from the past or taken from other contemporary contexts. This does not mean, however, that the argumentation is not new. Argumentation entails linking an advocated idea to a repertoire of commonplaces. If a significant change of the repertoire makes the environment conducive to the formation of a new advocacy, the argumentation for which this advocacy stands is innovative. If only in nuances, advocates need to invent a new link between the advocated idea and the evolving repertoire. Even in the rare case that the advocacy originates in an environment in which no major change of the repertoire occurred but only a revolutionary event, the argumentation is most likely to be innovative. It reflects novel attempts of agents to cope with a world in which this event has just occurred.

Although they may not perfectly mirror it, advocacies echo the reasoning through which advocates came to believe in their stance. Aristotle's *Art of Rhetoric* is about how to make up one's own mind and how to get this message across. To Aristotle, these are separate but interrelated tasks. First, elites reason about their conclusions. Then, they need to convince the masses. Aristotle deplores the fact that the masses do not reason in the same way that the supposedly more sophisticated elites do. He maintains, therefore, that elites have to learn the necessary *techne* to reach the masses. The *techne* helps the elites to translate their lines of reasoning into a language that is compelling for the masses. Albeit far less focused on differences of elite and mass reasoning, Martha Finnemore and Kathryn Sikkink (1998) make a similar claim in their research on norm advocacies. Advocates think strategically how to get their message across. Their reasoning is mediated by strategic considerations. They leave out certain aspects of their original reasoning if they think that this will not resonate with the audience. They simplify it, in order to make it easier to understand. Although made more palatable to a broader audience, however, the line of reasoning that developed when the advocacy formed is also at the core of its efforts to make it resonate beyond the advocacy network.

Power of argument I: persuasive argumentation

Innovative argumentations are initiated frequently but only a few of them succeed in persuading a broader audience. What makes an advocacy persuasive? Based on the process of reasoning outlined above, my explanatory strategy for this question is twofold. First, I identify the *topoi* that make for compelling abstract, comparative and appropriateness reasoning. Some ideas taken from the reservoir of commonplaces make for a more convincing argument than others. Second, I inquire into the opportunities that the use of certain *topoi* offers to advocates to assure the audience of their credibility.

This translates into four conditions that facilitate persuasive argumentation. First, arguments that invoke a fit between an advocated normative idea, the dominant episteme, and a nation's widely shared longing for the future facilitate persuasive argumentation. This proposition pertains to abstract reasoning. The conclusion of a syllogism presupposes a goal (major premise) and a cause–effect relationship (minor premise). A nation's widely shared longing for the future is a powerful *topos* for identifying the goal. The identity narrative sketches paths towards the nation's longing. Nations tend to project the achievement of their most important ideals into the future. In this way, nations are often incomplete by their own judgement (Meier, 1999). The identity narrative also contains cause–effect relationships. The episteme, however, provides a more compelling *topos* for the minor premise of the syllogism because the cause–effect relationship of the dominant episteme is situated at a deeper level of the web of taken-for-granted meaning.

Second, arguments that assert a match between widely accepted key events of the identity narrative, the dominant episteme and the normative idea make persuasive argumentation more likely. This kind of argumentative power stems from the salience of comparative reasoning. Nations interpret their identity narrative through the lens of the episteme. This lens makes actors emphasise certain key events of the identity narrative and predisposes them to make sense of these events in a particular way. Serving as analogies, key events make for powerful *topoi*, especially if the taken-for-granted lens through which actors look at these events – i.e. the episteme – is also explicitly invoked as a *topos*.

Third, arguments that postulate a link between identity-constituting norms, their justification by the dominant episteme and/or key events of the identity narrative, and the advocated idea facilitate persuasive argumentation. As outlined in the previous section, appropriateness reasoning may be underwritten by the justification of an institutionalised norm. A strong justification may revolve around the dominant episteme or key events of the identity narrative or both. Employing such a justification is expected to make for a more compelling argument than appropriateness reasoning that merely invokes an already institutionalised norm.

Fourth, advocates who have established a reputation with the audience of having persistently supported the *topoi* of their advocacy not only during the pursuit of this advocacy but also outside of it make persuasive argumentation more likely. Endorsing the *topoi* not only for a particular advocacy but having endorsed them beyond it lends credibility to communicators. It assures the audience that the speakers have not chosen the *topoi* of the advocacy for opportunistic reasons but because they actually believe in them.[9]

Power of argument II: compromise

If the power of an argument were confined to persuasion, norm selection through argumentation would be a very rare phenomenon. It is very unlikely that an argument persuades everyone. Yet the power of an argument is not confined to persuasion. I contend that an advocacy that succeeds in establishing a new majority view puts pressure on recalcitrant actors to comply.

Research on public opinion suggests that an argument, once it has become widely accepted, puts pressure on non-persuaded actors to conform (Nölle-Neumann, 1981). Focusing on norm selection, Finnemore and Sikkink (1998: 902) contend that an advocacy that succeeded in persuading a critical number of actors puts pressure on recalcitrant actors to rethink their position. This makes them amenable to be swayed into norm compliance by 'material sanctions and incentives' offered to them. What this really suggests is that the pressure of the

---

[9] For the link between perceived sincerity and credibility see Alice Eagly, Wendy Wood and Shelly Chaiken (1978).

newly established majority view makes recalcitrant actors sit down at the bargaining table. This contention begs two questions. First, when are actors prepared to sit down at the bargaining table? Most importantly, recalcitrant actors yield to the pressure of a successful advocacy independently of their beliefs that made them initially oppose the advocacy. Second, what happens at the bargaining table? What bargaining situation, with what implications for the bargaining outcome, does a successful advocacy create?

Successful argumentation only makes those recalcitrant actors willing to bargain whose repertoire of commonplaces contains the *topoi* that the advocates invoke in their argumentation. There are two levels of disagreement with an argument. The *topoi* employed by an advocate may be part of a recalcitrant actor's reservoir of commonplaces. The rift between arguments, however, may cut much deeper. The *topoi* picked by the advocate may not be part of the counter-advocate's repertoire of commonplaces. In the latter case, the recalcitrant actor refuses to bargain, even if this entails significant costs. Reaching an agreement with the advocate would require the unconvinced actor to violate his or her deepest held beliefs. If the *topoi* invoked by the advocate are also part of the recalcitrant actor's repertoire, by contrast, bargaining becomes possible.

What happens once advocates and counter-advocates sharing the advocacy's *topoi* sit down at the bargaining table? The occurrence of the persuasive argumentation stage of the norm selection mechanism makes clear who is eager to reach an agreement. The recalcitrant actors are desperate to overcome the costs resulting from their opposition. They seek a way out. Political parties, for example, are likely to act in such a way in order to avoid being punished at the polls for defending what has become an unpopular stance. From this eagerness it follows that the focal point – i.e. the outcome with the highest expected utility that each actor, locked into a game with the other, can achieve – and with it the likely outcome of the bargaining process is much more closely situated at the position of the successful advocates than at the stance originally embraced by the recalcitrant actors. I refer to such a bargaining success, triggered by the power of an argument, as compromise.[10]

---

[10] Note that this is only one among several possible conceptualisations of a compromise. A newly established majority view provides a weaker impetus to compromise on one's position than, say, an immanent threat of physical force. I am only concerned with the former.

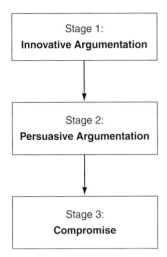

Figure 2.2 Ideal-typical three-stage norm selection mechanism

Figure 2.2 summarises the three-stage norm selection mechanism that I developed in the last three sections. Innovative argumentation, if a number of conditions are fulfilled, diffuses through persuasive argumentation, which in turn pressures recalcitrant actors into a compromise with the successful advocates.

These three stages are, of course, merely ideal-types. They are a means to conceptually cope with a world that is much more complex. The extent to which this simplification is leading or misleading ultimately depends on the degree to which the ideal-typical stages help provide a plausible answer to an important empirical question, in this study the peaceful settlement of irredentist disputes in Europe. Two more clarifications are in order. First, ideas can be selected as norms in various ways. Figure 2.2 merely captures one among many pathways. Some of these pathways may somewhat resemble this three-stage mechanism, including perhaps a reverse order of the last two stages. Other pathways, however, are very different. The logic of practice (Guzzini, 2000; Adler, 2005; Pouliot, 2008), for instance, provides such an alternative route towards norm selection. Due to the equifinality of norm selection, this study pays close attention to the conditions making these three stages possible. Second, the three-stage norm selection mechanism focuses on how agents link the taken-for-granted to normative ideas in order to reason, argue and persuade. This enables me to explain only a limited change of the pool of taken-for-granted ideas, i.e. the internalisation of a new norm. Explaining changes of the episteme, for instance, is outside of the scope of my study. (My empirical analysis of changing epistemes is descriptive.) Yet I maintain this focus because such a normative change may make a major difference in world politics and because it remains very ill-understood how agents assemble a coherent and to others convincing picture about the world out of the myriad (at times contradictory) clues provided by the social context of which they are a part.

Studying argumentation and compromise

How to study argumentation and compromise empirically? The three-stage norm selection mechanism contains a number of aspects that make for thorny methodological issues. In order to address these adequately, this section develops six methodological steps to bridge the theoretical and empirical realms. These steps pertain to examining (1) the repertoire of commonplaces, (2) innovative argumentation, (3) persuasive argumentation, (4) compromise, (5) norm internalisation and (6) alternative explanations.

There are two principal methodological options for analysing argumentation and the environment in which it is embedded. Formal argument analysis entails translating argumentative encounters into mathematical language and tracing the moves that each player makes in detail (Alker, 1988). Informal argument analysis (Crawford, 2002: 119–30), by contrast, is an interpretivist approach. It involves thickly describing the social context of argumentative processes, the specific beliefs invoked by advocates, and the success with which they link these beliefs to the advocated idea. Given the emphasis that the theoretical framework puts on the social environment in which actors – be they senders or recipients of a message – are embedded, the interpretivist approach is better suited than the more formal one. Yet the three-stage norm selection mechanism requires modifying Crawford's methodology, in order for informal argument analysis to be able to examine the conditions that give rise to these stages and the linkages between them.

This yields six methodological steps, which are summarised in table 2.2. The first task involves the analysis of the repertoire of commonplaces. The primary purpose of this analysis is descriptive. The means is thick description. The examination traces the evolution of controversies about and

Table 2.2 *Navigating argumentation and compromise*

---

1 Analysis of repertoire of commonplaces
   1.1 Trace evolution of and contestation about epistemes
   1.2 Trace evolution of and contestation about identity narrative
   1.3 Trace evolution of and contestation about already selected norms
2 Analysis of innovative argumentation
   2.1 Identify advocated idea
   2.2 Identify topos or topoi of argumentation
   2.3 Identify modes of reasoning (abstraction, comparison, appropriateness)
   2.4 Scrutinise environmental propositions on innovative argumentation
3 Analysis of persuasive argumentation
   3.1 Trace diffusion of argument (presence of 2.1, 2.2 and 2.3) from actor to actor (diffusion test)
   3.2 Correlate presence of topoi as used by advocates in 2.2 and support for 2.2 where data do not allow for 2.3 (congruence test)
   3.3 Scrutinise propositions on conditions of persuasive argumentation
4 Analysis of compromise
   4.1 Identify instances in which unconvinced actors forgo their opposition
   4.2 Scrutinise propositions on compromise (sequencing test)
5 Analysis of norm internalisation
   5.1 Identify situational circumstances that could spark debates about the newly selected norm
   5.2 Use absence of such a debate as indicator for norm internalisation
6 Discussion of alternative explanations

---

agreements on the three ideational forces that make up the repertoire of commonplaces: episteme, identity and already established norms. This shows whether there is a dominant repertoire at a particular moment in time, and, if so, whether this dominance is challenged. Thus, the analysis of the repertoire enables the researcher to reconstruct the reservoir of ideas available to advocates and their audience to reason.

There is a good reason for starting the empirical analysis with the repertoire instead of intermingling the analysis of the repertoire with the examination of the three norm selection stages. Argumentation and compromise cannot but occur on the basis of the ideas contained in the repertoire of commonplaces. Even the most savvy advocates stand on the intersubjective foundation of the repertoire and cannot manipulate it by free will. This makes it possible for the student of argumentation to keep the examination of the repertoire and the inquiry into norm selection separate, which ensures that the explanation does not become tautological. It separates those ideas that help to reason from those that are advocated.

The second task entails the analysis of innovative argumentation. This involves, in chronological order, identifying the advocated idea, the *topoi* that the advocates employ, and the modes of reasoning they use to link the *topoi* to the advocated idea. This enables me to determine whether innovative argumentation occurs or not. If it occurs, the environmental factors outlined in the theoretical framework are applied to the case: Has a revolutionary event occurred? Has the repertoire of commonplaces changed? How do these environmental factors affect agents struggling to make sense of the world?

The third task revolves around scrutinising persuasive argumentation. I employ what I label the diffusion and the congruence tests to determine the occurrence of persuasive argumentation. The diffusion test focuses on the spread of the intersubjective fit between repertoire and normative idea. If a particular argument, identified by the advocated idea as well as the *topoi* and the modes of reasoning employed, spreads from one communicator to another, it can be inferred from this that the former persuaded the latter through his or her argument. The reproduction of an argument, therefore, serves as indicator for persuasion. The congruence test, used when data – such as public opinion surveys – do not allow for the diffusion test, is slightly less demanding. If (1) an audience comes to accept a normative idea, (2) the *topoi* picked by the advocates are part of the audience's repertoire of commonplaces, and (3) the audience comes to agree with the advocates' argumentation without rewards and punishments being offered, I infer from this the occurrence of persuasive argumentation. If, according to these two tests, persuasive argumentation has occurred, I examine the conditions that made it possible. This examination is guided by the four propositions on persuasive argumentation developed in the theory sections above.

Fourth, I use a sequencing test as indicator for the occurrence of a compromise: at t_1 some players advocate selecting the idea as a norm whereas others argue against it; the former and the latter do not share the same repertoire of commonplaces or, if they do, they disagree about the linkage between the repertoire of commonplaces and the normative idea. Between t_1 and t_2, the costs of opposing the normative idea are mounting. At t_2 the opponents receive a concession by the domestic advocates and/or in the international arena that makes the normative idea, given the opponent's repertoire of commonplaces, less objectionable. At t_3 the opponents comply with the norm selection but they do not advocate a fit between the normative idea and the repertoire of commonplaces.

Fifth, I identify situational circumstances in the aftermath of persuasive argumentation and compromise that have the potential to spark renewed controversies about the normative idea. If, despite these circumstances, no new debate about the idea ensues, I infer from this that it has been internalised as a norm. Internalisation means that a norm develops a 'taken-for-granted quality'. This quality can be shown empirically by the extent of public debate on a selected norm. If it is internalised, it is 'no longer a matter of broad public debate' (Finnemore and Sikkink, 1998: 895).[11]

Finally, I address alternative explanations of my cases. This discussion is not concerned with what positivists would label control variables. Positivist research aims to discover the objective truth by employing variants of the controlled experiment as a methodological path to knowledge. I am sceptical about the epistemological assumptions that underpin this truth claim (even if qualified as merely approximating the objective truth) and this methodological pathway. Although I do not control for variables, discussing alternative explanations is of key importance for this study. My goal is to develop a plausible explanation for the peaceful settlement of irredentist disputes in Europe. Plausibility in this context has something to do with scholarly argumentation. This study engages in a debate with other scholars who have worked on the cases I choose and on the phenomenon that I seek to explain. Needless to say, debating involves not only dealing with one's own explanation but also with the explanations of others. This is why the discussion of alternative accounts is an important step on my road map for this research.

Case selection

Exploring the three-stage norm selection process requires an in-depth investigation of a limited number of cases. Otherwise it would be

---

[11] Internalised norms have become part of the repertoire of commonplaces and may serve as *topoi* for future arguments.

impossible to scrutinise the repertoire of commonplaces and trace the norm selection mechanism, especially its argumentation stages, in sufficient detail. I examine two claimants in detail – the FRG (West Germany) and the Republic of Ireland – because they allow for a demanding plausibility probe of my theoretical framework.

After the Second World War, the FRG claimed that Germany in its 1938 borders – i.e. after the territorial revisions of the Versailles Treaty and before Hitler's expansionism – continued to exist *de jure*. Thus, it refused to recognise the GDR (East Germany) (historical 'Central Germany') and the loss of East Prussia, Pomerania and Silesia (historical 'Eastern Germany') to Poland and the Soviet Union. Until the mid-1960s, there was a consensus in the West German public and among political elites that the GDR as well as the border between Poland and the GDR – the Oder–Neiße line – must never be recognised. This made the FRG the state with the most irredentist claims in post-Second World War Europe. In the early 1970s, however, Bonn recognised the territorial status quo in a series of bilateral agreements.

Until quite recently, the Republic of Ireland refused to recognise the United Kingdom's sovereignty over Northern Ireland. The 1921 Anglo-Irish Treaty established the Irish Free State. The Unionists of Northern Ireland seized upon the opportunity offered by the treaty, and six counties of the historical province of Ulster – Antrim, Armagh, Down, Fermanagh, Londonderry/Derry[12] and Tyrone – opted out of the Free State. In the South, the treaty triggered a civil war between those Nationalists in favour and those against signing it.[13] A party emerging from the latter group, Fianna Fáil, became the South's most powerful political force. While in power in 1937, it wrote a new Constitution for the Republic of Ireland. In Articles 2 and 3, the Republic codified its irredentist claim to Northern Ireland. According to these articles, the *de jure* territory of the Republic of Ireland encompassed the entire island of Ireland. More than half a century later, the Republic changed the Constitution and renounced its irredentist claim.

Studying these two cases, of course, cannot resolve the research puzzle of European irredentism once and for all. I examine the plausibility of the

---

[12] Nationalists refer to it as Derry, Unionists as Londonderry.
[13] I use these labels as they appear in Irish discourse: Nationalists share the ideal of a unified Ireland, whereas Unionists wish to remain a part of the United Kingdom. The overwhelming majority of the Republic's populace and a sizeable minority in the North are Nationalists. The majority in the North are Unionists.

three-stage norm selection mechanism for two out of twelve cases in post-Second World War Europe. Yet these two cases make for a demanding plausibility probe that can determine whether pursuing this research agenda further is worthwhile. There are two reasons for this. First, the FRG and the Republic of Ireland settled their irredentist disputes peacefully only after decades of determined irredentism. The two cases, therefore, not only tell us something about how settlements of irredentist disputes succeed. They also tell us something about how they fail. For the three-stage norm selection mechanism to provide a convincing explanation of the two cases, it has to be able to explain both success and failure. Second, in light of the theoretical framework introduced in this chapter the two cases amount to a puzzle within the puzzle. Within the grand puzzle of why Europe expelled the ghost of irredentism in the last half century through peaceful recognitions of existing borders, the timing of the FRG's and the Republic of Ireland's renunciation of irredentism poses a peculiar puzzle for a theory that puts identity at the centre of its inquiry. The FRG renounced its claims to the GDR as well as parts of Poland and the Soviet Union in the midst of the Cold War. The Republic of Ireland, by contrast, settled its dispute with the United Kingdom – a fellow member of the European Union – only a quarter of a century later. For a theoretical framework that takes the identification of nations vis-à-vis other nations seriously, this timing is puzzling. At least at first glance, it should have happened the other way round. The Republic of Ireland should have settled its conflict with a fellow member of the European Union much more easily than the FRG did with its Cold War adversaries across the Iron Curtain.

Sources

Ted Hopf (2002) encourages researchers interested in the ideational dimension of world politics to look inside the state. This is an important point that has far-reaching methodological repercussions for this research endeavour. In order to capture the domestic dynamics of norm selection – something that is of key importance for putting the three-stage norm selection mechanism under scrutiny – a variety of different sources are required.

On a theoretical level, the advocacy literature argues convincingly that the selection of a norm by a nation-state has, among other things, something to do with whether international and/or domestic advocates succeed in making a normative idea resonate with a nation. Yet much of the same literature tends to truncate domestic processes *qua* methodology. While its theoretical frameworks allow for the analysis of domestic dynamics, empirical research is largely confined to government elites. National identity is, for example, an important factor in Schimmelfennig's theory of rhetorical action, but he empirically investigates only elite representations of national identity and how elites, given these representations, act on behalf of the state (Schimmelfennig, 2000). In a similar vein, Jeffrey Checkel inquires into 'European identity change' (2001: 553) and 'national identity in contemporary Europe' (1999: 83) by studying changing representations of identity by small circles of elites. This is a risky methodological path. Identity representations by political elites, other elites and the public at large may be the same. But they may also be different. The extent to which they converge or diverge should be a matter of empirical analysis.

The prerequisite for such an analysis is a diversification of sources. The analysis of government documents, for example, is indispensable but only reveals government elite representations of the repertoire of commonplaces and merely gives access to arguments made and received by government elites. In order to avoid theorising about the nation and gathering evidence on a narrowly defined elite level, this study uses six clusters of sources. First, I analyse biographies, autobiographies and speeches of all German Chancellors who held office between 1949 and 1973, and of all Irish *Taoisigh* (Prime Ministers) who were in power between 1945 and 1998. Second, I scrutinise all parliamentary debates in the Deutscher Bundestag and the Dáil Éireann within the above-mentioned time periods that either deal with general principles of foreign policy or with the disputed territories. The German and Irish parliaments each have two chambers. The chambers chosen for analysis are the ones where decision-making power for foreign policy is concentrated. Third, I analyse the reactions to these debates in the editorials of major national newspapers that are representative of the political spectrum in each country.[14] Concerning the case of the FRG, I analyse the *Frankfurter*

---

[14] It is simply not feasible to analyse all newspaper editorials from five decades. Thus, I narrowed the analysis down to responses to the parliamentary debates that I examined. I analysed the first two newspaper editions following a parliamentary debate on the irredentist claims or general principles of foreign policy. See appendix III for more details. I partly borrow this design from Jeffrey Legro (2000).

Allgemeine Zeitung, Süddeutsche Zeitung, Die Welt and *Die Zeit*.[15]
With regard to the Irish case, I examine the *Irish Independent, Irish Times* and *Irish Press*.[16] Appendix III lists the subjects and dates of the parliamentary debates as well as the dates of the newspaper editions that I analyse. Fourth, I examine public opinion polls on the issues raised in these parliamentary debates and newspaper editions. Fifth, I identify *leitmotive* pertaining to identity discourses in political caricature, paintings, plays, films and fictional literature. Finally, I conducted elite interviews with high-ranking decision-makers and advocates who were actively involved in the norm selection processes.

The two principal tasks of the informal argument analysis, i.e. examination of the repertoire of commonplaces, as well as analysis of argumentation and compromise, translate into two empirical chapters on each of the two cases. The first deals with the repertoire of commonplaces, and the second with argumentation and compromise. I begin with an inquiry into the case of the FRG because its irredentist claims were settled prior to the Republic of Ireland's recognition of the territorial status quo. Chapter 3, entitled 'Broadening a vision for Europe', traces the evolution of the FRG's repertoire in the field of European security. I contend that the FRG began in the 1960s to project fragments of its vision of a peaceful Western Europe through co-operation and integration into the relations between Eastern and Western Europe. Chapter 4, 'Towards a new beginning', shows how advocates selected

---

[15] All four newspapers have a significant circulation throughout the country for the period analysed. The newspapers are representative of the dominant political spectrum. From the late 1950s onwards, the *Frankfurter Allgemeine Zeitung* developed into a paper that is situated at the conservative end of the centre of the political spectrum. *Die Zeit* occupies the liberal end of the centre of the spectrum, although the newspaper initially showed some strong conservative tendencies. The *Süddeutsche Zeitung* is situated slightly left of *Die Zeit*, *Die Welt* slightly right of the *Frankfurter Allgemeine Zeitung*.

[16] These are the only national newspapers (i.e. with significant circulation throughout the Republic of Ireland) in the analysed time frame. The *Irish Independent* and *Irish Times* were published throughout this period. Due to dwindling circulation in the 1990s, the *Irish Press* went out of print in 1995. The *Irish Times* is a liberal newspaper. Although the newspaper has its roots in Unionism in the nineteenth century and was Protestant-owned until 1974, it is a politically independent newspaper. The *Irish Independent* has its roots in Catholicism and shows affinities to Fine Gael. The *Irish Press*, established by Eamon de Valera and henceforth controlled by the de Valera family, by contrast, was affiliated with Fine Gael's principal – and often more powerful – political opponent, Fianna Fáil (Hussey, 1994: 340–3).

new *topoi* for debating the selection of the territorial status quo norm from the changing repertoire of commonplaces. Guided by the theoretical framework, I examine the generative mechanism that led to the selection of the territorial status quo norm in the early 1970s. Chapter 5, 'From exclusion to inclusion', traces the remarkable change in the Republic of Ireland's repertoire of commonplaces. Reinvented in the 1920s and 1930s, Irish nationalism became very exclusive. Its key defining feature was sharp demarcation of Irishness from Unionism, Britain and to a lesser extent the outside world. By the 1990s, the repertoire of commonplaces had changed towards inclusivity. The attempt to overcome these demarcations on the island of Ireland, the British Isles and Europe had become part of Irishness. Chapter 6, 'Constitutional change', examines how the change of the repertoire changed the *topoi* that actors employed to make sense of the Irish Question, and analyses the successes as well as failures of argumentation and compromise to bring about the recognition of the territorial status quo. In the concluding chapter, I compare the empirical results and discuss their significance for the study of irredentism as well as for the theoretical debate to find a middle ground between the logics of argumentation and consequences.

3 | Broadening a vision for Europe

The territorial revisions following the Second World War had severe repercussions for Germany. With Moscow incorporating East Prussia into the Soviet Union, and Poland (compensated for the loss of its eastern territories to the Soviet Union) annexing Pomerania and Silesia, Germany lost all its territories east of the Oder and Neiße rivers. Furthermore, with the Allies not being able to reach agreement on the future status of Germany, two German states came into being, which were separated by the Iron Curtain. The purpose of this chapter is descriptive: What were the perimeters within which West Germans tried to make sense of this situation and possible future improvements? The chapter traces the evolution of the repertoire of commonplaces pertaining to the German Question. This is the necessary first step of the argumentation analysis. Only after identifying the repertoire in this chapter can the next chapter then inquire into how agents pick *topoi* from the repertoire, link them to advocated ideas, and succeed or fail to win over an audience.

The analysis of this chapter reveals continuity and change. Four important aspects remained fairly constant from the late 1940s to the early 1970s. First, the identity narrative on Germany's homeland did not change. For most West Germans, the territories lost after the Second World War remained part of Germany's historical homeland, and East Germans were self-evidently regarded as fellow Germans. Second, the norm of peaceful resolution of disputes constituted a key norm, which served as a marker sharply differentiating Germany's militarist past from West Germany's present and future. Third, the FRG's identification with Western Europe was another major marker that drew an unambiguous line between the FRG and Nazi Germany. Fourth, and situated at a deeper level of the ideational fabric, most West Germans came to look at Europe through the episteme of the Idea of Europe. They took it for granted that Europe consists of distinct nations but that these nations are not autonomous from one another. Their fate was considered inescapably intertwined (ontological dimension). Europe had failed to understand this shared fate in the past, causing a series of disasters. Only by overcoming the divisiveness of Europe's nation-state borders through co-operation and integration would it be possible for Europe to prevent these tragedies from reoccurring (causal dimension).

Despite these continuities the repertoire of commonplaces did not stay the same. There were two important and interrelated changes. First, most West Germans came to tell a different narrative about themselves. Whereas they had cautiously circumvented any painful questions about Germany's past, they began to reflect more critically upon the Second World War and the Holocaust from the early 1960s onwards. This led to the desire to 'make good again' (*Wiedergutmachung*) with East Europeans. Second, the desire for *Wiedergutmachung* predisposed the Federal Republic to interpret the overtures of the Warsaw Pact to establish a new security regime in Europe (this culminated in the 1975 Helsinki Final Act) as the evolution of a common ground on how to make sense of and manage security in Europe. Based on this common ground, the FRG came to imagine and desire the creation of a – however rudimentary – community dictated by an inescapably shared fate across the East–West divide. The Federal Republic increasingly identified itself with the role of nurturing and promoting such a community.

This chapter is divided into two major parts. The first one discusses the continuities of the repertoire of commonplaces. I deal with the episteme, address the definition of the homeland, elaborate on the norm of peaceful resolution of disputes, and examine the FRG's positive identification with Western Europe. The second half uncovers the changing dimensions of the repertoire. It traces the evolution of West German identity vis-à-vis Eastern Europe chronologically: from sharp demarcation to the desire to build a community of fate (*Schicksalsgemeinschaft*).

The idea of Europe

Historically, the Idea of Europe has tended to become influential among intellectual elites all over Europe after major catastrophes.[1] They have

---

[1] An excellent overview of the evolution of the Idea of Europe can be found in Rolf Hellmut Foerster (1967).

used the Idea of Europe to make sense of what happened and to find ways to prevent disasters from reoccurring. Maximilian de Béthune, duc de Sully (2002 [1662]), wrote his *grand dessein* shortly after the Thirty Years War. He argued that Europeans were bound together by a common fate. In order to overcome a legacy of bloody wars, Europeans would have to replace the divisions that statehood had imposed on the continent with co-operation and integration. Later, the Enlightenment's belief in progress sparked an array of European unification plans, including those by the Abbé de Saint-Pierre (1986 [1712]), Jeremy Bentham (1974 [1789]) and Immanuel Kant (1871 [1791], 1995 [1795]).

After the unprecedented loss of life and destruction of the First World War, the Idea of Europe was no longer confined to intellectual circles, but was also embraced by political decision-makers, for example Eduard Beneš, Aristide Briand and Gustav Stresemann. After the Second World War had caused a catastrophe in Europe and the world that defied anything that – despite the experiences of the First World War – had been imaginable before 1939, the Idea of Europe gained increasing salience all over Europe. The idea became the episteme based on which actors – including powerful ones such as Winston Churchill (1946) and Charles de Gaulle (1971) – made sense of Europe's past, present and future. Europe had forgotten that it was one. European nations had embarked on atomism. Nationalism had ripped Europe apart. The divisions would have to be overcome in order for Europe to have a future.

The West German reading of the Idea of Europe echoed these deeply held beliefs. According to this reading, Europe consisted of distinct nations but these were far from autonomous from one another. Their fate was inescapably intertwined (ontological dimension). Europe, divided by impenetrable nation-state borders, failed to acknowledge this shared fate in the past. This caused a history of warfare that culminated in two world wars and threatened Europe's very existence. The only way to overcome this history of destruction was to take away the divisiveness of Europe's nation-state borders. Europeans would have to co-operate and integrate in order to survive (causal dimension).

Not all West Germans shared the episteme. A small minority continued to hold on to the epistemic understandings underpinning National Socialism. Fascist parties such as the German Empire Party (DRP) and its successor, the National Democratic Party of Germany

(NDP), looked at the world from a perspective that was diametrically opposed to the Idea of Europe. For them, it continued to be a given that world politics is the fighting ground of nations and races out of which the stronger emerge victoriously. Races and nations were considered to be living organisms that had to be nurtured in order to stand their ground on the battlefield of history (Rohlinger, 1969: 106). Fascist splinter groups, however, exerted little influence in the Bonn Republic. Only in 1949 were a small number of fascist candidates elected to the Bundestag. Afterwards, right-wing extremist parties did not succeed in entering parliament again.

The Communist Party of Germany (KPD) looked at world politics through a radically different lens. In line with the doctrines of Karl Marx and Vladimir Lenin, the party held that the world was divided into capitalist and socialist states. The former would always be imperialist and use nationalism to mobilise for war in the interest of the bourgeoisie. Peace would only be possible by overcoming capitalism (Kommunistische Partei Deutschlands, 1963 [1945]). Yet the KPD and its successor, the German Communist Party (DKP), were as marginalised in West German politics as the fascist splinter parties.

These peculiar sets of fundamental knowledge for looking at the world on the marginalised radical left and radical right notwithstanding, a far-reaching and taken-for-granted consensus on the Idea of Europe had developed by the mid-1950s. The episteme can be identified in parliamentary debates across party lines, in documents and speeches by high-ranking government officials independently of their party affiliation, as well as in the works of novelists and poets. The salience of the episteme can also be inferred from school curricula and public opinion polls.

In the Bundestag, the episteme was made explicit in the grand debates on general principles of foreign policy. Although there were sharp disagreements about the integration of the FRG into Western Europe and the North Atlantic Treaty Organisation (NATO) in the early years of the Bonn Republic and about policies towards Eastern Europe in the late 1960s and early 1970s, there was a far-reaching consensus across political parties on the Idea of Europe. There was consensus that Europe's nationalistic past had to be overcome. Günter Henle, foreign policy specialist of the Christian Democratic Union (CDU), for example, spoke of the changes in Europe brought about by the Second World War, 'which must make continuing national rivalries appear to be as anachronistic as the continuing warfare between the hellenic states or the

Italian city-states of the Middle Ages were'.[2] There was also consensus that overcoming the past could only be accomplished if Europeans came together as a community and overcame intra-European divisions. Hans Ewers, member of the German Party (DP), for example, praised Gustav Stresemann, Foreign Minister during the Weimar Republic, because of his efforts towards European co-operation and integration. His death, according to Ewers, was the beginning of a nationalist foreign policy that had ended in disaster.[3] Helmut Schäfer, foreign policy specialist of the Liberal Democratic Party (FDP) contended that peace in Europe could only be accomplished if Europe's divisions into nation-states could be overcome by the creation of 'real, cognitive, economic and personal contexts'[4] that transcend the nation-state.

German newspaper editorials also emphasised the need to replace intra-European divisions with co-operation and integration, in order to achieve peace. The episteme was the basis from which contemporary European affairs were interpreted and evaluated. In 1949, the *Süddeutsche Zeitung* wrote about the Second World War and the current state of Europe as the 'tragedy of sovereign nation-states'.[5] In the mid-1960s, *Die Zeit* advocated following de Gaulle's lead in increasing contacts with Eastern Europe, because it enabled Europeans to overcome the divisions that threatened the continent's security.[6] Also advocating détente, the *Frankfurter Allgemeine Zeitung* warned that, 'in the German view, the current state of world politics does not justify a splintering of Europe into nation-states'.[7] In 1973, *Die Welt* cautioned that France and Germany had to compromise on their different visions of the European unification process. Given the lessons of European history, European unification was 'damned' to be successful.[8]

[2] Günter Henle, *Verhandlungen des deutschen Bundestages* 1, 23 September 1949, p. 96.
[3] Hans Ewers, *Verhandlungen des deutschen Bundestages* 1, 21 September 1949, p. 47.
[4] Helmut Schäfer, *Verhandlungen des deutschen Bundestages* 1, 21 September 1949, p. 51.
[5] Franz Josef Schöningh, 'Deutschland und Frankreich', *Süddeutsche Zeitung*, 15 November 1949, p. 1.
[6] Marion Gräfin Dönhoff, 'Ostpolitik mit de Gaulle', *Die Zeit*, 3 December 1965, p. 1.
[7] Nikolas Benckiser, 'Die deutsche Plattform,' *Frankfurter Allgemeine Zeitung*, 25 March 1966, p. 1.
[8] Georg Schröder, 'In der Europa-Frage zum Erfolg verdammt', *Die Welt*, 14 September 1973, p. 4.

A detailed study on the content of German newspapers by Markus Kiefer confirms the salience of the Idea of Europe. Analysing the editorials of eight newspapers from 1949 to 1955, Kiefer (1993: 73) concludes that there was a broad consensus on the new ideational basis from which to construct European affairs:

There was a very clear change of ideas, terminology, values and beliefs when it came to evaluating traditional principles such as nation, nation-state, state sovereignty, national consciousness, patriotism etc. and to giving these terms new meaning based on the background of the historical break. A paradigm and perspective shift in favour of the Idea of Europe occurred, which was in principle advocated and actively shaped by all newspapers. Only differences in nuances existed. A voice in the newspapers that simply carried on within the frame of the traditional-nationalist world did not exist.

Speeches and writings by all West German Chancellors were shaped by the Idea of Europe. Sometimes, the episteme was explicit. The endorsement of the idea by Adenauer (CDU), in office between 1949 and 1963, has already been mentioned above. Ludwig Erhard (CDU), Chancellor from 1963 to 1966, argued that intra-European divisions led to conflicts and dispute, but could be overcome through economic co-operation and integration. His 1954 speech entitled 'European unity through functional integration' was heavily influenced by David Mitrany whose influential essay *A Working Peace System* is about overcoming national boundaries through functional co-operation to achieve peace (Erhard, 1965: 163–9; Mitrany, 1966 [1943]). During his Chancellorship from 1966–9, Kurt-Georg Kiesinger (CDU) emphasised that overcoming nation-statehood and achieving European integration was the precondition for peace in Europe:

For us, Europe … is an important matter, because we know very well that either the decision in this century is the European decision. Then all disputes over which we still quarrel today will lose their meaning. Or Europe does not find this way; then it vanishes. This is the alternative.[9]

Willy Brandt, long-time chairman of the Social Democratic Party (SPD), dedicated most of his time as Chancellor (1969–74) to trying to create a nascent form of a community encompassing all of Europe, as opposed to only its Western half. He juxtaposed past and present. Europe's past

---

[9] Kurt-Georg Kiesinger, *Verhandlungen des deutschen Bundestages*, 24 November 1949, p. 491.

consisted of 'destructive rivalry'. Instead, the present ought to be dedicated to creating a 'real, enduring community' in Europe. This would be the only way to maintain peace (Brandt, 1968: 152).

The remarkably far-reaching consensus on the Idea of Europe as episteme was not confined to Chancellors, Bundestag debates and newspapers. It went far beyond that. Teaching the communal episteme was an important goal of secondary education. Curricula for history included guidelines such as '[t]he pupils ought to understand that even nations, especially neighbouring nations, are interdependent' (Niedersächsische Landesregierung, 1964: 57–8). Furthermore:

[t]he history of the German nation is to be put into context with the development of other nations. A narrow nation-state perspective does not allow for understanding what nations have in common … Using selected examples, the essentials of a certain era and its political, cultural, social and economic interconnectedness are explained. Efforts for peace and concord among nations are to be put ahead of accomplishments at warfare. (Freie und Hansestadt Hamburg, 1960: 27)

For much of the academic community, the communal episteme was the taken-for-granted knowledge base from which to make sense of European politics. Shortly after the Second World War, the philosopher Karl Jaspers (quoted in Mommsen, 1990: 21–2) wrote 'that the doctrine of nation-statehood is the malaise of Europe and also of all other continents. While the doctrine of nation-statehood is today the most overpowering and destructive force on earth, we can begin to understand its roots and eliminate it.' Ernst Jünger (1994 [1945]) put it in similar terms. The central lesson of the Second World War and indeed the entirety of European history ought to be that intra-European divisions had to be overcome. Lothar Brock (1974: 13–32), echoing the convictions of many West German social scientists, embraced David Mitrany's logic of peace through co-operation and integration. Peace in Europe could only be achieved through broadening and deepening the functional co-operation among European states.[10]

Representations of the episteme can also be found in works by West German novelists and poets. Heinrich Böll's short fiction *Als der Krieg ausbrach* (When War Broke Out) is a story not only about the causes of

---

[10] This argument, as well as the predominant West German thinking about peace and war in general, is remarkably close to Mitrany's work on the origins of peace (Mitrany, 1966 [1943]).

war, but also about its prevention through overcoming existing boundaries that keep nations apart (Böll, 1978 [1961]). The same *leitmotiv* is
found in writings by authors as diverse as Walter Dirks (1994 [1946]),
Reinhold Schneider (1994 [1957]), Robert Jungk (1994 [1959] and
Carl Amery (1994 [1961]). Walter Helmut Fritz's work is about the
juxtaposition of borders and peace. His poem 'Das Wort Friede' ('That
Word Peace') puts this juxtaposition very succinctly (Van D'Elden,
1979: 183–4):

> Fences crisscross
> the earth
> That which has begun
> unhappiness
> continues.
> And yet the word peace wants
> to appear everywhere.

The public was slower than elites in adopting the Idea of Europe as an
episteme. Whereas the idea was already the seemingly natural perspective for making sense of Europe for most politicians, journalists and
intellectuals in the late 1940s, the public came to embrace the lens only
in the early 1950s. Emnid, one of the FRG's leading institutes for survey
research, asked the following question in the 1950s and 1960s: 'Which
one do you consider a happier solution for the future: the restoration
(*Wiederherstellung*) of Germany as an independent nation-state with its
own custom barriers or Germany as equal member of a European
unification?' (quoted in Glaab, 1999: 171). This question is a hard
test for the existence of the communal episteme because of the ambiguous meaning of the term *Wiederherstellung*. In public discourse, the
term was normally used in the context of reunification. Thus, the
question could be interpreted: German reunification or Europe?

    Despite this ambiguity, European unification scored consistently
higher than the nation-state option from 1950 onwards. After 1955,
half of the population or more believed that the unification of Europe
would provide for a happier future than the nation-state (Emnid,
quoted in Eberlein, 1968: 112). Figure 3.1 summarises the findings for
the 1950s.

    The trend towards embracing integration and rejecting the nation-
state continued in the 1960s. In 1966, when the question was asked for
the last time, almost two-thirds believed that European integration

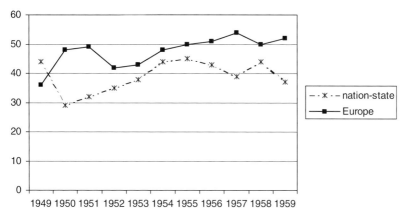

Figure 3.1 Happy solution for the future; nation-state or Europe?
Source: Emnid, quoted in Eberlein (1968: 112)

would provide a desirable future for Europe and less than a quarter
wanted to restore a German nation-state (Emnid, quoted in Glaab,
1999: 173).

The longing for reunification

Perhaps it is not too surprising that the Idea of Europe proved to be an
enduring episteme. Epistemes are deeply sedimented into the ideational
fabric of a collective. Major changes – similar to paradigmatic changes
in the academic realm – are quite rare. Yet the persisting dimensions of
the repertoire of commonplaces were not confined to the episteme.
Three crucial aspects of the identity narrative and its constituting
norms were also quite resistant to change: the definition of the homeland, the norms of peaceful resolution of disputes and national self-
determination as well as the FRG's European identity. This section deals
with the homeland. The following sections address the remaining two
aspects.

Germany's defeat in the First World War resulted in considerable
territorial losses. Most importantly, Germany lost Alsace-Lorraine to
France, and parts of its eastern territories – West Prussia, Posen and
parts of Pomerania – to the re-established Poland. Yet compared to the
end of the Second World War, the territorial implications of the
Versailles Treaty were rather moderate. After the Second World War,
Germany lost all its territories east of the Oder and Neiße rivers to

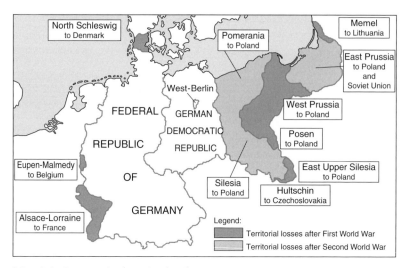

Map 3.1 Germany's changing borders

Poland and the Soviet Union, and was divided into two parts: the FRG in the West and the GDR in the East. Map 3.1 compares the borders of the German Empire of 1871, Weimar Germany, and the territorial changes following the Second World War.

What territory did West Germans consider their homeland after the end of the Second World War: every piece of territory that once belonged to the German state or only certain lost territories? There is no evidence that West Germans considered Alsace-Lorraine as part of the German homeland. A few political actors postulated that Austria ought to be part of Germany. The Bavarian Party (BP) and the Activist Movement of Independent Germans (AUD) shared very little in common, with the exception of their advocacy for a loose German confederation consisting of the FRG, the GDR and Austria. In the view of some AUD members, Vienna was the true German capital (Gieseke and Markert, 1996: 171).[11] Yet neither party has ever played a significant role in German politics.

---

[11] The best-known AUD member was probably the artist Joseph Beuys. At the end of the 1970s, the Green Party developed out of certain segments of the highly heterogeneous AUD. For an example of the BP's advocacy for reunification with Austria, see Franz Etzel, 'We want Germany. Yet, there can be no Germany without Austria' (Franz Etzel, *Verhandlungen des deutschen Bundestages* 1, 21 September 1949, p. 119).

Nevertheless, for most West Germans the national homeland went well beyond the borders of the Federal Republic throughout the period analysed in this study. It included the GDR and the Weimar Republic's post-1919 territories east of the Oder–Neiße line: East Prussia, Pomerania and Silesia. All of these territories had been part of the Holy Roman Empire, Wilhelmine Germany, and the Weimar Republic. Furthermore, the three areas had been integral parts of Prussia, the core state that unified Germany in 1871, for centuries.

With regard to the GDR, the narrative focused on people and not on land. East Germans were self-evidently regarded as co-nationals, and all Germans ought to live in one state. On a visit to Moscow, the FRG's long-time Chancellor, Konrad Adenauer (1984 [1955]), put it as follows: 'The division of Germany is abnormal, it is against divine and human law and against nature.' The Preamble of the *Grundgesetz* (Constitution) emphasised that the goal of the Federal Republic was to unify Germans again in one state. In giving themselves the *Grundgesetz*, West Germans 'have also acted on behalf of those Germans whose participation was not possible. The task for the entire German nation remains to complete the unity and freedom of Germany in an act of free self-determination.'[12] Public opinion surveys show that the desire for reunification of East and West was widely shared by the public. Glaab (1999: 129–32) compares opinion polls by eight survey institutes from 1945 to 1990 and finds that the desire for reunification was consistently around 80 per cent.

As far as the eastern territories were concerned, the discourse centred on land, and those people who were expelled from it. In March 1945, Poland annexed the territories east of the Oder–Neiße line and expelled an estimated 8–10 million Germans. Expellee organisations estimate that, combined with the expulsions from other East European countries including the Soviet Union, as many as 14–15 million people were expelled and 2 million died. The German expellees were part of almost 50 million people who were forced to leave their homeland during and in the aftermath of the Second World War in Europe alone.[13]

---

[12] The Preamble was only changed after reunification.
[13] These numbers are contested, although it seems that – at least in the German discourse – a near consensus on these numbers is evolving. I relied on expellee and non-expellee sources (Koschyk, 1989; Müller, 1990; Knopp, 2001).

The expulsions put a virtual end to German settlements east of the Oder–Neiße, which had started in the thirteenth century.[14] Yet the memory of the Eastern territories lived on. The far right formulated the attachment to them quite drastically. They are 'arch-German'.[15] Conservatives put it somewhat differently: 'we regard this territory as German homeland, as a territory that is attached to our soul.'[16] Yet the identification of the eastern territories as ancient homeland was not confined to a particular political spectrum, and it was not confined to the time prior to the settlement of the irredentist dispute. The novelist Martin Walser (1990 [1988]: 79) wrote about Königsberg, now Kaliningrad, the former capital of East Prussia: 'And if I think of Königsberg I get into a turmoil of history that makes my head spin and engulfs me.' The Social Democrat Willy Brandt, under whose leadership the Federal Republic recognised the territorial status quo with Poland, reflected on this recognition as follows: 'It could not be easy for anybody to cope with the fact that a quarter of German territory – within pre-Hitler borders – had been lost. Territory that held a lot of meaning for Prussian-German history and also for German culture' (Brandt, 1976: 526).

Expellee organisations kept the memory of the Eastern territories alive. They created museums, foundations, libraries, archives and memorials and also organised conferences and social gatherings. Academic writings continued to link the contributions of philosophers such as Immanuel Kant and Johann Gottfried Herder, and famous writers including Alfred Döblin, Hans Fallada, Joseph von Eichendorff and

---

[14] The settlement started in the thirteenth century, when Konrad of Masovia, a Polish prince, invited the Order of Teutonic Knights to settle north of its principality. Shortly thereafter, the Knights started their brutal conquest of what would later become East Prussia. Simultaneously, Brandenburg expanded east of the Oder–Neiße in a mixture of peaceful settlement by Germans, following invitations from Polish princes, and forceful conquest. The latter culminated in the three partitions of Poland in 1772, 1793 and 1815. One of the Prussian goals in these partitions was to connect Brandenburg and East Prussia (Kulski, 1976: 1–32).

[15] Franz Richter (Socialist Imperial Party), *Verhandlungen des deutschen Bundestages* 1, 21 September 1949, p. 82. Richter tried to hide his real identity due to his involvement with Nazi crimes. His real name was Fritz Rößler. His parliamentary immunity was revoked in 1952 and he was jailed. The Socialist Imperial Party (*Sozialistische Reichspartei*) was banned the same year. Since then no far right party has succeeded in entering the Bundestag.

[16] Hans Ewers (DP), *Verhandlungen des deutschen Bundestages* 1, 21 September 1949, p. 50.

Gerhard Hauptmann, to their lives in the old Germany east of the Oder
and Neiße rivers (Rothe, 1992). Furthermore, there has been a very
vibrant expellee literature. Some of the most influential post-Second
World War German novelists, such as Günter Grass, Siegfried Lenz and
Rolf Hochhuth, have been very critical about attempts to retrieve the
eastern territories, but by writing about them they have contributed to
keeping them in the collective memory of people.

The geographical incongruence between the homeland and the
Federal Republic had important repercussions for the Bonn Republic.
The FRG was constructed to be a provisional state. The *Frankfurter
Allgemeine Zeitung, Christ und Welt* and *Die Welt* wrote that the FRG
was a 'torso', while the *Süddeutsche Zeitung* and the *Deutsche- und
Wirtschaftszeitung* labelled it a 'fragment of a state' (quoted in Kiefer
1993: 113). The longing to replace the torso with the entire sculpture
was a defining element of West German identity. The Bonn Republic
was seen as incomplete and its *raison d'être* was to put together again
what belonged together. The German homeland was defined as the
FRG, the GDR, and the former eastern territories. This was often put
into the formula 'Germany in the borders of 1937', i.e. the borders
before the start of Hitler's expansionism. Nowhere else was the provisional character of West Germany and its commitment to reunification
formulated more clearly than in the Preamble of the Constitution: the
purpose of the Constitution was to create 'a new order for a transition
period'. The Bundesverfassungsgericht (Supreme Court) ruled in 1973
that Germany within the borders of 1937 was merely defunct, but had
never ceased to exist. According to the court's decision, the FRG aspired
to the re-establishment of this Germany.[17] This is exactly how the
drafters of the Constitution had interpreted the Preamble.

Hence, the longing for reunification, ingrained in the identity narrative, was very resistant to change. Territories under the (by Bonn not
recognised) sovereignty of the GDR, Poland and the Soviet Union were
considered part of the German homeland although they were not part of
the Federal Republic. Dealing with identity-constituting norms, the next
section continues the overview of those aspects of the repertoire of
commonplaces that proved resistant to change.

---

[17] BVerfGE 36,1, 31 July 1973. The ruling is included in Helmut Kistler (1982:
131–40).

Key norms

Of the many norms that constituted the dominant repertoire of commonplaces, two were especially important and were as enduring as the
definition of the homeland and the Idea of Europe. The norm of
national self-determination channelled the longing for unity into an
internationally recognised norm while the norm of peaceful resolution
of disputes clearly circumscribed the means for attaining reunification.
These two norms persistently featured prominently in public discourse.

The Preamble of the *Grundgesetz* invoked the right to national self-
determination when it stated that the *raison d'être* of the FRG was to
reunify Germany as an act of national self-determination of all
Germans. The SPD and CDU/CSU disagreed on many aspects of foreign
policy and steps towards reunification but both emphasised the right to
national self-determination again and again. Willy Brandt, for instance,
made the right to national self-determination the centre-piece of his
elaborations on the German Question in his inaugural address to the
Bundestag as newly elected Chancellor in 1969. Deputies from the
CDU/CSU vehemently criticised Brandt's reasoning but they built
their rejoinders also on the right to national self-determination.[18]

No matter how much progressive intellectuals and expellee organisations at times criticised one another, they converged around the norm of
self-determination. Karl Jaspers fully endorsed the 'inalienable right to
[national] self-determination' (Jaspers, 1969 [1960]: 38), and the
Federal Convention of the Association of Expellees appealed to the
international community to ensure that the Germans' right of national
self-determination would not be violated. Related to this norm, expellee
organisations also stressed the expellees' right to return to their homeland (*Heimatrecht*) (Marzian, 1968: 151).

The FRG's strong commitment to the norm of peaceful resolution of
disputes was another important normative dimension of the repertoire
of commonplaces. German bellicosity had caused havoc in Europe and
the world. A strong commitment to resolving disputes peacefully was
part of constructing a new German identity in diametrical opposition to

---

[18] Willy Brandt, *Verhandlungen des deutschen Bundestages* 6, 28 October 1969,
pp. 31–2; Rainer Barzel, *Verhandlungen des deutschen Bundestages* 6, 20 March
1970, p. 2094; Werner Marx, *Verhandlungen des deutschen Bundestages* 6,
17 June 1970, p. 3222.

Nazi Germany. Adenauer's formula, 'reunification in peace and free-dom', for example, made clear that the FRG would not seek to pursue its foreign policy goals by force. Public opinion surveys show that the public fully concurred: in 1953, more than three-quarters refuted the idea of resorting to war for reunification; in 1959, more than four-fifths did so. Expellee organisations were often criticised as being radical. Yet expellees were not more war-prone than non-expellees (Allensbach, quoted in Glaab, 1999: 232). A 1964 public opinion poll unequivocally put peace ahead of reunification. Ranking the importance of political tasks, 91 per cent thought that protecting peace was a very important political task; 63 per cent considered reunification as a priority (Emnid, quoted in Eberlein, 1968: 119).[19]

The commitment to the norm of peaceful resolution of disputes was so firm that it even gave rise to doubts on an issue that is usually self-evident to nations: the need for a military force. Despite the onset of the Cold War and the threats that this entailed for the FRG, it proved very difficult for Adenauer to win over the public for his plans – fully supported by the FRG's allies – to re-establish a military force. In the mid-1950s, there were arduous debates about rearmament. According to Allensbach data, the public was split quite evenly about the question. Only from May 1955 onwards did Adenauer's advocacy for a West German military pay off and a small majority endorsed the establish-ment of the Bundeswehr (Nölle and Neumann, 1957: 296).[20]

The nuclear taboo, closely attached to the norm of peaceful resolution of disputes in public discourse, however, remained untouched during these discussions. Between 1957 and 1960, less than 20 per cent of the population was in favour of providing the new military with nuclear capabilities. The smallest percentage of the opponents was 62 per cent (Divo, 1962: 15). When the Bundeswehr was finally created, Bonn renounced the possession of nuclear, biological and chemical weapons.

---

[19] More precisely, they regarded reunification as 'very important'. The exact question asked was the following: 'I have here a deck of cards. A political task is written on each of them. Please read the cards and tell me whether the task is very important, important, not that important or unimportant at the moment.'

[20] This tenuous majority, however, was dependent on the question asked. The question 'Are you in favour of or against the establishment of a new army in West Germany?' yielded a small majority. A different question (Nölle and Neumann, 1957: 296) resulted in a majority for the opponents for most of 1956: 'Do you approve or not that the establishment of a new German army has started in West Germany?'

Poets made the peaceful settlement norm a subject of their works. In 'The Fatherland' by Wolfgang Weyrauch (1963), Germany only had a right to exist if it renounced the use of force:

> There it lay, totally asunder,
> a carcass, because it had desecrated,
> I regret this, because Hölderlin
> and a somebody in Salzderhelden
> did not betray it, they were good people,
> like others somewhere else, perhaps in Birmingham,
> and as it lay there I thought,
> what lies now will stand again, however, what's up,
> how goes it, whereto, to new shadows,
> to justice for you, which means, you have
> as much right as anyone else,
> as long as you injure no one.
> If it is otherwise, fatherland: go and lie down
> and never arise again.

This poem describes the importance of peaceful resolution of disputes very vividly. The norm was a cornerstone of West German identity. Germany, in the shape of the Federal Republic, had got another chance to show that it had changed fundamentally. If it spoiled this chance, it would no longer have a right to exist.

A European identity

Not only the episteme, but the longing for unity and the norms of national self-determination and peaceful resolution of disputes were also quite resistant to change. The FRG's rejection of nationalism and its corresponding European identity were also important continuities of the repertoire of commonplaces.

The post-Second World War construction of West German identity was not undisputed. The extreme right and left poles of the political spectrum envisaged different national identities than the mainstream. The KDP and DKP emphasised the antagonism between bourgeoisie and proletariat as well as between capitalist and socialist states and deliberately played down any conception of national identity (Kommunistische Partei Deutschlands, 1963 [1945]). At the extremist right-wing margin of the political spectrum, the DRP and later the NDP propagated essentially the same nationalistic fervour that had given rise to the Second World War and the Holocaust. The foreign policy goal was to rebuild a Greater Germany that would exert hegemony in Europe and lead the fight against 'Bolshevism'. The key domestic aim was to restore a jingoistic and narcissistic nationalism. In the view of the fascist right, the right measure of nationalism was taken away from Germans by the occupying powers (Sowinski, 1998: 211–83).

The extremist right-wing representations of German identity had little resemblance to the identity that the overwhelming majority embraced. West Germans sought to demarcate themselves sharply from the past. In juxtaposing today's with yesterday's Germany, mainstream identity representations did not go as far as those at the left pole of the political spectrum. The nation remained a source of identification. Yet the nation was domesticated by two twin traits, which were rooted in the demarcation from Germany's past: scepticism against the national and nationalism, as well as a European identity.

The scepticism centred on German and European tragedies, in particular the Franco-German enmity and the two world wars. Seen through the Idea of Europe, most West Germans regarded the Second World War as a lesson that nationalism only leads to disaster. This lesson was a key aspect of national identity. It was frequently invoked, in particular on annual commemoration days such as 1 September (Germany's attack against Poland in 1939) and 8 May (Germany's unconditional surrender in 1945). As Volker Hauff (SPD) put it in the Bundestag on one of these occasions: 'fleeing back into short-sighted nationalism does not offer any solutions but only new, greater difficulties. For me, this is the certain lesson of 8 May 1945.'[21]

This lesson from history tabooed the construction of a nationalistic identity. Most West Germans defined themselves as anti-nationalist. In parliament, terms such as 'nationalism', 'nationalistic', 'nationalist' and frequently even 'national' were used to discredit the political opponent. This strategy was first employed by the conservative coalition under Adenauer, chairman of the Christian Democratic Union (CDU), against the Social Democratic opposition. When the opposition opposed Adenauer's policy to integrate the FRG into the North Atlantic Treaty Organisation (NATO), Adenauer accused them of a nationalistic attitude. In a similar vein, *Die Zeit* chastised Kurt Schumacher, chairman

---

[21] Volker Hauff, *Verhandlungen des deutschen Bundestages* 6, 8 May 1970, p. 2570.

of the Social Democratic Party (SPD), that 'he seems to lapse into nationalism'.[22] The opposition responded by blaming the coalition for being nationalistic, and pointed to incidents of a supposed lack of co-operation with European states as evidence for this claim. A furious Schumacher countered the allegations by accusing Adenauer of being nationalistic:

> I quote ... Chancellor Adenauer. In 1946, for example, he explained that the Social Democrats run the risk of being perceived as lackeys of His Majesty the King of Great Britain by the German people. This is nationalism. The Chancellor wrote in June ...: Given the events of the London Conference, German honour commands us to refuse co-operation with the allies. This is nationalism.[23]

During the debates about *Ostpolitik* in the late 1960s and early 1970s, it was the coalition under the leadership of the Social Democrats that accused the conservative opposition of being nationalistic. This time, the conservatives refuted the allegation emphatically by emphasising how important they considered European unification to be. Franz-Josef Strauß, long-time leader of the Christian Social Union (CSU) and widely regarded as belonging to the conservatives' right wing, said:

> Since I started to get involved in politics ... I have considered nationalism to be the gravedigger of our people and Europe ... I am still of the opinion that the revival of nationalistic ideas here and elsewhere ... and the pursuit of national interests, without any consideration for others by decrepit administrative structures or backward politicians, are among the most serious obstacles on our way to European unification.[24]

Forgoing nationalism was one side of the coin. Europhilia was the other. Like the scepticism of the national, the European identity trait was linked to the Idea of Europe. Establishing communal ties with other European states was the only conceivable response to the horrors of two world wars. Quotes such as the following by Helene Wessel of the Centre Party (Z) were representative for virtually all members of parliament:

---

[22] Ernst Friedlaender, 'Schumachers nationaler Sozialismus', *Die Zeit*, 17 November 1949, p. 1.

[23] Kurt Schumacher, *Verhandlungen des deutschen Bundestages* 1, 15 November 1949, p. 447.

[24] Franz Josef Strauß, *Verhandlungen des deutschen Bundestages* 6, 29 October 1969, p. 70.

I believe that – drawing from the experiences that we have made in this country, and encouraged by everything that we have understood about our own nation – we have to actively continue the work of *rapprochement* in Europe without surrendering to the difficulties that still stand in our way. [T]his attitude, it seems to me, is shared by all parties, unless anybody would want to attempt to reactivate a Prussian-German nationalism despite all the misery that it caused.[25]

Adenauer (1972b [1951]: 191) put it in similar terms:

The catastrophe made the German nation understand that peace had always been destroyed by an excessive nationalism in the past. This generated the knowledge that our existence and the existence of all other European nations can only be secured within a community that transcends national boundaries.

Adenauer (1965: 41) defined himself as German and European: 'I am a German, but I am and always was a European, and I have always felt like a European.' The Europeanness of Germanness was an identity representation that the four most influential political parties, which were elected to the Bundestag in all elections from the late 1940s to the early 1970s, shared. The manifestos of these parties (especially those of the CDU, 1963 [1961], CSU, 1963 [1957], FDP, 1963 [1952] and SPD, 1963 [1952]) all postulated this European identity trait.

Europhilia and scepticism of the national were identity representations that were not confined to political elites. They were shared by intellectuals and the public. When the newly founded NPD came close to getting enough votes to enter parliament in the mid-1960s, intellectuals mobilised against the threat from the right. Heinrich Böll, a well-known novelist and political activist, was among them. Böll (1969: 35) made explicit the connection between German identity and the rejection of the NPD: 'I am German, I speak, I write German, I even read German, and exactly because of this the NPD is out of the question for me.' The majority of the public was similarly opposed to the rise of the NPD. Less than 10 per cent wished such a party to become stronger in the future. Almost three-quarters were opposed (Emnid, quoted in Eberlein, 1968: 122).

The anti-nationalistic and European identity traits can also be inferred from a public opinion survey on 'great Germans', depicted in figure 3.2. West Germans replaced their heroes of the 1950s and early

[25] Helene Wessel, *Verhandlungen des deutschen Bundestages* 1, 15 November 1949, p. 433.

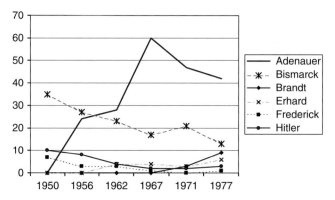

Figure 3.2 'Great Germans'
Source: Nölle-Neumann (1981: 430)

1960s. Public figures who were connected to German nationalism and militarism were replaced by individuals who embraced the FRG's European identity trait. In 1950, Otto von Bismarck, glorified as the unifier of the German nation, led the list; 35 per cent of West Germans regarded him as a 'great German'. Bismarck was followed by Adolf Hitler; a shocking 10 per cent still considered him a national hero. Finally, Frederick the Great, symbolising Prussia's past glory and military might, scored 7 per cent. This changed remarkably throughout the 1950s and 1960s. Adenauer became *the* 'great German' for West Germans.[26] The support for Hitler and also Frederick the Great decreased sharply, and two of Adenauer's successors as Chancellor, Ludwig Erhard and Willy Brandt, completed the rise of anti-militarist and European-minded heroes (Nölle-Neumann, 1981: 200).[27] It is interesting to note that, judging by this opinion poll, the public lagged behind the reconstruction of national identity as it did with regard to the epistemic change. Identity representations changed first on the elite level. Then, they changed on the mass level. The pattern of epistemic change, as described above, was similar.

---

[26] In 2004, Germans – like many other nations around the globe – crowned their national hero in a popular television show. Who is the greatest German? Adenauer finished first, followed by Martin Luther and Karl Marx.
[27] This Allensbach survey consistently asked the following question: Which great German has, in your opinion, done the most for Germany?

Not only did West Germans regard Adenauer as a national hero, they also widely endorsed his main political project: European unification. A 1962 survey, conducted in all member states of the European Economic Communities (EEC), illustrates this quite clearly: 81 per cent of the West German populace were in favour of European unification. Only the Netherlands scored slightly higher (Emnid, quoted in Eberlein, 1968: 117–18).[28]

In short, the story that West Germans told about Germany focused on major disasters. It identified nationalism as the major culprit of these disasters. In line with this narrative, West Germans defined themselves as anti-nationalistic and European. The Federal Republic's European identity trait was almost constant throughout the time period analysed. The overwhelming majority of political elites had come to embrace this identity by the late 1940s. The public followed in the early 1960s. Continuity, however, is only one aspect of a repertoire of common-places. The other is change. The key change of the repertoire pertained to the FRG's self-positioning vis-à-vis Eastern Europe. The next three sections trace these identity changes.

But Europe ends at the Elbe

For most of the 1950s, the Europe in the minds of most West Germans had little to do with the geographical Europe. Despite some dissenting voices, a small Europe was constructed that ended at the Elbe river, i.e. the border between the FRG and the GDR. West of the border was the supposedly true Europe. Western Europe was seen as a community of shared values (*Wertegemeinschaft*) and a community based on the historical lesson that European nations, their fate being inescapably intertwined, would have to co-operate and integrate across nation-state borders (*Schicksalsgemeinschaft*). Eastern Europe, by contrast, or more precisely Eastern European governments, were portrayed as the antithesis of Europe's values and accused of not having learnt the lesson of two world wars.

Art is often seen as transcending boundaries. With regard to the East–West divide, however, this by no means applied to West German art in

---

[28] Emnid asked the following question: 'To what extent do you favour efforts directed at the unification of Europe? Are you very much in favour, in favour, against or very much against?'

the 1950s. Painters, for example, painted against the East. They abandoned Realist art after 1945 and chose Abstraction as their means of expression. Realism, prevalent in Eastern Europe and the Soviet Union, was equated with totalitarianism. Abstraction was seen as its antithesis: the language of freedom and a means to build bridges among free nations. Selecting Abstraction and attaching this specific meaning to it, West German painters sought a maximum of demarcation from Eastern Europe and identification with the West (Hermand, 1991; Schmied, 1995; Belting, 1999).

In a similar vein, politicians and public opinion identified as strongly with the West as they vigorously rejected the East. Adenauer was a key proponent of the small Europe. His phrase 'Asia stands at the Elbe River' (quoted in Altmann, 1993: 33) was a standard formulation that appeared in several speeches. He also repeatedly emphasised shared Western values and juxtaposed them to the East: 'There is no doubt in our mind that we belong to the Western European world according to our origin and mentality.'[29] The West European identity gave rise to a far-reaching consensus on foreign policy. A fourfold agreement was widely shared by public opinion: yes to the unification of Western Europe, yes to the alliance with the West, yes to NATO membership and yes to the fight against communism. In a 1961 public opinion survey, only 3 per cent disagreed with the West European unification process, 2 per cent with the alignment with the West, 5 per cent with NATO membership and 8 per cent with fighting communism (Emnid, quoted in Eberlein, 1968: 141).[30] Figure 3.3 gives a more detailed overview of these data.

West Germans anchored their demarcation from the East in three main dichotomies. First, the peace-loving West was juxtaposed to the menacing East. This juxtaposition was produced and reproduced by the FRG's perception that the policies of Warsaw Pact states, especially the Soviet Union, were diametrically opposed to the lessons Western Europe had learnt from the history of fighting and destroying one another. While the West had built a *Schicksalsgemeinschaft* on the

---

[29] Konrad Adenauer, *Verhandlungen des deutschen Bundestages* 1, 20 September 1949, p. 29.

[30] Emnid asked the following question: 'Were the policies pursued by the federal government in the following issue areas good and right, only partly good and right or wrong: Europe, alliance with West, NATO membership, fight against communism, international aid, re-unification?'

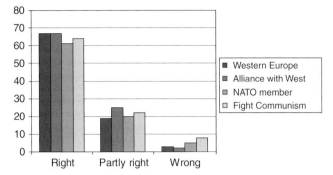

Figure 3.3 Fourfold consensus on foreign policy
Source: Emnid, quoted in Eberlein (1968: 141)

collectively held Idea of Europe, the East's practices were perceived as a violation of the West's episteme, i.e. a violation of the most deeply embedded set of beliefs on how European affairs work and ought to work.

Perceived violations of deeply held beliefs trigger very strong reactions. The FRG demarcated itself from the East in the sharpest terms. In West German discourse, the Soviet Union was still part of Europe's dark era that West Europeans strove to overcome. This would put Europe at enormous risk. Adenauer (1975 [1950]) warned that the Soviet Union and the Warsaw Pact were only waiting for a window of opportunity to extend their conquest into Western Europe. An editorial in the *Süddeutsche Zeitung* accused the East German regime of being 'nationalistic, not patriotic'. Its 'anti-Western aggressiveness is reminiscent of Hitler's nationalism'.[31] *Die Zeit* repeatedly accused the Soviet Union of being an inherently aggressive power, equated Stalin with Hitler, and juxtaposed the menacing East with the peacefulness of the West.[32]

A second dichotomy, freedom versus slavery, reinforced the FRG's demarcation from the East. Western Europe was not only seen as a *Schicksalsgemeinschaft* but also as a community based on shared values

[31] 'Das Streiflicht', *Süddeutsche Zeitung*, 17 February 1950, p. 1.
[32] See, for example, Marion Gräfin Dönhoff, 'Atlantische Defensive: Von Narvik bis Gibraltar', *Die Zeit*, 22 September 1949, p. 3; J.C., 'Atom-Wettrennen', *Die Zeit*, 29 September 1949, p. 1; Marion Gräfin Dönhoff, 'Im englischen Spiegel', *Die Zeit*, 22 October 1953, p. 1. A political caricature visualised the epistemic demarcation even more vividly. Stalin looks in a mirror and sees Hitler (*Die Zeit*, 7 October 1948, in Marienfeld, 1990: 54).

(*Wertegemeinschaft*). It was praised as part of the free world, whereas communism was condemned for enslaving people by denying individuals their human rights and nations the fundamental right to national self-determination. There was agreement on this juxtaposition in West German newspapers. *Die Zeit* complained how 'unbearable' it was 'that millions of innocent people remain stripped of their rights' in Eastern Europe.[33] The *Süddeutsche Zeitung* wrote that freedom of religion had been replaced with a new totalitarian religion in Eastern Europe.[34]

In the Bundestag, which usually had a very hard time agreeing on matters of foreign policy, invoking the freedom versus slavery dichotomy persistently guaranteed applause across party lines. Adenauer earned stormy applause when he juxtaposed the FRG and the Soviet-backed East German regime by means of the national self-determination norm:

I emphasise the following. There is no free will of the German population in the Soviet Zone … The population does not agree to and therefore does not legitimise what is happening there now … The Federal Republic legitimises itself through the freely articulated will of circa 23 million Germans who are entitled to vote. (Adenauer, 1972c [1959]: 155, 156)

Herbert Wehner (SPD), later an influential advocate of détente and the renouncement of irredentist claims, read a joint declaration of all parties (excluding the KPD) in the Bundestag in 1950: 'The communist system means destruction of human rights, enslavement of the working people, misery and exploitation. The communist dictators are the true war agitators against their own people.'[35] The protocol of this parliamentary session annotates that deputies of all parties – with the exception of the Communist Party of Germany (KPD) – reacted with 'stormy applause'. The applause increased further when Wehner juxtaposed the communist system with the Western values of peace and liberty (Auswärtiges Amt, 1972: 163).

The third dichotomy, the Christian *Abendland* (occident) versus Asia, also pertained to the Western *Wertegemeinschaft* and the supposed

---

[33] Ernst Friedlaender, 'Es gibt keine Flucht vor den Flüchtlingen', *Die Zeit*, 22 September 1949, p. 1.
[34] S., 'Osteuropa und das Heilige Jahr', *Süddeutsche Zeitung*, 23 November 1949, p. 3.
[35] Entschließung des Deutschen Bundestages zur nationalen Einheit, 14 September 1950, read by Herbert Wehner (in Auswärtiges Amt, 1972: 163–4).

denial of its values by the East. Communist regimes were portrayed as something alien to the European *Wertegemeinschaft* and equated with Asia. Germany was regarded as part of the *Abendland*, whereas the Soviet Union was an Asian power. Adenauer (quoted in Altmann, 1993: 33) called the Soviet regime 'a dictatorship with an Asian element'. During an early parliamentary debate on the German–Polish border, Günter Götzendorff, member of the Economic Reconstruction Coalition (WAV), harshly criticised Max Reimann, chairman of the KPD: 'It seemed to me as if not only Reimann had stood here, but as if a megaphone had stood here, a megaphone behind which grins the Asian grotesque face of the red dictators.'[36]

The *Abendland* versus Asia dichotomy was much weaker than the freedom-loving versus menacing and freedom versus slavery dichotomies. Of the eight newspapers that Kiefer analyses, he finds that only two constructed Western Europe as the *Abendland*: the *Frankfurter Allgemeine Zeitung* and *Rheinischer Merkur*. It was imagined to be 'an ideational, Christian-based security and cultural community that has its roots in the times of the ancient Greek and the Roman civilisations, and the religious traditions of the *Abendland*'.[37] Five of the eight newspapers analysed by Kiefer either did not use the term *Abendland*, or did not construct it as Western Europe. Indeed, a number of writers attached a fundamentally different meaning to the term. For Reinhold Schneider (1994 [1957]), for example, the concept was the unifying bond for the whole of Europe.[38] Moreover, Kiefer also finds that one of the newspapers he analyses argued vehemently against the *Abendland* concept. The *Spiegel* warned that it was the task of European politics to generate ideas for European unification that 'go beyond the usual romancing of the unity of the *Abendland* culture'.[39]

---

[36] Günter Götzendorff, *Verhandlungen des deutschen Bundestages*, 23 September 1949, p. 126.

[37] Konrad Legat, 'Zum Tode von Dr. F. A. Kramer', *Rheinischer Merkur*, 18 February 1950 (quoted in Kiefer, 1993: 85).

[38] Stephen Brockmann (2002) argues that the *Abendland* was constitutive of West German identity as a whole. He overlooks how divisive this idea was. While the *Abendland* concept appealed to conservative segments of the electorate immediately after the Second World War, some actors ignored it and others argued vehemently against it – at least the way Adenauer defined it (i.e. in sharp juxtaposition to the East).

[39] Jens Daniel (pseudonym of Rudolf Augstein), 'Stolpergang nach Straßburg', *Der Spiegel*, 6 April 1950 (quoted in Kiefer, 1993: 86).

Although the sharp demarcation of the FRG from the Soviet Union
and Eastern Europe dominated the political discourse, there were a
significant number of dissenting voices, who opposed the sharp demarcation from the Soviet Union. Alexander Abusch (1996 [1948]: 225)
criticised the 'crusade of the *Abendland* against the East European
people's democracies and the Soviet Union'. Thomas Mann (quoted in
Peitsch, 1996: 228) distanced himself from the 'hysterical persecution of
communists and war agitation'. Several authors, such as Hans-Werner
Richter (1996 [1948]), Alfred Andersch (1994 [1946]) and Reinhold
Schneider (1994 [1957]), advocated a truly European community,
including rather than excluding Eastern Europe and the Soviet Union.
They saw Germany as the bridge between East and West. Due to its
geographic location, it would be able to facilitate the creation of such a
community. In order to fulfil this role, Germany would have to be
neutral. Prominent politicians envisioned this role for Germany,
amongst them the leading Christian Democrat Jacob Kaiser and the
chairman of the SPD, Kurt Schumacher.

Maintaining the borders of the *Wertegemeinschaft*

As much as the FRG's self-positioning vis-à-vis the East changed in the
1960s, the borders of the *Wertegemeinschaft* continued to be drawn at
the Elbe river. They were reproduced by the freedom–slavery dichotomy
even though the *Abendland*–Asia dichotomy lost most of its influence.

The latter dichotomy, which, even in the early years of the Federal
Republic, was mainly confined to the conservative political spectrum,
lost further significance in the 1960s and 1970s. While the concept was
mentioned quite frequently in parliamentary debates and the
Frankfurter Allgemeine Zeitung in 1949, its use declined throughout
the 1950s. When the 'statesman of the *Abendland*', as the philosopher
Karl Jaspers (1969a [1960]: 86) called Adenauer sarcastically, retired as
Chancellor in 1963, the *Abendland*–Asia dichotomy lost its main protagonist and ceased to play a significant role in the West German
identity discourse.

The freedom versus servitude dichotomy, by contrast, continued to be a
dominating strand of discourse on the relationship between Eastern and
Western Europe. It maintained the borders of the *Wertegemeinschaft*. On
the one hand, there was the image of Western Europe, united by its liberal-
democratic values. On the other hand, there was the counter-image of

Eastern Europe, whose communist values were seen as the antithesis of liberal-democratic values. From 1961 onwards, the discourse focused to a considerable extent on the Berlin Wall. A West German memorandum to the 1962 Conference of Non-Aligned States in Belgrade even invoked a comparison with concentration camps: 'The 16 million Germans who remained in the Soviet occupied zone are now imprisoned in a single, huge concentration camp. Their protests are ruthlessly suppressed by Soviet troops and the police of the Eastern zone.'[40] Foreign Minister Heinrich von Brentano put it in similar terms:

Ladies and Gentlemen, the Soviet Union is responsible for the fact that 17 million Germans have to live in the slavery of an inhuman system. The Soviet Union is responsible for the fact that a wall cuts through the living body of the city of Berlin and that watchtowers and barbed-wire entanglements inhibit the interaction of Germans with Germans.[41]

West Germans also sharply criticised the Soviet Union for grossly violating individual and group rights in the whole of Europe. Werner Marx, foreign policy specialist of the CDU, explained:

In our political everyday life, we must forget Eastern Europe not for a single moment, the people there, their cultural and historical accomplishments. We know that they have to be silent, that they are cooped up by the doctrines of the conqueror, by its soldiers and weapons.[42]

Particular emphasis was put on the Soviet crushing of the uprisings in the GDR in 1953, Hungary in 1956 and Czechoslovakia in 1968.[43]

Adding an identity dimension: *Wiedergutmachung*

In the 1950s, the three dichotomies upon which West Germans demarcated themselves from the East were unmitigated. There was a

[40] Bundesregierung, 'Zweites deutsches Memorandum an die Teilnehmer der Konferenz blockfreier Staaten in Belgrad, 22 August 1961' (in Auswärtiges Amt, 1972: 459).
[41] Heinrich von Brentano, *Verhandlungen des deutschen Bundestages* 4, 11 October 1962, p. 1676.
[42] Werner Marx, *Verhandlungen des deutschen Bundestages* 7, 24 January 1973, p. 200.
[43] For a detailed analysis of the impact of 17 June 1953 on West Germany's self-understanding vis-à-vis the Soviet Union and Warsaw Pact states see Martin Krämer (1996).

diametrically opposed Us versus Them. The Us (West Germans), self-identifying as good, blamed Them (the East) for all of Europe's major problems. Yet in the 1960s, a discourse emerged that broke the clear-cut Us versus Them division. West Germans, coming to understand that they had to ask painful questions about their past, developed a desire for 'making good again' (*Wiedergutmachung*). This desire applied, *inter alia*, to Eastern Europe and ran counter to the long-standing tendency unambiguously to vilify the East.

In 1951, Adenauer (1989 [1951]: 37) reflected a majority view when he claimed that the Holocaust was committed by a small circle of Nazi elites and that the overwhelming majority of Germans had nothing to do with it. From the end of the Second World War to the late 1950s, West Germans distanced themselves from Nazi Germany but they were very reluctant to ask painful questions about who was responsible for the rise of the Nazi regime, the war, the atrocities committed by the German military, and the horrors of the Holocaust. West Germans (and East Germans) fled from the daunting task of confronting the past. When they did deal with the past, West German identity – despite its many peculiarities – proved to be no exception to the rule. Nations have a strong tendency to portray themselves as victims rather than perpetrators (Judt, 2002). West Germans saw themselves as victims of Nazi terror.

A brief survey of West German cinema in the 1950s illustrates these two easy ways out of addressing the past – avoiding dealing with it and rejecting the role of perpetrator. Most movies were meant to offer light entertainment. They celebrated those monarchs who were free of the shadow of German history such as Ludwig II of Bavaria (*Monarchenfilm*), romanticised the simple rural life (*Heimatfilm*), or followed the everyday life of a helpful physician (*Arztfilm*). There were several films dealing with the Second World War, including Helmut Käutner's *Des Teufels General* (The Devil's General) and *Die letzte Brücke* (The Last Bridge), Alfred Weidemann's *Der Stern von Afrika* (Star of Africa) and Harald Reinl's *Kapitänleutnant Prien* (Lieutenant Commander Prien). These movies continue to be extraordinarily powerful in their anti-war message, but they answer the question of guilt in a simplistic way. Everything was Hitler's fault (Höfig, 1980: 25).

In the late 1950s and early 1960s, this convenient answer came under critical scrutiny by a young generation that questioned older generations about their actions and inactions during Hitler's rule. The process of *Vergangenheitsbewältigung* (coping with the past) began. The attempt to come to terms with the past focused on the Holocaust and the Second World War. West German intellectuals were the protagonists of this process. The political establishment followed. Widely read authors such as Heinrich Böll, Rolf Hochhuth, Günter Grass, Siegfried Lenz, Martin Walser, Peter Weiss and Hans Magnus Enzensberger dealt with the question of responsibility and guilt. Attempting to cope with the past became a *leitmotiv* of West German literature.

In 1962, the Young German Film constituted itself in the Oberhausen Manifesto. The manifesto's main goal was to break away from 'grand-dad's cinema'. This break included a variety of stylistic elements. But break also meant a radical change in substance. The new directors pulverised the juxtaposition of the good and innocent German mass on the one hand, and the small, solely responsible Nazi clique around Hitler on the other. The films showed – implicitly and explicitly – that without mass support and an attitude of looking the other way, National Socialism and its atrocities would not have been possible (Pflaum, 1990: 17).

Vergangenheitsbewältigung – as contested and incomplete as it may have been – had many important repercussions for the ways in which the FRG positioned itself vis-à-vis other nations. One of them was the desire for *Wiedergutmachung* with the East. This desire called for a repositioning of the FRG vis-à-vis those European nations from whom it demarcated itself. The poet Wolfdietrich Schnurre (1994 [1967]: 160) put this quite succinctly, when he wrote about the German division and West German policies towards Eastern Europe:

[W]hat we suffer from today is the consequence of the immense suffering that we caused for Russia and the peoples of Europe. And it is based on this insight that, I believe, one should try to make policy in West Germany today. [I]t is high time that we now begin to become more prudent; at least more prudent than our gloomy holding on to the confines of the Cold War and our much too dramatic claims indicate.

The desire for *Wiedergutmachung* did not make the FRG suddenly change its outlook on the East. Yet it predisposed the Federal Republic to no longer dismiss conciliatory signals by Warsaw Pact states outright and to test out the waters for how to overcome the enmity between East and West.

Imagining the possibility of a *Schicksalsgemeinschaft* beyond the Elbe

An inescapably shared fate alone does not make for a *Schicksalsgemeinschaft*. In order for a community to form around a common fate, the members of this community need to share, in the perception of each member, the acknowledgement of this shared fate and a view of how to act in accordance with it. In the 1960s, predisposed by its desire for *Wiedergutmachung* and encouraged by Warsaw Pact proposals to increase co-operation across the East–West divide in order to safeguard peace, the FRG repositioned itself towards the East. The freedom-loving versus menacing dichotomy, underwritten by the East's supposed rejection of the Idea of Europe, came to be replaced by the perception of a common ground on fundamental issues of European security.

This change was not brought about by a sudden shift but a decade-long process that was characterised by a number of setbacks. The evolution began with West German reactions to the 20th Party Congress of the Communist Party of the Soviet Union (CPSU) in 1956. The Report of the Central Committee of the CPSU to the Congress was a landmark document, because it closely intertwined three components of a new European order for the first time. First, the report emphasised that war was no longer inevitable. Prior to this, Lenin's doctrine that there would always be war as long as capitalist systems existed had long been an unquestioned orthodoxy. Second, the report outlined in detail the concept of peaceful coexistence. Countries with different social systems, such as capitalist and communist states, 'can do more than just live side by side. It is necessary to proceed further, to improve relations, strengthen confidence between countries, and co-operate' (Khrushchev, 1956: 39). Economic, cultural and scientific contacts between states with different social systems furthered such co-operation (Khrushchev, 1956: 46). Third, the Soviet Union advocated co-operation beyond these 'soft' issues. It called for the establishment of a collective security system in Europe (Khrushchev, 1956: 31). The second and the third points had been made before, but the first point lent it new credibility.

West German newspapers argued that the CPSU's Party Congress showed the development of some common ground between the FRG and the Eastern bloc. First and foremost, the newspapers stressed that the Warsaw Pact wanted peace. The East was no longer vilified as a menace. Instead, the *Süddeutsche Zeitung* wrote that the Soviet Union wished to initiate another détente.[44] The *Frankfurter Allgemeine Zeitung* quoted Khrushchev's speech at the 20th Party Congress: 'War is not fatalistically inevitable.'[45] *Die Welt*, which had been a staunch Cold Warrior, expressed hope that 'there will soon be again talks on the highest levels about peace in this world'.[46] Newspapers also emphasised that there was common ground about the pathway to peace. Given the Soviet suggestions, there was room for a more peaceful order in Europe. As the *Frankfurter Allgemeine Zeitung* put it, 'peaceful reconciliation' is possible'.[47] *Die Zeit* criticised not the East but Adenauer for making this reconciliation impossible due to the 'harshness of his arguments against the world of communism'.[48]

Parliamentary debates showed little change to the identity discourse in the aftermath of the CPSU's 20th Party Congress. Yet the new manifesto that the FDP gave itself in 1957 envisaged a fundamentally new role for the FRG in European politics. One of the ten sections dealt exclusively with the appropriate response to the Soviet proposals for a European security conference. It was the duty of the FRG, the paper argued, to actively contribute to a peaceful European order. To this end, it was necessary 'to free the Idea of Europe of its previous narrowness and to widen its meaning … to the Idea of "Greater Europe"' (Freie Demokratische Partei, 1976 [1957]: 87).

There was also some movement in the SPD. Willy Brandt, mayor of Berlin, argued that East and West had finally understood that, whether Europeans wanted it or not, their fate was inescapably inter-twined. Given new weapon technologies, they would survive or perish together. East and West ought to seize the opportunity of this common understanding. Without building a *Schicksalsgemeinschaft*, Europe and possibly mankind would vanish in a Third World War.[49] These developments constituted a remarkable break from the FRG's dominant

---

[44] bm, 'Chruschtschows Kalkulationen', *Süddeutsche Zeitung*, 7 November 1957, p. 3.

[45] 'Eine schicksalsbedingte Unvermeidlichkeit von Kriegen gibt es nicht', *Frankfurter Allgemeine Zeitung*, 5 November 1957, p. 1

[46] H.Z., 'Hartes Spiel', *Die Welt*, 6 November 1957, p. 1.

[47] Hansjakob Stehle, 'Rußland gestern – Sowjetunion heute', *Frankfurter Allgemeine Zeitung*, 5 November 1957, p. 1.

[48] Robert Strobel, 'Nur kleine Experimente: Zur Regierungserklärung Dr. Adenauers', *Die Zeit*, 31 October 1957, p. 2.

[49] Willy Brandt, 'Die Welt, in die wir hineingestellt sind', *Willy Brandt Archiv* (Friedrich Ebert Stiftung, Bonn: Mappe 78 of the Archiv der Sozialdemokratie).

identity discourse of the early 1950s. The Federal Republic had started to reposition itself vis-à-vis Eastern Europe.

This process was temporarily halted by three crises. In November 1958, Khrushchev threatened to cut the access routes to West Berlin unless Berlin was transformed into a 'Free City'. In August 1961, the East German government – with Moscow's approval – built the Berlin Wall. Finally, the Cuban Missile Crisis brought the world to the brink of nuclear war in the autumn of 1962. As a consequence, the image of the Soviet Union as a menace for Europe and, given the construction of the Berlin Wall, the freedom–servitude dichotomy temporarily dominated all other identity aspects. There was a unanimous and strong condemnation of the Soviet Union.

Soon after the Cuban Missile Crisis was over, Czechoslovakia, Hungary, Poland and Romania began to articulate their desire to increase economic and cultural ties with Western Europe, and emphasised the importance of such ties for more stability in Europe. Partly based on earlier Soviet proposals for a European security conference, Adam Rapacki, Polish Foreign Minister, made an important proposal in 1958. He suggested the establishment of a nuclear-weapons-free zone in Central Europe and called for a dialogue between East and West to enhance security in Europe. Confronted with the Berlin Crisis, the FRG hardly reacted to this proposal. Any co-operation with the East was widely regarded as impossible. In 1964, Władysław Gomułka revived the plan, proposing a European security conference. The purpose of the conference should be to enhance European stability through various measures, among them increased co-operation in trade and scientific research as well as more cultural exchange in Europe. A year later, the Warsaw Pact endorsed the proposal. The plan was also included in subsequent Warsaw Pact declarations.[50]

The West German parliament engaged with this development.[51] All parties welcomed the proposals to increase contacts among European states. The positive reaction was anchored in the perception that the

---

This article was originally published in August 1956 in the Munich journal *Deutsche Jugend*. See also: Willy Brandt, 'Jahreswende-Weltenwende', *Willy Brandt Archiv* (Friedrich Ebert Stiftung, Bonn: Mappe 78 of the Archiv der Sozialdemokratie). This is a speech given in December 1956 in Berlin.

[50] A concise overview of these developments can be found in John Freeman (1991: 33–54).

[51] Some parliamentarians emphasised positive aspects of the Soviet proposals already in 1954. See, for example, Erich Ollenhauer (SPD), *Verhandlungen des deutschen Bundestages* 2, 7 October 1954, p. 2237.

Soviet Union had come to share – albeit in a limited way – the Idea of
Europe. Only co-operation across Europe's national and ideological borders could safeguard peace. Chancellor Erhard (CDU) welcomed the
Gomułka plan and stressed how important it was for European stability
to 'further develop the relations with the Eastern European states, to
promote trade, increase cultural contacts and achieve mutual understanding'.[52] Fritz Erler (SPD) spoke about the necessity to 'intensify our relations
with the East European states'.[53] Numerous parliamentarians explicitly
referred to the East European willingness to strive for a more stable
European order through increased contacts and co-operation. Walter
Scheel (FDP) pointed out that '[t]he desire of European nations for closer
co-operation among each other cannot be inhibited and will be impossible
to inhibit in the future'.[54] Wolfgang Mischnick (FDP) suggested using the
Rapacki plan as a point of departure for creating a new Europe:

> Is it not necessary to have the courage to think once again about Rapacki's
> proposals, to put under scrutiny whether there are not some useful elements,
> whether these should be amended by us and whether we in this way would not
> move a step forward towards a European security system …?[55]

Friedrich Zimmermann (CSU) pointed out that a communal Greater
Europe was a goal that seemed almost too far away to be imaginable.
Yet he argued that the East's willingness to change interaction towards
more co-operation and contacts would make it possible to achieve that
goal. These 'thoughts', as he labelled the Idea of Europe, were no longer
confined to Western Europe:

> The fact that those thoughts appear even in states with socialist social systems
> is proven by an article in the Prague newspaper *Svobodne Slovo*, which wrote
> a couple of days ago: Close, long-term co-operation of all European states in
> economic and cultural matters, and increasingly even in political matters is
> without doubt a firm basis for European security.[56]

---

[52] Ludwig Erhard, *Verhandlungen des deutschen Bundestages 5*, 10 November
1965, p. 29.

[53] Fritz Erler, *Verhandlungen des deutschen Bundestages 5*, 29 November 1965,
p. 103.

[54] Walter Scheel, *Verhandlungen des deutschen Bundestages 5*, 26 September 1968,
p. 10103.

[55] Wolfgang Mischnick, *Verhandlungen des deutschen Bundestages 5*, 14 March
1968, p. 8318.

[56] Friedrich Zimmermann, *Verhandlungen des deutschen Bundestages 5*, 14 March
1968, p. 8322.

Knut von Kühlmann-Stumm (FDP) emphasised the compatibility of the FRG's episteme with the proposals of a Soviet note to the Bonn government in 1966. This note ought to be

made a reference point for further German-Soviet contacts ... Particularly interesting in this context is, it seems to me, the part of the note that deals with the 'possibilities for initiation and development of mutual advantageous peaceful political, economic, technological-scientific, cultural and other ties among all European states'. We also largely agree with the Soviet government that the termination of the Cold War and its painful aftermath would constitute a safe path towards creating an atmosphere 'that would facilitate the solution of the pressing questions that affect European nations'.[57]

The perception that Eastern Europe was willing to overcome some of Europe's divisions in order to build a more stable regional order was reinforced by the successes of détente. After the Cuban Missile Crisis, East–West relations changed considerably. Within Western Europe, France under Charles de Gaulle was the protagonist of détente. *Die Zeit* stressed that 'the many threads that he has spun in the last 18 months across the dividing line that cuts Europe into two parts – to Warsaw, Bucharest and Moscow' showed that Eastern European states genuinely wanted more interaction with Western Europe.[58] Similar lessons were drawn by the *Frankfurter Allgemeine Zeitung*, the *Süddeutsche Zeitung* and, more cautiously, *Die Welt*.[59]

The Soviet Union was still considered as a primary security threat. Given the signals by Warsaw Pact states and their interpretations by the FRG, however, the perception of the Soviet Union as a menace – an immediate and alarming threat – decreased significantly during the 1960s. The *Süddeutsche Zeitung* wrote 'that the imminent threat from

---

[57] Knut von Kühlmann-Stumm, *Verhandlungen des deutschen Bundestages 5*, 25 May 1966, p. 2034.
[58] Marion Gräfin Dönhoff, 'Ostpolitik mit de Gaulle', *Die Zeit*, 3 December 1965, p. 1.
[59] See, for example, Jürgen Tern, 'Die neuen Akzente nach draußen', *Frankfurter Allgemeine Zeitung*, 16 December 1966, p. 1; Anonymous, 'Das Streiflicht', *Süddeutsche Zeitung*, 2 February 1967, p. 1. *Die Welt* did not doubt that some Eastern European countries wanted more co-operation with the West, but was very cautious in expecting a major change in interaction patterns between East and West from this: Lothar Ruehl, 'De Gaulles Ostpolitik enthüllt ihre Schwäche', *Die Welt*, 19 October 1968, p. 4; Lothar Ruehl, 'Beziehungen zu den Osteuropäern nützlich – aber zweitrangig', *Die Welt*, 21 October 1968, p. 4; Dieter Zeylon, 'Garantie der Hegemonie Moskaus', *Die Welt*, 18 June 1970, p. 4.

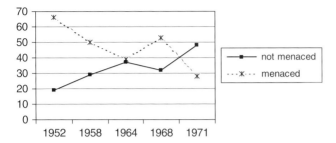

Figure 3.4 Is the Soviet Union a menace?
Source: Nölle-Neumann (1981: 430)

the East has stopped'.[60] *Die Zeit* called 'our panic fear of communism completely anachronistic'.[61] A public opinion survey captured the perceived change of the Soviet threat as well. In 1952, two-thirds of West Germans considered the Soviet Union a menace. Only 19 per cent disagreed. Thereafter, and despite Moscow's invasion of Hungary in 1956, the construction of the Berlin Wall in 1961 and the Cuban Missile Crisis in 1962, fewer and fewer people regarded Moscow as a menace. The crushing of the Prague Spring led to a momentary increase in threat perception. Three years later, however, those who did not regard the Soviet Union as a menace outnumbered those who did by 20 per cent (Nölle-Neumann, 1981: 109). Figure 3.4 shows this development.

Towards a European peace order

With the peace-loving versus menace dichotomy undermined, the FRG came to embrace a community-building identity that was based on the idea of an all-European *Schicksalsgemeinschaft* and the perception of at least moderate co-operation by the East to build such a community. By the mid-1960s, the FRG had come to see itself as the protagonist of a European peace order, that is, of a (however limited and tenuous) community of fate across the East–West divide.

Gone were the times in which the FRG identified itself merely as a Western European state. Citing Churchill as an exemplary advocate of

---

[60] Hermann Proebst, 'Vom Ernst der Lage', *Süddeutsche Zeitung*, 26 March 1966, p. 4.
[61] Marion Gräfin Dönhoff, 'Ostpolitik mit de Gaulle', *Die Zeit*, 3 December 1965, p. 1.

the pan-European idea, Thomas Dehler (FDP) inveighed against Western Europe as the 'Small Europe'.[62] Herbert Wehner (SPD) argued against 'bloc thinking' with the Warsaw Pact on the one hand and NATO on the other.[63] Hans-Dietrich Genscher (FDP) and Kurt-Georg Kiesinger (CDU) cautioned against establishing a 'North Atlantic Empire'.[64] Erich Mende (FDP) hoped for a 'loosening of the inflexible fronts of the regional alliance systems in Europe'.[65] Strong demarcation from Eastern Europe was subject to criticism in parliament. Helmut Schmidt posed a rhetorical question: 'Could we really not think together about ways to put an end to this simply too cheap and actually cowardly manner in which this country often deals with communism?'[66] Mischnick criticised past electoral campaigns of the CDU/CSU due to their 'invention of the villain of communism'.[67]

West German painters stopped painting against the East. Realism re-emerged in the FRG in the early 1960s (Schmied, 1995). The political cabaret show of a major Berlin radio station, *Die Insulaner* (The Islanders), highly successful in the 1950s, lost its popularity in the early 1960s because it was considered too anti-Soviet. In 1963, the show was terminated. In 1968, the radio station put the show back on air, but dropped it shortly afterwards. The main protagonist of the show was criticised for being a Cold Warrior (van Sweringen, 1989). Many West German novelists of the 1960s and 1970s included East Europeans, especially Poles, as key characters and showed a strong tendency to portray them positively. Among the best known among these writers are Horst Bienek (1986 [1975]), Günter Grass 1986 [1959]), Hans Lipinsky-Gottersdorf (1982 [1961]) and Siegfried Lenz (1986 [1978], 1997 [1960]).[68]

---

[62] Thomas Dehler, *Verhandlungen des deutschen Bundestages 5*, 16 December 1966.

[63] Herbert Wehner, *Verhandlungen des deutschen Bundestages 5*, 5 October 1966, p. 2953.

[64] Hans-Dietrich Genscher, *Verhandlungen des deutschen Bundestages 5*, 14 March 1968, p. 8337; Kurt-Georg Kiesinger, *Verhandlungen des deutschen Bundestages 5*, 11 March 1968, p. 8169.

[65] Erich Mende, *Verhandlungen des deutschen Bundestages 5*, 16 December 1966, p. 3864.

[66] Helmut Schmidt, *Verhandlungen des deutschen Bundestages 5*, 30 November 1965, p. 220.

[67] Wolfgang Mischnick, *Verhandlungen des deutschen Bundestages 5*, 14 March 1968, p. 8312.

[68] This is only a short selection. For an interesting overview of German expellee literature from a Polish perspective, see Martin Sander (1989).

Instead of sharply demarcating itself from the East, the FRG described itself as a community-creating state in Europe. It would be a protagonist for the establishment of a peaceful order in Europe and possibly even a future friend of all European states in such an order. *Die Zeit* wrote that Germany had been the bridge between East and West for centuries and now desired to play this role again.[69] The *Süddeutsche Zeitung* and the *Frankfurter Allgemeine Zeitung* described the FRG's role in Europe with the same metaphor.[70] Richard Stücklen (CSU) spoke about the 'desire for a real partnership' with all European states.[71] Kiesinger (CDU) identified friendship as the ultimate goal: 'We want to get to know and understand each other, then we want reconciliation and co-operation, and finally, as far as we are concerned, friendship.'[72]

Public opinion widely shared this desire for partnership and even friendship with the East. In 1971 and 1972, Emnid asked the question whether the FRG should seek to strengthen its relations with the Soviet Union and to create, if possible, a friendship. The public overwhelmingly endorsed this desire: 78 per cent were in favour in August 1971. This figure increased to 83 per cent by February 1972 (Emnid, 1972: 4).[73]

The Federal Republic's self-definition as a community-builder across the East–West divide was embodied in the key concept of foreign policy at the time: the European peace order (*Europäische Friedensordnung*).[74] By the mid-1960s, the term became the key concept of foreign policy

[69] Rolf Zundel, 'Eine Debatte ohne Form und Richtung: Der Bundestag und die deutsche Außenpolitik', *Die Zeit*, 20 October 1967, p. 4. For the same argument see also: Kurt-Georg Kiesinger, *Verhandlungen des deutschen Bundestages 5*, 13 December 1966, p. 3662.

[70] Immanuel Birnbaum, 'Nicht allzu kleine Schritte', *Süddeutsche Zeitung*, 16 December 1966, p. 4; Jürgen Tern, 'Die neuen Akzente nach draußen', *Frankfurter Allgemeine Zeitung*, 16 December 1966, p. 1. *Die Welt* did not describe the FRG as a bridge or with a similar metaphor, but also encouraged 'a policy of peace and détente'. Schr., 'Bewegung?' *Die Welt*, 17 December 1966, p. 1.

[71] Richard Stücklen, *Verhandlungen des deutschen Bundestages 5*, 26 September 1968, p. 10116.

[72] Kurt-Georg Kiesinger, *Verhandlungen des deutschen Bundestages 5*, 1 February 1967, p. 4170.

[73] The wording of the question was as follows: 'Do you agree or disagree: The government should attempt to strengthen its relations with the Soviet Union and, if possible, attain a friendship?'

[74] Joyce Marie Mushaben (1998: 147–9) deals with this concept in more depth.

vis-à-vis Eastern Europe. Kiesinger (CDU) and his successor as Chancellor, Brandt (SPD), used it very frequently to describe the FRG's role in European affairs. Kiesinger's predecessor, Erhard (CDU), also employed the redefined concept at the end of his chancellorship in 1966.[75] Newspapers and parliamentarians across all parties regularly used the concept.

The evolution of the meaning of the concept mirrored the change of the FRG's positioning vis-à-vis Eastern Europe. The concept originated with Heinrich von Brentano, Foreign Minister from 1955 to 1961. Writing at the very beginning of the West German search for a new identity vis-à-vis Eastern Europe and the Soviet Union, Brentano defined the concept atomistically. Every nation, regardless of its social system, ought to have the right to pursue its security as it deems appropriate, as long as it does not harm another nation. Brentano envisaged a negative peace among nations who would keep apart, but respect their mutual right of existence. This aspect of the European peace order, as defined by Brentano, was similar to the concept of peaceful coexistence as outlined at the 20th Party Congress of the CPSU.

By the mid-1960s, the definition of the concept had changed profoundly. The vision for the future was no longer a negative peace of keeping apart, but a positive and active peace through promoting communal ties. Brentano had defined the task of the FRG as the management of the sharp boundary between East and West. The redefined concept, by contrast, envisioned a very different role for the FRG in European politics. It would have to contribute to overcoming this divide eventually, even if only in the distant future, by creating a community encompassing all of Europe.

Discussion of findings

This chapter set the stage for the analysis of argumentation and compromise that follows in the next chapter. To this end, I identified the pool of ideas – in technical language the repertoire of commonplaces –

---

[75] See, in particular, Kiesinger's and Brandt's *Große Regierungserklärungen* after they were elected Chancellor: Kurt-Georg Kiesinger, *Verhandlungen des deutschen Bundestages* 5, 13 December 1966, pp. 3661–4; Willy Brandt, *Verhandlungen des deutschen Bundestages* 6, 28 October 1969, pp. 31, 32. Erhard started to use the redefined concept only in 1966. See, for example, *Verhandlungen des deutschen Bundestages* 5, 5 October 1966, p. 2941.

from which actors could draw to reason about the German Question. There was a dominant repertoire throughout the analysed time period from the late 1940s to the early 1970s. This repertoire exhibited both continuity and change.

From the mid-1950s onwards, there was a far-reaching consensus on the Idea of Europe as the FRG's episteme. The idea became the seemingly self-evident perspective from which to interpret European affairs. Elites – both in the official political realm as well as in civil society – held that perspective from at least 1949 onwards. Opinion polls suggest that the public followed the lead of the elites quickly. By the mid-1950s, there was a widely shared consensus on the episteme.

While the episteme remained, once firmly established, resistant to change, the evolution of West German identity and its constituting norms showed continuity and change. Throughout the analysed time period, the Federal Republic identified positively with Western Europe. The flip side of the coin of the Western European *Wertegemeinschaft* was the persistent demarcation from the East on the basis of the freedom versus slavery dichotomy. The norm of peaceful resolution of disputes, frequently invoked in public discourse, was always constitutive of West German identity. Finally, the construction of the FRG as a torso did not change. The territories lost in the wake of the Second World War – East Germany, East Prussia, Silesia and Pomerania – were still regarded as German homeland.

Other aspects of the repertoire of commonplaces changed significantly. In the 1960s, first intellectuals and then the political establishment adopted a more critical attitude towards the actions and inactions of ordinary Germans during National Socialism. No longer limiting issues of responsibility and guilt to a small circle of Nazi elites required *Vergangenheitsbewältigung*. And this, in turn, necessitated *Wiedergutmachung* for the victims of Germany's war of aggression. Among these were East European states, in particular Poland. The desire for *Wiedergutmachung* predisposed the FRG to no longer easily dismiss any conciliatory proposals by the Warsaw Pact states. Making sense of these proposals, the Federal Republic came to perceive a tenuous convergence of East and West on the Idea of Europe, and, based on this perception, came to understand itself as the builder of a *Schicksalsgemeinschaft*. Despite the ongoing sharp demarcation from communist values, it sought to fundamentally reshape European affairs by establishing partnerships across the East–West divide and, if possible, eventually even friendships.

These continuities and changes of the repertoire of commonplaces serve as the starting point for the analysis of argumentation and compromise in the next chapter. Although it goes beyond the descriptive purpose of this chapter, it is too tempting not to point briefly to two important empirical findings that are suggestive for the study of identity formation. First, the episteme, neglected in studies of identity formation, plays a critical role for the construction of identity. The episteme delineates a range of imaginable identity narratives. Given the internalisation of the Idea of Europe, a return to an identity of racial supremacy intertwined with a destiny to rule the world was entirely inconceivable for most West Germans. Only those who still held on to the Social Darwinist episteme of the past also held on to the National Socialist identity. The episteme is of crucial importance for identifying with others. Not only does it delineate to what extent mutual identification with other nations is imaginable in principle but it also critically affects processes of identification with particular nations. Mutual identification is impossible if actors perceive that the other violates the episteme that they take for granted. West Germans reacted with vigorous demarcation to what seemed to them the Warsaw Pact's rejection of the Idea of Europe. When the FRG started to perceive a convergence on the idea – even a fragile one – it began to believe in the chance to build a rudimentary community.

Second, the formation of national identity cannot be understood by accounts that overlook the international dimension or bracket domestic processes. There is evidence for the salience of symbolic interactionism as suggested by Alexander Wendt (1999). The FRG (and other NATO members) on the one hand, and Warsaw Pact states on the other, changed their identification vis-à-vis one another through symbolic interaction. Most importantly, the latter's proposals for a collective security scheme across the East–West divide made the FRG see the East, and with it the FRG's role in Europe, in a new light. Yet this is only half of the story. The Federal Republic's preparedness to engage in symbolic interaction that moved its identity away from the enmity pole of the identity spectrum towards partnership cannot be explained without looking inside the state. The desire for *Wiedergutmachung*, generated primarily on the domestic level, cannot be explained by a systemic theory that black-boxes the state. Theories of nations and nationalism, especially those that seek to explain changes of nationness over time, provide important insights on these domestic dynamics (Billig 1995; Brubaker 1996; Calhoun 1997; Hastings 1997; Hall 1998).

4 | *Towards a new beginning*

The previous chapter described the reservoir of ideas upon which West Germans drew to reason about European security. Building on this discussion, this chapter inquires into the mechanism through which ideas are selected as norms and whether such a mechanism can explain the FRG's forgoing of irredentism in the early 1970s.

I contend that the empirical findings lend evidence to dispute settlement through norm selection in general and the three-stage norm selection mechanism in particular. First, environmental change made actors embark on innovative argumentation in favour of the idea of a territorial status quo norm. The building of the Berlin Wall was the revolutionary event that made it clear to the advocates that the old ways of doing things had become obsolete and the changing repertoire of commonplaces, in particular the change from unequivocal demarcation from the East to the desire to form a *Schicksalsgemeinschaft*, provided the clues for what the new should look like.

Second, advocates who had already established a reputation for persistently supporting the *topoi* of their advocacy even outside of the advocacy succeeded in persuading large segments of the elites and the public. They accomplished this persuasive argumentation by linking the advocated idea of a territorial status quo norm to the nation's longing for unification and the Idea of Europe (abstract reasoning); to Germany's past crimes and the historical lesson of the need for reconciliation (comparative reasoning); and to the already established norms of peaceful resolution of disputes and national self-determination, including the episteme and the key events of the identity narrative that justified these norms (appropriateness reasoning).

Third, those recalcitrant actors whose repertoire of commonplaces included the *topoi* invoked by the advocates for the territorial status quo norm sat down at the bargaining table with the proponents of the normative idea. Eager to rid themselves of the costs arising from their opposition to the newly established majority view, they accepted a compromise with the advocates, even though the compromise clearly favoured the advocates' position. As a result of this norm selection through argumentation and compromise, the FRG renounced its irredentist claims.

This chapter is organised chronologically. First, I deal with *Ostpolitik* (policy towards the East) and the taboo against recognition in the 1950s. Second, I address the emergence of the advocacy for the idea of a territorial status quo norm. Third, I trace the diffusion of the argumentation in favour of the territorial status quo. Fourth, I scrutinise the compromise stage of the norm selection mechanism. Finally, I discuss the results of this investigation.

The taboo against recognition

In the late 1940s and throughout the 1950s, the overwhelming majority of West Germans vowed never to recognise the territorial status quo. The resolve never to recognise was more than a norm. It was a taboo. The few advocates for the territorial status quo norm were vilified as traitors.

It was unthinkable for most West Germans to recognise the borders between the FRG and the GDR as well as the one between the GDR and Poland. With the exception of the KPD, there was consensus across the parties in the Bundestag never to recognise the territorial status quo. Chancellor Adenauer (CDU) vowed that the 'German nation will never recognise the so-called Oder–Neiße border'.[1] Heinrich von Brentano (CDU) repeated his Chancellor's resolve and explained 'that the Bundestag and the federal government will never be prepared to recognise the Oder–Neiße line'.[2]

Newspapers mirrored the very strong consensus that, as *Die Zeit* put it, '[n]ot only the refugees and expellees, but also all other Germans are incapable of ever recognising the wrong border at the Oder and Neiße, and the faulty *limes* at the Elbe'.[3] The public shared this strong

---

[1] Konrad Adenauer, *Verhandlungen des deutschen Bundestages* 2, 20 October 1953, p. 20.

[2] Heinrich von Brentano, *Verhandlungen des deutschen Bundestages* 2, 28 October 1953, p. 31.

[3] Ernst Friedlaender, 'Es gibt keine Flucht vor den Flüchtlingen', *Die Zeit*, 22 September 1949, p. 1. See also similar arguments such as: Herbert von Borch, 'Das Versagen der Westmächte', *Frankfurter Allgemeine Zeitung*, 20 October 1953, p. 1; Werner Friedmann, 'Des Kanzlers zweiter Start', *Süddeutsche Zeitung*, 21 October 1953, p. 1.

commitment not to recognise the existing borders. Several opinion polls were conducted in the 1950s by various institutes. The highest score of those in favour of accepting the Oder–Neiße as a border and recognising the GDR as a state was a mere 12 per cent, both in 1958 (Allensbach in Glaab, 1999: 242, 246).

This orthodoxy never to recognise the post-Second World War borders extended beyond the 1950s to the early 1960s. In 1963, Willy Brandt (SPD), under whose chancellorship the FRG eventually recognised the Oder–Neiße border in 1970 and the GDR in 1973, still equated recognition with treason:

Breslau, Oppeln, Gleiwitz, Hirschberg, Glogau, Grünberg [former German cities east of the Oder–Neiße, MK]: these are not only names, they are living memories, which are rooted in the souls of generations and knock incessantly on our conscience. Relinquishing would be treason; who would want to dispute that. (Brandt in Jahn, 1985: 29)

Everyday language describing the disputed borders also reflected the taboo against recognition. The Polish–German border was never referred to as a border, but simply as line, the so-called border, or demarcation line. The lost territories in Poland and the Soviet Union were often referred to as *Ostdeutschland* (Eastern Germany). Likewise, East Germany was never referred to as the German Democratic Republic or GDR, but 'SBZ' (Soviet occupied zone), 'zone', '*Mitteldeutschland*' (Central Germany), 'so-called GDR', '"GDR"', 'Pankow' (after a *quartier* in East Berlin), or even 'phenomenon' (Pötzsch, 1997: 147).[4]

The taboo against recognition was buttressed by a number of *topoi*. The 1950 Joint Declaration of all parties (excluding the KPD) in the Bundestag, for instance, used three established norms to bolster the resolve never to recognise the territorial status quo.[5] First, public discourse connected the taboo to the right to national self-determination and emphasised that the German people's right to national self-determination had been trampled upon. According to this argumentation, every nation

---

[4] A brief clarification in order to prevent these difficulties with directions for this study: I refer to what some actors referred to as *Mitteldeutschland* as East Germany or GDR, and I use the terms territories east of the Oder–Neiße and Eastern territories to describe the historical *Ostdeutschland*.

[5] Entschließung des Deutschen Bundestages zur nationalen Einheit, 14 September 1950, read by Herbert Wehner (Auswärtiges Amt, 1972: 163–4).

had the right to determine its own future. Germany, however, was divided into East and West against the will of Germans in East and West. Second, the taboo was reinforced by the territorial integrity norm. This argument stressed that, although currently defunct, the Weimar Republic had never ceased to exist as a territorial entity. The Potsdam conference never condoned the dismemberment of Germany. On the contrary, it gave all four occupying allies the responsibility for Germany as a whole. Third, there was widespread agreement that the expulsions violated international law. The millions of expellees from east of the Oder–Neiße had the right to return. This right could never be taken away from people. In Adenauer's reading, this was even a divine law (Adenauer, 1963 [1950]: 84).

The FRG reacted to those who violated the taboo against recognition with fury. In 1950, the GDR and Poland signed the Görlitz Treaty, in which East Berlin recognised the territorial status quo. The Preamble stated that the border agreement was meant to make a contribution to a stable peace among peace-loving states.[6] The treaty was remarkably similar to the one that Bonn and Warsaw would sign twenty years later. In 1950, however, the Bundestag condemned the recognition of the Oder–Neiße border as a 'crime against Germany and against humanity' (quoted in Auswärtiges Amt, 1972: 164).

There was only one deputy in the Bundestag who tried to advocate the recognition of the territorial status quo. Max Reimann, chairman of the KPD, argued that the recognition of the Oder–Neiße line was a necessary contribution to peace in Europe. The taboo, however, made it virtually impossible for him to pursue this advocacy. In a speech at the Bundestag in 1949, the supposedly impartial Speaker of parliament interrupted and vented his anger against him: 'It is a provocation of the overwhelming majority of this House when you make such remarks. Therefore, I call you to order.'[7] The taboo against recognition was too strong to allow for the articulation of an advocacy for recognition.

---

[6] Abkommen über die deutsch-polnische Staatsgrenze zwischen der DDR und der Volksrepublik Polen (Görlitzer Abkommen), 6 July 1950 (in Jacobsen and Tomala, 1992: 72–3).
[7] Erich Köhler (CDU), *Verhandlungen des deutschen Bundestages*, 22 September 1949, p. 66.

Debating about reunification policies

Throughout the late 1940s and early 1950s, the normative consensus on the German Question – never to recognise the current borders and never to attempt to retrieve the lost territories through the use of force – was the basis of West German foreign policy towards the East. Beyond this broad consensus, however, there remained a lot of room for heated controversies about reunification policies. The two main protagonists of this debate were the CDU on the one hand and the SPD on the other.

With few exceptions, the CDU followed Adenauer's logic for reunification. In his view, reunification would be the result of a Politics of Strength (*Politik der Stärke*). Only a strong FRG could make the Soviet Union agree to concessions in negotiations about reunification. Thus, joining NATO was more than a means of securing the FRG – as essential as Adenauer considered this to be; it was also a means for reunification (Adenauer, 1958: 90). When the FRG joined NATO in 1955, Adenauer was very optimistic that NATO would bring about reunification:

We are now part of the greatest and most powerful military alliance of all times … The whole of the Transatlantic community will now vigorously pursue our goal, i.e. re-unification; the re-unification in peace and freedom will soon become a reality. (Adenauer quoted by Heinemann, 2004)

The only notable counter-advocate to Adenauer in the CDU was Jakob Kaiser, who had been a key figure in the creation of the CDU. He advocated a neutral Germany, performing the function of a bridge between East and West. This reasoning was close to that of those who were sceptical of the Politics of Strength in the FDP, and in particular to the thinking about reunification in the SPD. To most Social Democrats, the Politics of Strength was an entirely implausible and counter-productive policy. They sharply criticised Adenauer for deepening the German division instead of trying to overcome it. By firmly integrating the FRG on the Western side of the East–West conflict, the German Question would become intractable. Reunification would only be possible if the FRG and the GDR left their respective military blocs. In this case, reunification would not mean a growth of power for either of the two blocs. No military alliance would be threatened, and this would make NATO and the Warsaw Pact agree to reunification. In 1959, the SPD summarised its thoughts on the path for reunification in the

Germany Plan (*Deutschlandplan*), which outlined several steps for reunification. These included the creation of a demilitarised zone in Central Europe, Bonn's withdrawal from NATO, and diplomatic relations with Warsaw Pact states. The East and West German governments would negotiate the terms of reunification.

The public preferred the Germany Plan to the Politics of Strength. Public support for the Germany Plan oscillated between 43 and 46 per cent in the late 1950s, whereas less than a quarter of the population backed the Politics of Strength. Arguably, however, what is most important about these surveys is the high number of undecided people. Approximately 40 per cent of the populace did not know what to answer (Divo, 1962: 34).[8] This is an indicator of how unsure West Germans were about how to work towards reunification.

West German foreign policy in the 1950s was made by the party in power, i.e. the CDU. Based on the sharp demarcation from the Soviet Union, it rejected any Soviet offers of negotiations for the reunification of Germany. The Soviet Union was seen as an expansionist menace that only waited for a window of opportunity to continue its conquest further into the West. Negotiation offers were interpreted as Soviet attempts to create such a window of opportunity. Most importantly, the Adenauer government rejected the 1952 Stalin Note outright. Stalin offered Bonn the reunification of the GDR and FRG under the condition that Germany would be neutral. When Stalin renewed the offer a month later, he signalled that he would be prepared to make compromises, including the date for free, all-German elections.[9] For Adenauer (1965: 548), however, the Note remained a trick to lure Germany away from the West into the hands of the Soviet Union. Public opinion concurred with Adenauer's rejection of the Stalin Note. In 1958, only a quarter of the West German populace thought that a closer scrutiny of the

---

[8] The question was phrased as follows: 'Recently, a number of suggestions have been made how to attain reunification. Please tell me whether you agree or disagree with the suggestions below: A. The four great powers should be induced to release the two parts of Germany from their military alliances with the aim of embedding all of Germany in a security pact that they guarantee. B. West Germany should continue to increase its military capabilities as a part of NATO, in order to be able to conduct meaningful negotiations with the Soviet Union in due time.'

[9] There is a lively debate to this date about whether the Stalin Note was a chance for reunification. For a brief summary of this debate see Christian Hacke (1997: 70–1).

Soviet proposals could have resulted in progress towards reunification; 50 per cent disagreed (Nölle and Neumann, 1965: 485).

Under Adenauer's chancellorship, the FRG conducted virtually no *Ostpolitik* at all. There were only two notable exceptions. First, Adenauer visited Moscow to negotiate the release of German prisoners of war in 1955. In exchange for their release, the FRG agreed to initiate diplomatic relations with the Soviet Union. Yet Bonn hardly made any use of these new diplomatic channels for the remainder of the 1950s. Instead, the Adenauer government was concerned with the possible precedent which its diplomatic relations with the Soviet Union could set. Suddenly there were two German ambassadors in Moscow, one from the East and one from the West. This lent the GDR a legitimacy that Bonn was not prepared to grant to East Berlin. For the FRG, the GDR was not a state, but a zone that was against the will of the people, and illegally and illegitimately occupied. Thus, Bonn announced what would become known as the Hallstein Doctrine, named after one of Adenauer's closest advisers. In principle, the FRG would cease diplomatic relations with any country that recognised the GDR.

Second, the FRG reacted in a limited way to the signals of détente. In 1959, Bonn offered Poland and Czechoslovakia bilateral treaties about the renunciation of force. Apart from the emphasis that the FRG – having learnt the lessons of the past – would settle all its disputes peacefully and in accordance with the principles of the UN Charter, the proposal for these treaties also contained a paragraph about the FRG's refusal to recognise Poland's western border and other disputes.[10] Poland and Czechoslovakia criticised this paragraph harshly. They accused the FRG of continuing to be revanchist and nationalistic.[11] The 1959 offer for the renunciation of force, therefore, can hardly be considered a success.

New environment and innovative argumentation

The shifting repertoire of commonplaces, especially the turn towards critical reflection on the recent past and the interrelated lessening of the

[10] 'Wortlaut einer von der Bundesregierung abzugebenden Erklärung über das Angebot eines Gewaltverzichtsvertrages mit Polen und der Tschechoslowakei, 20. Juli 1959' (in Auswärtiges Amt, 1972: 408–10).
[11] Of course, this again provoked anger on the West German side. See, for instance, Konrad Adenauer (1972c [1959]).

demarcation from the East, provided clues for how a new European order ought to look. In the late 1950s, a small number of intellectuals started to argue that there was a need to recognise the Oder–Neiße border. The building of the Berlin Wall showed painfully and clearly that the old ways of doing things had become obsolete, and the advocacy was extended to the recognition of the GDR.

In the late 1950s and early 1960s, a number of intellectuals – some cautiously, others more vigorously – broke the taboo that West Germans must never recognise the Oder–Neiße line. The two most outspoken of them were the philosopher Karl Jaspers and the historian Golo Mann. In 1960, Jaspers published his book *Freiheit und Wiedervereinigung* (Freedom and Reunification), which argued for the recognition of the Oder–Neiße border. Jaspers used two supporting arguments. First, he linked *Wiedergutmachung* and recognition. Germany had to learn the lessons of history and contribute, as much as possible, to a new Europe that was fundamentally different from the old. This included *Wiedergutmachung* and reconciliation with Poland. Without the recognition of Poland's borders such a reconciliation would be impossible: 'Good neighbourliness with Poland ... can only be achieved by recognising the Oder–Neiße line' (Jaspers, 1969a: [1960] 35). Second, Jaspers connected the Idea of Europe to the FRG's longing for reunification with East Germany. The FRG's contribution to a new Europe, in which the rigidity of nation-state borders and the East–West divide would be replaced by co-operation and integration, would eventually offer a chance for German reunification.

Golo Mann's advocacy echoed the historical lesson that Jaspers emphasised. The loss of the 1937 borders was Germany's own fault: 'If we had wanted to keep the borders of 1937, then we should have been satisfied with them in 1937' (Mann, 1963 [1958]: 951). It was now time not for retaliation but to put an end to the vicious cycle of territorial wars. Bearing in mind Germany's role in the Second World War, it was Bonn's duty to seek reconciliation with those states and nations that it had targeted. Instead of engaging in old border disputes, it should settle its territorial conflicts peacefully and contribute to a European order 'under which political borders increasingly lose their evil significance; break out of the cursed cycle of wars, mutual expulsions and torture' (Mann, 1963 [1958]: 952).

In many ways, Jaspers's and Mann's reasoning was the innovative blueprint for the advocacy in favour of the territorial status quo norm that formed in the early 1960s. The two writers called for the recognition of the Oder–Neiße line and showed a new path towards unification. Yet they did not call for the recognition of the German–German border. Translated into the conceptual language of this study, Jaspers's and Mann's argumentation combined three modes of reasoning: abstraction, comparison and appropriateness.

The abstract reasoning was confined to Jaspers and still lacked an advocacy for the recognition of the German–German border. Linking the *topoi* of the Idea of Europe and the FRG's longing for unity, he contended that the episteme showed a path towards reunification. Germany could eventually be reunified when Europe was transformed from a divided continent into a co-operating and integrating community. The FRG's key contribution to the beginning of the evolution of such a new order would have to be the recognition of the Oder–Neiße border.

The comparative reasoning is apparent in Jaspers's and Mann's argumentation. Both authors linked the recognition of the Oder–Neiße line to the *topoi* of Germany's atrocities during the Second World War and *Wiedergutmachung*. Germany would have to learn the lessons of history and do everything possible to help break the cycle of instability and crises that had plagued Europe for centuries. In particular, Germany had to seek reconciliation with its former victims. This required Bonn to recognise Poland's western border.

While the abstract and comparative modes of reasoning carried the argument for recognition, the appropriateness mode circumscribed and supported it at the same time. On the one hand, it circumscribed it by the principle of national self-determination. Jaspers stressed that Germans would have, like any other nation, the right to self-determination. Alluding to critical aspects of the identity narrative, Jaspers chastised Germany's partition as 'rape' (Jaspers, 1969a [1960]: 38). The FRG ought to recognise existing borders without, however, forfeiting the Germans' right to national self-determination. On the other hand, the appropriateness mode unequivocally supported recognition by emphasising the norm of peaceful resolution of disputes as demarcation from Germany's past. Breaking out of Europe's cycle of instability and war, for which Germany had been responsible to a great extent, required settling disputes peacefully.

Three years went by before the three modes of reasoning became an argumentation for the recognition not only of the Oder–Neiße line but also the German–German border. A key event during these three years marked a watershed for West German politics. On 13 August 1961, the building of the Berlin Wall began. Confronted with a mass exodus of people, the East German regime sealed the last remaining hole in the Iron Curtain. Families were torn apart. East German border patrols were ordered to shoot at those trying to climb over the Wall. Trying to escape from East to West meant risking death. The border shootings provoked outrage in the FRG. This peaked with the death of Peter Fechter in 1962. Having been shot by a border guard, he was left bleeding to death on the eastern side of the Wall, but visible from the West, for almost an hour.

While the immediate reaction to the Berlin Wall was one of outrage, it was one of reflection in the medium and long term. For many, the Wall was seen as proof that West German policies towards the East would have to change radically. Adenauer's *Ostpolitik* had failed. The old ways of doing things had become impossible. It is no coincidence that the architects of a new *Ostpolitik* start their *ex post facto* contemplations about their new approach with 13 August 1961. Willy Brandt (1976: 17) refers to the Wall as the background of his policies towards the East: 'What one has labelled my *Ostpolitik* was shaped by this background.' Klaus Schütz maintains that Brandt's fundamental reorientation with regard to policies towards the East was 'because of the building of the Wall'.[12] Egon Bahr (1996: 125) concurs: 'The old arguments and common desires of East and West met, crushed into the new fact of a Wall. After the storm was over, fundamental changes began to appear, from which nobody could run away.'[13]

Given the locus of Berlin in the East–West confrontation and the Wall that cut through Berlin, Willy Brandt, mayor of Berlin, and his advisers Heinrich Albertz, Egon Bahr and Klaus Schütz, 'were forced to think of the East'.[14] The Wall triggered a fundamentally new reasoning about East–West relations and norms pertaining to territorial claims.[15] While the Berlin SPD around Brandt made some use of the comparative reasoning sketched by Jaspers and Mann, it initially focused primarily

---

[12] Interview with Klaus Schütz, 7 July 2003.
[13] A 1968 caricature by Ernst Maria Lang (in Dollinger and Klein, 1989: 96) captured this metaphor very graphically. It shows Kiesinger and Strauß crashing into the Wall and Brandt showing them the damage they caused.
[14] Interview with Egon Bahr, 15 July 2003.
[15] Interview with Klaus Schütz, 7 July 2003.

on the abstract mode of reasoning. In many ways it followed Jaspers's reasoning, but, going beyond the philosopher's earlier argumentation, linked the recognition of East Germany to the longing for unity and the Idea of Europe.

The Idea of Europe was omnipresent in Brandt's reasoning on European affairs. In his 1962 speech at Harvard, for example, Brandt (quoted in Görtemaker, 1998: 52) emphasised the necessity to transform relations in Europe. The communal episteme was very explicit:

We have to look for forms that transcend and penetrate today's blocs. We need as much interaction and as much meaningful communication as possible ... What is at stake is a politics of transformation. Real political and ideological walls have to be slowly and steadily taken down.

Brandt firmly believed that only a Europe that grew together and overcame the divisiveness of state borders would offer a chance for reunification in the distant future. This fundamental transformation demanded from the West in general and from the FRG in particular that they 'come to be open to contributions from the other side'. This hinted already at the necessity to be prepared to make painful concessions. In his 1963 Tutzing speech, Bahr indicated what one of the concessions could be. The FRG should explore all modes of recognising the GDR below the threshold of recognising it as a foreign state.

Strategic considerations mitigated Brandt's argumentation to some extent. Brandt and his advisers were very cautious in presenting their abstract mode of reasoning to the public. Especially in the first half of the 1960s, Brandt did not expect that the vision of an all-European community able to transcend the borders of states and thus making German unification possible would resonate with a wider audience. He was very much aware of the risk that this vision could easily be discredited as utopian. In order to argue effectively for a new *Ostpolitik*, therefore, he resorted to two strategies. First, he probed the persuasiveness of his argumentation by encouraging his advisers to test out the limits of resonance. In 1963, for example, Brandt and Bahr gave speeches at Tutzing. Brandt's speech contained little novelty. Bahr's speech, by contrast, based on the Idea of Europe, presented the vision for a fundamental reorganisation of European politics and, embedded in it, the relations between East Germany and West Germany. Second, based on these probes and other evidence on the limits of resonance, Brandt occasionally censored himself and his advisers. This is most evident with regard to Bahr's book manuscript *Was nun?* (What now?), written in 1965. The book revolved around an ambitious eight-stage plan for German reunification. Germany would eventually be reunited, but only after an all-European collective security system replaced the Warsaw Pact and NATO. This was a bold vision. It would have been easy to attack it as utopian. Brandt, therefore, talked Bahr out of publishing the manuscript (Vogtmeier, 1996: 90).

In short, a new advocacy for the recognition of the territorial status quo had formed by the early 1960s. Intellectuals, drawing upon a shifting repertoire of commonplaces, delivered the blueprint for this advocacy. Following the construction of the Berlin Wall, the Berlin SPD struggled to make sense of the shocking new situation. They did so, like the intellectuals a few years earlier, by applying the new aspects of the repertoire of commonplaces to the new situation. This made the Berlin SPD elaborate on the earlier reasoning of the intellectuals – cautiously when addressing a larger audience and in a more visionary fashion when reasoning about the nexus of recognition and a new European order in private.

Resonance in political parties

Soon after the Berlin Wall was built, two of the three political parties represented in the Bundestag, the SPD and the FDP, began to change their views on the German Question and European security. By the late 1960s, the endorsement of the territorial status quo norm had become their official party policy. This section traces the processes through which the parties came to join the advocacy for the territorial status quo.

Brandt's advocacy gained momentum in the mid-1960s. In 1964, he wrote a memorandum entitled 'About the relations with the East European states and nations'.[16] The memorandum argued that, given Germany's history and the current East–West divide, achieving good relations with East European countries constituted a primary goal of German foreign policy. In order for the FRG to fulfil the role of a protagonist for a new Europe, it would have to recognise Poland's need to live within secure borders. Additionally, the Berlin SPD, in particular Bahr, argued in increasingly explicit terms for the recognition of East Germany as an independent but not foreign state. Bonn should

---

[16] For a more detailed overview of this paper, see Bingen (1998).

recognise, in Bahr's view, that there were two German states. These states could not be foreign to one another because there was only one German nation. In 1964, he outlined a two-step model for reunification. The first phase would consist of military détente, the second of political détente. The latter would have two purposes: reconciliation and friendship with East European states as well as the loss of significance for rigid nation-state borders; and reunification, based on a Europe that left rigid nation-state borders behind. This new Europe was conceptualised as the European Peace Order, which was discussed in some detail in the previous chapter (Vogtmeier, 1996: 73).

Thus, in the view of Bahr and other advocates of the new thinking within the SPD, recognition did not contradict Germany's right to national self-determination. Recognising existing borders did not mean bidding farewell to the desire for reunification. On the contrary, it was seen as the precondition for setting a process in motion that could culminate in the reunification of Germany. Adenauer's expectation of achieving unity through strength was replaced by the expectation of achieving unity, if at all, through co-operation and integration in Europe.

By the mid-1960s, the innovative argumentation that had formed in the late 1950s and early 1960s had persuaded some influential FDP members. Echoing the argumentation of the Berlin SPD, they started an advocacy aimed at persuading their party. This was a difficult task. In the mid-1960s, the FDP still insisted on the re-creation of Germany in the borders of 1937, thus reunifying the FRG with the GDR and the former territories east of the Oder–Neiße line.

In 1966, the FDP's chairman, Erich Mende, requested Wolfgang Schollwer to draft a white paper on the FDP's *Ostpolitik* options. The Schollwer study became public a year later. It contended that the FRG, given its history and its position in the East–West conflict, had a duty to seek reconciliation with the East. The recognition of the Oder–Neiße border was a necessary step for the reconciliation. The same year, the FDP's treasurer, Hans Wolfgang Rubin, published an article echoing the reasoning of Schollwer. He also followed Bahr's argumentation on the recognition of the GDR. Rubin called for the recognition of all existing borders in Europe and for the GDR as second German state. This step would not mean forgoing the aspiration of national unity and the principle of national self-determination. On the contrary, it would be the beginning of a process that could develop into a chance for reunification in the future (Kistler, 1982: 21; Jahn, 1985: 373–80).

The advocacy within the SPD and the FDP may again be grouped into three modes of reasoning: abstraction, comparison and appropriateness. Abstract reasoning postulated that the Idea of Europe provided the key to the German Question. Germany could be reunified by transcending the borders separating Europe's states and nations, and cutting through Germany. The comparative aspect centred on the lessons to be learned from the Second World War and the atrocities committed by Germany. Reconciliation with the East, especially with Nazi Germany's first and major victim Poland, would be indispensable for establishing a level of stability and security that made the reoccurrence of the disasters of the past impossible. Finally, the appropriateness dimension focused on the right to national self-determination and the norm of peaceful resolution of disputes. Even if the FRG recognised the GDR as a state, the Federal Republic would continue to aspire to unify Germany through an act of national self-determination by Germans in East and West. The norm of peaceful resolution of disputes buttressed the case for recognition. Demarcating itself from its own past, the FRG was determined to resolve its disputes peacefully in present and future. This included the border disputes.

This argumentation proved to be very powerful. By the late 1960s, the advocacy within the SPD and the FDP met with success. Recognition became official party policy. Although the dynamics of change differed across the SPD and the FDP, there was also a critical similarity. It was primarily persuasive argumentation – as measured by the diffusion of an argument (see chapter 2) – that made party members change their minds.

There was some contestation in the SPD about the new course in the early and mid-1960s. The two most influential sceptics were Fritz Erler and Herbert Wehner. Erler criticised Brandt's and Bahr's new thinking quite strongly. In Erler's view, the recognition of the territorial status quo could never lead to reunification. It would cement the division of Germany and would lead to the loss of West Berlin. Before 1966, Wehner was also a gatekeeper preventing the new thinking from entering official SPD documents (Schirmer, 1988: 150).

Erler and Wehner, however, soon changed their opposition to full endorsement of the new reasoning. Mirroring the argumentation of Brandt and his advisers, they became important advocates for the new *Ostpolitik* in the latter half of the 1960s. In March 1965, the SPD leadership endorsed a memorandum by the Evangelical Church, which is discussed in detail below, to recognise the Oder–Neiße border. The party was in principle prepared to recognise the border as a contribution to a more peaceful European order. Based on this memorandum, Erler proposed starting negotiations with Poland about settling the border dispute.

By 1968, there was a far-reaching consensus in the party on the new thinking. The party congress in Nuremberg dealt with the new *Ostpolitik* in detail. The recognition of the GDR as a sovereign but not a foreign state (one German nation but two German states) as well as the indication that creating a path towards a European Peace Order would be worth the sacrifice of the recognition of the Oder–Neiße line became part of the new party platform. The debate on these issues at the party congress shows that the arguments in favour of recognising the territorial status quo had diffused. Not a single speaker was against recognition. All of them joined the chorus of the familiar argumentation. They connected the recognition to the Idea of Europe, the longing for unification, Germany's role in the Second World War, the desire for *Wiedergutmachung*, the norm of peaceful resolution of disputes and the principle of national self-determination (SPD, 1968: 703–27). In short, the SPD followed the lead of Brandt, who had been elected its chairman in 1964.

The FDP did not follow its chairman. Argumentative success within the party led to the downfall of the party's leadership. Only thereafter did the party endorse the recognition of existing borders. The party leadership around its chairman Erich Mende distanced itself from the initiatives of Schollwer and Rubin. Frustrated with the rejection of the initiatives by the party leadership, the proponents of the new *Ostpolitik* leaked the memoranda to the press. The news magazine *Stern*, which fully backed the new *Ostpolitik*, published the documents. At the 1967 party congress in Hanover, the progressive-liberal and the national-liberal wings of the party quarrelled about the party's future stance on *Ostpolitik*. Progressive liberals followed the reasoning of the advocates of the new *Ostpolitik* and many individuals of this wing became important advocates for recognition. The national-liberal wing, by contrast, rejected the argumentation for the territorial status quo.

At the 1968 party congress in Freiburg, the progressive wing won a decisive victory. Erich Mende was replaced by the reform-minded Walter Scheel with 216 of 251 possible votes. Other progressive liberals, among them Ralf Dahrendorf, Hans-Dietrich Genscher, Hildegard

Hamm-Brücher and Wolfgang Michnick, were elected into the party's executive. At the 1969 party congress, the recognition of the GDR and, phrased more indirectly, the recognition of the Oder–Neiße as a necessary sacrifice for a European Peace Order became part of the official party platform.[17]

More advocates

The advocacy for the territorial status quo norm was not confined to political parties. It grew stronger and stronger. The three modes of reasoning of the argument diffused to churches, interest groups and the media. The abstract mode was further reinforced by a changing international constellation.

The Evangelical Church was at the forefront of those calling for the recognition of the Oder–Neiße line. Focusing on the norm of peaceful resolution of disputes and juxtaposing it with Germany's past, it emphasised the appropriateness modes of reasoning. As early as in 1962, the Tübinger Memorandum, written by eight leading laymen of the Evangelical Church, linked the norm of peaceful resolution of disputes to the recognition of the Oder–Neiße line. Without the FRG's recognition, a peaceful settlement would be impossible. A paper by the Evangelical Church in Germany (EKD) endorsed the Tübinger Memorandum in 1965. Three years later, the Roman Catholic Church confirmed the peace-through-recognition logic in a paper by the Bensberger Kreis, a group of leading members of the Catholic Church.[18] Public opinion concurred with this argumentation. According to an Emnid survey in 1966, 45 per cent of those people informed about the EDK paper agreed with it. Only 24 per cent disagreed and 26 per cent were undecided (Emnid, 1966: 1).[19]

A number of influential journalists fully supported the view that Germany, given its past, had a particular responsibility to learn the lessons of history. Recognition was considered a central lesson, without which Europe might relapse into another catastrophe. Rudolph Augstein, editor of the *Spiegel*, the FRG's leading news magazine,

---

[17] For more details on the FDP and *Ostpolitik*, see Hans Edgar Jahn (1985: 373–80).

[18] For more details on these church initiatives, see Dieter Bingen (1998: 87–8).

[19] The wording of the question was as follows: 'Do you essentially agree with the memorandum, essentially not agree with it, or is your opinion situated in between these two views?'

started his advocacy in favour of the territorial status quo in 1962.[20] He chastised the Federal Republic for its claim to the former eastern territories and even welcomed the existence of the GDR in this context. In his view, East Germany constituted some kind of a *cordon sanitaire* between the Federal Republic and the disputed territories in the East. Otherwise, Germany would start the vicious circle of territorial claims and acquisitions anew: 'Without it [the GDR, MK] the old game – Poles out of Breslau, Russians out of Lemberg – would start again' (Augstein, 1967: 19). Augstein's message was that the FRG, if it was serious about breaking with Germany's past, fostering reconciliation and seeking *Wiedergutmachung*, had to recognise existing borders, including the German–German border.

Many of Augstein's fellow journalists fully concurred with him. Sebastian Haffner (quoted in Roth, 1995: 32) cautioned that the refusal of recognition constituted 'anachronistic politics' that would threaten 'Europe's peace and the survival of Europe in an again increasingly more dangerous environnment'.[21] Theo Sommer (1966) warned that the only alternative to the new *Ostpolitik* was conflict and war: 'The alternative to this policy is, in my view, continued stagnation, perpetuated division and, at worst, war.' Several journalists such as Peter Bender (1966) and Martin Jänicke (1966), used this argument to explicitly advocate the recognition of the territorial status quo. Günter Gaus (quoted in Roth, 1995: 32) argued in a similar vein: The 'recognition of the GDR and the Oder–Neiße border' is the only means for 'the establishment of the kind of peace that is at all feasible'.

Marion von Dönhoff, editorial writer for *Die Zeit*, also employed the comparative mode of argumentation. She was one of the most remarkable advocates for recognition. She grew up in East Prussia and continued to identify not only with Germany but also with Prussia and its East Prussian province. In 1964, she wrote: 'Nobody who comes from the East will ever give up land.' A year later, she stated: 'Without exaggeration and considered *sine ira et studio*: it would be easier for me to cope with the news that I would have a deadly accident within the next three days, than coming to terms with the loss of my East Prussian home.' Yet despite these deeply held sentiments, von Dönhoff warned

[20] Jens Daniel (alias Rudolf Augstein), 'Nehmt Ulbricht in die Arme', *Der Spiegel*, 15 August 1962, p. 14.
[21] For a very similar reasoning see also Willy Brandt (1976: 220).

that the tragedies of history must not be repeated. She advocated reconciliation with the East, especially Poland. In the late 1960s, she began to argue for the recognition of the territorial status quo. In her view, this was the only possible path to reconciliation and peace in Europe (von Kuenheim, 2003).

The abstract mode of reasoning was also prevalent in public discourse. Even the Indivisible Germany Curatory (*Kuratorium Unteilbares Deutschland*), a movement for German reunification, embarked on the argumentation for recognition. In 1967, Wilhelm Wolfgang Schütz, its chairman, wrote a memorandum entitled *Was ist Deutschland?* (What is Germany?). He elaborated on Bahr's Tutzing proposals about the status of the GDR. He argued that there were two German states, but they could not be foreign countries to one another. Thus, West Germany should recognise the GDR *staatsrechtlich* (law pertaining to the interaction of states in world politics), but not *völkerrechtlich* (law pertaining to the interaction of nations in world politics).

The German nation would be represented by two states in international affairs. These states would not interfere in each other's affairs. Yet the relations between them would be special relations of a German community rather than relations between two foreign states. There would be two German states, but not two foreign states (Meyer, 1997: 401). This recognition would not make a peaceful reunification impossible. On the contrary, it would offer a chance, by contributing to a fundamental reordering of Europe, for Germans to exercise their right to national self-determination in the future.[22] Thus, the abstract reasoning was intermingled with the appropriateness mode. The principle of national self-determination was a key *topos* for the advocates of recognition as it was for those buttressing the taboo against recognition in the 1950s. Journalists such as Marion von Dönhoff (1962) and Paul Sethe (1966) argued in a similar vein. Only recognition would make the creation of a new, co-operative Europe a possibility. And only such a Europe could safeguard peace and generate a chance for reunification through a peaceful act of national self-determination in the distant future.

---

[22] When Wilhelm Schütz made this proposal, he was not yet a member of the SPD, but nevertheless quite closely affiliated with the party. His suggestion was well received by leading Social Democrats, including Brandt, Bahr, Klaus Schütz and Wehner.

From the mid-1960s, abstract reasoning was reinforced by the changing international constellation. After the Cuban Missile Crisis, the antagonism between East and West declined and a period of détente began. This change played into the hands of those advocates who focused on the abstract mode of reasoning. Creating a fundamentally new order in Europe that would eventually offer a chance for German unification did not seem as far fetched as it had done a few years earlier. Helmut Schmidt (SPD), for instance, welcomed the détente and postulated that West Germany ought to position itself 'in the vanguard of détente in Europe' in order to contribute to a more peaceful order in Europe and, thus, to a chance for reunification in the future. Yet a more peaceful order would require recognising the current 'demarcation lines'.[23] Similar arguments were made in *Die Zeit* and the *Süddeutsche Zeitung*, but not in the *Frankfurter Allgemeine Zeitung* or *Die Welt*.[24]

Ostpolitik in transition

Although the advocacy for the territorial status quo norm grew from 1962 to 1969, it had little impact on Bonn's foreign policy. The governing CDU/CSU rejected recognition. Nevertheless, post-Wall *Ostpolitik* was not the same as pre-Wall *Ostpolitik*. It became more conciliatory.

Adenauer (CDU) retired as Chancellor in 1963. Ludwig Erhard (CDU) became his successor. Two years earlier, Adenauer's long-time foreign minister, Clemens von Brentano, had been replaced by Gerhard Schröder. With Erhard and Schröder, *Ostpolitik* became more flexible. Schröder emphasised that the FRG sought reconciliation with Eastern Europe as well as a more positive peace through increased contacts and co-operation. He set up trade missions in Warsaw, Bucharest, Budapest and Sofia. The FRG's isolation from the East slowly eroded. Erich Mende, Erhard's Minister for All-German Affairs, argued in favour of diplomatic relations with Warsaw Pact states. In his opinion, the Hallstein Doctrine was a hindrance to the establishment of more contacts with the East.

---

[23] Helmut Schmidt, *Verhandlungen des deutschen Bundestages* 5, 13 March 1968, p. 8307.
[24] Marion Gräfin Dönhoff, 'Ostpolitik mit de Gaulle', *Die Zeit*, 3 December 1965, p. 1; Immanuel Birnbaum, 'Nicht allzu kleine Schritte', *Süddeutsche Zeitung*, 16 December 1966, p. 4.

In 1966, *Ostpolitik* gained more momentum. Erhard (CDU) sent the Peace Note (*Friedensnote*) to East European governments. Many parts of the note are reminiscent of the *topoi* employed by the advocates of the territorial status quo. The FRG, bearing in mind its history, would seek to contribute to the prevention of a new war. This would only be possible by increasing contacts across the East–West divide. The Federal Republic wanted reconciliation with the Eastern countries. Poland and Czechoslovakia were explicitly mentioned in this context. The thrust of the note consisted of the reassurance that the FRG would never resort to aggressive foreign policies again and would pursue its goals only by peaceful means. The note proposed to Warsaw Pact states the bilateral renunciation of force treaties. However, the document did not connect the *topoi* it invoked, such as Germany's responsibility for the Second World War, reconciliation, and peace through overcoming the rigidity of borders, to the recognition of present borders. On the contrary, the document clearly rejected the recognition of the territorial status quo. It supported this rejection with a legal argument. According to the allies' decision at the Potsdam Conference, Germany continued to exist in its 1937 borders. The allies had the responsibility for Germany as a whole until a peace treaty with Germany as a whole was concluded. Only such a peace treaty, or a democratically elected all-German government, could change the legal borders of Germany (Auswärtiges Amt, 1972: 561).

The electoral support for the CDU/CSU, although still the strongest caucus in the Bundestag, decreased in the 1960s. Following the 1961 and 1965 elections, the party needed a coalition partner in order to govern. Before 1966, it formed a coalition with the FDP and thereafter with the SPD. By the time the SPD joined the coalition, the Social Democrats had already completed much of the transformation towards Brandt's new *Ostpolitik*. Brandt became foreign minister. The recognition of the territorial status quo was still a taboo for the CDU/CSU and the new Chancellor, Kurt-Georg Kiesinger (CDU). Although this complicated the decision-making in the coalition, the two parties managed to reach agreements on several important foreign policy issues because they made sense of many foreign policy challenges in a similar way.

For the most part, the CDU and the SPD shared the same repertoire of commonplaces. Parliamentary debates during the so-called Great Coalition reveal that both parties shared the belief that Germany, because of its past, had a particular duty to learn the lessons of history and to seek reconciliation with the East. Peace was synonymous with a European Peace Order, i.e. the overcoming of borders that kept nations, states and military blocs apart.[25] Such a European Peace Order would also offer the chance for German reunification. The CDU's Bavarian sister party, the CSU, was outside of the shared repertoire of commonplaces but failed to exert much influence on the *Ostpolitik* during the Great Coalition. The CSU's chairman, Franz-Josef Strauß, understood himself as the heir of Adenauer's Politics of Strength. On this view, the Soviet Union and its satellite regimes remained menacing enemies that could only be kept at bay by a preponderance of power (Clemens, 1989: 41–44).

The most tangible outcome of the *Ostpolitik* of Kiesinger and Brandt was the erosion of the Hallstein Doctrine. The FRG offered diplomatic relations to all East European states except the GDR.[26] Romania and Yugoslavia responded favourably and diplomatic relations were established. The recognition of the GDR as a state by another state no longer made Bonn sever diplomatic ties with the recognising state.

Persuasive argumentation

In the late 1960s and early 1970s, the advocacy for the recognition of the territorial status quo continued. The argumentation had a major impact on public opinion. By the end of the 1960s, the public was in favour of recognition. The advocacy for recognition resonated with a majority of West Germans.

Laurence Whetten (1971:6) claims that *Ostpolitik* was the decisive factor that decided the 1969 elections in favour of the SPD and the FDP. While this may be an exaggeration, *Ostpolitik* was an important factor. For the first time in the history of the FRG, the CDU/CSU was confined to the role of the opposition. The SPD gained its hitherto best result and formed a coalition government with the FDP under Chancellor Brandt.

The new government, especially Brandt and Bahr, who remained Brandt's closest adviser, continued to employ the three modes of reasoning for their advocacy against the irredentist claims. The abstract mode kept on linking recognition, the Idea of Europe and the longing for

---

[25] This cross-party consensus is very clear in the debate about Kiesinger's Regierungserklärung in 1966: *Verhandlungen des deutschen Bundestages 5*, 13–16 December 1966, pp. 3565–879.

[26] Kurt-Georg Kiesinger, *Verhandlungen des deutschen Bundestages 5*, 13 December 1966, pp. 3661–4.

reunification. Through increasing interaction, communal bonds would develop among European states. Borders, including the German–German border, would gradually lose their divisive nature. Eventually, European states could come to see each other as friends. This was precisely Bahr's definition of *Ostpolitik*. It was the path to 'stable peace', to 'security through friendship'.[27] In the distant future, this path could offer a chance for reunification.[28] The necessary first step to initiate the process towards this new quality of European relations would be the FRG's recognition of the existing borders. Hence, only the recognition of the territorial status quo would make it possible to overcome this status quo in the future. In the words of Brandt: 'If we want European borders to lose their divisive function over time in a historical process, then we have to acknowledge the existing borders first, *de facto* and politically.'[29]

Brandt and Bahr also emphasised the comparative mode of reasoning. Brandt frequently made the link between the lessons of history, reconciliation and *Ostpolitik* explicit. Given the war of aggression that Hitler had waged, it was Germany's duty to help 'overcome the consequences of the catastrophe' that Germany had caused in Europe (Brandt, quoted in Meissner, 1970: 383). Nothing captures Brandt's desire for *Wiedergutmachung* and reconciliation as vividly as his famous kneeling in front of the memorial of the Warsaw ghetto, when he was on a state visit in Poland in 1969. In his numerous drafts for Brandt's inaugural speech as Chancellor, Bahr emphasised the link between *Wiedergutmachung*, reconciliation and the recognition of the territorial status quo. The Oder–Neiße border would have to be recognised, 'if one wants a politics of peace and reconciliation'.[30]

Finally, the new government also employed the appropriateness mode of reasoning for its advocacy for the recognition of the territorial status quo. The advocates of recognition did not surrender the emphasis on the principle of national self-determination to the opponents of

[27] *Egon Bahr Depositum of the Archiv der Sozialdemokratie*, Ordner 398/Mappe 1 (Bonn: Friedrich Ebert Stiftung).
[28] Interview with Egon Bahr, Berlin, 15 July 2003.
[29] Willy Brandt, *Verhandlungen des deutschen Bundestages* 6, 17 June 1970, p. 3216.
[30] *Egon Bahr Depositum of the Archiv der Sozialdemokratie*, Ordner 115/Mappe 1. This file contains suggestions for Brandt's inaugural speech as Chancellor in October 1969.

recognition. They stressed that the recognition of existing borders did not impinge on this principle. On the contrary, it would make it possible to pursue its implementation in a meaningful way.[31] Brandt and Bahr also frequently invoked the norm of peaceful resolution of disputes. In contrast to its past, the FRG defined itself as a peaceful state, determined to settle its disputes without resorting to force.[32]

It is doubtful whether this threefold argumentation would have had the overwhelming success that it had in the late 1960s and early 1970s if Brandt's reputation had not changed as fundamentally as it did. To be sure, the argumentation was very strong. The key advocates used all three modes of reasoning, and they used *topoi* – the longing of the nation, the episteme, highly influential lessons from the past, and critical norms – that make for a very compelling argument. Yet the persuasiveness of this argument was also strongly facilitated by the reputation Brandt gained in the 1960s.

In the early 1960s, his visions of a new *Ostpolitik*, which encompassed a fundamentally new European order and not merely the advocacy for the territorial status quo, were shocking to large segments of the political establishment and the public. The idea of a *Schicksalsgemeinschaft* transcending the East–West divide was ridiculed and dismissed. Conservative segments of society singled Brandt out as a traitor. At that time, Brandt used a different compass to navigate Europe than the majority. The repertoire of commonplaces upon which he drew contained a different identity narrative than the one cherished by the majority.

While using a different compass caused a number of setbacks in the short run, it earned him a strong reputation and impenetrable aura in the medium and long run. When the dominant repertoire shifted in the mid-1960s, the majority came to share Brandt's lifeworld, in particular a different understanding of the FRG's history and a different positioning vis-à-vis the East. Many influential actors and the public looked for help in orientating themselves in this new environment. Brandt, as one

---

[31] This appropriateness aspect was usually intertwined with the abstract mode of reasoning. See, for example, *Egon Bahr Depositum of the Archiv der Sozialdemokratie*, Ordner 398/Mappe 1 (Bonn: Friedrich Ebert Stiftung).

[32] This appropriateness aspect was usually intertwined with the comparative mode of reasoning. See, for instance, Brandt (1968: 28).

of very few leading politicians, provided this orientation because he had
been an outspoken protagonist of the novel aspects of the repertoire of
commonplaces at a time when they had still been fiercely contested.
Public opinion polls show this trust in Brandt very clearly. As early as
1967, an Allensbach survey determined that 45 per cent of the population considered Brandt best qualified in the field of *Ostpolitik*. The
Chancellor under whom Brandt served at the time, Kiesinger, scored
only 33 per cent (Koppel, 1972: 179). In the early 1970s, two-thirds
thought that Brandt had deservedly received the Nobel Prize for
Ostpolitik (Infas, 1974: 266). Daniela Münkel captures this transformation of the 'traitor to the fatherland' to the 'cult figure' very well with
her expression 'Brandt-fever' (Münkel, 2000: 33). In a similar vein, the
caricaturist Horst Baerenz (1988 [1971]: 200) sketched Brandt as a
secular saint who was entirely immune to the attacks from his critics.[33]

By the late 1960s, the advocacy had come to resonate with a majority
of influential actors. In the Bundestag, the FDP and SPD caucuses fully
supported the advocacy for forgoing irredentism.[34] Recognition was
also widely supported in the newspapers. Of the four analysed newspapers, only *Die Welt* opposed recognising the GDR. The reason for
this criticism was not that *Die Welt* opposed steps towards a European
Peace Order. Rather, *Die Welt* argued that recognition would make
reunification more difficult, if not impossible, and that recognition
would not contribute to a more peaceful Europe.[35] *Die Zeit*, the
Süddeutsche Zeitung and the *Frankfurter Allgemeine Zeitung*, by

---

[33] Harsh criticism continued from those who had not come to embrace the novel
aspects of the repertoire of commonplaces. The newspaper of the CSU, the
Bayernkurier, for instance, continued to vilify Brandt as a traitor.

[34] See, for instance, two key figures of the coalition: Herbert Wehner,
Verhandlungen des deutschen Bundestages 6, 29 October 1969, p. 59; Wolfgang
Mischnick, *Verhandlungen des deutschen Bundestages* 6, 29 October 1969,
p. 54.

[35] Georg Schröder, 'Bilanz einer großen Woche', *Die Welt*, 1 November 1969,
p. 2; Matthias Walden, 'Barfuß auf dem Wege der Annäherung?' *Die Welt*,
1 November 1969, p. 2; Ernst-Ulrich Fromm, 'Warnungen und Ermutigungen an
die Adresse Brandts', *Die Welt*, 1 November 1969, p. 4; Dieter Cylon, 'Moskau
verhandelt mit Bonn nach Lenins Prinzipien', *Die Welt*, 17 April 1970, p. 4;
Georg Schröder, 'Das neue Deutschland meldete sich am 8. Mai zu Wort', *Die
Welt*, 9 May 1970, p. 4; Dieter Cylon, 'Garantie der Hegemonie Moskaus', *Die
Welt*, 18 June 1970, p. 4; Bernt Conrad, 'Was Brandt nicht sagte, ist politisch
aufschlußreich', *Die Welt*, 20 January 1973, p. 4.

contrast, supported recognising the territorial status quo. This support was unqualified in the *Süddeutsche Zeitung* and *Die Zeit* and sometimes accompanied by increasingly sharp criticism of opponents of recognition.[36] For the most part, the *Frankfurter Allgemeine Zeitung* supported recognition. One editorial writer, Ernst-Otto Maetzke, initially cautioned that the kind of recognition of the GDR would have to be more clearly defined. Yet the more *Ostpolitik* progressed, the more critical the *Frankfurter Allgemeine Zeitung* became of opponents of recognition.[37]

By the late 1960s, the argumentation in favour of the territorial status quo also resonated with the public. According to a survey by the Allensbach Institute, a majority of West Germans were prepared to recognise the Oder–Neiße border in the case of reunification with the GDR from 1966 onwards (Allensbach, quoted in Glaab, 2000: 45). Figure 4.1 shows this evolution of public opinion from 1959 to 1969.

In 1969, there was for the first time a majority in favour of accepting the German–Polish border, independently of a reunification of the GDR and the FRG. As figure 4.2 shows, public opinion on this issue shifted

---

[36] Hans Heigert, 'Immer noch das deutsche Trauma?' *Süddeutsche Zeitung*, 30 October 1969, p. 4; bm, 'Gifttropfen im Friedensbecher', *Süddeutsche Zeitung*, 30 October 1969, p. 4; re, 'Wehners schwarze Stunde', *Süddeutsche Zeitung*, 16 April 1970, p. 4; Hans Heigert, 'Bilanz der Vorschlußrunde', *Süddeutsche Zeitung*, 17 June 1970, p. 4; Immanuel Birnbaum, 'Vom Osten her gesehen', *Süddeutsche Zeitung*, 17 June 1970, p. 4; Hans Heigert, 'Noch in den alten Schatten', *Süddeutsche Zeitung*, 15 September 1973, p. 4; Theo Sommer, 'Deutsch sein zu zweit', *Die Zeit*, 31 October 1969, p. 3; Marion Gräfin Dönhoff, 'Geöffnet nach Osten', *Die Zeit*, 31 October 1969, p. 3; Marion Gräfin Dönhoff, 'Der Dialog beginnt', *Die Zeit*, 7 November 1969, p. 3; Theo Sommer, 'Sicherheit für die Bundesrepublik', *Die Zeit*, 1 November 1969, pp. 11, 12; Kurt Becker, 'Das deutsche Nadelöhr', *Die Zeit*, 27 March 1970, p. 1.

[37] Ernst-Otto Maetzke, 'Deutsche Haupt- und Nebensätze', *Frankfurter Allgemeine Zeitung*, 30 October 1969, p. 1; Jürgen Tern, 'Kritisches Echo', *Frankfurter Allgemeine Zeitung*, 21 March 1970, p. 1; Walter Henkels, 'Zaungast in Erfurt', *Frankfurter Allgemeine Zeitung*, 21 March 1970, p. 2; Jürgen Tern, 'Generalkonsulate', *Frankfurter Allgemeine Zeitung*, 23 March 1970, p. 1; Hermann Pörzgen, 'Bahrs Moskau-Aufenthalt intensivierte Gespräche', *Frankfurter Allgemeine Zeitung*, 23 March 1970, p. 2; Dettmar Cramer, 'Bonn und Warschau', *Frankfurter Allgemeine Zeitung*, 18 June 1970, p. 2; n.b., 'Die Opposition', *Frankfurter Allgemeine Zeitung*, 19 January 1973, p. 1; Fritz Ullrich Fack, 'Die Handschrift Brandts', *Frankfurter Allgemeine Zeitung*, 19 January 1973, p. 1.

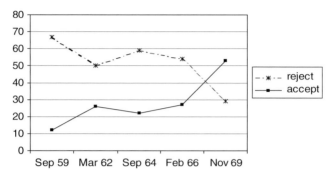

Figure 4.1 Acceptance of Oder–Neiße border in exchange for reunification of
East and West Germany
Source: Allensbach, quoted in Glaab (2000: 45)

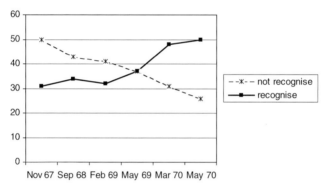

Figure 4.2 Recognition of Oder–Neiße line as final border
Source: Allensbach and Ifak, quoted in Glaab (1999: 244)

towards recognition from 1969 onwards. In May 1970, 50 per cent of
the populace opted for the Oder–Neiße line as the final border
between Poland and Germany (Allensbach and Ifak, quoted in Glaab,
1999: 244).[38]

[38] Allensbach asked the following question: 'What do you think about the following
issue: Should the Federal Republic recognise the Oder–Neiße line, which now
separates Germany from Poland, as the final Eastern border of Germany or not?'
Glaab takes all the data in this table from Allensbach except for 1970, where she
uses data from Ifak. This institute asked a slightly different question: 'You are
surely familiar with the view that the Federal Republic should no longer hesitate
to recognise the Oder–Neiße line as the final German border. Do you think that
the Federal Republic should recognise the Oder–Neiße line now or not?'

It is worth mentioning that the shift in public opinion even included expellees. In 1969, 44 per cent of expellees rejected the border and 44 per cent accepted the border. A year later, a majority of 57 to 33 per cent opted for acceptance (Allensbach, quoted in Glaab, 1999: 242).

The public opinion shift with regard to recognition of the GDR is somewhat more difficult to trace, because the questions asked in the surveys changed very frequently and are often not easily comparable. Yet the available data strongly suggest that the public opinion shifts on the issues of the recognition of the GDR and the Oder–Neiße are very similar. In 1955, less than 10 per cent favoured the recognition of the GDR, whereas almost two-thirds were opposed. In October 1970, an equal percentage of West Germans favoured and opposed the recognition. From 1971 to 1973, approximately two-thirds favoured recognition (Allensbach, quoted in Glaab, 1999: 246). Moreover, according to four opinion polls by Infas in 1970, over 80 per cent of West Germans favoured entering negotiations with the GDR, whereas less than 10 per cent were opposed (Infas, quoted in Glaab, 1999: 260–76). The electorate considered the SPD, who advocated recognition, as opposed to the CDU/CSU, who opposed it, to be much more competent with regard to *Ostpolitik*. An Infas opinion poll conducted before the 1969 federal elections showed that over 50 per cent regarded the prospect of having a CDU/CSU government as harmful for achieving a more peaceful order in Europe, whereas more than 50 per cent thought an SPD government would make a positive contribution to bringing about peaceful co-operation between East and West (Infas, quoted in Koppel, 1972: 306). Another Infas survey from 1971 showed that almost two-thirds of the populace – 63 per cent to be exact – agreed with Brandt's *Ostpolitik* (Infas, 1974: 6).

In short, the argumentation for the territorial status quo norm was highly successful. More and more social actors and the majority of the public embraced the argumentation in favour of recognition. What repercussions did this successful argumentation have for recalcitrant actors? The next section deals with the reaction of the CDU/CSU to the widespread endorsement of recognition.

Compromise

The success of the argumentation put pressure on the opponents to comply with the majority view. Those who shared the repertoire of commonplaces of the advocates of the territorial status quo norm were willing to compromise. This compromise made it possible for the FRG to forgo irredentism. Those opponents who did not share the repertoire of commonplaces, however, were absolute opponents. They were not prepared to accept a compromise.

Despite harsh criticism from the opposition, the SPD/FDP coalition government pushed its agenda forward very quickly. In May 1969, Poland offered the FRG talks about the Oder–Neiße border independently of other problems such as the recognition of the GDR. Two months later, the Soviet Union declared that it was prepared to enter negotiations with the FRG about a treaty on the renunciation of force. In January 1970, Bahr began talks with the Soviet foreign minister, Andrei Gromyko. A month later, German–Polish talks started. In March, Brandt visited the GDR. In May, Willy Stoph, the East German Prime Minister, came to the FRG. In July, Walter Scheel, foreign minister, travelled to Moscow, and finalised the German–Soviet negotiations. In August, Brandt signed the Moscow Treaty.

The treaty consisted of three key aspects. First, the two parties signed the accord in order to contribute to peace in Europe and in the world. Second, they would settle their disputes only by peaceful means. Third, they agreed 'that Europe's peace can only be kept if nobody puts the current borders into question'. Based on this belief, the parties 'declare that they do not claim territory of any state and will refrain from doing so in the future as well'. More precisely, they

consider the borders of all states in Europe today and in the future as inviolable ... including the Oder–Neiße line, which is the Western border of the People's Republic of Poland, and the border between the Federal Republic of Germany and the German Democratic Republic. (Auswärtiges Amt, 1972: 761–2)

In December 1970, four months after the Moscow Treaty, the FRG and Poland signed the Warsaw Treaty. The treaty dealt with the same three aspects as outlined above. The FRG renounced its claim to Pomerania, Silesia and East Prussia by recognising the Oder–Neiße border. In June 1972, negotiations between the FRG and the GDR began. In December, the two German states signed the Basic Treaty (*Grundlagenvertrag*). The two parties affirmed that the purpose of the treaty was to make a contribution to peace in Europe, and that a precondition for this was to recognise the existing borders. In addition to this, the treaty emphasised that the United Nations Charter was the basis for the relationship between the FRG and the GDR. In accordance with the Charter, the two parties would settle their disputes only peacefully, not interfere in each other's affairs, respect each other's territorial integrity and independence, and would not act in the name of the other. Yet, in the West German interpretation, the GDR and the FRG were not foreign states to one another, and the FRG continued to aspire to the reunification of the two parts of Germany.[39]

Of the political parties in the Bundestag, only the CDU/CSU opposed the recognition of the territorial status quo. Three camps within the conservative caucus may be identified. First, there was a group that Geoffrey Pridham (1975) aptly labelled 'absolute opponents'. A minority, rallying around the CSU's chairman Franz-Josef Strauß and Karl Theodor von Guttenberg as well as a few CDU members such as Alfred Dregger, opposed any kind of recognition. In contrast to the two other groups, the absolute opponents did not share the dominant repertoire of commonplaces of public discourse. They continued to seek sharp demarcation from the East not only in terms of human rights, but also with regard to epistemic understandings. The Soviet Union was still portrayed as a menace who had learnt nothing from history and merely waited for an opportunity to conquer the whole of Europe. Eastern Europe was still seen as the antithesis of Western Europe in every respect. Peace with the enemy beyond a negative peace secured by deterrence was considered utopian. Recognising a deeply unjust status quo would amount to something akin to treason.[40] Second, another minority within the CDU supported recognition. Walther Leisler-Kieps, Norbert Blüm, as well as the CDU's youth organisation, *Junge Union*, for example, supported the view that recognition would open the way to a more peaceful order in Europe, in which Europe's pressing problems such as Germany's partition could be eventually solved. Third, there was a group of ambivalent opponents that changed into ambivalent supporters between 1970 and 1973. The most prominent figures in this group were Rainer Barzel, the CDU's chairman, Kurt-Georg Kiesinger, Helmut Kohl, Werner Marx, Gerhard Schröder and Richard von Weizäcker.

[39] The *Grundlagenvertrag* can be found in Helmut Kistler (1982: 121–3).
[40] As mentioned above, this is also the position that *Die Welt* advocated.

The latter group did not doubt by any means the role that the FRG should play in Europe and in the world. Indeed, many in this group had contributed substantially to redefining West German identity as a community-creating identity in all of Europe. This focus on peace remained during the debates. Von Weizäcker, for example, explained: 'Our geographical location at the centre of the continent assigns us the task to find a path towards a European Peace Order.'[41] Moreover, there was an emphasis that the FRG would have to be prepared to make sacrifices, in order to contribute to such an order. Barzel, for instance, spoke about the German Question as the FRG's 'chance to historically compensate Europe for what Hitler has done to it. Our preparedness to even make painful sacrifices for a European Peace Order complies with this duty.'[42] The group did not disagree with the SPD and FDP about what a European Peace Order should look like. There would be a dense web of co-operation on many different levels and in many different issue areas. As a consequence, borders would lose their divisive nature, and this would, *inter alia*, offer a chance for reunification.

The ambivalent opponents also wanted bilateral treaties with Warsaw Pact states. They believed that Germany's contribution to peace in Europe should consist of renunciation of force treaties with Warsaw Pact states. This would be the stepping stone for entering 'true negotiations'[43] with the Soviet Union, Poland and the GDR that would lead towards the establishment of a European Peace Order by developing economic, scientific and cultural ties across the Iron Curtain.[44] The Eastern countries were 'partners' in this process (Barzel, 1998: 74).

The ambivalent opponents, however, did not share the SPD's and FDP's reasoning on the effect of recognising the territorial status quo. They were convinced that such a recognition would be entirely counter-productive. They argued that recognition would contribute to the exact antithesis of such a peace order, i.e. the strengthening of borders. This would make a

---

[41] Richard von Weizäcker, *Verhandlungen des deutschen Bundestages 6*, 8 May 1970, p. 2568.
[42] Rainer Barzel, *Verhandlungen des deutschen Bundestages 6*, 20 March 1970, p. 2092. A very similar argument is made by Richard von Weizäcker, *Verhandlungen des deutschen Bundestages 6*, 8 May 1970, p. 2568.
[43] Kurt-Georg Kiesinger, *Verhandlungen des deutschen Bundestages 6*, 16 June 1970, p. 3241.
[44] 'Alternativentwurf der Opposition für einen Vertrag mit der Sowjetunion, 1972' (in Kistler, 1982: 103–4).

European Peace Order, and with it reunification, impossible. While establishing a European Peace Order was about overcoming borders, recognition would carve them into stone and thus perpetuate conflicts instead of resolving them. In Weizäcker's words: 'Not a Europe of walls, but a continent that takes away the separating character of its borders will be prepared for the future.'[45] In a similar vein, Werner Marx warned against 'an inflexible, decrepit, nineteenth-century, reactionary nation-state character of a border'.[46] Instead, the character of all European borders should be modelled after the Western example – open and not dividing. Yet the government would pursue a policy of respecting borders 'that are truly defined ... by walls, mine fields and watch towers for machine guns'.[47]

Thus, the *topoi* for reasoning on the German Question were not in dispute between the supporters and most of the opponents (with the sole exception of the small minority of absolute opponents). They employed the same *topoi*, such as the Idea of Europe, *Wiedergutmachung* and the longing for reunification. What was in dispute, however, was the link between these *topoi* and the territorial status quo norm. Kiesinger put this quite succinctly when he distinguished between the positions of the opposition and the government: 'What is the contribution that we have to make for Europe's peace, more precisely our own ... indispensable contribution? Indeed, this is what is at stake, this is the key issue of the *Ostpolitik*, and this is the key issue between us.'[48] In short: yes to a European Peace Order, yes to negotiations with the East, but no to the recognition of the territorial status quo. Barzel (1998: 47) summarised this in the formula: 'Not "no", but "not like this".'

Although the ambivalent group in the CDU argued against the reasoning in the SPD and the FDP that the recognition of borders could ultimately contribute to overcoming them, it signalled its will to compromise. These signals were due to the realisation that the CDU was out of touch with public opinion. As Christian Hacke (1975: 38) explains, the party attempted to avoid the 'odium of the destructive naysayer'. By

[45] Richard von Weizäcker, *Verhandlungen des deutschen Bundestages* 6, 8 May 1970, p. 2568.
[46] Werner Marx, *Verhandlungen des deutschen Bundestages* 6, 17 June 1970, p. 3227.
[47] Werner Marx, *Verhandlungen des deutschen Bundestages* 6, 17 June 1970, p. 3222.
[48] Kurt-Georg Kiesinger, *Verhandlungen des deutschen Bundestages* 6, 17 June 1970, p. 3241.

the early 1970s, the competence that the public ascribed to the CDU and SPD in foreign policy issues had reversed:

The SPD, once considered inexperienced and potentially unreliable in foreign policy matters in the 1950s and early 1960s, developed due to the debates about the treaties with the East into the favoured guarantor for a new and realistic policy towards Eastern Europe, whereas the Union [CDU, CSU; MK] came to be perceived as a party unwilling to face reality and sometimes even as hostile to détente. (Hacke, 1975: 56)

Soon after Bahr began to negotiate in Moscow, the CDU's ambivalent opponents tried to push for a *junctim*. The FRG's concessions should be related to progress on issues concerning the partition of Germany. For example, there were demands that the East German regime should withdraw the order to shoot those trying to escape from the East to the West, and that it should clear the mine fields that were part of the border strip. The CDU complained that the government's negotiation strategy was inadequate because it offered everything – recognition of the territorial status quo – without asking for anything important first. Brandt was targeted in particular, because he *de facto* recognised the GDR in the Bundestag before even starting negotiations with the East (Tiggemann, 1998: 49–50).

By 1972, the Moscow and Warsaw treaties were pending ratification by the Bundestag. This ratification was more than a formality. As a consequence of *Ostpolitik*, four Bundestag deputies switched from the FDP to the CDU/CSU caucus: Wilhelm Helms, Erich Mende, Heinz Starke and Siegfried Zoglmann. Herbert Hupka left the SPD and joined the CDU. Thus the majority of the SPD and the FDP shrunk to one deputy. Given this virtual parity and the explosiveness of the issue, a majority for the treaties was by no means guaranteed. The ratification was in the hands not only of the government, but also of the opposition.

In his memoirs, Barzel, the leader of the opposition, outlines four instruments that he used or at least considered using. First, in early 1970 he considered an appeal to the Supreme Court. In his view, the treaties would have to be ratified by a two-thirds majority in both houses of parliament, Bundestag and Bundesrat, as opposed to the government's position that the ratification required only a simple majority in the Bundestag. Barzel (1998: 78) was confident that the treaties would never have received such a double two-thirds majority. Yet he discarded this option, 'because I wanted a *rapprochement* with Moscow, and not the failure but the improvement of the treaty'. Second, Barzel travelled to Moscow to achieve these improvements, i.e. to rid the treaty of the recognition of the territorial status quo. He failed. Third, upon his return to Bonn, the CDU/CSU employed the sharpest weapon available to the parliamentary opposition: a no-confidence vote to replace Brandt with himself as Chancellor. He was defeated by two votes.[49] Fourth, Barzel tried to influence the interpretation of the treaties through negotiating a joint statement on the interpretation with all parties in the Bundestag.

With this last instrument, he succeeded. All Bundestag parties reached a consensus on how to interpret the treaties. The Joint Statement was in many ways a success for the opposition. The CDU/CSU succeeded, against the wishes of the coalition government, in including two issues in the document that it considered of great importance. First, the recognition of the territorial status quo was part of a *modus vivendi*. The treaties recognised the current borders without carving them into stone for ever. The FRG would never unilaterally change a border, but peaceful change was still possible. In particular, the statement emphasised that the treaties did not contradict the goal of peaceful reunification through free self-determination in the future. Second, the recognition of the borders did not constitute a basis for the current borders in international law. The current borders were provisional until France, Great Britain, the Soviet Union and the United States defined these borders in a future peace treaty with all of Germany.

Barzel was satisfied with the compromise. The joint statement was passed with the agreement of the CDU/CSU. Barzel also tried to convince the absolute opponents to agree to the ratification of the treaties in the Bundestag. He failed, however. Led by Franz-Josef Strauß, the absolute opponents pressured the numerically much stronger ambivalent opponents into abstaining from the vote (Barzel, 1998: 157). Nevertheless, this abstention made the ratification possible.

The pattern of the ratification controversy about the *Grundlagenvertrag* was similar to the one about the Moscow and Warsaw treaties. Absolute opponents and ambivalent opponents within the CDU debated the course of action. The opposition voiced its disapproval but stopped short of blocking ratification. Due to its peculiar nature, the treaty required the ratification of the second chamber of parliament, the

---

[49] It surfaced after reunification that the pro-Brandt vote of one of the CDU deputies, Julius Steiner, was bought by the East German secret police.

Bundesrat. The Christian Democrats used their majority in this chamber
to vote against the treaty but – in a historically unique move – did not
send the treaty to the arbitration panel of the Bundestag and Bundesrat,
although this had been the firmly established procedure for decades.
Thus, the Bundesrat did not formally reject the ratification of the treaty.
Soon thereafter, the absolute opponents in the CSU called on the CDU-
controlled provincial governments to prepare a lawsuit against the federal government at the Supreme Court. In the CSU's opinion, the federal
government had violated the Basic Law by recognising the GDR. The
CSU, however, could convince no other provincial government. Thus,
only Bavaria took legal action. The Supreme Court ruled that the
Grundlagenvertrag did not violate the Constitution.

Argumentation and compromise made the FRG forgo irredentism.
Yet renouncing irredentism was not merely a policy change. It also
reflected a normative change. Not to claim territory became a taken-
for-granted norm. It was a key principle of the 1975 Helsinki
Agreement that the FRG signed and ratified. Even when the *rapprochement* between East and West started to crumble after Helsinki, and it
became more and more obvious that the daring vision of a European
peace order had been overly optimistic, there was not even a debate any
more about reviving the territorial claims. The territorial status quo
norm had become internalised. When the CDU/CSU returned to power
in 1982, the norm continued to be a seemingly self-evident foundation
of *Ostpolitik*. Franz-Josef Strauß, in the early 1970s still a harsh critic of
Ostpolitik, fully engaged in it in the 1980s. The CDU/CSU were still in
power when the Berlin Wall fell and Germany was reunified. This could
have sparked a new irredentism. The reunified Germany could no
longer hide behind the formula that it was up to the German people as
a whole to determine the legitimate borders of Germany. The reunified
state had to decide upon which borders it recognised and which ones it
did not. Yet irredentism – and even contemplating irredentism –
remained a thing of the past. Under the chancellorship of Helmut
Kohl (CDU), the reunified Germany confirmed the Oder–Neiße line as
the border between Poland and Germany.[50] Eighty-one per cent of the

---

[50] Vertrag zwischen der Bundesrepublik Deutschland und Republik Polen
über gute Nachbarschaft und freundschaftliche Zusammenarbeit, 17 June
1991 at: http://provinz-sachsen.de/krr/rechtsfundstellen/1950–2002/
grenzanerkennungsvertrag 1991.html

populace agreed with the recognition of Germany's borders (Ipsos, quoted in Glaab, 1999: 245).

Discussion of findings

Was the territorial status quo norm selected in three ideal-typical stages as hypothesised? If so, do the hypothesised conditions explain why these stages occurred? Does the norm selection mechanism, especially if compared to alternative explanations of the case, provide a convincing explanation for why the FRG renounced its irredentist claims?

The FRG's selection of the territorial status quo norm followed the ideal-typical three-stage process outlined in the theoretical framework: an innovative argumentation formed in the late 1950s and early 1960s, comprised of intellectuals and a small circle of politicians. The advocacy succeeded in persuading more and more segments of society, and managed to establish a new majority view by the late 1960s. In the early 1970s, a number of important recalcitrant actors succumbed to the pressure emanating from the new majority view. This is not to claim, of course, that every single interaction among actors followed three clear-cut stages. The FDP's national-liberal wing, for instance, was not persuaded to select the territorial status quo norm in the mid-1960s but was toppled from many powerful positions and silenced by the progressive wing. Yet the three stages are heuristically useful ideal-types that help us make the process of norm selection more intelligible. Figure 4.3 provides a schematised overview.

What conditions gave rise to the three stages of the norm selection mechanism? The empirical investigation supports the hypothesised conditions. Chapter 2 proposed that a fundamental change of the environment provides the impetus for innovative argumentation. In the case of the FRG, a shifting repertoire of commonplaces, coupled with a shocking event, provided a highly conducive environment for the formation of a new advocacy. When the Berlin Wall was built in 1961, it became obvious to many actors that the old ways of doing things had to be replaced by something new. The novel aspects of the repertoire, especially the desire for *Wiedergutmachung* and the interrelated repositioning towards the East, provided new clues for how the new ought to look.

The advocates developed a very strong argument, encompassing all three modes of reasoning as well as compelling *topoi*. The abstract reasoning linked the longing for unification, a key component of the

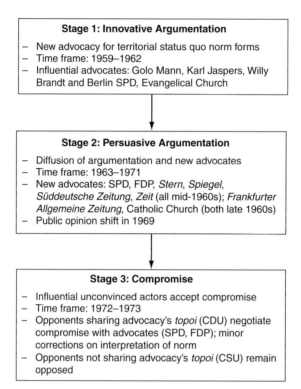

Stage 1: Innovative Argumentation
 − New advocacy for territorial status quo norm forms
 − Time frame: 1959–1962
 − Influential advocates: Golo Mann, Karl Jaspers, Willy
   Brandt and Berlin SPD, Evangelical Church

Stage 2: Persuasive Argumentation
 − Diffusion of argumentation and new advocates
 − Time frame: 1963–1971
 − New advocates: SPD, FDP, *Stern, Spiegel,*
   Süddeutsche Zeitung, Zeit (all mid-1960s); *Frankfurter*
   Allgemeine Zeitung, Catholic Church (both late 1960s)
 − Public opinion shift in 1969

Stage 3: Compromise
 − Influential unconvinced actors accept compromise
 − Time frame: 1972–1973
 − Opponents sharing advocacy's *topoi* (CDU) negotiate
   compromise with advocates (SPD, FDP); minor
   corrections on interpretation of norm
 − Opponents not sharing advocacy's *topoi* (CSU) remain
   opposed

Figure 4.3 Schematised three-stage norm selection process

dominant identity narrative, and the dominant episteme of the Idea of Europe to the recognition of the territorial status quo. The comparative reasoning connected the need to learn the lessons of history, which was also a highly salient aspect of the identity narrative, the Idea of Europe and the recognition of the territorial status quo. Finally, appropriateness reasoning not only invoked the norms of national self-determination and peaceful resolution of disputes but also buttressed them with their underlying justifications revolving around the self-identification as an unjustly partitioned nation and the Idea of Europe, respectively. Figure 4.4 illustrates the components of the successful argumentation. Each circle describes a form of reasoning and identifies its *topoi.*

A message – no matter how well crafted – also needs a convincing messenger in order to resonate with an audience. Brandt was the public face of the advocacy and his reputation proved to be crucial. Initially, his reputation was a hindrance for the advocacy. Being a protagonist of

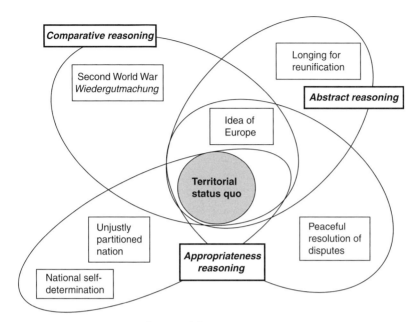

Figure 4.4 Components of successful argumentation

the novel aspects of the repertoire of commonplaces prior to their becoming dominant exposed him to severe criticism. Yet once these new aspects had come to be embraced by large segments of the society, the public and many influential social actors sought orientation from those who had been in the vanguard of this change. This bolstered Brandt's reputation, in particular in the field of *Ostpolitik*.

Finally, there is also empirical evidence for the conditions hypothesised to explain the occurrence of a compromise. Those recalcitrant actors who shared the *topoi* invoked by the advocacy sat down at the bargaining table with the advocates. Given the mounting costs of their counter-advocacy against what had become a majority view, they agreed to a compromise with the advocates. Since the costs made the recalcitrant actors very eager to compromise, the result of the compromise was much closer to the stance of the advocates than the position of the counter-advocates. Those recalcitrant actors, by contrast, whose repertoire of commonplaces did not include the *topoi* invoked by the advocates refused to bargain their position away.

What about alternative explanations? Are there other, more compelling accounts? Several authors contend that *Ostpolitik* was a function of international pressure. The FRG's political elites recognised the territorial status quo because of pressure from its allies (Besson, 1970; Haftendorn, 1985; Hacke, 1988). The problem with this argument is twofold. First, a focus on elites alone cannot explain the FRG's recognition of the territorial status quo. Some of these elites were pressured into recognition by public opinion. It is the interplay of elites and masses that explains the recognition of the existing borders. Second, the external pressure argument overlooks the fact that Bonn's *rapprochement* and its visions for a new European order went so far beyond the positions of Bonn's allies that the Brandt government aroused their suspicions. Given the fast pace and the far-reaching visions of *Ostpolitik*, allied states, in particular the United States, questioned – usually behind closed doors – whether Brandt's new approach could lead to another Rapallo (Joffe, 1973; Steffens, 1989).

William Griffith (1982) contends that the FRG recognised the territorial status quo because of Soviet preponderant power. He holds that the Federal Republic did not have the option to reunify the country. This could only be achieved through military might, which the FRG was lacking. Yet this argument cannot explain why the FRG was completely opposed to recognition in the 1950s and came to accept it in the early 1970s. This shift occurred although the FRG's military position vis-à-vis the Warsaw Pact improved following rearmament and its accession to NATO.

Another argument about the causes of *Ostpolitik* focuses on the attempt to ease the practical repercussions of partition for the people affected by it. Authors such as Roger Engelmann (1993) contend that the protagonists of *Ostpolitik* tried to make partition bearable, especially by allowing visits across the divide of the Iron Curtain. Undoubtedly, *Ostpolitik* started, *inter alia*, with this motivation.[51] This applies in particular to the Berlin SPD. Brandt's *Ostpolitik* started when he was still governing mayor of Berlin. In 1963, Brandt successfully negotiated an agreement with East Berlin that made it possible for families to reunite for Christmas. Yet from the mid-1960s onwards, *Ostpolitik* was firmly embedded in the European context and the concept of a European Peace Order. Görtemaker (1998: 53) captures this well:

---

[51] Interview with Klaus Schütz, 7 July 2003.

But Brandt and his fellow-advocates aimed at more than making the division more bearable in the shadow of the Wall. What they really wanted was a fundamental re-shaping of the relations between East and West – at least for Germany and Europe.

Hence, there are certain limitations of an argument that exclusively focuses on easing the consequences of partition for people. Nevertheless, it was an important reason for some actors.

Peter Bender (1972) argues that *Ostpolitik* was the outcome of a learning process. The Berlin Wall demonstrated the failure of Adenauer's Politics of Strength. Thus, the new *Ostpolitik* was, as Bender puts it in the sub-title of his book, the 'art of the self-evident'. This explanation, however, is incomplete. It is a plausible contention that the Wall provided an important impetus for changing the foreign policies towards the East. Yet it is not clear in Bender's account how the Wall translated into the *Ostpolitik* of the early 1970s. The three-stage norm selection mechanism and the empirical analysis allude to the significance of the Wall for *Ostpolitik* without reducing everything to 13 August 1961. The building of the Wall was the revolutionary event that made advocates feel compelled to seek a new beginning. Coupled with the changing repertoire of commonplaces, it sparked a new reasoning on *Ostpolitik*. Yet for this reasoning to generate the power to change entrenched policies and even the normative fabric, it required persuasion and compromise as well.

Ulrich Scheuner (1970) argues that a public opinion change caused the FRG to recognise the territorial status quo. Bonn renounced its irredentist claims when a majority of the public supported this step. Scheuner's argument is important, because the shift in public opinion was clearly of significance in the case of the FRG, and because public opinion is a factor that is routinely neglected by students of world politics. Public opinion is an important force in the three-stage mechanism. It makes recalcitrant actors seek a compromise. Yet public opinion alone does not explain the recognition of the territorial status quo. The public opinion shift came from somewhere and influenced decision-makers in certain ways. This study, in contrast to Scheuner, deals with these processes.

Finally, a number of authors contend that *Ostpolitik* was a policy of peace. The FRG, seeking to address its past, tried to make a contribution to a more peaceful order in Europe (Ackermann, 1992; Garton

Ash, 1993). This study's examination of the case of the FRG shows that peace and *Wiedergutmachung*, after the atrocities committed by Germany in the Second World War, were important factors contributing to *Ostpolitik*. The *topoi* of the Second World War and *Wiedergutmachung* were part of the eventually successful argumentation. Yet the application of the three-stage norm selection mechanism reveals that there were also other important *topoi* and modes of reasoning. Furthermore, it shows that there was considerable domestic contestation about what a politics of peace ought to look like, and that this contestation eventually nudged the less radical of the opponents into compromising on their convictions. A politics of peace argument glosses over these important domestic dynamics.

5 | *From exclusion to inclusion*

The Republic of Ireland found it even more difficult than the FRG to come to terms with the territorial status quo. Rejecting the partition of Ireland resulting from the 1921 Anglo-Irish Treaty, the Irish Free State and later the Republic of Ireland steadfastly refused to withdraw its *de jure* claim to Northern Ireland for almost eight decades. Being a cornerstone of the identity narrative in the Republic, the claim even featured prominently in the Constitution. In 1998, however, the Republic changed its Constitution and recognised the territorial status quo. How did this become possible?

The following two chapters seek to find a plausible answer to this question. Analogous to the third chapter, the purpose of this chapter is descriptive. It traces the evolution of the repertoire of commonplaces upon which actors in the Republic of Ireland drew to reason on the Irish Question. The chapter thereafter uses the findings of this chapter as a starting point for its examination of which *topoi* advocates of normative ideas about the territorial status quo picked from this repertoire of commonplaces and with what success.

How did the repertoire evolve? In a nutshell, the identity narrative, an important ingredient of the repertoire, exhibited a highly salient continuity throughout the analysed time period from 1921 to 1998. The Republic's longing for the unification of North and South persistently constituted a key aspect of the repertoire of commonplaces. In some ways, however, the repertoire changed radically: the colonial episteme, including the axioms that nations are homogeneous and have to defend their uniqueness against outside interference, was replaced by the Idea of Europe in the 1980s. Shortly thereafter, the dominance of the exclusive identity discourse, focusing on Gaelicism and Catholicism, waned and was increasingly replaced by a more inclusive type of nationalism. The longing for the authentic Self was replaced by the vision of an integrative Self – pertaining to relations between Nationalists and Unionists on the island of Ireland as well as to the Republic of Ireland in European affairs.

Normative change was intertwined with the change of the episteme and the identity narrative. Long-standing norms concerning the Republic's self-positioning vis-à-vis other nations, such as the neutrality norm, eroded. Other norms, such as the norm of peaceful resolution of disputes, gained increasing dominance when the Republic started to reflect more critically on the legacy of the violence that had once earned the South its independence.

A few words on terminology: I use the terms Nationalist and Unionist to describe the two predominant traditions on the island of Ireland. Nationalists, the overwhelming majority in the Republic of Ireland, aspire to the unity of Ireland, whereas Unionists, the majority in Northern Ireland, wish to remain within the United Kingdom. This distinction is more useful than the labels Catholic and Protestant. Even though most Catholics are Nationalists and most Protestants are Unionists, there have been a number of prominent Protestant Nationalists in the South who had a major impact on the construction of Irish identity.

This chapter is organised as follows. First, I describe the Republic's colonial episteme. Second, I outline the key tenets of exclusive nationalism. Third, I investigate the Republic's longing for the unification of North and South. Fourth, I examine the contestation between the old orthodoxies on the one hand and the Idea of Europe and inclusive nationalism on the other. Fifth, I scrutinise the evolution of the dominance of the Idea of Europe and inclusive nationalism. Finally, I discuss the findings of this chapter.

The Republic's colonial episteme

From the 1920s to the 1950s, the colonial episteme constituted the almost uncontested lens through which actors in the Republic made sense of Irishness, including the positioning of Ireland vis-à-vis the outside. The colonial episteme consisted of four orthodoxies: nations are ancient, homogeneous, have easily identifiable borders, and need to preserve their authentic Self against outside interference.

Epistemes rarely ever stop abruptly at the borders of a nation. Usually, they are internationally shared understandings of the world with a peculiar national twist. Ireland's colonial episteme shows this quite clearly. In many ways, the episteme resembles the lens upon which the Age of Romanticism founded the invention of nations and nationalism in continental Europe. Johann Gottlieb Fichte's writings provide a glimpse into the ontological and causal dogmas of this lens.

His work formulates four key beliefs about nations. First, nations are ancient. Nations are not new but ancient, and, provided that they have the freedom to live according to their customs, eternal (Fichte, 1978 [1808]: 130). Second, nations are homogeneous as well as ethnically and linguistically distinct from one another. A nation is constituted by a distinct race. This race speaks the same language. People who speak the same language naturally form a nation. Homogeneous nations – and this is, of course, an immensely dangerous belief – must preserve their homogeneity in order to flourish: co-nationals

understand one another, they are able to communicate with one another more and more clearly, they belong together, they are naturally one, and an inseparable whole. Such a nation cannot include a nation with a different descent and language and cannot want to intermix with it, without – at least at first – confusing itself and disrupting the harmonious development of its culture. (Fichte, 1978 [1808]: 207)

Third, nations have 'truly natural boundaries'. In Fichte's view, the world is divided into homogeneous nations. Their settlement area is easily and objectively identifiable (1978 [1808]: 207). Finally, a nation can only flourish if it is free of outside interference. Only then can it craft a political order that is tailored to its unique needs. For Fichte (1978 [1808]: 214), this is the 'highest law of the spiritual world'.

An Irish interpretation of these four key beliefs constituted the dominant episteme through which the inventors and reinventors of the Irish nation looked at the world from the late nineteenth to the mid-twentieth century. The four key beliefs are ubiquitous in the speeches and writings of the three most influential early twentieth-century reinventors of Irishness: Eamon de Valera, author of the *Bunreacht na hÉireann* (Constitution) and long-time *Taoiseach* (Prime Minister); William Butler Yeats, the famous poet; and Douglas Hyde, writer and translator of fictional literature as well as the Republic's first President.

The ontological dimension of the episteme guided the builders of the Irish nation in making sense of what a nation actually is. There was no question for the twentieth-century reinventors of the Irish nation that looking for nationness meant to look for something ancient. Nations were not understood as products of modernity. They were considered as quintessential human communities that originated at the 'dawn of history' (de Valera, 1980d [1933]: 235). Nation-builders also took the homogeneity of nations for granted. Homogeneity was seen as the necessary glue holding nations together over the millennia. Especially Hyde (1986 [1892]: 159) emphasised the salience of a shared physiognomy in this context. Finally, it was an unquestionable dogma for the builders of the Irish nation that nations are territorially bounded and that there are always clear-cut geographical markers that define the borders of a nation, such as mountains and the sea. Thus, de Valera (quoted in Bowman, 1982: 302) even believed that the borders of nations are drawn by God.

The causal dimension of the episteme was intertwined with the ontological dimension. De Valera, Hyde and Yeats strongly believed that the uniqueness of nations required a unique form of polity. A nation ensures its survival as a nation only if it manages to tailor a state around the very specific needs of this nation. The need for creating and safeguarding such a state was the focus of Yeats's political writings, it was the *raison d'être* of de Valera's political career, and it was the impetus for Hyde's struggle to revive the Gaelic language. Of course, the idea of the uniqueness of a nation and the connected claim to national self-determination is nothing extraordinary. Yet what is distinctive in the case of the Republic of Ireland, along with other nations that had just broken free from colonial rule, is that defending the nation's uniqueness against the outside was equated with fending off major powers. Small states would always be threatened by powerful nations. The latter would try to manipulate and subjugate smaller nations. There was far-reaching agreement on this aspect of the colonial episteme in parliament. Seán Flanagan (FF) put it as follows:

I am very chary of any organisation which is tied hand and foot to a major Power because I have nothing but suspicion for all major Powers, if only because history teaches us that we must be suspicious of nations which control too much power in their own hands.[1]

Peadar Cowan (CnaP) argued in a similar vein. In his view, any alliance between a small and a great nation was synonymous with 'subservience'.[2] Frank Aiken (FF), Liam Cosgrave (FG), Gerald Boland (FF), Seán MacBride (CnaP) and de Valera (FF) all warned that great nations could never be trusted. They would merely aim to exploit and interfere

---

[1] Seán Flanagan, *Dáil Éireann Debates* 138, 29 April 1953, col. 815.
[2] Peadar Cowan, *Dáil Éireann Debates* 138, 29 April 1953, col. 835.

with smaller nations.[3] In a similar vein, Seán Flanagan (FF) criticised great powers as being imperialist.[4] Reflecting on the grand ideas explaining Irish foreign policy, Garret FitzGerald (1991a: 1) refers to this aspect of Ireland's colonial episteme as an 'inferiority complex'. Joseph Lee (1989: 627) calls it a 'dependency syndrome'.

Hence, these four axioms – ancient nation, homogeneity, clear-cut boundaries and uniqueness versus imperialism – constituted the episteme through which the builders of the Irish nation looked at the world. In contrast to the Idea of Europe, the colonial episteme was atomistic. It was a system of beliefs that centred on the assumption of sharp differences among homogeneous nations and the necessity to guard these differences in order for the nation to survive.

Exclusive nationalism – the national dimension

Given the colonial episteme, only the construction of an exclusive national identity was conceivable for the early twentieth-century nation-builders. On the national level, there was no attempt to build bridges between different communities on the island of Ireland. There was no room for those not believing in the authentic Gaelic and Catholic Self. On the international level, the nation sharply demarcated itself from the outside world. This section deals with the national level. The section thereafter addresses the international level.

Early Irish nationalism was not exclusive. In the late eighteenth century and inspired by the French Revolution, the United Irishmen under the leadership of Theobald Wolfe Tone vowed to fight British rule in order to safeguard *liberté*, *égalité* and *fraternité* on the island of Ireland. Tone (quoted in McGuirk, 2000:1) emphasised that this required building an inclusive Irishness that would 'unite the whole people of Ireland ... abolish the memory of past dissensions, and ... substitute the common name of Irishman in the place of Protestant, Catholic and Dissenter [Presbyterian, MK]'. In the early twentieth century, John Redmond was an influential protagonist of such an

[3] Frank Aiken, *Dáil Éireann Debates* 146, 12 July 1955, cols. 550–1; Liam Cosgrave, *Dáil Éireann Debates* 146, 12 July 1955, col. 585; Gerald Boland, *Dáil Éireann Debates* 159, 4 July 1956, cols. 216–17; Seán MacBride, *Dáil Éireann Debates* 156, 10 July 1956, cols. 601–2; Eamon de Valera, *Dáil Éireann Debates* 156, 10 July 1956, cols. 611–12.
[4] Seán Flanagan, *Dáil Éireann Debates* 159, 11 July 1956, col. 628.

inclusive Irish nationalism, supported by prominent Irish writers in exile such as James Joyce and Oscar Wilde.

The dominance of the colonial episteme in the late nineteenth and early twentieth century, however, made such an inclusive identity inconceivable for most Nationalists. Redmond was vilified as a traitor and, guided by the colonial episteme, the vast majority of Nationalists looked for a nationness that was ancient, homogeneous and radically different from Britain. This gave rise to an exclusive identity narrative that focused on the revival of the authentic Irish Self. The authenticity was defined by Gaelicism and Roman Catholicism.

Nation-builders found their 'true' Ireland in the myths of the Gaelic past. The remote and Gaelic-speaking west of Ireland, in particular the Aran Islands, became a national shrine. Literature on Ireland's Gaelic past, such as Thomas Moore's *Irish Melodies* (Moore, 1823 [1821]), served as a window into an imaginary past that ought to be revived. Yeats, being fascinated with ancient Celtic saga and mythology wrote a number of influential books, for example the *Wanderings of Oisien* and *The Celtic Twilight*, that helped the Irish nation define itself. In his 1890 book *Beside the Fire*, Hyde translated fifteen Irish folk tales into English, making Gaelic myth accessible to a broader audience. James O'Grady popularised the revivalist notion of Irish history in his fictional historical novels *The Coming of Cuculain, Ulrick, the Ready, In the Gates of the North* and *The Triumph and Passing of Cuculain*.

The celebration of the Gaelic included the attempt to revive the Gaelic language. Hyde was among those who strongly advocated for the Gaelic language to replace English. In 1892, he gave a lecture entitled 'On the Necessity for De-Anglicizing the Irish People'. Only in this way, he argued, could the Irish nation distinguish itself from Britain. In a similar vein, D. P. Moran (quoted in Cahalan, 1993: 159) advocated that the Irish could not be a nation without Gaelic as a shared language: 'The foundation of Ireland is the Gael, and the Gael must be the element that absorbs. On no other basis can an Irish nation be reared.'

Another defining aspect of the Gaelic Revival was the rejection of modernity. Sharply demarcating themselves from Britain, the Revivalists celebrated the simple, rural life. Yeats (quoted by Garratt, 1989: 38), for instance, writes:

We Irish, born into that ancient sect.
But thrown upon this filthy modern tide

And by its formless spawning fury wrecked,
Climb to our proper dark, that we may trace
The lineaments of a plummet-measured face.

How appealing this attempt to turn an imaginary Gaelic past into present reality was to political leaders is illustrated by de Valera's vision for an independent Ireland (de Valera, 1980c [1922]: 94):

Let us turn aside for a moment to that ideal Ireland that we would have. That Ireland which we dreamed of would be the home of a people who valued material wealth only as the basis of right living, of a people who were satisfied with frugal comfort and devoted their leisure to the things of the spirit – a land whose countryside would be bright with cosy homesteads, whose fields and villages would be joyous with the sounds of industry, with the romping of sturdy children, the contests of athletic youths and the laughter of comely maidens, whose firesides would be forums for the wisdom of serene old age. It would, in a word, be the home of a people living the life that God desires that man should live.

Gaelicism was one of the pillars on which the nation was built. Roman Catholicism was the other. For de Valera, Catholicism was a defining feature of the Irish nation. The 1937 Constitution, of which he was the main author, made this quite clear. Catholic social doctrine under-pinned the Constitution, and it reserved a 'special role' for the Catholic Church.[5] While Gaelicism was seen as the constant essence of Irishness, Roman Catholicism was seen as a defining element that was added somewhat later. Frank Gallagher's influential *The Indivisible Island*, published in 1957, stressed that the Irish nation became a Catholic nation in the fifth century, when St Patrick returned to Ireland, travelled through all parts of Ireland and set up his Episcopal See at Armagh in Ulster. Irish monasteries flourished, and brought back the word of God to Europe after the collapse of the Roman Empire.

The imagination of the Irish as a Gaelic and Catholic nation con-stituted the nation as an ancient and homogeneous one. It was not denied that new settlement populations had arrived over the centuries but it was claimed that these blended into the ancient nation. Gallagher wrote that the Anglo-Norman invaders were absorbed by the Gaelic population: 'The Norman families turned Irish' (Gallagher, 1957: 19). In the nineteenth and twentieth centuries, however, Britain prevented

[5] Yet the Constitution stopped short of making Catholicism a state religion.

Unionists from being absorbed into the Irish nation by a policy of divide and rule. Exploiting confessional differences, Britain made Unionists forget that they are Irish. Pádraic Pearse, the leader of the 1916 Easter Rising, echoed this conviction. Unionists had forgotten that they are Irish due to their interaction with Britain:

> they have spent so much of their lives parleying with the English, they have sat so often and so long at English feasts, that they have lost communion with the ancient unpurchaseable faith of Ireland, the ancient stubborn thing that forbids, as if with the voice of fate, any loyalty from Ireland to England, any union between us and them, any surrender of one jot or shred of our claim to freedom. (Pearse, 1916: 80)

In retrospect, the Easter Rising was the Nationalists' first great victory. The uprising was crushed brutally by the British. As a consequence of this oppression, Irish nationalism became stronger and stronger. Sinn Féin, the nationalist party, overwhelmingly won the general elections in 1918. Three years later, the Anglo-Irish Agreement established the Irish Free State as a self-governing dominion, excluding Northern Ireland. Sinn Féin failed to reach a consensus on how to respond to this treaty. The minority, under the leadership of Michael Collins and Arthur Griffith, opted in favour of the treaty. The majority, led by Eamon de Valera, opposed it. The disagreements escalated into the Irish Civil War. Michael Collins was assassinated.

As much as they fought one another, however, the warring factions never questioned exclusive nationalism. Collins fully shared de Valera's ideal of a Gaelic and Catholic Ireland (Boyce, 1995: 351). The quarrel was about how to attain it. Collins opted for a temporary co-operation with Britain, being convinced that partition would not last. De Valera, by contrast, opted against compromising on the issue of Irish independence in any way. In particular, he was not prepared to accept any kind of partition scheme – whether conceived of as provisional or not.

The few remaining voices who dared to question exclusive nationalism were silenced by a rigid censorship regime, introduced between 1923 and 1929. The 1929 Censorship of Publications Act established a censorship board that was chaired by a priest. It had the power to prohibit the sale and distribution of any material that it judged to be 'in its general tendency indecent or obscene' (quoted in Cahalan, 1993: 212). The censorship regime started to erode only in the 1950s.

Exclusive nationalism – the international dimension

The colonial episteme delineated not only the national but also the international dimension of national identity. It circumscribed the Free State's and later the Republic's positioning of the Irish nation vis-à-vis other nations. The identity narrative emphasised again and again that Ireland had suffered terribly at the hands of invaders, especially Britain, and that the newly independent state ought to distance itself from the outside world in order to ensure that it would be the master of its own destiny at last.

Ireland sharply distanced itself from Britain's role in world politics. This demarcation was based on the interrelated normative complexes of human rights, national self-determination and decolonisation. Discourse in the Republic strongly emphasised that Britain had caused horrible suffering in Ireland and elsewhere in the world. Several authors have shown that the catastrophic element of Irish history, mostly caused by Britain, is a critical trait of Irish nationalism (Gibbons, 1996; Kennedy, 1996). Dáil deputies from all parties stressed that Britain's abuse of power in the past very much resembled that of the present. In their view, Britain continued to be an imperialist nation that abused the human rights of the people it subjected. Con Lehane (CnaP), for instance, accused Britain of having carried out pogroms against Catholics in Belfast in the past and claimed that it continued to hold Northern Ireland 'in servitude by armed force and by armed force alone'.[6] Criticism against Britain was not confined to the Northern Ireland issue. Patrick Browne (FG) accused Britain of having committed atrocities in Nyasaland and Kenya,[7] and the Cyprus problem featured very prominently in the Dáil.[8] All three analysed newspapers, the *Irish Independent*, *Irish Press* and *Irish Times*, were highly critical of Britain and its role in world politics.[9]

---

[6] Con Lehane, *Dáil Éireann Debates* 113, 14 December 1948, col. 1515.

[7] Patrick Browne, *Dáil Éireann Debates* 176, 7 July 1959, col. 658.

[8] See, for example, the debate on decolonisation and Cyprus in *Dáil Éireann Debates* 159, 10 July 1956, cols. 599–606.

[9] 'British Ministers Talk of "Plot"', *Irish Independent*, 14 July 1950, p. 6; 'Printed Humbug', *Irish Press*, 1 May 1953; 'The True Aspect', *Irish Times*, 13 July 1955, p. 5. Yet, the *Irish Times* was far less critical of Britain than the political elite. This issue will be addressed below.

The Republic of Ireland came to define its proper place in the world in juxtaposition from Britain. Until at least the late 1950s, Dublin's self-positioning vis-à-vis other nations was defined by three elements: neutrality, Christianity and full endorsement of the United Nations Charter.[10] The key norm for Irish foreign policy was neutrality. Being Irish meant standing apart from other nations, and in particular keeping away from great powers. This norm was put to the ultimate test when Churchill offered de Valera the unification of the Republic with Northern Ireland in exchange for Ireland joining the allies in 1940. De Valera declined. For him, neutrality was synonymous with independence. Giving up neutrality would be the end of independence and liberty. And the independence of the Republic was to him even more important than ending partition:

Although freedom of a part of this island is not the freedom we want – the freedom we would like to have, this freedom for a portion of it, freedom to develop and to keep the kernel of the Irish nation is something and something I would not sacrifice ... [not] even [for] the consideration of a united Ireland. (de Valera quoted in Fanning, 1990: 9–10)

De Valera did not stand alone with his emphasis on neutrality. There was a very strong agreement on neutrality during the Second World War. When the Dáil voted on the matter, only one member, James Dillon, opposed neutrality. As a consequence of his vote, he was expelled from his party, Fine Gael (Doherty, 2002: 34). When Hitler shot himself in 1945, de Valera went to the German embassy and offered his condolences. He did this not because he sympathised with Nazi Germany, but because he considered this the appropriate thing to do as the leader of a neutral country. The gesture caused considerable irritation in Europe (Douglas, Harte and O'Hara, 1998: 216). Ireland continued to guard its neutrality after the Second World War. It continued to oppose any participation in military alliances. Dublin rejected offers to join the North Atlantic Treaty Organisation (NATO) and the Western European Union (WEU) in the late 1940s and early 1950s.

---

[10] These three principles of foreign policy were outlined by Liam Cosgrave while in office as Minister of External Affairs: Liam Cosgrave, *Dáil Éireann Debates* 159, 3 July 1956, cols. 142–4. The Dáil agreed with these principles, but some deputies resolved the tensions between these three principles differently from Cosgrave. These debates are addressed below.

Neutrality clashed at times with another key element of Irish foreign policy, i.e. the Republic's self-definition as a Christian nation. While neutrality was a key norm of Irish foreign policy, the advent of the Cold War caused controversy about the exact definition of neutrality. The lowest common denominator was uncontested. At a minimum, neutrality meant abstaining from military alliances. Yet should Ireland take sides in the Cold War? This question was hotly disputed in the Dáil and in Irish newspapers. The debate was shaped by the tensions between neutrality and Ireland's self-understanding as a Christian nation. There was consensus in the Dáil that Ireland was a Christian nation. Anthony Esmonde (FG) went so far as to argue that Ireland was 'fundamentally the most Christian nation in the world'.[11] There was also a consensus that this would have to reflect Ireland's role in international politics. William Norton (LB) even called for a missionary role for Ireland on the world stage. Ireland ought to demonstrate again 'to the world the sense of Christian values which inspire our people to-day, just as we did when our missionaries brought light and knowledge to a dark Europe in the generations which have now passed from us'.[12] There was further agreement that being Christian meant being anti-communist. Seán Flanagan (FF), for instance, was adamant about this dichotomy.[13]

Yet there was disagreement between the two major parties, Fianna Fáil and Fine Gael, about the implications of abiding and strengthening Christian principles in world politics for Ireland's positioning vis-à-vis Western Europe. Fine Gael argued that Ireland, without entering any military alliances, should make clear that it belonged to the Western world. Fianna Fáil, by contrast, wanted to pursue a more independent course. This debate culminated in 1957, when the newly elected Fianna Fáil government joined the international advocacy to include the People's Republic of China in the United Nations. Remarkably, the *Irish Times*, usually quite critical of Fianna Fáil, agreed with the government.[14] Fine Gael, however, argued vehemently against this support for a communist country.[15] Foreign minister Frank Aiken (FF) defended

---

[11] Anthony Esmonde, *Dáil Éireann Debates* 176, 2 July 1959, col. 508.
[12] William Norton, *Dáil Éireann Debates* 97, 18 May 1945, col. 732.
[13] Seán Flanagan, *Dáil Éireann Debates* 159, 11 July 1956, col. 629.
[14] 'Routine Exercise', *Irish Times*, 8 July 1959, p. 7.
[15] Seán MacBride, *Dáil Éireann Debates* 117, 13 July 1949, col. 747; Liam Cosgrave, *Dáil Éireann Debates* 159, 3 July 1956, cols. 142–4; Declan Costello, *Dáil Éireann Debates* 159, 4 July 1956, cols. 211–12.

Fianna Fáil's stance. Given the lessons of Irish history, he argued, Ireland must pursue its own course in international affairs:

I see no reason to regret anything … Indeed, in view of the struggles and sacrifices of our compatriots, from Colmcille to Columbanus, to Tone and Davis and to Pearse and MacSwiney, I should have regarded myself as betraying our national traditions had I allowed myself to be pushed, persuaded or palavered into adopting a contrary course or a contrary approach.[16]

Neutrality and Christianity were key aspects of the Republic's self-positioning in world politics. The commitment to the norms of the United Nations Charter completed the normative triad through which Ireland defined itself in the world. Ireland defined itself as a nation that stood for the rule of law in world politics. Emphasis was put on key Charter norms such as the peaceful settlement of disputes.[17] Beyond this, Ireland stressed less traditional norms that many other states fully endorsed only much later, if at all: in particular, human rights norms, the principle of national self-determination and the decolonisation norm. Ireland chastised imperialism and unequivocally criticised French, British and Portuguese colonialism, China's annexation of Tibet, as well as South Africa's apartheid rule and occupation of Namibia. In particular, during Aiken's time as External Minister, Ireland was very active at the United Nations in pushing for the self-determination of colonised peoples.

Longing for a united Ireland

Much of this chapter is about change. It will show that the Idea of Europe replaced the colonial episteme as the dominant episteme and that the identity narrative became increasingly inclusive. An important dimension of the identity narrative, however, remained largely unchanged. The longing for the unification of North and South was a key article of faith in the creed of exclusive Nationalists, and it remained a defining identity trait even when the identity narrative changed fundamentally.

---

[16] Frank Aiken, *Dáil Éireann Debates* 164, 28 November 1957, cols. 1205–16.
[17] Liam Cosgrave, *Dáil Éireann Debates* 159, 3 July 1956, cols. 138–43; Frank Aiken, *Dáil Éireann Debates* 159, 3 July 1956, cols. 146–7.

Many maps of historic Ireland, relying on information contained in a map by Ptolemy, suggest that the island was divided into four loosely confederated kingdoms: Ulaidh, Connachta, Laigin and Erainn. This corresponds to the four modern provinces of Ulster, Connaught, Leinster and Munster. Of course, it is very difficult – if not impossible – to determine the historical accuracy of accounts of the island's ancient territorial order. Ptolemy compiled material for a map of Ireland without ever setting foot in Ireland and by relying on what people told him about the island. And, of course, other maps of Ireland depict a different territorial order. What really matters for the purposes of this study, however, is not the objective but the intersubjective dimension. The four ancient provinces were a central pillar upon which the authors of traditional nationalism built the narrative of the Irish nation. The four ancient kingdoms provided a critical link between past, present and future.

Britain sought to bring the guerrilla war that followed the 1916 Easter Rising to an end by a political settlement. The 1920 Government of Ireland Act granted 'Southern Ireland', as the document put it, the status of a co-equal member of the Commonwealth, comparable to the Union of South Africa. Southern Ireland would have its own parliament – a Senate and a House of Commons – and it would have the rights of an independent country. Yet members of parliament would have to swear the oath of allegiance to the British crown and Irish diplomats would be accredited by the British monarch. A parliament would also be created for 'Northern Ireland'. North and South were purposefully divided in such a way to ensure a Unionist majority in as large a territorial entity as possible. The six counties of Antrim, Armagh, Down, Fermanagh, Londonderry/Derry and Tyrone, in some of which Nationalists outnumbered Unionists, became Northern Ireland. This divided not only the island of Ireland, but also the province of Ulster. Three of its counties – Cavan, Donegal and Monaghan – became part of Southern Ireland. The 1920 Act also included provisions for the unification of North and South. 'With a view to the eventual establishment of a Parliament in the whole of Ireland', the Act created a Council of Ireland. North and South would be represented in the Council. It was designed to further co-operation between the two parts of Ireland. Britain would not object to the unification under two conditions. First, there would have to be a double majority. The absolute majority of members of parliament in North and South would have to opt for unity. Second, the unified Ireland would keep its ties, such as the oath of allegiance and the crown in parliament, with Britain (Hughes, 1994: 32).

In 1921, the Anglo-Irish Treaty established the Irish Free State. Northern Ireland seized the opportunity offered by the treaty and opted out of the Free State. Furthermore, the Free State had to cede three ports – Cobh, Berehaven and Lough Swilly – to Britain. The Council of Ireland was ineffective and finally buried in the 1925 Anglo-Irish Agreement. The 1921 treaty split Sinn Féin, the party that served as protagonist of Irish nationalism in the early twentieth century. A civil war ensued between its two main factions. Those in favour of the treaty considered it as a stepping stone towards a free and united Ireland. Those opposing it regarded it as treason, because it abandoned the principle of a united Ireland.

The anti-Treatyists won the struggle for power in the Free State. In 1926, de Valera formed a new party, Fianna Fáil. Anti-Treatyists formed the nucleus of the party. By the late 1930s, Fianna Fáil had become the dominant political force in the South. De Valera became the country's most influential politician. He was the main author of the 1937 Constitution, *Bunreacht na hÉireann*. In contrast to the Government of Ireland Act, the Anglo-Irish Treaty and the Constitution of the Irish Free State, the new Constitution did not distinguish between North and South. The fundamental premise of the Constitution was that there was only one Ireland. *De facto*, however, the island of Ireland remained territorially divided between the Republic and Northern Ireland. Map 5.1 shows what has been the territorial status quo since the early 1920s.

There has been a strong desire in the Republic and among the Nationalist community in Northern Ireland to reunify Ireland. Public opinion data, available only after 1970, reveal a far-reaching consensus on unity. Seven times between 1970 and 1991, the Irish Marketing Surveys (IMS) and the Market Research Bureau of Ireland (MRBI) asked comparable questions about the approval for unity.[18] The desire

---

[18] IMS survey, 25 May 1970 (JN:1452 RJA/mec); the exact question was as follows: 'Would you prefer to see the border stay or go?' MRBI survey, 2–16 February 1983 (21st Anniversary Poll); wording: 'Do you think that a united Ireland in North and South is (a) something to hope for or (b) something that you would prefer not to happen?' MRBI survey, 23 June 1987 (25th Anniversary Poll); identical wording. MRBI survey, 15–16 April 1991 (MRBI/3950/91); identical

Table 5.1 *Public opinion on approval and disapproval of Irish unification*

	1970	1974	1983	1984	1987	1989	1991
Support	70	61	76	74	67	73	82
Oppose	29	16	15	10	19	17	13

Map 5.1 The Republic of Ireland and Northern Ireland

for unity did not abate over time. On the contrary, it even increased. In 1970, 70 per cent of the populace expressed approval for the goal of Irish unification. Four years later, the approval temporarily decreased to 61 per cent. Yet in the 1980s, the approval oscillated between two-thirds and three-quarters. In 1991, more than four-fifths desired reunification. Table 5.1 gives an overview of this development.

wording. MRBI survey, 15–16 April 1991 (MRBI/3950/91); identical wording. The survey results for 1974 and 1984 are taken from Mair (1987: 90). 1974 was an MRBI, 1984 a MORI poll. The author does not provide the wording of the questions. These survey results are comparable, because the questions asked for clear-cut yes or no answers. Two later surveys in the 1990s gave several options and specified several conditions for unification.

All political parties in the Republic have regarded Irish unity as an important political goal. When Fine Gael was founded, it called itself The United Ireland Party – Fine Gael. Unity was always an important part of the party's political agenda. Fianna Fáil emerged as a non-Treatyist party and the non-recognition of the border was at the core of its identity as a political party. Smaller parties such as Labour, the Progressive Democrats, the Workers' Party and Sinn Féin have had very different visions of a united Ireland, but they have shared the goal of unification (Herz, 1989: 45–80). Few intellectuals have criticised traditional Irish nationalism with as much vehemence and endurance as Conor Cruise O'Brien. But despite all his reservations, he shared the goal of unity: 'I would be absolutely overjoyed if Ireland were to become united peacefully and by consent' (O'Brien quoted in Herz, 1989: 69). The aim of reunification was also ubiquitous in Ireland's three major newspapers, the *Irish Independent*, *Irish Press* and *Irish Times*.

The last three sections provided an overview of exclusive nationalism: the resolve to return to the imagined Gaelic and Catholic roots of the ancient nation; the demarcation from other nations, in particular major powers; and the longing for unity. While the latter was the key continuum of the repertoire of commonplaces, the episteme and with it much of Irish nationalism and its constituting norms changed significantly. The remainder of this chapter traces these changes chronologically.

More dissenting voices

A certain repertoire of commonplaces may be dominant at a particular moment in time, but there is hardly ever an all-encompassing agreement on it. In the Irish case, this applies even to the heyday of the colonial episteme and exclusive nationalism from the 1930s to the late 1950s. There was a far-reaching agreement on the repertoire of commonplaces, but this consensus was never complete. Alternative ideas existed, some of which came from outside Ireland. Gaining some measure of influence between the late 1950s and early 1960s, these alternative ideas started to challenge the dominant repertoire of commonplaces.

Prior to the early 1960s, alternatives to the colonial episteme existed but they were marginalised. There were two counter-paradigms, both of which had come from outside Ireland. The first counter-paradigm was Revisionism. As early as in the 1930s, a group of historians began to make sense of the Irish nation not through the colonial episteme, but through a scientific epistemology. Robert D. Edwards, Theodor W. Moody, David B. Quinn and Desmond Williams were educated outside of the Irish Free State, most of them at the Institute of Historical Research in England. There they had been socialised into a theory of knowledge according to which history would have to be told in a value-free way. It ought to consist of objective facts, and not myths. This required the researcher to stand apart from the object of study. A nationalist was seen as a bad historian *qua* his or her values. These values would inevitably distort the true history to be told. Delineated by these epistemological premises, Revisionists, as this group of scientists came to be known, rejected the commonplace belief that Irish history was nothing but the struggle of an ancient and homogeneous nation against an external enemy. For Revisionists, this was merely a myth. They traced the origins of the Irish nation to the nineteenth century, and focused on the differences among Irish people as well as elements of co-operation and confrontation between different Irish communities (Boyce, 1996). The influence of Revisionism grew steadily from the 1930s onwards.

The Idea of Europe constituted the second, even more influential challenge. While in office as External Minister, Seán MacBride taught the Dáil (lower chamber of parliament) the episteme that he had learned in numerous meetings at the Council of Europe in the late 1940s. He spoke about the evolution of the Idea of Europe over the centuries. In many ways, the Idea, as interpreted by MacBride, was the opposite of the colonial episteme: plurality versus homogeneity (nation) and integration versus demarcation (across nations). In order to prevent disaster from reoccurring in Europe, European nations had to acknowledge their internal plural character as well as replace the impenetrability of their nation-state borders by co-operation and integration.

The Idea made new identity formations imaginable. MacBride called for Ireland to open up to Europe.[19] Sharply contradicting the firmly established neutrality norm and the self-positioning as a nation that stands apart, he contended that the Irish ought to understand themselves as a European nation and cease to seek isolation. One of the Republic's three national newspapers supported this point of view. Several editorials in the *Irish Times* (1949, 1950) endorsed the Idea of Europe and a European identity as early as the late 1940s and early 1950s.

---

[19] Seán MacBride, *Dáil Éireann Debates* 117, 12 July 1949, cols. 695–709.

While alternative perspectives on how to make sense of Irish identity and alternative identities were marginalised prior to the late 1950s, they became more influential thereafter. One of the reasons for this was the relaxation of censorship in the 1960s. Another factor that made this development possible was the public discussion of the European dimension of Irish politics. In 1959, de Valera stepped down as *Taoiseach* and was replaced by Seán Lemass. Partly because he really believed in the cause of European unification and partly because he sought a way out of Ireland's economic problems, Seán Lemass attempted to break out of the Republic's international isolation. Dublin applied for membership in the European Economic Community (EEC) in 1961. The application caused a heated debate.

During this debate, a considerable number of parliamentarians came to draw upon the Idea of Europe to make sense of European affairs and the situation on the island of Ireland. Lionel Booth (FF), Liam Cosgrave (FG), Declan Costello (FG), James Dillon (FG) and Noel Lemass (FF) were the main advocates for entering Europe because of the belief in the Idea of Europe.[20] In their reading, the Idea consisted of a national and an international dimension. The national dimension rejected the homogeneity assumption of the colonial episteme. It no longer took for granted that nations are monolithic entities but conceived of them as pluralistic communities. Only embracing the diversity within nations would make it possible for European nation-states to leave their violent domestic nation-building struggles behind. The international dimension focused on the relations among nation-states. European nations ought to replace rigid nation-state borders with co-operation and integration in order to put an end to the wars and instabilities that had plagued Europe in the past. In short, Europe would have to safeguard 'diversity and unity', as James Dillon (FG) put it, in order to prevent the tragedies of the past from reoccurring – diversity and unity within as well as across nations.[21]

[20] Lionel Booth, *Dáil Éireann Debates* 176, 7 July 1959, cols. 639–44; Lionel Booth, *Dáil Éireann Debates* 201, 3 April 1963, cols. 995–6; Liam Cosgrave, *Dáil Éireann Debates* 194, 5 April 1962, cols. 1356–8; Declan Costello, *Dáil Éireann Debates* 191, 11 July 1961, cols. 560–1; Declan Costello, *Dáil Éireann Debates* 201, 3 April 1963, col. 949; James Dillon, *Dáil Éireann Debates* 198, 13 December 1962, col. 1354; Noel Lemass, *Dáil Éireann Debates* 194, 5 April 1962, cols. 1370–1.
[21] James Dillon, *Dáil Éireann Debates* 198, 13 December 1962, col. 1354.

The Idea had repercussions on interpretations of the Irish Question. Most importantly, the alternative episteme unveiled the diversity of the people of Ireland for those who had selected this episteme. Seán Lemass, for example, passionately argued for Irish unity. Yet the conception of this unity was different from the Gaelic Ireland of which de Valera had dreamt. There was no question in Lemass's mind that there was only one Irish nation, but equally important to him were the different identities of Unionists and Nationalists. This difference would have to be safeguarded. Unionists would have autonomy, 'very especially in regard to educational and religious matters' (Lemass, 1959: 9). Lemass also envisaged a radically different relationship between the Republic of Ireland and the United Kingdom. Based on the communal episteme, some Fine Gael deputies started to argue against too strong a demarcation from Britain. Thaddeus Lynch (FG), for example, harshly criticised Aiken. He alleged that the foreign minister's anti-British sentiment 'would cloud the Minister's judgment'.[22] James Dillon (FG), one of the most eloquent supporters of the Idea of Europe, even called for an economic community between Britain and Ireland. In his view, this would 'make a substantial contribution to better understanding between ourselves and the British'.[23] This was a dramatic departure from the entrenched view that virtually any kind of co-operation with the former coloniser would lead to the neo-colonialisation and renewed exploitation of Ireland.

Continuing dominance of the old

Between the late 1950s and the mid-1960s, some actors questioned long-cherished beliefs. Yet this was a still a small minority. The colonial episteme, exclusive nationalism and its constituting norms remained dominant. Three political events made this very clear: the festivities for the fiftieth anniversary of the Easter Rising, the widespread scepticism against the Republic's membership application to the European Union, and the debate about the Anglo-Irish Trade Agreement.

The Republic and the Nationalist community in Northern Ireland celebrated the fiftieth anniversary of the Easter Rising in 1966. The celebrations included a television documentary of the Rising, and many small celebrations in Ireland's cities, towns and villages (Keogh, 1995:

[22] Thaddeus Lynch, *Dáil Éireann Debates* 176, 2 July 1959, col. 581.
[23] James Dillon, *Dáil Éireann Debates* 201, 3 April 1963, col. 1012.

289). The anniversary was a celebration of traditional nationalism as envisioned by de Valera. Dublin's Garden of Remembrance, which was opened during the festivities, shows this quite clearly. Its centre-piece is a statue by Oisín Kelly. It depicts four people being resurrected and four swans flying away.

The sculpture tells Irish history through the Irish legend 'The Children of Lir'.[24] Lir, lord of the sea, and his wife, Eva, had four children: Conn, Fiachra, and the twins Fionnuala and Aodh. Eva died while giving birth to the twins, and the father married Aiofe, Eva's sister. One day, while the children played joyfully in the water, the jealous step-mother destroyed the idyll and cast a spell on the children that turned them into swans. According to the spell, they would remain swans for 900 years, until the bell of a new God would turn them into humans again. They would spend the first 300 years at Lough Derravaragh, the second on the Straits of Moyle and the last on the Isle of Inish Glora.

The years on the Straits of Moyle were especially hard. The frequent storms often separated them, but they always managed to reunite. After having spent almost 900 years as swans, they saw an old man. They asked him whether he was a follower of the new God. The man answered in the affirmative and told the children that St Patrick had brought the new faith to Ireland many, many years ago. The old man built a chapel for the children and told them about God. When he was about to complete the bell for the house of prayer, a warrior stormed into the chapel wanting to take the children away. Yet when the warrior ordered his men to take the children away, the bell rang and at this moment the swans turned back into humans. This moment of liberation is captured in the sculpture.

The analogies to Irish history as traditionally told are obvious. The four children stand for the four provinces of the ancient nation: Connacht, Leinster, Munster and Ulster. An external force (the step-mother) destroys the idyll. Having suffered a long time of injustice, they are eventually liberated. This liberation is the will of God. Roman Catholicism (St Patrick) brought God to Ireland. The sculpture also alludes to the ideal of a Gaelic Ireland. According to the legend, the four children were the last descendants of the *Tuatha De Danann*, a Celtic tribe.

---

[24] The following description is taken from: http://www.ireland-information.com/articles/thechildrenoflir.htm

The political debate about accession to the EEC lacked the poetic beauty of this legend. Yet it shows the salience of traditional national-ism, as underwritten by the colonial episteme, equally clearly. The few Europhiles who advocated EEC membership for ideational reasons were a small minority. There was another small minority that categori-cally rejected the membership application. This minority warned that neutrality did not allow Ireland to join a political community of states. Frank Sherwin (IND), for example, initially postulated that 'we should not become involved politically in any sense of the word'.[25] Brendan Corish (LB) argued in a similar vein. He posed the rhetorical question: '[M]ust we sell our neutrality for economic advantage?'[26]

The overwhelming majority view on Ireland's EEC application was that exactly this economic factor forced the Republic to join Europe. Yet the dominance of the colonial episteme and exclusive nationalism allowed only for a very lukewarm reception of the application. The EEC was seen as a necessary evil. The Republic would have to apply because Britain was applying for membership. The British and the Irish econo-mies were interdependent to such a high degree that this would force Ireland to join the EEC as well. Anything else would cause an economic disaster for Ireland.[27] Even Sherwin soon reversed his critical attitude and adopted the majority view.[28] Dillon did not succeed in making his enthusiasm about Europe resonate within his party. When he sum-marised the position of Fine Gael, Dillon stuck to the majority view: 'we in *Fine Gael* decided that it was the right policy for this country to enter the Common Market if Great Britain entered it, so as to protect the vital economic interests of our own people'.[29] Given the weight of the old orthodoxies, not even Fine Gael, persistently more Europhile than other parties, saw the Common Market, as the EEC was usually referred to, as anything but dictated by economic necessity.[30]

---

[25] Frank Sherwin, *Dáil Éireann Debates* 191, 11 July 1961, col. 569.
[26] Brendan Corish, *Dáil Éireann Debates* 201, 3 April 1963, col. 987.
[27] See, for example, Brendan Corish, *Dáil Éireann Debates* 198, 13 December 1962, col. 1372.
[28] Frank Sherwin, *Dáil Éireann Debates* 194, 5 April 1962, col. 1374.
[29] James Dillon, *Dáil Éireann Debates* 198, 13 December 1962, col. 1337.
[30] This perception of being forced into the EEC is well captured by a caricature in the *Dublin Opinion*: British Prime Minister Macmillan stands at the edge of a diving board and is ready to jump into the Common Market pool. Lemass stands behind him with his right leg tied to Macmillan's (in Douglas, Harte and O'Hara, 1998: 251).

Finally, the 1966 debates about an Anglo-Irish trade agreement high-lighted Ireland's demarcation from Britain as underpinned by the colonial episteme. Britain's and Ireland's EEC applications failed. This necessitated a trade agreement between the two countries. Opposition parties harshly attacked the deal negotiated by the Fianna Fáil government. The colonial episteme is very obvious in these debates. The government was accused of having negotiated a highly disadvantageous deal for the Republic. This was explained by the nature of the relations between Britain and the Republic. Major powers would always seek to exploit smaller nations. Britain, in particular, would continue to try to take advantage of the unequal power relations between Ireland and Britain. Patrick Lindsay and Eileen Desmond harshly criticised the agreement as yet another British scheme to exploit Ireland.[31] Maurice Dockrell (FG) argued that the trade agreement was a 'disastrous document'.[32] He explained that such an exploitative agreement could only come about due to Britain's imperial aspirations and centuries of experience in dictating unequal treaties.[33] Gerard L'Estrange (FG) accused the government of failing to curb Britain's exploitative and imperi-alist tactics: 'I suppose next time the *Taoiseach* goes over they will have a party and they will sit together with the Union Jack wrapped around them, or perhaps sing "Rule, Britannia".'[34]

Old convictions under siege

The escalation of violence between Nationalists and Unionists in Northern Ireland in the late 1960s shook the Republic's beliefs about Irishness to their very foundations. Within six years of clashes between Nationalists and Unionists in the North, criticism against the colonial episteme and exclusive nationalism multiplied, and alternative ideas, most importantly the Idea of Europe and inclusive nationalism, gained unprecedented strength.

On 5 October 1968, a Catholic civil rights association defied a police ban and marched through the Unionist area of Londonderry/Derry in Northern Ireland.[35] The Protestant-dominated police intervened and

---

[31] Patrick Lindsay, *Dáil Éireann Debates* 219, 5 January 1966, cols. 1281–2; Eileen Desmond, *Dáil Éireann Debates* 219, 6 January 1966, col. 1534.
[32] Maurice Dockrell, *Dáil Éireann Debates* 219, 6 January 1966, col. 1504.
[33] Maurice Dockrell, *Dáil Éireann Debates* 219, 6 January 1966, col. 1503.
[34] Gerard L'Estrange, *Dáil Éireann Debates* 219, 7 January 1966, col. 1722.
[35] Unionists refer to the city as Londonderry, Nationalists as Derry.

clashed with the demonstrators. This event marked the beginning of what the Irish somewhat euphemistically call the 'Troubles', i.e. violent conflict between Nationalists and Unionists in Northern Ireland. Further marches and clashes occurred throughout 1969. In the same year, the Provisional Irish Republican Army broke away from the Official Irish Republican Army (IRA). It started its terrorist campaign in 1971. Patrick Hillery, Dublin's foreign minister, travelled to London and to the United Nations in New York in order to convince Britain and the world of the need for an impartial peacekeeping force. The efforts did not yield any success. Instead, London sent troops in an attempt to stabilise the situation. In January 1972, British troops opened fire on a civil rights march in Londonderry/Derry and killed thirteen people. The incident has become known as Bloody Sunday. In March 1972, Britain suspended the Northern Ireland regime and introduced direct rule. Yet the violence continued. According to official British statistics, the Troubles left almost 2,500 people dead and injured close to 27,000 people between 1971 and 1986. Civilian deaths accounted for half of the casualties and two-thirds of the injured (Day, 1992: 128).

In the South, the overwhelming immediate reaction to the beginning of the Troubles was outrage about the treatment of the Catholic minority and the deployment of British troops in the North. The anger peaked shortly after Bloody Sunday. Demonstrators burned down the British embassy in Dublin, the Republic withdrew its ambassador from London, and Hillery (quoted in Keatinge, 1978: 119) accused Britain of pursuing 'lunatic policies'. The medium and long-term effect of the violence in the North, however, has been something entirely different. The civil-war-like situation sparked a heated debate about how to make sense of Irish identity, especially the relationship between Nationalists and Unionists, and the relationship between Ireland, Britain and Europe at large.

During this debate, the dominant consensus on the colonial episteme and exclusive nationalism was broken. Two nationalisms started to compete against one another. Traditional republicanism, as embraced by Fianna Fáil, defended de Valera's orthodoxies. The *Irish Press*, affiliated with Fianna Fáil, continued to look at the world through the colonial episteme and to defend exclusive nationalism. In its editorials, the newspaper argued that Ireland's problems stemmed from its lack of independence from other countries, in particular Great Britain. Without London's interference in Irish affairs in Ulster, there would be no problems between Catholics and Protestants. The Irish nation continued to be portrayed as a homogeneous, ancient Celtic and Catholic nation, which remained beleaguered by Unionism and British colonialism.[36] *Taoiseach* Jack Lynch attempted to soften this identity narrative, but was pushed by his party, Fianna Fáil, to a response to the Troubles that was more in line with the party's dominating definition of Irishness. In a 1969 radio address, he asserted that violence in Northern Ireland was a function of Britain's occupation of Northern Ireland. The conflict was caused by outside interference and by outside interference alone (Keatinge, 1978: 116).

Traditional nationalism was challenged within Fine Gael and the Labour Party, and, to a limited extent, even within Fianna Fáil. The challenge was preceded by an increasing adoption of the Idea of Europe as episteme. After having applied for more than ten years, Ireland finally became a member of the European Community (EC) in 1973. Throughout the application process, the Idea of Europe became an important part of Irish political discourse. More and more people ceased to look at the world through the lens of the colonial episteme, and replaced it with the Idea of Europe. Parliamentarians such as John O'Connell (LB), Conor Cruise O'Brien (LB), Maurice Dockrell (FG), James White (FG) and Garret FitzGerald (FG) drew upon the Idea of Europe to reflect on Irish identity and make sense of the conflict in Northern Ireland.

Given the newly taken-for-granted beliefs in the necessity of acknowledging the heterogeneity of nations and the need for overcoming the impenetrability of nation-state borders, partition and violence were not puzzling to these actors. They were convinced that the Republic's isolation and inward-looking nationalism as well as the refusal to acknowledge the diversity of the Irish nation stood in the way of a resolution of the Irish Question. The Republic would have to embrace the diversity of the Irish nation as well as seek ways and means to make the border between the Republic and Britain/Northern Ireland more penetrable in order to overcome the sharp boundaries separating Unionists and Nationalists in Northern Ireland and on the island of Ireland as a whole.[37]

[36] 'After Newry', *Irish Press*, 7 February 1972, p. 10.
[37] John O'Connell, *Dáil Éireann Debates* 256, 8 May 1973, col. 642; Garret FitzGerald, *Dáil Éireann Debates* 256, 9 May 1973, cols. 740–1; Maurice Dockrell, 9 May 1973, *Dáil Éireann Debates* 256, col. 785; James White, *Dáil Éireann Debates* 260, 18 April 1972, cols. 613–14. Conor Cruise O'Brien emphasised this in his book *States of Ireland* (1972).

Freed from the colonial perspective and marked out by the European episteme, some intellectuals began to reflect critically on Irish nationalism and to (re-)invent a different Irish identity. Peter Lennon made one of the most controversial contributions to this reflection. His 1968 documentary *The Rocky Road to Dublin* chastised the old dogmas. In Lennon's view, Ireland was 'a country with its future in the hands of people who think in terms of the past' (quoted in Browne, 1996). The documentary harshly criticised the role of the Catholic Church and post-1916 politicians, especially de Valera. The film starts with the following commentary: 'This is an attempt to reconstruct in images the plight of an island community which survived nearly 700 years of English occupation and then nearly sank under the weight of its own heroes – and clergy.' The film's critique culminated with Seán O'Faoláin's contribution. O'Faoláin was an influential fiction and non-fiction writer as well as a political activist. He had fought on the side of de Valera against those of the Republican movement who agreed to the 1921 Anglo-Irish Treaty. O'Faoláin, however, was highly dissatisfied with the society that evolved out of the liberation struggle. In particular, he vilified the Catholic Church and de Valera's ideal of a rural Ireland. The following quote, taken from *The Rocky Road to Dublin*, shows his disdain:

It was a society of what I would call urbanised peasants. A society without real moral courage, constantly observing a self-interested silence, never speaking in moments of crisis and in constant alliance with a completely obscurantist, repressive, regressive and uncultivated church. I often feel that if those dead men of 1916, before the bullets crashed into their heads and before the rope tightened around their necks, had seen the kind of reward that would come out of their sacrifice, they would have felt only that their efforts had been betrayed and that their sacrifice had been in vain. (quoted in Browne, 1996)

This was a strong claim by one of those whose participation in the armed struggle for an independent Irish Republic had made him a hero in the eyes of many Irish people. O'Faoláin accused Ireland's ruling elite of betrayal. O'Faoláin was not the only fiction writer criticising traditional nationalism. In *Poor Lazarus*, for example, Maurice Leitch (1969) juxtaposed exclusive nationalism with an inclusive variant. The novel reveals the myth of the homogeneity of Irish identity, and deals with cultural crossovers between North and South as well as Protestant and Catholic.

During their long careers as high-ranking politicians and influential commentators on Ireland, Garret FitzGerald (FG) and Conor Cruise

O'Brien (LB) have disagreed over many issues. Yet the two important books that they published in 1972 – FitzGerald's *Towards a New Ireland* and O'Brien's *States of Ireland* – show important agreements. The dedication of FitzGerald's *Towards a New Ireland*, 'To the "New Irelanders", North and South, Protestant and Catholic', sums up the purpose of both books. The books are highly critical of the Nationalists' strong demarcation from the Unionist tradition. FitzGerald and O'Brien advocated constructing Irish identity anew. In their view, the exclusive Irish identity as constructed after independence had to be replaced by an inclusive Irish identity that would leave room for heterogeneity and would make reconciliation between Nationalists and Unionists possible.

The emphasis of O'Brien's book is on the Irish identity narrative. In his view, the way in which Nationalists remembered their history caused disaster. '[B]ad history, rancorous commemorations and ... murderous violence' are inseparable from one another (O'Brien, 1972: 9). According to O'Brien, the Irish – Nationalists and Unionists – had to thoroughly scrutinise and revise Irish history. It had to be stripped of the myths that kept Nationalists and Unionists apart. Without such a process, violence would never end. This argument stands in the tradition of the beginnings of the Revisionist school in the 1930s. Yet it makes a different argument about what the myths do. To early Revisionist historians the myths represented a distraction from the truth about history. To O'Brien, the myths were more than that. They killed.

FitzGerald's study was less concerned with the past and how to deal with it. The bulk of his book outlined a vision for a future Ireland, which was heavily influenced by the Idea of Europe. FitzGerald argued that Ireland's participation in Europe would change Irish identity. It would become more inclusive. Europe would make it possible for Ireland to be united in diversity and for Nationalists and Unionists to become 'New Irelanders'. FitzGerald's distinctly European perspective was no coincidence. After several failed attempts, the Irish Council of the European Movement (ICEM) was founded in 1954 and relaunched in 1959. FitzGerald was its first chairman.

The tide turns – the international dimension

By the mid-1990s, the Idea of Europe and inclusive nationalism assumed the status of a new orthodoxy. Both have an international and a national aspect. The international dimension emphasises the need for co-operation and integration (episteme) as well as self-definition as a European nation (identity narrative). The national dimension stresses the heterogeneity of nations (episteme) and the plural character of Irishness (identity). The change of the international dimension, traced in this section, preceded the shift of the national dimension by half a decade.

For Fine Gael, the Idea of Europe became the lens through which to make sense of the Republic's role in Europe from the early 1970s onwards (Goodman, 1996: 200). For deputies such as Martin Deasy (FG), Patrick Harte (FG), FitzGerald (FG) and Peter Barry (FG), it was axiomatic that co-operation and integration was the only pathway to sustainable peace among states. They applied this insight to the Irish Question. Only through increasing political, economic and cultural contacts between North and South could the Irish Question be resolved. Fine Gael expected that the divisiveness of the border could be overcome through integrative structures, bringing the Republic, Northern Ireland and Britain closer together.[38]

Looking at inter-state relations through the international dimension of the Idea of Europe, Fine Gael increasingly came to distance itself from earlier attempts to ensure that the Republic stood apart from other nations. Instead, the party firmly committed itself to the European unification process. It began consistently to emphasise the European trait of Irish identity (Goodman, 1996: 200). The *Irish Times* and the *Irish Independent* fully supported this departure from de Valera's ideal of strict neutrality and isolationism towards a European identity. The lessening of demarcation from and increase of identification with other nations included Britain, the former coloniser. This was a major change in the Republic's self-positioning in the world.[39]

It took the other major political party, Fianna Fáil, much longer to complete this transition. Within its radical republican wing, there was no movement away from the colonial episteme and exclusive nationalism. This wing consistently believed that Ireland ought to keep its

[38] Martin Deasy, *Dáil Éireann Debates* 317, 13 December 1979, col. 1685; Patrick Harte, *Dáil Éireann Debates* 317, 13 December 1979, cols. 1689–90; Charles Haughey, *Dáil Éireann Debates* 321, 29 May 1980, col. 1063; Garret FitzGerald, *Dáil Éireann Debates* 321, 29 May 1980, col. 1068; Peter Barry, *Dáil Éireann Debates* 360, 4 July 1985, col. 610.
[39] 'A Challenge', *Irish Independent*, 30 May 1980, p. 10; 'Shadow and Substance', *Irish Times*, 30 May 1980, p. 11.

distance from other nations. Denis Lyons (FF), for instance, firmly believed that Ireland's problems were entirely due to its continuous dependency on the outside. In his view, Britain caused most of these problems, most importantly partition. Some members of Fianna Fáil's radical republican wing, anxious to preserve de Valera's ideals in an even purer form than the party's mainstream, left Fianna Fáil in the early 1970s, and were also determined to defend the old orthodoxies.[40]

Charles Haughey, Fianna Fáil's long-time chairman, was in many ways an upholder of the traditional republican tradition. Yet he and with him the mainstream of Fianna Fáil moved slowly and with many setbacks towards the international aspect of the Idea of Europe. Interpretations of the practices of the Republic's significant other – Britain – and socialisation in international forums were important factors for this development.

This process started in 1979. When Haughey was elected *Taoiseach*, he embarked on a bilateral negotiation process with Britain. Initially, he was highly satisfied with this process. Haughey's interaction with Britain changed his outlook on the Irish Question. After the 1980 Anglo-Irish summit, he informed the Dáil that he was confident that, similarly to the relations of other West European states, 'old differences between our peoples [Irish and British, MK] – who have so much in common and whose interests are so inextricably linked – can be eliminated and forgotten' (Haughey, 1986g [1980]: 411). The creation of integrative institutions binding the two countries together would be the means by which to achieve this goal (1986g [1980]: 413).

Several of his speeches affirmed Ireland's European identity trait. Haughey (1986d [1980]: 161) welcomed Ireland's 'historic opportunity' to assume its 'place among the nations of Europe'. He emphasised Ireland's support for European integration: 'Ireland, however, does not today act in isolation. We are a member State of the European Community; and as such we are committed to working with our partners towards European integration' (Haughey, 1986e [1980]: 348). The *Irish Press*, as much a guardian of traditional republicanism as Fianna Fáil, supported Haughey's view.[41]

---

[40] Neil Blaney, *Dáil Éireann Debates* 325, 11 December 1980, col. 996; Denis Lyons, *Dáil Éireann Debates* 361, 20 November 1985, col. 2953.
[41] 'House Divided', *Irish Press*, 30 May 1980, p. 8.

Haughey's move towards integration and Europeanness was reversed, however, when his interpretation of Britain's practices changed. Between 1981 and 1989, he saw Britain again in the old light. This was due to two chains of events: Britain's handling of the hunger strikes by IRA inmates and the Falklands War. For Haughey, these events confirmed the colonial episteme. In the mid-1970s, IRA prisoners arrived at Maze, an infamous prison in Northern Ireland. Seeing themselves as prisoners of war, they immediately began protesting against their treatment as ordinary inmates. The protests culminated in two hunger strikes: one in 1980 and another in 1981. Britain refused to make any concessions. Eleven prisoners died. This caused public outrage in the Republic and among the Nationalist community in Northern Ireland. In Dublin, protests turned violent and the British embassy could only be protected by a massive deployment of police.

The outbreak of the Falklands War in 1982 confirmed, in the view of traditional Nationalists, that Britain had remained an imperialist power. In early May, Argentina invaded the Falkland Islands/Las Malvinas. The Republic, then a non-permanent member of the UN Security Council, supported a resolution calling for the immediate withdrawal of Argentina from the islands. Dublin initially also supported an EEC trade embargo against Argentina, but did so reluctantly. Yet Haughey, then in office as *Taoiseach*, changed his policy when Britain sank an Argentine battleship, causing the loss of hundreds of lives. After the incident, Ireland called for an immediate cessation of hostilities at the UN and withdrew from the EEC embargo. This caused a furious verbal exchange between Britain and Ireland. British media, in particular, responded to Ireland's neutral stance with harsh criticism. An article in Britain's *Sunday Telegraph* put this criticism in acerbic language: 'It is tempting to yearn for a return of the Vikings to plunder Ireland's coastal area and rape her nuns so that we, too, can have an opportunity to declare high-minded neutrality and demand a diplomatic solution' (quoted in Dwyer, 1995: 227–9). In the course of these exchanges between Britain and Ireland, Neil Blaney (IFF) – as the only Dáil deputy – went so far as to advocate Ireland's support for Argentina (Dwyer, 1995: 228).

When Maze and the Falklands ceased to dominate political discourse in the Republic and Haughey – along with several aides from his party – discussed the future of Europe with his European counterparts, his outlook on the Republic's place in the world changed again. Haughey participated as *Taoiseach* in the negotiation and approval of the

Maastricht Treaty in 1991 and the Paris Summit of the Conference on Security and Co-operation in 1990, which issued the Charter for a New Europe. These diplomatic encounters left their mark.

Haughey moved increasingly towards the international aspect of the Idea of Europe. He celebrated European unification efforts in the Dáil and juxtaposed Europe's dark history with the prospect of a new, co-operative and integrative beginning after the end of the Cold War. Parallel to these taken-for-granted beliefs, he emphasised again Ireland's European identity trait.[42] Smaller parties such as Labour, the Workers' Party and the Democratic Left took even longer than Fianna Fáil to embrace Europe and the international aspect of the Idea of Europe, but by the early 1990s the shift had occurred (Goodman, 1996: 200–1).

Public opinion polls indicate – albeit in an indirect manner – that the public agreed with abandoning de Valera's ideal of an Ireland standing apart from the rest of the world. The public supported Ireland's involvement in Europe. A 1979 survey shows that FitzGerald's Europhilia – which went far beyond economic cost–benefit calculations – resonated with the public. Forty-six per cent thought that he was the Republic's best leader to handle Ireland's relations in Europe. Jack Lynch, then leader of Fianna Fáil, followed with only 39 per cent.[43] Considering the fact that Fianna Fáil was consistently more successful at national elections than Fine Gael, FitzGerald's clear lead against Lynch in this issue area is rather remarkable.

Another 1979 survey indicates a similar pro-European attitude. As figure 5.1 shows, half of the populace opted for 'going much further towards economic and political union in Europe'. A third of the interviewees indicated that they had no opinion on the issue and only 16 per cent disagreed.[44] This indicates a major shift away from the colonial episteme and exclusive nationalism, which had been a virtually unquestioned orthodoxy in the 1960s.

By the late 1980s and early 1990s, the public's positive attitude towards Europe had increased even further. The results of the Republic's referenda on European issues confirmed the public's strong support for Europe. More than two-thirds of the Irish electorate voted

---

[42] Charles Haughey, *Dáil Éireann Debates* 403, 28 November 1990, col. 461.
[43] MRBI survey, 1979 (MRBI/1848/79). No exact date available.
[44] IMS survey, 10–21 March 1979. No code name available.

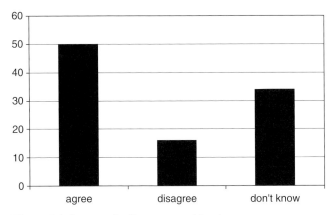

Figure 5.1 Support for European unification
Source: IMS survey, 10–21 March 1979

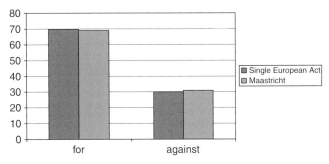

Figure 5.2 Referenda on the Single European Act and Maastricht
Source: http://www.electionsireland.org

for the Single European Act in 1987 and the Maastricht Treaty in 1992.
Whereas the governments of other member states struggled to sway
public opinion in favour of major steps towards European unification,
the strong support for European unification in the Republic made
referenda merely a formality. Figure 5.2 compares the outcomes of the
referenda on the Single European Act and Maastricht.

A very significant increase in pro-European attitudes is evident from
public opinion surveys on a question that is, arguably, the hardest test
for the salience of a European identity. Should Ireland be part of a
United States of Europe with a fully functional central European government including the power to determine Europe's foreign policy? In

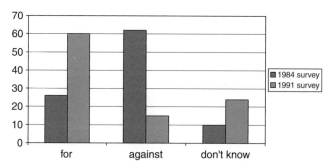

Figure 5.3 Establishment of the United States of Europe
Source: MRBI, 6–12 March 1984; IMS, 5–7 December 1991

1984, the Republic's populace was still overwhelmingly opposed to such a step. Twenty-six per cent agreed with a central European government, 62 per cent opposed this idea. By 1991, this relationship had been more than reversed. Sixty per cent agreed with a central government and only 15 per cent opposed it. Figure 5.3 shows this development.[45]

Incomplete change – the national dimension

The previous section traced a remarkable change. Within a few decades, the Republic turned from an inward-looking nation into a strong supporter for tearing down the barriers separating Europe's states and nations. Compared to the increasing support for the international aspect of the Idea of Europe and the Europhile identity trait, however, the adoption of the national aspect of the Idea and the imagination of a heterogeneous nation lagged behind.

Not everyone who supported the international dimension of the Idea of Europe also embraced its national dimension. This applies in particular to Fianna Fáil. In the 1980s and early 1990s, the party came to adopt the international but not the national aspect of the Idea. Haughey

---

[45] MRBI survey, 6–12 March 1984 (MRBI/3265/84) and IMS survey, 5–7 December 1991 (CMC/mcJ.1S393). Note that the questions were slightly different. In 1984, the question was: 'Would you be in favour, or against Europe having one Central Government, determining things like foreign policy, and economic policy, with each member state having less power than at present?' The 1991 survey asked the question: 'There is a lot of talk these days about European Unification. Would you be in favour or opposed to Ireland becoming part of a federal United States of Europe comparable to the United States of America?'

could not conceive of a pluralistic nation. To him, a nation was some-thing natural, historic and homogeneous. His characterisation of the border between the Republic and Northern Ireland made this quite clear: 'Northern Ireland is not a natural geographical or historical unit. Its boundaries do not reflect any underlying reality of race or culture' (Haughey, 1986c [1980]: 363–4). Yet this view was vehemently criticised. The political debates of the 1980s were dominated by a sharp controversy about how to imagine an Irish nation. Haughey was the key proponent of the old episteme, and FitzGerald the protagonist of the national aspect of the Idea of Europe.

In FitzGerald's view, the presumption of the homogeneity of nations made the construction of post-independence Irishness in the Republic go fundamentally wrong. The Catholic majority had tried to impose its understanding of Irishness. In this way, the Republic had become 'a sectarian state'. It represented only the majority but not the minority: '[T]he fact is our laws and our Constitution, our practices, our attitudes, reflect those of a majority ethos and are not acceptable to Protestants in Northern Ireland' (FitzGerald, quoted in Keogh, 1995: 357). FitzGerald called for respecting the diversity of the Irish nation. There was an urgent need, in his view, to rethink what it means to be Irish. Amending the Constitution would be the crucial instrument to con-struct a New Ireland. At the beginning of his term as *Taoiseach* in 1981, FitzGerald (quoted in Keogh, 1995: 357) announced: 'I want to lead a crusade, a republican crusade, to make this a genuine republic.' The choice of words is very interesting. FitzGerald was a progressive critic of the old republican ideals and as such vulnerable to being accused of betraying the ideals on which the Republic was founded. Yet by arguing that his goal was to establish a true republic and by invoking religious imagery for his cause, he put his effort in the context of the cherished ideals of Irish nationalism – albeit, of course, a radically redefined one. In FitzGerald's reading, a republic is a polity that embraces diversity.

In Haughey's perception, FitzGerald crusaded not in order to estab-lish, but in order to destroy a true republic. Haughey emphatically rejected FitzGerald's portrayal of Ireland as a sectarian state. Continuing to take the homogeneity of the Irish nation for granted, FitzGerald's criticism did not make any sense to Haughey. He clung to the orthodox heroic narrative of the Irish nation and Irish nationalism, and resolutely rejected any criticism against it: 'I cannot accept this self-abasement, this suggestion that we in the Republic have something to be ashamed of' (quoted in O'Clery, 1999: 168). To Haughey, the believer in traditional nationalism, FitzGerald's efforts were anything but a crusade: It would be 'the first time in history that a crusade was started by the infidels' (quoted in Herz, 1989: 58).

FitzGerald had the support of Fine Gael and also increasingly of Labour and other smaller parties such as the Progressive Democrats.[46] Haughey was backed by his Fianna Fáil. Apart from party politics, the two political rivals had support from different societal segments for their views on Irish identity. Intellectuals tended to support FitzGerald. Revisionist historians, for instance, backed FitzGerald. By the time FitzGerald started his constitutional crusade, Revisionist historiography had left the margins of academia and come to constitute the mainstream. In 1986, Roy Foster (1986: 5), an influential Revisionist, could proclaim about historians in Ireland: 'We are all Revisionists now.' Influential Revisionist studies on Irish history before 1987 included David Fitzpatrick's *Politics and Irish Life*, Ronan Fanning's *Independent Ireland*, Oliver MacDonagh's *States of Mind*, Paul Bew's *C. S. Parnell*, F. S. L. Lyons's *Charles Stuart Parnell*, Roy Foster's *Modern Ireland* and Joseph Lee's *Ireland*. Apart from debunking the image of the ancient and Gaelic Irish nation as a myth, Revisionists argued that Irish nationalism was originally inclusive. When it originated in or shortly before the nineteenth century, it had 'to cater for disparate political minds' (Fitzpatrick, 1977: ix). Only after the Easter Rising in 1916 did Irish nationalism become exclusive and seek demarcation from Protestantism. This retold Irish history supported and influenced FitzGerald's argument. Revisionists criticised exclusive nationalism and went back to history to uncover what they considered the original, inclusive nationalism.

Haughey received some support from intellectuals such as Micheal O'Cuinneagain,[47] but his main support came from public opinion. For most Irish people in the Republic, the Irish – whether Nationalist or

[46] Barry Desmond, in particular, argued powerfully for the respect of plurality. Barry Desmond, *Dáil Éireann Debates* 361, 20 November 1985, col. 2886. To a large extent, this was due to his involvement with the Irish trade unions. These have been among the few formal political organisations that encompass North and South, and include Nationalists as well as Unionists. This environment inspired trade unionists such as Desmond, who comes from a traditional republican background, to advocate respect for diversity. Interview with Barry Desmond, Dublin, 27 January 2004.
[47] O'Cuinneagain (1986) criticised the 'tragic decline in the standards of honesty, truth and respect for God's laws, so evident in our land'.

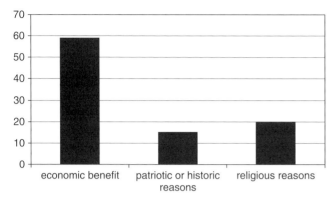

Figure 5.4 Perception of why Unionists want to stay with Britain
Source: IMS, 9 March 1978

Unionist – were one nation without any major identity differences. IMS conducted an interesting survey in 1978, asking people in the Republic what, in their opinion, was the most important reason for the majority in Northern Ireland to opt for union with Britain. Almost 60 per cent thought that Unionists stayed with Britain due to the economic benefits of the union. Only 20 per cent conceived of religious reasons and a mere 15 per cent considered patriotic or historic reasons as being paramount.[48] Figure 5.4 shows these results.

Brian Girvin (1994: 23) dismisses the result of FitzGerald's crusade: 'Most of Fitzgerald's initiatives were disastrous, in particular over the abortion and divorce referenda. What these events demonstrated was that in the Republic there was a majority for the defence of traditional politics and the constitution.' Undoubtedly, Girvin's evaluation is correct as far as the short-term consequences were concerned. FitzGerald lost two key referenda aimed at making the Republic's Constitution more acceptable to Unionists. In 1982, two-thirds of the Republic's electorate voted in favour of including the ban on abortion in the Constitution. Four years later, almost two-thirds rejected lifting the constitutional ban against divorce.[49] In the long run, however,

---

[48] IMS survey, 9 March 1978 (CMC/md/J.780/6). The exact question was as follows: 'Thinking of the majority in Northern Ireland, which of these reasons do you think is the most important to them at the moment in wanting Northern Ireland to remain linked to Britain?'

[49] The results of all referenda are available at: http://www.electionsireland.org

FitzGerald's crusade was an important success. It was the beginning of a change of Irish national identity towards the recognition of diversity and pluralism.

Inclusive nationalism

By the mid-1990s, the Idea of Europe and inclusive nationalism – including their national aspect – had come to dominate their long-standing atomistic and exclusive rivals. Influential actors such as Fianna Fáil and the public at large completed the far-ranging change of the repertoire of commonplaces that had begun in the early 1970s.

In 1992, Charles Haughey was forced to resign as *Taoiseach* due to allegations of corruption and involvement in tapping the phone lines of two journalists. Albert Reynolds succeeded him as *Taoiseach* and chairman of Fianna Fáil. With the demise of Haughey, traditional nationalism had lost its most vigorous defender. Fianna Fáil was voted out of power in 1994 and succeeded by a coalition government of Fine Gael, Labour and the Democratic Left.

Two years later, the coalition government, headed by John Bruton, published Ireland's first White Paper on Foreign Policy. The White Paper itself, as well as the Dáil debate that it triggered, showed very clearly the dominance of the new repertoire of commonplaces. At its core was the episteme that formed the basis of FitzGerald's, O'Brien's and the Revisionists' new thinking about the Irish nation two decades earlier. The consensus on peace through co-operation and integration continued, and was widened to include the constitution of nations as pluralistic communities. According to the White Paper, Europe's past taught two important lessons. First, nationalism brought about horrible wars between states: 'Twice in this century, terrible global wars have been fuelled by competing national claims' (Government of Ireland, 1996: 48). Second, the Holocaust and, more recently, ethnic cleansing during the violent break-up of Yugoslavia taught another lesson. Nation-states are not homogeneous. Attempts to homogenise them have resulted in some of the worst of Europe's catastrophes: 'Millions of people have been murdered in campaigns driven by the urge to establish the ethnic purity of states' (Government of Ireland, 1996: 48). According to the White Paper, these lessons allowed for only two inferences about the workings of world politics. One of these inferences concerns the relations among nation-states: 'These events have highlighted the instability of an international order made up of competing nation-states' (Government of Ireland, 1996: 48). The other inference addressed primarily intra-state relations.

[T]he limitations of the nation state are clearly seen in the difficulties which arise from attempting to define the human or territorial borders of a nation ... Much conflict has resulted from the lack of distinct boundaries between nationalities, from efforts to incorporate into a nation state people who do not identify with that state, and from attempts to create an artificial nation state where none exists. (Government of Ireland, 1996: 48)

This insight is diametrically opposed to Fichte's dictum that nations have obvious and natural boundaries – a belief that had shaped traditional Irish nationalism for decades. The borders of a nation are unclear. A nation ought not to force people into the nation who do not identify with it. This is an implicit but strong criticism against the claim made by traditional Nationalists that the borders of the Irish nation are obvious and natural, and that Unionists simply do not understand that they are Irish.

The White Paper stated that nation-states, despite their defects, would be likely to remain the 'essential building block of the international order for some time to come' (Government of Ireland, 1996: 47). Yet these nation-states would have to perform two critical roles: accommodate domestic diversity and overcome the borders of nation-states through co-operation:

If the nation state is to serve as a basis for peaceful and prosperous co-existence ... it must be accompanied by arrangements for the recognition and accommodation of internal diversity, and be situated within a framework providing for dialogue, consultation and cooperation between states. (Government of Ireland, 1996: 48)

Given these epistemic understandings, the Irish nation continued to imagine itself as a European nation. The White Paper put it as follows: 'Irish people increasingly see the European Union not simply as an organisation to which Ireland belongs, but as an integral part of our future. We see ourselves, increasingly, as Europeans' (Government of Ireland, 1996: 8).

Between 1993 and 1998, Dáil debates on foreign policy focused on the White Paper and negotiations for peace in Northern Ireland. The first tangible outcome of the negotiations was the Downing Street Declaration in 1993. This was followed by the Framework Agreement in 1995. The negotiations culminated in the 1998 Good Friday

Agreement, which fundamentally redefined the institutional make-up of Anglo-Irish relations and the relations between the Republic and Northern Ireland. The next chapter includes a more detailed analysis of the negotiations leading to the Good Friday Agreement.

What is crucial for the purposes of this chapter is that the Dáil debates about the White Paper and the peace process show that there was – apart from some disagreement about neutrality – a far-reaching consensus on a new repertoire of commonplaces. The integrative and diversity aspects of the Idea of Europe became the taken-for-granted lens to look at European affairs in general and Anglo-Irish relations as well as the Irish Question in particular. To John Bruton (FG), for example, the traditional nation-state was an 'obsolete hangover from the 19th century'.[50] States, he emphasised, are not containers of homogeneous societies. '[T]here can be different allegiances held by people living in the same territory at the same time.'[51] Derek McDowell (LB) made the same argument and warned that Bosnia showed what happened if leaders thought that nations are homogeneous.[52] There was nobody in parliament who argued against this epistemic understanding. Instead, it marked out the taken-for-granted cognitive and discursive space for making sense of Irishness. Declan Bree (LB) contended that Irishness ought to be the opposite of sectarianism, i.e. an identity that left room for different political aspirations.[53] Richard Spring (LB) assured Unionists that Nationalists would respect the Unionists' aspirations: 'We are not an enemy of your rights and aspirations; we aspire to be your friends and partners.'[54] Bertie Ahern (FF) emphasised that the Irish nation provided a home for both Nationalism and Unionism.[55] Echoing FitzGerald, Proinsias De Rossa (DL) explained that respect for minorities was a defining feature of republicanism. A true republic 'is based on the principle not that the majority takes all but that it defends and protects the rights of minorities within its borders and must have respect for all.'[56]

---

[50] John Bruton, *Dáil Éireann Debates* 437, 17 December 1993, col. 1243.
[51] John Bruton, *Dáil Éireann Debates* 437, 17 December 1993, col. 1246.
[52] Derek McDowell, *Dáil Éireann Debates* 449, 22 February 1995, col. 1497.
[53] Declan Bree, *Dáil Éireann Debates* 449, 22 February 1995, cols. 1524–5.
[54] Richard Spring, *Dáil Éireann Debates* 437, 17 December 1993, col. 1348.
[55] Bertie Ahern, *Dáil Éireann Debates* 437, 15 December 1993, cols. 747–8.
[56] Proinsias De Rossa, *Dáil Éireann Debates* 437, 17 December 1993, col. 1287.

Outside of the formal political realm, the Idea of Europe and inclusive nationalism also assumed dominance in the 1990s. The contrast between old and new is particularly stark with regard to school text-books. In the 1970s, the colonial episteme and exclusive nationalism were taught. A standard textbook by Noonan (1976: 41–2) was very sceptical about the possibility and benefits of European unification. Another history textbook glorified exclusive nationalism as a liberating force from colonialism (Foley and Enright, 1977: 223).

By the 1990s, however, the history taught in the Republic's schools had changed considerably. O level and H level history papers were equally divided between questions about Ireland and Europe. The Idea of Europe was taught. In O'Leary's textbook, for example, the Idea is explained in detail. The book argues that the catastrophe of the Second World War made statesmen adopt the Idea of Europe. The Second World War had made obvious that the nation-state was an inappropriate form of political organisation in the modern era. The post-war era showed that functional integration proved to be the means to turn hostility into friendship. The textbook presents those who over-came Europe's division into nation-states as heroes. There are short biographical descriptions of the protagonists of integration such as Robert Schuman, Jean Monnet and Konrad Adenauer. The book pos-tulates that 'one has to applaud the statesmanship of the leaders who brought together the former enemies in the harmony of the ECSC' (O'Leary, 1996: 220).

Irish film-makers continued to distance themselves from de Valera's and Yeats's mythical Ireland. This criticism had come into full swing in the 1980s. Bob Quinn's work, in particular, chastised the myth of the homogeneous Gaelic and Catholic Ireland of which the early twentieth-century nation-builders had dreamed. In a three-part television docu-mentary, entitled *Atlantean*, Quinn (1983) ridiculed the conviction of traditional nationalists that Ireland is the land of the Gael. He countered this longing for authenticity with his provocative assertion that many traditions that are seen as defining Irishness were actually imported from North Africa. In *Budawanny* (1987) and *The Bishop's Story* (1994), Quinn criticised the gap between the formal organisation of the Catholic Church and the religious practices of the people. Not coincidentally, the setting of the two films is the west of Ireland, the former shrine of the writers of Revivalist nationalism (McLoone, 2000: 133). Neil Jordan's *The Crying Game* (1992) is a film about the transgression of boundaries – between North and South and between Unionists and Nationalists. This is also a *leitmotiv* of fictional literature, such as in Bernard MacLaverty's *Cal* (1983), Glenn Patterson's *Burning Your Own* (1988), Patrick Quigley's *Borderland* (1994) and Joan Lingard's *Across the Barricades* (1995).[57]

Public opinion also completed the transformation from the hegemony of the colonial episteme and exclusive nationalism to the predominance of the Idea of Europe and inclusive nationalism. The public overwhelmingly supported the peace process that started with the 1993 Downing Street Declaration. As the next chapter will discuss in detail, redefining the Irish nation to encompass Nationalists and Unionists, and applying the lessons of European unification to Nationalist–Unionist, South–North as well as British–Irish relations were central to the Good Friday Agreement in 1998. No referendum in the Republic was ever carried with such an overwhelming majority: 94 per cent agreed with the accord, only 6 per cent rejected it.[58]

The newly dominant episteme and identity had normative repercussions. The agreement on the norms of the UN Charter remained largely unaltered. In particular, the emphasis on the norm of peaceful resolution of disputes, human rights and the rule of law in international affairs proved to be resistant to change (Government of Ireland, 1996: 15–18). The neutrality norm, however, changed profoundly. Strict neutrality as postulated by exclusive nationalism was brushed aside. The norm came to be interpreted increasingly loosely. All major political parties in the Republic campaigned in favour of the Amsterdam Treaty in 1998. They argued that the treaty did not affect Irish neutrality, although it contained stipulations about an EU capacity for peacekeeping, peacemaking and rescue missions. The referendum was carried by 62 per cent to 38 per cent of the votes. Even before the referendum a debate had started in parliament whether Ireland should drop neutrality altogether. Deputies such as Michael McDowell (PD) and Proinsias De Rossa (DL) argued against Irish neutrality.[59] Without regret, Bertie Ahern (FF) contended that neutrality had become *de facto* largely inconsequential for Irish foreign policy.[60] When Charles Haughey defended Irish

---

[57] For a good overview, see Cleary (2002: 77–115).
[58] http://www.electionsireland.org
[59] Michael McDowell, *Dáil Éireann Debates* 429, 28 April 1993, col. 1668; Proinsias De Rossa, *Dáil Éireann Debates* 429, 28 April 1993, col. 1675.
[60] Bertie Ahern, *Dáil Éireann Debates* 463, 28 March 1996, col. 1316.

neutrality as an integral part of Irish nationalism,[61] Alan Dukes dismissed this argument simply with the words: 'utter rubbish'.[62] Even though neutrality continued to be a norm informing Irish foreign policy-making, its interpretation was increasingly stretched and even the stretched version was more and more exposed to criticism.

Discussion of findings

Some aspects of the repertoire of commonplaces remained constant. The longing for unification of North and South persisted. The Republic's emphasis on key norms of the UN Charter, in particular human rights, peaceful resolution of disputes and the rule of law in international relations, remained constitutive of its identity. All in all, however, the history of the evolution of the repertoire of commonplaces is a history of change.

Twentieth-century contestations about Irishness may be simplified by juxtaposing two variants of Irish nationalism, one epitomised by de Valera and the other by Redmond. Following the Easter Rising, de Valera's exclusive nationalism gained the upper hand over Redmond's inclusive version. Yet things began to change in the 1970s. Kevin Boland (IND), a determined guardian of de Valera's ideals, criticised the nascent identity change in 1974 in acerbic manner: 'Redmondism ... has become rampant ... Venal politicians with a vested interest in the status quo ... have blasphemed the cause that dead generations of Ireland served' (quoted in O'Clery, 1999: 143). By the mid-1990s, inclusive nationalism was no longer subject to such vilification. Exclusive nationalism had become marginalised. The Republic came to identify itself as a European nation, and respecting a considerable degree of diversity of the Irish nation had developed into an important trait of the dominant variant of Irish nationalism. Parallel to the change of the identity narrative, the neutrality norm changed profoundly. De Valera's narrow interpretation of the norm was so sacrosanct to him that it even compelled him to mourn Hitler's suicide. In the 1990s, by contrast, the process of reinterpretation had come so far that the Republic did not even exclude itself from the European Union's steps towards a common security policy.

[61] Charles Haughey, *Dáil Éireann Debates* 463, 28 March 1996, col. 1336.
[62] Alan Dukes, *Dáil Éireann Debates* 463, 28 March 1996, col. 1336.

The focus of this study is on how actors assemble clues provided by their repertoire of commonplaces to reason about the world and not on how the parts of the repertoire interact with one another. Yet albeit not at the centre of this research endeavour, it is worth drawing attention to the ways in which this chapter has highlighted the salience of the episteme. The episteme explains what made the reinvention of Irishness possible. The nation came to imagine a different kind of nationness. The shared background knowledge about what a nation is and what it ought to do changed. The construction of the exclusive variant of Irishness was delineated by the colonial episteme. Given this episteme, it was axiomatic that nations are homogeneous and have to defend their uniqueness against outside interference. This made the invention of a Gaelic and Catholic authentic Self standing apart from the world imaginable. It precluded the construction of a national identity that embraced plurality and sought to overcome borders among nation-states. The more widespread the Idea of Europe became, however, the more the exclusive identity turned into an implausible and beleaguered identity construct. It developed from an ideal to a being responsible for violence. The Idea delineated a new cognitive and discursive space in which an inclusive identity variant emerged.[63]

This chapter has laid the foundation for the analysis of argumentation and compromise in the next chapter. While this chapter has described the evolution of the repertoire of commonplaces available to actors to reason about the Irish Question, the next chapter traces the processes through which actors came to link this repertoire to normative ideas pertaining to the territorial status quo.

---

[63] To some extent, my findings about the evolution of Irish identity and its constitutive norms echo studies on the change from exclusive to inclusive Irishness (Gibbons, 1996; Kearney, 1997; O'Mahony and Delanty, 1998; Tonge, 1998; Girvin, 1999; Tondra, 1999; Gilland, 2000; Hanafin, 2001; Harris, 2001). Yet these studies overlook the epistemic dimension. The episteme was not only a key component of the repertoire of commonplaces. It also helps explain the evolution of identity narrative and its constitutive norms (Kornprobst, 2005).

6 | *Constitutional change*

The previous chapter traced the evolution of the repertoire of common-places in the Republic of Ireland. I contended that there was continuity and change. The longing to overcome partition as well as a number of identity-constituting norms remained unaltered. However, the epis-teme, important aspects of the identity narrative involving the reposi-tioning vis-à-vis Unionists, Britain and Europe, as well as the neutrality norm changed fundamentally. This chapter examines how the changing repertoire of commonplaces influenced the formation of an advocacy for recognising the territorial status quo, how and with what success the advocates linked their arguments to the repertoire of commonplaces, and what role the repertoire played for bargaining processes between advocates and recalcitrant actors.

Only shortly after the Troubles started, advocates such as FitzGerald and O'Brien, who already embraced the novel aspects of the repertoire of commonplaces, challenged the taboo against the recognition of Britain's sovereignty over Northern Ireland. Using these novel aspects as clues for a new approach, they argued that the Republic had to learn an important lesson from history. The Unionists' fear of being forced into unification with the Republic had caused them to opt out of the Republic and explained their resolve to defend partition. Overcoming partition required reducing this fear and the recognition of the territorial status quo would be a key contribution to this reduction (comparative reasoning). Additionally, FitzGerald contended that the Unionists' fear could be gra-dually overcome through a process of co-operation and integration, mod-elled after the European unification process. In order for such a process to be initiated, the Republic would have to recognise existing borders (abstract reasoning). According to these two lines of reasoning, therefore, recognition did not mean burying the dream of Irish unity. It meant pursuing it. But pursuing it without a legal territorial claim to the North.

Throughout the 1970s, FitzGerald and O'Brien were harshly criti-cised by traditional Nationalists for their advocacy of dropping the

179

irredentist claim. They were accused of betrayal and treason. By the mid-1980s, however, the advocacy increasingly resonated with influential actors and public opinion. From the late 1980s onwards, appropriateness reasoning, focusing on the norm of peaceful resolution of disputes and the norm complex of the 1975 Helsinki Final Act, reinforced abstract and comparative reasoning. From 1992 onwards, public opinion favoured forgoing irredentism. Some actors, however, remained unconvinced. These opponents of change, in particular Fianna Fáil, compromised on their stance only when they were beleaguered by public pressure, and when the United Kingdom and the Unionists of Northern Ireland offered a comprehensive peace agreement on Northern Ireland that provided many benefits to the Republic and the Nationalist community in the North.

I develop this argument chronologically. First, I describe the taboo never to recognise the border between North and South. Second, I trace how the shifting repertoire of commonplaces, coupled with the onset of the Troubles in the North, contributed to the weakening of this taboo and the rise of an innovative argumentation advocating recognition of the existing border. Third, I inquire into the process through which the advocacy gained momentum, culminating in the endorsement of the advocates' argumentation by the public. Fourth, I examine the conditions that explain the compromise between the advocates and many of their opponents.

Taboo against recognition

Between the inauguration of the 1937 Constitution and the early 1960s, recognition of British sovereignty over Northern Ireland was inconceivable for Irish Nationalists. The recognition of the territorial status quo was a taboo. Underlying this orthodoxy, routinely invoked during commemorations and at international forums, was a twofold justification of the taboo that revolved around appropriateness and comparative reasoning.

The irredentist claim was axiomatic. In parliament, there was not a single voice questioning irredentism. Partition meant, in de Valera's words, 'cutting out Ireland's heart' (quoted in Bowman, 1982: 301). Without Northern Ireland, Ireland would not be Ireland:

There is Armagh, the See of St. Patrick; Downpatrick, his burial place, where lies also the body of Brian who drove out the Danish invaders; Bangor, the site of one of the greatest of Ireland's ancient schools; Derry of St. Columcille; Tyrone of the O'Neills; MacArt's Fort, where Wolfe Tone swore to work for Irish freedom; Belfast, the birthplace of the Irish Republican movement. (de Valera quoted in Boyce, 1995: 296)

No government, therefore, ought ever to be ambiguous about the irredentist claim. As Con Lehane (CnaP) put it:

[N]o act of the Minister's and no act of any servant or soldier of the Irish people shall be calculated in any way to permit of its being understood that we give even the most limited acquiescence to this wrong upon our country and this violation of our territory.[1]

Bunreacht na hÉireann, the Republic's 1937 Constitution, codified the territorial claim into law. At the very beginning of the Constitution, Articles 2 and 3 formulated in unambiguous terms that the Republic's *de jure* sovereignty encompassed North and South:

Article 2: The national territory consists of the whole island of Ireland, its islands and the territorial seas.
Article 3: Pending the re-integration of the national territory, and without prejudice to the right of the Parliament and Government established by this Constitution to exercise jurisdiction over the whole of that territory, the laws enacted by that parliament shall have the like area and extent of application as the laws Saorstát Éireann (Irish Free State) and the like extra-territorial effect.

As explained by the Supreme Court, these Articles formulated a claim of legal right to Northern Ireland (Boland vs. *Taoiseach*, 1974; McGimpsey vs. Ireland, 1988). Article 2 formulated the irredentist claim. *De jure*, it stated, Northern Ireland is part of the Republic of Ireland. Article 3 affirmed this by stating that the Republic's parliament and government would have the right to exercise jurisdiction in North and South, although it would refrain from doing so until partition was overcome.

At times, comparative reasoning was invoked to buttress the taboo against recognition. It linked the taboo against recognition to the *topoi* of the colonial episteme and exclusive nationalism. Northern Ireland 'was viewed as the last British outpost on the island of Ireland, a remnant of the old colonial structure' (O'Malley, 2001: 1). The

---

[1] Con Lehane, *Dáil Éireann Debates* 113, 14 December 1948, col. 1512.

comparative reasoning made an analogy between past anti-colonial struggles and future anti-colonial struggles. Generations of Irish people, despite and because of the atrocities committed by Britain, never ceased to pursue their dream of a free Ireland, governed by the Irish in the spirit of Irish Republicanism as laid down by Wolfe Tone. After centuries of liberation struggle, the 1916 Rebellion triggered events that culminated in the liberation of the Southern part. If the Irish continued to work for unity with the same resolve, the coloniser would eventually withdraw from the Northern part as well.

While in office as *Taoiseach*, John Costello introduced the motion 'Protest against Partition' in the Dáil in 1949. The comparative aspect was his main argument in favour of the motion, which was passed unanimously. Thanks to the glorious struggle of generations of Irish Nationalists, he argued, the South had become free. The present generation owed it to the nation's past heroes not to falter until the Republic succeeded in freeing Northern Ireland of British occupation.[2] Emmet's epitaph was frequently employed to link past sacrifices, the successful partial liberation of Ireland and the need for determination to complete the task that the forefathers had begun. Robert Emmet took part in a rebellion against British rule in 1803. He was sentenced to death for treason the same year. Before he died, he proclaimed that his epitaph must not be written before Ireland rids itself of British rule. The epitaph remained uncompleted despite the creation of the Republic in the South. As Costello put it: 'While Partition persists we cannot claim that Emmet's epitaph can be written in full.'[3]

Appropriateness reasoning also reinforced the taboo against recognition. While actors invoked a number of norms as *topoi*, they focused on the principle of national self-determination. All *Taoisigh* in power between the mid-1930s and the mid-1960s regularly appealed to Ireland's right to national self-determination. This *topos* was not only employed by the chief protagonist of Irish republicanism, Eamon de Valera (FF), but also by his reform-minded successor Seán Lemass (FF).

We wish to see the reunification of Ireland restored. By every test Ireland is one nation with a fundamental right to have its essential unity expressed in its political institutions. The unit for self-determination is the whole country and we do not accept that a minority has a right to vote itself out of the nation on

---

[2] John Costello, *Dáil Éireann Debates* 115, 10 May 1949, cols. 786–9.
[3] John Costello, *Dáil Éireann Debates* 113, 24 November 1948, col. 391.

the ground that it is in disagreement with the majority on a major policy issue. We cannot and will not depart from that position. (quoted in Ivory, 1999: 85)

This appropriateness reasoning also included the definition of the Irish nation as ingrained in the identity narrative. Actors provided two aspects of this definition as justification for their claim that the Irish nation as a whole – and not the Unionists on their own – had a right to national self-determination. First, the Irish nation was seen as a homogeneous nation without a racial or religious minority. In de Valera's view, Britain had divided this homogenous nation: 'Britain is fundamentally responsible for the partitioning of our country ... there is no distinct racial minority here ... Fundamentally, it [the Unionist population, MK] is not a religious minority either.'[4] De Valera discarded Unionist appeals to a distinct identity as entirely fictitious: 'This Ulster is a thing of the mind only, non-existent in the world of reality' (quoted in Bowman, 1982: 301). De Valera's political archrival, John Costello (FG), argued in a similar vein. In his view, partition was an 'unnatural division between the Irish people, the Irish race' (Costello, 1948: 26).

Second, geography made it obvious to Nationalists that Ireland was an indivisible whole. The sea naturally demarcated Ireland's borders. Anthony Esmonde (FG), for example, believed that this made its borders the most obvious in the world: 'There is no country in the world whose boundaries are as clearly defined as ours. Every schoolboy in every part of the world knows what the Irish nation is.'[5] Some actors attached religious meaning to the geographical dimension. Cardinal Joseph MacRory, for instance, argued that God created one island of Ireland and that it was God's will that this island was inhabited by one nation. The island was '[a]n ancient land, made one by God' (MacRory, quoted in O'Clery, 1999: 91–2).

While it was very clear to the Republic that it would never recognise partition, it was entirely unsure about how the country could be reunified. The majority agreed that it ought not to be achieved through the use of force. Only two Dáil deputies advocated a military invasion of the North. Peadar Cowan (CnaP) urged 'that there is only one way to end Partition and that is by the armed might of the youth of our

---

[4] Eamon de Valera, *Dáil Éireann Debates* 122, 12 July 1950, col. 1540.
[5] Anthony Esmonde, *Dáil Éireann Debates* 138, 29 April 1953, col. 847.

country'.[6] Roderick Connolly (LB) called for the 'reconquest of the Six North-Eastern Counties'.[7] Yet Declan Costello (FG) was right when he stated that there was 'near unanimity' in the Dáil on ruling out force.[8] Cowan later rescinded his view on force and urged a peaceful solution, because force could not lead to true national unity.[9] De Valera was among the most vigorous advocates for a peaceful solution. He is even on record asserting that he would fight on the side of the Unionists if they were coerced into unification (Bowman, 1982: 306). The *Irish Press*, in which the partition issue featured even more prominently than in other newspapers, argued that force could not be an option because that would involve Irish people shooting Irish people: 'Force has been abjured for the compelling reason that every man that fell in the struggle would be an Irishman.'[10]

While there was far-reaching agreement on how unity ought not to be achieved, there was no agreement on how it could be attained. It was widely accepted that Britain was the key to unity. British imperialism had caused partition and only the end of its imperial designs on Ireland could lead to unity. Dietmar Herz (1989: 10) does not exaggerate when he writes about Ireland's 'perception of Great Britain as the *deus ex machina* for the solution of the Irish Question'. This widespread perception, however, did little to facilitate a solution of the problem. It was very unclear to actors in the Republic how Britain could be made to agree to Irish unity. John Costello, *Taoiseach* from 1948 to 1951 and from 1954 to 1957, and Seán MacBride, Costello's Minister of External Affairs, frequently raised the Irish Question in international organisations. They appealed to Ireland's right to national self-determination and believed that Britain would eventually have to reverse the injustice of partition due to the pressure of world opinion.[11]

The *Irish Press*, usually quite critical of Fine Gael, fully supported raising the partition issue at international forums:

At every international gathering where she [Britain, MK] and we are represented, the story of our imposed territorial disunity must be told ... It is by

[6] Peadar Cowan, *Dáil Éireann Debates* 117, 13 July 1949, col. 770; for a similar call to arms see Peadar Cowan, *Dáil Éireann Debates* 126, 19 July 1951 col. 1560.
[7] Roderick Connolly, *Dáil Éireann Debates* 122, 12 July 1950, col. 1557.
[8] Declan Costello, *Dáil Éireann Debates* 142, 12 July 1955, col. 566.
[9] Peadar Cowan, *Dáil Éireann Debates* 122, 29 April 1953, col. 836.
[10] 'The Road to Unity', *Irish Press*, 30 April 1953, p. 6.
[11] Seán MacBride, *Dáil Éireann Debates* 122, 12 July 1950, cols. 1523–5.

getting the existence of this wrong more widely known in Europe and America and the threat to all liberty that lies at the core of it better appreciated, that progress will be made.[12]

Costello and MacBride raised the partition issue regularly at the Council of Europe. But when it became obvious that this practice was ineffective, it was discarded (Doherty, 2002: 45). De Valera stressed that overcoming partition was the primary goal of Irish politics: 'until I die, Partition will be the first thing in my mind' (quoted in Bowman, 1982: 299). Yet he was also very unsure about how this could happen and was very frank about the impasse. In a speech at the Dáil (1980f [1951]: 543) he explained:

If I am asked, 'Have you a solution for it?' in the sense, 'Is there a line of policy which you propose to pursue, which you think can, within a reasonable time, be effective?', I have to say that I have not and neither has anybody else.

De Valera was severely criticised for this acknowledgement of not having a solution for the Irish Question. John McQuillan (IND) inter-rupted de Valera's above-quoted admission with the sarcastic words 'hoping for a miracle' (de Valera, 1980f [1951]: 543). A 1938 caricature in the *Dublin Opinion*, entitled 'The Doctor', illustrated this criticism. De Valera, depicted as a physician, examines the personified Éire. Sitting in the north of the island, she has a severed arm that autono-mously beats an Orange Lambeg drum across the partition fence in Northern Ireland. De Valera examines her with a stethoscope and offers a vague hope for a remedy in the future: 'It's a very peculiar case, Miss Rosaleen, but I am not without hope that I will be able to do something to bring you and your other arm together.' The caricature hinted that de Valera might not only have no solution to the problem, but that he might also misdiagnose it. After all, it is not quite clear how a stetho-scope could give clues as to why Éire's left arm was severed.

One Dáil deputy, Patrick Cogan (IND), consistently looked at the Irish Question from a fresh perspective. Having internalised the Idea of Europe as the lens through which to make the Irish Question intelligible to himself, he reached very different conclusions as to why Ireland was divided and how partition could be overcome. In his opinion, partition was caused by the Unionists' fear of the Republic. They were afraid that

---

[12] 'The Road to Unity', *Irish Press*, 30 April 1953, p. 6.

a unified Ireland would leave no room for their identity. This fear could be overcome through gradual integration of North and South, modelled after the (then West) European unification process. Functional co-operation would start in the economic realm and then spill over into other spheres. This process would reduce Unionist fear and eventually culminate in unification.[13] The *Irish Times* – in contrast to the *Irish Independent* and the *Irish Press* – fully supported this analysis.[14]

Yet this abstract reasoning, linking the *topoi* of the Idea of Europe and the longing for unity, was not an advocacy to forgo irredentism. There was no call to break the taboo on renouncing the claim to Northern Ireland. It was also far from being a successful advocacy. It did not even come close to resonating with a broader audience. The Idea of Europe was still far from becoming a widely shared commonplace. Instead, it was the colonial episteme that made partition intelligible to the overwhelming majority of Nationalists, and Cogan's argument was far removed from the perimeter of reasoning that this episteme made intelligible.

Debating diagnosis and cure of the Irish Question

When Lemass was in power between 1959 and 1966, a debate about diagnosis and cure of the Irish Question started to develop. The increasing support for the Idea of Europe made more actors approach the Northern Ireland issue similarly to Cogan. The new reasoning on the causes and dynamics of partition began to erode the argumentation on which the determination never to recognise Northern Ireland was built. Yet the resolve never to give up the claim to the North remained intact. There was no advocacy for recognising the territorial status quo yet.

A considerable number of Dáil deputies continued to regard the Northern Ireland problem as a colonial issue. In their opinion, Britain alone was responsible for partition and could put an end to it from one moment to the next. William Norton (LB) put this quite succinctly. He argued that Britain could resolve the issue

tomorrow by offering two sentences of advice to the Six-County Government and by withdrawing from that Government, in the event of its failing to take

---

[13] Patrick Cogan, *Dáil Éireann Debates* 159, 3 July 1951, cols. 1999–2000.
[14] 'Council of Europe', *Irish Times*, 14 July 1949, p. 5.

that advice, the generous subsidies without which the Six Counties as an administrative unit could never exist.[15]

Yet this view was challenged by those who conceived of the Irish nation as a non-homogeneous people. Among these challengers were the leaders of the two most influential political parties, Seán Lemass (FF) and Liam Cosgrave (FG). The challengers held that partition was originally brought about by Britain. Cosgrave dismissed those downplaying the British role as 'pseudo-historians or pseudo-propagandists'.[16] In a similar vein, Lemass (1959: 3–4) emphasised the role Britain played in the partition of Ireland. Yet the diagnosis of partition did not stop there. Partition was sustained by the Unionists' fear of the Republic. This added the Irish component to the British dimension of partition. The Irish nation was imagined as being diverse. Most importantly, there were two distinct and fully legitimate 'communities' or 'sections', as they were often labelled: Nationalists and Unionists. The latter would be averse to joining the Republic, because they feared that they would lose their identity and be disadvantaged. Lionel Booth (FF) emphasised the role of fear again and again:

We must face the fact that there are inherent differences which are basic both in religion and political loyalty which divided the communities long before the Border was ever set up and that the Border really only recognises a division which was already there.[17]

The controversy about the reasons for partition triggered a new debate about how Ireland could be reunited. The two positions about the causes of partition translated into two clusters of positions on how to overcome it. First, those contending that Britain was the sole cause of partition warned against seeking reconciliation with Unionists. In the view of Patrick McGilligan (FG), not 'antagonising' Unionists would be 'defeatist'. Reconciliation would carve the false border into stone.[18] Instead, Ireland should mobilise world opinion against Britain in order to compel the latter to withdraw from Northern Ireland. The United Nations, in particular, was seen as a crucial international forum for this issue.[19] Some Dáil deputies continued to argue that even the use

[15] William Norton, *Dáil Éireann Debates* 176, 7 July 1959, col. 675.
[16] Liam Cosgrave, *Dáil Éireann Debates* 201, 3 April 1963, col. 956.
[17] Lionel Booth, *Dáil Éireann Debates* 176, 7 July 1959, col. 644.
[18] Patrick McGilligan, *Dáil Éireann Debates* 176, 7 July 1959, cols. 625–6.
[19] William Norton, *Dáil Éireann Debates* 176, 7 July 1959, col. 675.

of force would still be an option for attaining unification. Frank Sherwin (IND) contended that unity would be impossible to achieve without force. The ruling clique in the North would never be prepared to give away its privileges peacefully. Unfortunately, Ireland would be too weak at the moment to conquer Northern Ireland. But the balance of power between Britain and Ireland would not always be to Ireland's disadvantage. If 'Britain becomes weak ... we shall be able to walk in'.[20]

Those actors who focused on fear and divisions within the Irish nation as the cause of partition advocated a fundamentally different solution of the problem. The key word was 'healing'. The history of antagonism and violence between Nationalists and Unionists was understood as a wound that would have to be healed. If this healing process succeeded, unity would become a possibility. Lionel Booth (FF) was the most ardent advocate of this view in the Dáil. He emphasised that the path to unification that he supported was diametrically opposed to the Republic's previous and current policies towards the North. These exacerbated the inner-Irish divisions instead of trying to overcome them, and, therefore, were counter-productive:

> The fact remains that the country is divided in itself and we have done nothing to heal that division. We must face the fact that we have made no progress towards unity of minds and that it is because too many loud and impassioned speeches have been made on both sides.[21]

In Booth's opinion, one aspect of healing involved a change of vocabulary. Southern politicians should not refer to Northern Ireland as 'Six Counties', 'North-Eastern Counties' or use 'terms of abuse such as "bigotry", "occupied territory", "puppet government" and "police state"' but call it 'by the name they have taken for themselves' – Northern Ireland.[22]

Other actors added a functionalist dimension to this thinking. In Lemass's view, for example, fear could be decreased by developing contacts across the border. There would be no quick results, because the 'barriers of fear and suspicion ... are too strong to be demolished quickly'. But it would be the only possible path towards unity (Lemass, 1959: 13). Britain would play an important role in this process. Lemass

---

[20] Frank Sherwin, *Dáil Éireann Debates* 194, 5 April 1962, col. 1377.
[21] Lionel Booth, *Dáil Éireann Debates* 176, 7 July 1959, col. 644.
[22] Lionel Booth, *Dáil Éireann Debates* 176, 7 July 1959, col. 647.

(1959: 14) called upon London 'to encourage progress on these lines'. Furthermore, he wanted a British declaration to clarify that Britain would not have a selfish interest in preventing or discouraging Irish unity (Lemass, 1959: 3). Cosgrave's view was remarkably similar to Lemass's.[23] The leaders of the two largest political parties in the Republic – Fianna Fáil and Fine Gael – agreed on the basic parameters of the partition problem.

This process, borrowed from the European unification process, was particularly appealing to Fine Gael. Integration was expected to dramatically increase contacts and transactions across the Irish border. Eventually, this would render the border 'ridiculous', as James Tully (FG) put it.[24] Garret FitzGerald (FG), although a bit less over-optimistic than Tully, argued in a similar vein (Goodman, 1996: 212–13). James Dillon (FG), similarly to the *Irish Times* earlier, called for an integration scheme, modelled after the Rome Treaty, that would erode borders between the United Kingdom, Northern Ireland and the Republic.[25] Those identifying Britain as the sole culprit of partition disagreed with this expectation. In their view, Europe would not make any difference for Ireland's unification.[26]

This controversy about the diagnosis of and cure for the Irish Question undermined the taboo never to recognise the territorial status quo. Without questioning the taboo itself, it initiated the erosion of the reasoning on which it was built. Those arguing for healing as a prerequisite for unity undermined three central tenets of the irredentist argumentation that had been nearly unanimous from the 1930s to the 1950s. First, they forcefully rejected the assumption of the homogeneity of the Irish nation. While traditional republicanism emphasised the homogeneity of the ancient Irish nation and based the demand for the self-determination of all people living on the island of Ireland on the premise of this homogeneity, advocates of healing argued there were two fully legitimate traditions on the island, Nationalism and Unionism. Second, instead of framing the Irish Question in the traditional language of struggle and liberation, the new thinking rejected the notion that

[23] Liam Cosgrave, *Dáil Éireann Debates* 176, 2 July 1959, col. 504; Liam Cosgrave, *Dáil Éireann Debates* 194, 5 April 1962, cols. 1367–8.
[24] James Tully, *Dáil Éireann Debates* 194, 5 April 1962, cols. 1381–2.
[25] James Dillon, *Dáil Éireann Debates* 201, 3 April 1963, col. 1012.
[26] See, in particular, Brendan Corish, *Dáil Éireann Debates* 201, 3 April 1963, col. 987.

Britain was the sole culprit of partition. Instead it stressed the Unionists' legitimate fear of being forced into a united Ireland that would not leave room for their tradition. Third, the new approach was forward- and not backward-looking. Instead of emphasising Ireland's colonial past again and again, it borrowed from the European unification process to envision a process through which Ireland could be reunited.

During his years in office, Lemass attempted to pursue a policy towards Northern Ireland that was in agreement with his beliefs about diagnosis and cure of partition. His policy differed fundamentally from that of de Valera. He sought to normalise Anglo-Irish relations (Keogh, 2000). When speaking about the North, he was the first *Taoiseach* to use the term 'Northern Ireland' (Kennedy, 1999: 85), and he approached it as a neighbouring state, with which he sought to establish good neighbourly relations (Keogh, 1995: 287). In 1965, he travelled to Belfast to meet the Northern Irish Premier Captain O'Neill. This was the first meeting between the two Irish Prime Ministers since 1922. Northern Ireland had ceased to be a non-entity for the Republic.

In 1966, the Dáil followed Lemass's proposal to set up an all-party committee to review the Constitution. A year later, the committee published its final report. It made no recommendations to change Article 2. It continued to be self-evident to the actors involved that the Republic's *de jure* territory encompassed the entire island of Ireland. There was no advocacy to drop the irredentist claim. Aiming to lessen Unionist fear, however, the committee made a recommendation to change the wording of Article 3. The new Article should make clear that the Republic would not coerce Unionists into a unified Ireland. According to the recommendation, Article 3 should start with the following sentence: 'The Irish nation hereby proclaims its firm will that its territory be reunited in harmony and brotherly affection between all Irishmen' (quoted in Arnold, 1977: 1–2). However, Lemass's efforts to change the Constitution came to naught. The Dáil did not act upon the recommendations. Fianna Fáil deputies, in particular, were opposed to constitutional change.

New environment and half-hearted change

In 1968, the Troubles began. The violence in Northern Ireland was a shock to the Republic and triggered, facilitated by the changing repertoire of commonplaces, a debate in which even some of the most

cherished assumptions of Irishness were scrutinised. During this scrutiny, the Republic came to assure the Unionists that it would not seek
unification against the wishes of the majority in Northern Ireland
(principle of consent). Yet the Republic insisted on its irredentist
claim, even at the risk of the collapse of a comprehensive peace process
for Northern Ireland and the island of Ireland as a whole.

Initially, the Troubles made Anglo-Irish and North–South relations
on the island of Ireland reach an all-time low. In office as *Taoiseach*,
Jack Lynch (FF) warned in a 1969 speech that the Republic 'can no
longer stand idly by and see innocent people injured and perhaps worse'
(quoted in Keogh, 1995: 306). Lynch (1972) emphasised that action
would exclude the use of force. Yet there was no complete consensus on
this. Neil Blaney (FF) and Desmond Foley (FF) were the most outspoken
advocates for taking force at least into consideration.[27] Justin Keating
(LB) did not rule out the use of force either.[28] Blaney (quoted in Keogh,
1995: 304) put it like this:

[N]o-one has the right to assert that force is irrevocably out. No political party
or group at any time is entitled to pre-determine the right of the Irish people to
decide what course of action on this question may be justified in given
circumstances.

This advocacy earned Blaney the dubious reputation 'Bang Bang Blaney'
(Keogh, 1995: 305). Charles Haughey and Kevin Boland did not state
their views on violence in the Dáil but made clear within Fianna Fáil
decision-making circles that they were in favour of sending the
Republic's army into Derry and Newry in Northern Ireland (Walsh,
1986: 96). Yet the military option was rejected by a large majority in
the Dáil. Parliamentarians gave two different reasons against the use of
force. Some deputies gave a power-based explanation. Ireland would
stand no chance against the British military machinery.[29] For others,
not using force was a matter of principle. Among them was Jack Lynch.
Achieving unity by force would mean that Nationalists work themselves

[27] Desmond Foley, *Dáil Éireann Debates* 258, 4 February 1972, col. 1081. For
Blaney, see below.
[28] Justin Keating, *Dáil Éireann Debates* 252, 3 March 1971, col. 257. Keating
argued that force would be justifiable if necessary for defending the Nationalist
community in Northern Ireland.
[29] See, for example, Patrick Harte, *Dáil Éireann Debates* 258, 4 February 1972,
col. 1076.

'into the role of the overlord'. It would subjugate and tyrannise the Unionist minority. Yet this kind of rule would be an 'abomination'. It would contradict everything that Ireland stood for (Lynch, 1972: 4–9). Yet Lynch was not able to forge a consensus on the exclusive use of peaceful means in his own party. In 1970, he sacked two senior ministers, Neil Blaney and Charles Haughey. In what became known as the Arms Crisis, both were charged with conspiring to import arms and ammunition into the Republic and exporting these to the IRA in Northern Ireland. The trial ended with the acquittal of the two prominent politicians. In the next elections, both were re-elected. The republican wing of Fianna Fáil, led by Haughey, was alive and well. It continued to challenge Lynch.

When the dust of the onset of the Troubles had settled, however, many Nationalists, trying to understand the causes of the violence, started to reflect upon previously taken-for-granted beliefs. Foreshadowing more far-reaching change, the first tangible outcome of these reflections was the increasing support for the principle of consent. The principle qualified the right to national self-determination of the Irish nation as a whole. Not only ought the Irish nation as a whole to decide about whether unification should occur or not, but the majority of the people living in Northern Ireland would have to consent to this step as well. Thus, Unionists would not be forced into the unification of Ireland.

The argumentation for this normative idea combined two modes of reasoning. The appropriateness aspect focused on the norm not to use force in order to attain unification. Liam Cosgrave (FG) and Jack Lynch (FF), for example, interpreted the principle of consent as the logical corollary to the peaceful resolution of disputes norm. A unity other than by consent would be a unity by force and that was not worth having (Ivory, 1999: 92). The comparative dimension of the argumentation related the principle of consent to the *topoi* of the Idea of Europe, the Troubles and healing. Advocates argued that the Troubles taught the lesson that Unionists reacted with violence if threatened by Nationalists. Healing the rift between Unionists and Nationalists would only be possible if Nationalists made it clear that they would not coerce Unionists into a unified Ireland but that they would respect their tradition and seek only a unification by consent. Advocates such as Conor Cruise O'Brien and Garret FitzGerald combined the appropriateness aspect with the comparative dimension (Ivory, 1999: 89–90).

The appropriateness aspect of the argumentation was compatible with the old repertoire of commonplaces. Prompted by the Troubles, even some actors not yet embracing the new aspects of the repertoire of commonplaces qualified the previously cherished national self-determination norm with the normative idea about consent, which they linked to the *topos* of peaceful resolution of disputes. The comparative aspect, by contrast, was only made possible by the shifting repertoire of commonplaces. Only those actors embracing the Idea of Europe and inclusive identity argued forcefully for the principle of consent as one among several means of increasing contacts between North and South, overcoming fears and suspicions, and respecting different cultural traditions.

Among the Republic's three most influential political parties, the support for the principle of consent was greatest in the party that endorsed the new aspects of the repertoire of commonplaces with the most resolve and weakest in the one that rejected them most vigorously. By 1969, Fine Gael had embraced the principle of consent. Its founding manifesto of 1933 had already emphasised that Fine Gael 'stands for the voluntary reunion of the Irish nation as the paramount Constitutional issue in Irish politics' (quoted in Gallagher, 1985: 59). At the same time, however, the manifesto had contradicted the principle of consent by postulating, in the tradition of exclusive nationalism, the right to national self-determination for the Irish nation as a whole (Gallagher, 1985: 59). By the late 1960s, it was the principle of consent that qualified the principle of national self-determination and not vice versa. In the party's reading, the Republic aspired to the unification of Ireland, but it would not force Unionists into unity. Unification would only occur if a majority in Northern Ireland agreed to this step (Ivory, 1999: 89–90).

The principle of consent caused acrimonious debates within Labour. O'Brien, Barry Desmond, Brendan Corish and Michael O'Leary argued forcefully in favour of the principle of consent. Traditional nationalists, however, such as David Thornley and Seán Treacy were vigorously opposed to the principle. Their main target was O'Brien, because he advocated not only for the principle of consent but also for abandoning irredentism. In 1972, however, the party's annual conference put an end to the controversy. Labour adopted the principle of consent, but not O'Brien's more far-reaching demands for dropping the irredentist claim. The beleaguered O'Brien remained Labour's spokesperson on the North (Gallagher, 1982: 136–43).

Jack Lynch failed to win Fianna Fáil over to adopt the principle of consent. The principle was omnipresent in his speeches on Irish unity

(Lynch, 1972), but traditional republicanism in the party was too strong for the principle to be adopted. For the most part, Fianna Fáil chastised the principle of consent as a Unionist veto. Such a veto would contradict the right to national self-determination of the Irish nation. Its self-determination would be in the hands of the small Unionist minority, which was entirely unrepresentative of the Irish nation.[30]

The media were split in their attitude towards the principle of consent. By the late 1960s, the *Irish Independent* and the *Irish Times* consistently argued in favour of the principle of consent.[31] The *Irish Press*, by contrast, was opposed to it. This rejection was underpinned by a perception of the Northern Irish problem as a colonial issue and a reluctance to acknowledge the plurality of the Irish nation.[32]

The continuing dominance of the colonial episteme and exclusive nationalism hampered the advocates' attempts to change the majority view in favour of the principle of consent. Yet when the advocates were elected into power in 1973, the Republic's policies came to reflect the principle of consent. A Fine Gael-led government replaced Fianna Fáil and Cosgrave became *Taoiseach*. The same year, the Republic agreed to the principle of consent in what was envisaged to be an international treaty. In December 1973, representatives of the Unionists and Nationalists from Northern Ireland as well as the Republic and Britain met in Sunningdale to conclude their discussions of a comprehensive peace process. Fully in line with the position of his party, Cosgrave offered the principle of consent but he was not prepared to forgo irredentism as demanded by Brian Faulkner, the representative of the Ulster Unionist Party. Yet even without this concession, the parties concluded a comprehensive peace agreement. Within Northern Ireland, a power-sharing executive would make sure that the rights of the Nationalist minority were upheld. A Council of Ireland, modelled after the 1920 Government of Ireland Act and comprised of representatives from North and South, would deal with all-Ireland affairs. Finally,

---

[30] Blaney (IFF) was an outspoken critic of this 'Unionist veto'. See, for example, his argument that Britain should 'get the hell out of this country'. Neil Blaney, *Dáil Éireann Debates* 275, 6 November 1974, cols. 116–17.

[31] See, in particular, 'About Partition', *Irish Independent*, 4 March 1971, p. 12; 'Continuing Process', *Irish Times*, 27 February 1974, p. 11.

[32] 'A Plural Society', *Irish Press*, 10 March 1971, p. 10; 'Peace in Newry, or...', *Irish Press*, 5 February 1972, p. 10.

opaque wording on the constitutional status of Northern Ireland did not require the Republic to recognise British sovereignty over the North.

London did not encounter any problems in selling this deal to the British public. The public, weary of the Northern Ireland problem, hoped for a solution to the conflict. It was also no problem for Cosgrave to sell the peace agreement. There was a widespread hope that the Council of Ireland could be the nucleus of an all-Ireland government, and the Republic had not renounced its claim to Northern Ireland. Faulkner, however, faced a mission impossible. Unionists were outraged that the Republic refused to withdraw the irredentist claim. The Council of Ireland reinforced their suspicions. Unionists feared that the Council was a Trojan horse, which would be the beginning of the Nationalist take-over of power on the whole island (Herz, 1989: 194–201).

In January, the Ulster Unionist Council rejected Sunningdale. Faulkner resigned. In March, the Republic's Supreme Court, prompted by a lawsuit launched by Kevin Boland (IND) against the government,[33] confirmed that the opaque wording of the Communiqué did not violate the Constitution, because the government had recognised Northern Ireland merely *de facto* but not *de jure*. Following this decision, the peace processes unravelled further. The Northern Irish power-sharing executive resigned in May. The Sunningdale process had collapsed. The Sunningdale Agreement was never ratified as an international treaty. The Troubles remained unresolved. Britain reintroduced direct rule (Herz, 1989: 201–5).

New environment and innovative argumentation

The Troubles and the failures to resolve them were a shocking series of events that continued to provoke a fundamental debate about the Irish Question. At the same time, the increasing influence of the Idea of Europe and inclusive nationalism provided new clues for making sense of partition and violence. In the aftermath of the breakdown of

---

[33] Boland was a confidant of Eamon de Valera, as well as a long-term Minister of Defence, Social Welfare, and Local Government. He resigned when Lynch sacked Haughey and Blaney. After running for the Dáil as an independent in 1973, he founded his own party, Aontacht Éireann. The party's focus was on ending partition. Yet it failed to attract other prominent politicians and did not gain much electoral support.

Sunningdale, an advocacy formed that argued for more than the principle of consent. Advocates such as FitzGerald and O'Brien began to make their case for constitutional change. The Republic's legal claim to Northern Ireland ought to be replaced by an aspiration for unity.

FitzGerald started his explicit advocacy for recognising the territorial status quo after the failure of Sunningdale. Prior to the collapse of the peace agreement, his contributions on Northern Ireland had already hinted that it might be necessary to renounce the irredentist claim. In 1969, with the beginning of the Troubles very much on his mind, FitzGerald started to actively engage in Fine Gael's Northern Ireland policy. He wrote a draft policy statement that circulated within the party. The statement postulated that the Republic, by changing its Constitution, ought to develop a more inclusive Irishness that, instead of threatening them, would attract Unionists by safeguarding their rights and traditions. When the Sunningdale process collapsed and the Troubles continued, FitzGerald made explicit what this reasoning meant for the claim to the North. If the South wanted to make a meaningful contribution to reducing Unionist fear, breaking out of the cycle of violence in the North and embarking on a process that could, modelled after the European unification process, culminate in the unification of North and South, Dublin would have to renounce its claim of legal right to Northern Ireland (FitzGerald, 1991b: 222–3).

O'Brien's advocacy for abandoning the territorial claim began prior to the collapse of Sunningdale. During the negotiation stage, he warned that Faulkner might not be able to sell the Sunningdale accord to his Unionist constituencies unless the Republic revoked its territorial claim to the North (O'Brien, 1999: 348–51). Yet even independently of this problem, O'Brien postulated that the Republic ought to drop its irredentist claim. His advocacy for forgoing irredentism was always connected to his sharp criticism of exclusive nationalism, as formulated in his 1972 book *States of Ireland*.[34] Exclusive nationalism would have to be replaced by an inclusive variant. The claim of legal right to the North symbolised for O'Brien the opposite of inclusivity: namely the Nationalists' disrespect for the Unionist tradition and their resolve to impose their tradition. In O'Brien's view, this attempted imposition threatened Unionists, fuelled the violence in the North, and made a unification of North and South impossible (O'Brien, 1972).

---

[34] The book is discussed in detail in the previous chapter.

Translated into the language of argumentation analysis, FitzGerald and O'Brien employed two modes of reasoning: abstract and comparative. There was an abstract element in FitzGerald's reasoning, linking the *topoi* of longing for unity and the Idea of Europe to forgoing irredentism. Unity could only come about through a process resembling European unification. Contacts and co-operation between North and South would increase. Over time, the border would become meaningless and this would offer a chance for unification. In order to start the evolution of such a process, however, the Republic would have to drop the claim of legal right to Northern Ireland.

The *topoi* of comparative reasoning, employed by FitzGerald and O'Brien, were the Idea of Europe, partition and the Troubles. Seen through the Idea of Europe, a fundamental lesson had to be learnt from Irish history: in the twentieth century, the majority (Nationalists) had tried to impose its conception of Irishness onto the minority (Unionists). As a consequence, the minority felt threatened. This fear entrenched partition and fuelled violence in the North. Taking this historical lesson seriously meant redefining Irishness in a more inclusive manner and dropping the irredentist claim. This would assure Unionists that they would not be forced into the Republic, lessen their fears, and uphold a chance for unification by consent in the future.

FitzGerald and O'Brien succeeded in establishing an advocacy network among a small group of Dáil deputies. Michael O'Leary (LB), Frank Carter (FG) and Richard Burke (FG) echoed their reasoning in the Dáil. Reflecting *ex post facto* on Sunningdale, O'Brien believed that Labour would have supported a referendum on changing Articles 2 and 3 of the Constitution from a legal claim to an aspiration in 1973 (O'Brien, 1999: 348). Burke even went beyond FitzGerald's and O'Brien's argumentation by making a case for erasing the vision of a united Ireland from the Constitution completely. In his view, the claim of Articles 2 and 3 of the Constitution should not even be reformulated into an aspiration for unity.[35]

Burke's argument shows the salience of comparative reasoning very clearly: the *topoi* of Burke's comparative reasoning were the 1922 Irish

---

[35] Michael O'Leary, *Dáil Éireann Debates* 260, 18 April 1972, cols. 477–93; Conor Cruise O'Brien, *Dáil Éireann Debates* 265, 8 May 1973, col. 597; Frank Carter, *Dáil Éireann Debates* 275, 6 November 1974, col. 1185. Especially FitzGerald (1972) called for a comprehensive revision of the Constitution.

Free State Constitution, the 1937 Constitution of the Republic, the Troubles and the Idea of Europe. The 1922 Constitution, which did not contain a claim of legal right to the North, respected the diversity of the Irish nation. Nationalists did not attempt to force Unionists into a Celtic and Catholic Ireland. De Valera's 1937 Constitution, by contrast, was deeply sectarian. Partition and the Troubles were the price that the Irish had to pay for it.[36]

The advocacy for dropping the irredentist claim started at a time when the new aspects of the repertoire of commonplaces underpinning this advocacy were still far from being widely accepted. Initially, this rendered the advocacy rather ineffective. Given the continued salience of the colonial episteme, exclusive nationalism and its constituting norms, the advocacy to forgo irredentism was to most people implausible at best and a betrayal at worst.

The counter-advocacy, based on appropriateness and comparative reasoning, drew upon the old repertoire of commonplaces. The appropriateness aspect connected the defence of irredentism to the *topos* of national self-determination. The Irish nation as a whole had the right to national self-determination. This right was inalienable. Britain illegally and unjustly occupied a part of Irish territory contrary to the will of the Irish people. Additionally, the comparative dimension linked the *topoi* of partition and Troubles to the colonial episteme. Partition was caused by Britain. Violence in the North was a function of partition. A deeply unjust territorial status quo had given rise to the Troubles. It was time for Unionist and British decision-makers to comprehend that partition was to blame for violence, and that only unification could bring stability to the North. Thus, it was not the Republic that had to learn a lesson from history, but the United Kingdom. British imperialism was to blame for partition and violence and not Irish Republicanism. In the Dáil, these counter-arguments against recognition were made across party lines, most forcefully by Patrick Harte (FG), Jack Lynch (FF), Liam Cosgrave (FG), Desmond Foley (FF), Seán Moore (FF) and Neil Blaney (FF).[37]

---

[36] Richard Burke, *Dáil Éireann Debates* 252, 3 March 1971, cols. 249–50.

[37] Patrick Harte, *Dáil Éireann Debates* 252, 9 March 1971, col. 544; Jack Lynch, *Dáil Éireann Debates* 256, 20 October 1971, cols. 5–19; Liam Cosgrave, *Dáil Éireann Debates* 258, 1 February 1972, cols. 826–8; Desmond Foley, *Dáil Éireann Debates* 258, 4 February 1972, cols. 1079–88; Seán Moore, *Dáil Éireann Debates* 275, 6 November 1974, col. 1102; Neil Blaney, *Dáil Éireann Debates* 275, 6 November 1974, cols. 1109–10.

An embittered debate between the advocates for dropping the legal claim from the Constitution and the defenders of the Constitution developed. For ardent traditionalists, recognition of the territorial status quo was treason. As Blaney alleged, recognition would be 'a blatant betrayal of the half million people in the Six Counties who have never abandoned the claim their fathers established, as did our fathers ... to be part of a free and independent Ireland'.[38] Foley singled out FitzGerald as a traitor: 'Deputy FitzGerald's contribution was similar to speeches we have heard from his predecessors, from a type of individual who would promote British propaganda and British Imperialism in this country.' Foley vowed to 'eradicate' this 'type of attitude'.[39]

The advocates for constitutional change countered these allegations by blaming orthodox Nationalists for the lack of progress in resolving the conflict in the North and in bringing about unification. They alleged that traditional Nationalists had learnt nothing from history. Instead of trying to heal divisions by making urgently needed constitutional changes and supporting a new policy towards Northern Ireland, they would exacerbate an already precarious situation with their belligerent rhetoric.[40]

In the late 1960s and early 1970s, the radical opponents of constitutional change enjoyed a considerable amount of public support. Prior to Blaney's dismissal during the Arms Crisis, dealt with in the previous chapter, the public considered him to be the best Fianna Fáil candidate for the next general elections. Thirty-seven per cent regarded him as the best of four possible candidates.[41]

Persistent irredentism in the midst of the departure from the old

Between the mid-1970s and the mid-1980s, the advocacy for abandoning irredentism remained confined to small advocacy networks. Albeit waning, the persistent dominance of the colonial episteme and

---

[38] Neil Blaney, *Dáil Éireann Debates* 270, 26 February 1974, col. 1712.
[39] Desmond Foley, *Dáil Éireann Debates* 258, 4 February 1972, cols. 1079–80.
[40] See, for example, Garret FitzGerald, *Dáil Éireann Debates* 270, 26 February 1974, cols. 1699–1705; Conor Cruise O'Brien, *Dáil Éireann Debates* 270, 26 February 1974, cols. 1682–3; Liam Cosgrave, *Dáil Éireann Debates* 270, 26 February 1974, cols. 1533–44.
[41] The IMS survey (code name: JN:1452 RJA/mec) was carried out on 25 May 1970.

exclusive nationalism still hampered the advocacy's success. Yet during FitzGerald's tenure as *Taoiseach*, the new thinking underpinning the advocacy had repercussions for the Republic's Northern Ireland policies.

Fianna Fáil radicalised its views on Northern Ireland after the collapse of the Sunningdale process. The party's radical republican wing around Haughey gained the upper hand over reformist members such as Lynch. In 1975, Michael O'Kennedy drafted a statement on the part of the Fianna Fáil caucus in the Dáil that demanded British withdrawal from Northern Ireland. Against the wishes of Lynch, the document became official Fianna Fáil policy (Herz, 1989: 69). In 1979, the reformers within the party were further weakened when Haughey replaced Lynch as chairman of Fianna Fáil and *Taoiseach*. In his first speech as chairman at an *Ard Fheis* (annual party convention), Haughey reiterated the call for British withdrawal.

He buttressed this claim with the orthodox appropriateness and comparative reasoning. Haughey claimed that British colonialism violated the Irish right to national self-determination. Furthermore, he maintained that the Troubles were a logical consequence of the British occupation of Northern Ireland. Britain had carved out an artificial polity. According to Haughey (1986a [1980]: 334), this artificiality made violence inevitable: '[T]he very entity itself is artificial and has been artificially sustained. In these conditions, violence and repression were inevitable.' Haughey repeated his call for British withdrawal at the 1983 *Ard Fheis*, and earned minutes of standing ovation for it from his party (Arnold, 1993: 217).

It came as no surprise that Haughey, when he became *Taoiseach* in 1979, attempted to initiate bilateral talks with Britain about partition. Following his understanding of the Irish Question as a colonial issue, Haughey thought that the key to unity lay in London and not in Belfast. Given his earlier calls for British withdrawal, however, it was surprising to many observers that he was successful in starting negotiations with Margaret Thatcher about Ireland. The first meeting between Haughey and Thatcher took place in May 1980. The joint Communiqué emphasised the 'unique relationship' between Britain and the Republic, and the two governments agreed to hold regular summit meetings and meetings at the ministerial level. The second meeting occurred in December 1980. There was agreement to set up the Joint Studies. These were designed to explore a bilateral institutional arrangement that would allow for a significant increase in co-operation between the United Kingdom and Ireland.

Haughey, however, oversold this success. He claimed in interviews that these new institutional arrangements could be a stepping stone towards unity. These far-reaching conclusions angered Thatcher. The constitutional status of Northern Ireland was never part of the discussions (Herz, 1989: 215–17). The relationship between Haughey and Thatcher was eventually damaged beyond repair when Haughey pursued a neutral stance during the Falklands/Islas Malvinas War.

FitzGerald defeated Haughey in the 1981 elections and succeeded him as *Taoiseach*. His argumentation about Irish unity and irredentism did not change over time. Partition and violence in Northern Ireland were due to Unionist fear of losing their identity. They were a beleaguered community. Nationalists had to attempt to take this fear away, in order to resolve the dispute in Northern Ireland and the dispute between North and South. This required changing the legal claim to Northern Ireland into an aspiration. This comparative reasoning, taking the partition and the Troubles as *topoi* seen through the diversity aspect of the Idea of Europe, was complemented by abstract reasoning. In FitzGerald's view, the European unification process showed how Irish unity could evolve over time. An increasing web of co-operation and integration could eventually culminate in the unification of Ireland. This process, however, could only succeed if the Irish Constitution became less sectarian. Among other things, the irredentist claim would have to be withdrawn.[42]

FitzGerald, however, was well aware of the problem that there was no majority for dropping the territorial claim. The constitutional change that he envisaged would have required a broad majority. Supported by his Fine Gael and Labour, therefore, he focused on other aspects of making Irishness more inclusive. In 1983, he invited all influential Nationalist political parties of North and South, excluding Sinn Féin, to the New Ireland Forum. All parties, except for the Workers' Party, accepted the invitation. The title of the conference was paradigmatic for its purpose as understood by FitzGerald. Irish nationalism would have to be refounded. A new, inclusive idea of Ireland should replace the old, exclusive one. Only this would make it possible to reach the goal that all Nationalists pursued: Ireland's unity.

---

[42] For a very clear-cut argumentation of these two aspects see Garret FitzGerald, *Dáil Éireann Debates* 321, 29 May 1980, cols. 1068–82 as well as Garret FitzGerald, *Dáil Éireann Debates* 325, 29 May 1980, cols. 976–82.

The majority of representatives shared FitzGerald's view. There was a divide between representatives from Fine Gael, Labour and Northern Ireland's Social Democratic and Labour Party (SDLP) on the one hand and Fianna Fáil on the other. As John Hume, chairman of the SDLP, put it, the Forum should not be a 'revival mission' of exclusive nationalism. On the contrary, it should prepare the way for a new society that broke with 'some of our most cherished assumptions' (Kearney, 1988: 8). Fianna Fáil, led by Haughey, however, was determined vigorously to defend these assumptions.

The Forum did not succeed in bridging the divide. Exclusive and inclusive Nationalists remained worlds apart. On several occasions, it seemed that no compromise could be reached on a final report. There were the two usual bones of contention: diagnosis of and cure for partition. Fianna Fáil insisted that Britain was the cause of partition, and unity would only be attained if Britain withdrew from Northern Ireland. Fine Gael, Labour and the SDLP, by contrast, argued that partition was a function of fear and suspicion among the Irish and could only be overcome by reducing this fear. This would require nothing less than a redefinition of Irishness. It ought to become an identity that embraced the diversity on the island of Ireland. This contention between exclusive and inclusive nationalism also had repercussions for envisioning the process of Irish unification. Haughey wanted a unitary Irish state, whereas FitzGerald's preferred option was a joint authority of the Republic and Britain over Northern Ireland. FitzGerald thought that this was the only realistic option for the time being and believed that it could be the beginning of a more far-reaching change of the constitutional status of Northern Ireland.

In 1984, the parties reached a compromise that demanded painful concessions from all of them. Since the different positions were not easily combined, the New Ireland Forum Report is a remarkably incoherent document. It combined Haughey's reasoning about the causes of partition with FitzGerald's view on how unity could be achieved and endorsed Haughey's preference of a unitary state. The inconsistencies of the New Ireland Forum Report mirrored the deep rift between exclusive and inclusive variants of Irish nationalism instead of overcoming it.

FitzGerald, however, kept on pushing his agenda for the 'New Irelanders', as he had put it in the early 1970s. When he succeeded Haughey as *Taoiseach* in 1981 and again in 1982, FitzGerald built on the bilateral negotiations – in particular the Joint Studies – with Britain that

Haughey had started. The outcome of this process was the Anglo-Irish Agreement. The accord, signed in Hillsborough in 1985, echoed the passages of the Forum Report that were authored by Fine Gael and Labour and excluded those components that were written by Fianna Fáil. Two passages in the Preamble read almost as paraphrases. First, there was an emphasis on the European dimension and Anglo-Irish relations within it. Britain and the Republic wished 'further to develop the unique relationship between their peoples and the close co-operation between their countries as friendly neighbours and as partners in the European Community' (Anglo-Irish Agreement, 1985). Second, the Preamble emphasised that two communities with different identities and aspirations lived on the island of Ireland. Peace could only come about if each community respected the identity and aspirations of the other (Anglo-Irish Agreement, 1985).

The Agreement provided for an Intergovernmental Conference, including a permanent secretariat. Through this institution, the Republic had the right to put forward proposals on the administration of Northern Ireland to the British government. Although this fell short of joint authority over Northern Ireland, the Intergovernmental Conference constituted a significant break from the past. Whereas Britain had previously often criticised the Republic for interfering with its domestic affairs, it agreed in the Hillsborough Agreement to institutionalise this interference.

With regard to the irredentist claim, however, the Agreement did not make any progress. Forgoing irredentism required a referendum on Articles 2 and 3 of the Constitution. In many ways, FitzGerald's constitutional crusade, aimed at making Irishness more inclusive, was rather daring. In 1986, for example, he risked a referendum on the legalisation of divorce, which he lost. Yet FitzGerald did not risk a referendum on the irredentist claim in the mid-1980s. It seemed too obvious to him that such a referendum would not be carried. During the negotiations on the Anglo-Irish Agreement, FitzGerald explained to Thatcher that he would take the risk of holding a referendum to change Articles 2 and 3 if he could show to the Irish public a more comprehensive peace agreement with a stronger Irish component such as joint authority over Northern Ireland. Under these circumstances he perceived a chance of a referendum against irredentism succeeding.[43] Thatcher, however, vehemently and

---

[43] Interview with Garret FitzGerald, Dublin, 24 June 2003. He did not explicitly mention joint authority. This is my interpretation.

publicly rejected such far-reaching changes (O'Clery, 1999: 178). Hence, the Hillsborough Agreement phrased the constitutional status of Northern Ireland as vaguely as the Sunningdale Communiqué.

The treaty caused a passionate debate in the Dáil. Fine Gael and Labour – in a more qualified way also the Workers' Party – considered the Hillsborough Agreement an important breakthrough for Anglo-Irish relations and, more importantly, for inter-Irish relations. FitzGerald emphasised the importance of the principle of consent as well as respect for the aspirations of the Nationalist and the Unionist communities on the island. He considered the principle of consent and respect for Unionist aspirations an important step towards the reduction of Unionist fear.

Fianna Fáil rejected the accord, because the party interpreted it as a breach of Articles 2 and 3 of the Constitution. Yet Fianna Fáil's reaction was not completely monolithic. Mary Harney voted in favour of the accord. Consequently, she was expelled from the party and co-founded a new party, the Progressive Democrats (PD). Apart from this exception, there was a qualified and an unqualified rejection of the Hillsborough Agreement. Bertie Ahern criticised the constitutional aspect, but also maintained that there were positive aspects that would facilitate the reconciliation of Nationalists and Unionists.[44] Haughey, by contrast, completely rejected the Agreement. In addition to his conviction that the treaty constituted a breach of Articles 2 and 3, he argued against the principle of consent. If Britain withdrew, he postulated, Ireland would be unified, independently of the wishes of the Unionists.[45] Gerard Collins (FF), Brian Lenihan (FF) and Michael O'Kennedy (FF) also rejected the agreement in its entirety.[46] Blaney (IFF) went so far as to call for the prosecution of those who were involved in negotiating the Hillsborough Agreement. Delegates from other parties responded to these attacks with vehement criticism. John Kelly (FG) and Alan Shatter (FG) accused Fianna Fáil of being the key obstacle to improving relations between the Unionist and the

---

[44] Bertie Ahern, *Dáil Éireann Debates* 361, 20 November 1985, cols. 2826–67.
[45] Charles Haughey, *Dáil Éireann Debates* 361, 19 November 1985, cols. 2584–2659.
[46] Gerard Collins, *Dáil Éireann Debates* 361, 19 November 1985, cols. 2612–15; Brian Lenihan, *Dáil Éireann Debates* 361, 21 November 1985, cols. 3113–20; Michael O'Kennedy, *Dáil Éireann Debates* 361, 20 November 1985, cols. 2726–7.

Nationalist traditions on the island.[47] Desmond O'Malley (PD) compared Fianna Fáil to 'a fundamentalist sect'.[48]

Throughout these debates, the *Irish Independent* and the *Irish Times* sided with Fine Gael and Labour, whereas the *Irish Press* supported Fianna Fáil's position. The *Irish Independent* asserted that it was important to uphold the aspiration for unity. Yet a claim of legal right would sustain Unionist fear, and, therefore, would be counter-productive for the goal of unity.[49] The *Irish Times* argued in a similar vein and combined it with strong criticism against Fianna Fáil.[50]

While these quarrels resembled the heated controversies about Sunningdale to some extent, the mid-1980s was clearly not the early 1970s. Fianna Fáil had become an increasingly isolated guardian of the traditional view on Northern Ireland. Most other political parties criticised Fianna Fáil heavily. Even within Fianna Fáil, the resistance against the new started to crumble. Furthermore, Fianna Fáil was out of step with public opinion. As figure 6.1 shows, the public overwhelmingly approved of the Anglo-Irish Agreement: 69 per cent of the Republic's populace was in favour of the treaty. Only 20 per cent opposed it.[51] Fifty-six per cent thought that it would improve relations between the Republic and Northern Ireland, while only 34 per cent disagreed.[52] A majority expected the treaty to improve the life of Nationalists and the overall situation in Northern Ireland.[53] Finally, more than two-thirds

---

[47] John Kelly, *Dáil Éireann Debates* 361, 19 November 1985, cols. 2603–6; Alan Shatter, *Dáil Éireann Debates* 361, 21 November 1985, cols. 2971–80.

[48] Desmond O'Malley, *Dáil Éireann Debates* 361, 21 November 1985, col. 2986.

[49] 'Debate starts', *Irish Independent*, 20 November 1985, p. 12; 'Anglo-Irish Agreement', *Irish Independent*, 21 November 1985, p. 7; 'Approved', *Irish Independent*, 22 November 1985, p. 8; 'Poll', *Irish Independent*, 23 November 1985, p. 8.

[50] 'Conciliation', *Irish Times*, 22 November 1985, p. 9.

[51] MRBI survey, 3–4 February 1986 (MRBI/3420/86). The exact wording was as follows: 'As you are probably aware, an Agreement was signed between the Irish and the British Governments, regarding Northern Ireland. Do you approve or disapprove of the Irish Government signing this Agreement?'

[52] MRBI survey, 3–4 February 1986 (MRBI/3420/86). 'Do you think that this Agreement will: Promote better relations between Northern Ireland and the Republic of Ireland?'

[53] MRBI survey, 19–20 November 1986 (MRBI/3410/85). 'Do you think that this Agreement will improve life for the Nationalists/Catholics in Northern Ireland?' MRBI survey, 3–4 February 1986 (MRBI/3420/86). 'Do you think that this Agreement will: Promote better relations between the two communities in Northern Ireland?

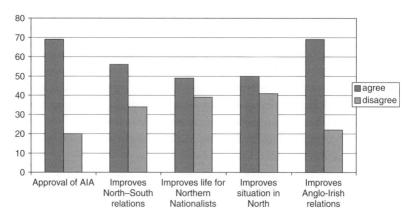

Figure 6.1 Approval of Anglo-Irish Agreement
Sources: MRBI, 3–4 February 1986; MRBI, 19–20 November 1986

thought that the Agreement would improve Anglo-Irish relations.[54] These results correspond to the findings of the previous chapter. From the mid-1980s onwards, exclusive nationalism increasingly failed to resonate with the public, and Fianna Fáil's objections to the Anglo-Irish Agreement were based on exclusive nationalism.

Persuasive argumentation

From the late 1980s onwards, the advocacy for the recognition of the territorial status quo increasingly resonated with a broader audience. Fianna Fáil was beleaguered in the Dáil for continuing to resist constitutional change. The *Irish Times* and *Irish Independent* criticised the party harshly for holding onto the irredentist claim. Most importantly, argumentation in favour of dropping the irredentist claim came to persuade the public. From 1992 onwards, there was a majority for recognising the territorial status quo.

With the new repertoire of commonplaces establishing its hegemony over the old one, FitzGerald's reputation changed markedly. He became a very popular and virtually untouchable figure by the time he left politics in 1992. Having adopted the new outlook on Northern Ireland decades before most other actors, FitzGerald provided

---

[54] MRBI survey, 3–4 February 1986 (MRBI/3420/86). 'Do you think that this Agreement will: Promote better relations between Ireland and Britain?'

much-needed orientation and guidance for those who later came to adopt the new tools to understand the Irish Question. None of his political heirs, such as Peter Barry and John Bruton, ever came close to FitzGerald's popularity, although they echoed his reasoning. To this very day, traditional Nationalists are very unsettled by his popularity. Joe Keenan (2006), for example, angrily ridicules FitzGerald's image as the 'great', the 'good' and the 'wise'. Deservedly earned or not, this image greatly facilitated the advocacy for recognition. FitzGerald – much more so than O'Brien – was the public face of the advocacy.

By the late 1980s, the argumentation against Articles 2 and 3 became more nuanced. Three modes of reasoning may be distinguished. First, advocates linked the advocated territorial status quo norm to already institutionalised norms. They buttressed these established norms by invoking key aspects of the inclusive identity narrative. The irredentist claim was considered 'un-European' and, therefore, inappropriate. According to this view, the Republic, being a member of the European Community and a signatory to the 1975 Helsinki Final Act, ought not to claim territory from another state.[55] Furthermore, the advocated normative idea was related to the norm of peaceful resolution of disputes. Abandoning irredentism was seen as a necessary demarcation from the IRA's violent pursuit of Irish unity. The irredentist claim became associated with an aggressive nationalism with which the overwhelming majority of Southern Nationalists wanted nothing to do. Irredentism was portrayed as a constitutive element of an aggressive nationalism.[56]

Second, the comparative reasoning, originating with FitzGerald and O'Brien in the early 1970s, continued to be employed by advocates for constitutional change. Partition and violence were still seen as historical lessons on the repercussions of Unionist fear. Only by reducing this fear and respecting Unionist identity could the Republic make a contribution to peace in Northern Ireland and create a chance for

---

[55] This argument was made, in particular, by Fine Gael deputies: John Bruton, *Dáil Éireann Debates* 403, 28 November 1990, col. 471; Peter Barry, *Dáil Éireann Debates* 404, 18 December 1990, col. 71.

[56] John Murphy, *Seanad Éireann* 124, 16 November 1988, col. 720; Shane Ross, *Seanad Éireann* 384, 16 November 1988, col. 721; David Norris, *Seanad Éireann* 124, 16 November 1988, col. 935; Proinsias De Rossa, *Dáil Éireann Debates* 429, 1 April 1993, cols. 67–8; Mary Harney, *Dáil Éireann Debates* 437, 17 December 1993, col. 1259; Michael McDowell, *Dáil Éireann Debates* 437, 17 December 1993, col. 1274.

unification. Forgoing irredentism continued to be seen as an important step towards reducing fear.[57]

Third, the abstract reasoning, powerfully introduced by FitzGerald in the early 1970s, continued to be used as an argument against the irredentist claim. According to the adherents of this argumentation, there was a chance for unification in the future through increasing contacts and co-operation. The European unification process showed the possibility of overcoming borders through increasing contacts. In order for such a process to be initiated on the island of Ireland, however, it would be essential to stop threatening Unionists with the annexation of Northern Ireland. Thus, the irredentist claim would have to be withdrawn.[58]

The advocates vilified Fianna Fáil's opposing stance in harsh words. For the *Irish Independent*, irredentism was a remnant of the old nationalism that was partly responsible for partition and violence. Fianna Fáil was criticised severely for holding onto the territorial claim.[59] The *Irish Times* argued in a similar vein. For the sake of peace on the island, the demise of old nationalism had to be followed by constitutional change, including a change of Articles 2 and 3. *Taoiseach* Albert Reynolds (FF) was criticised for defending the Constitution. The latter, in its unamended form, was seen as facilitator of violence:

Worse, in a speech, parts of which were more evidently addressed to *Fianna Fáil* backbenchers than to the burning problem on the floor of the *Dáil* [Articles 2 and 3, MK], he claimed that the 1937 Constitution 'took the gun out of politics on this side of the Border' and declared that 'all Irish people now want another framework that will take the bomb and bullet out of the politics of the entire island'. The claim for the Constitution is unbearably complacent and historically inaccurate.[60]

---

[57] Bruce Arnold, 'The Fianna Fail Dilemma', *Irish Independent*, 3 April 1993, p. 10; 'Still Waiting for Leadership', *Irish Times*, 2 April 1993, p. 13. John Murphy, *Seanad Éireann* 124, 16 November 1988, cols. 720–1; John Bruton, *Dáil Éireann Debates* 403, 28 November 1990, col. 471; Peter Barry, *Dáil Éireann Debates* 404, 18 December 1990, col. 71; Michael McDowell, *Dáil Éireann Debates* 429, 1 April 1993, col. 52.

[58] With regard to the central place of the European unification process in his thinking, John Bruton was the political heir of FitzGerald: John Bruton, *Dáil Éireann Debates* 403, 28 November 1990, cols. 471–4; John Bruton, *Dáil Éireann Debates* 437, 17 December 1993, cols. 1243–56. Yet others also argued in a similar vein. See, for example, Proinsias De Rossa, *Dáil Éireann Debates* 437, 17 December 1993, col. 1287.

[59] Bruce Arnold, 'The Fianna Fáil Dilemma', *Irish Independent*, 3 April 1993, p. 10.
[60] 'Still Waiting for Leadership', *Irish Times*, 2 April 1993, p. 13.

Table 6.1 *Public opinion on amending Articles 2 and 3*

	1981	1992	1993	1995
Support	35	41	39	60
Oppose	46	39	32	20
Don't know	17	20	29	20

Public opinion data show that the argumentation for constitutional change began to resonate with the public in the early 1990s. There is a plethora of public opinion data on the amendment of Articles 2 and 3. Most of the questions, unfortunately, are difficult to compare with one another because of considerable differences in their wording. Nevertheless, the comparable opinion polls show that a highly significant shift occurred in 1992. Table 6.1 depicts the results of opinion polls on changing (as opposed to simply omitting) Articles 2 and 3 from a territorial claim to an aspiration for unity, and includes only opinion polls that did not connect the constitutional question to the outcome of the negotiations for a comprehensive peace settlement for Northern Ireland, which had started in the early 1990s.

In 1981, almost half of the populace was opposed to amending the Constitution.[61] In 1992, by contrast, there was a majority in favour of amendment for the first time: 41 per cent wished the territorial claim to be replaced by an aspiration for unity, whereas 39 per cent rejected this option.[62] In 1993, the margin between those in favour of amendment and those against increased to 7 per cent: 39 per cent preferred amendment while 32 per cent were opposed.[63] By 1995, the support for

---

[61] IMS survey, 14–15 October 1981 (j.8041); wording: 'The Irish Constitution claims jurisdiction over the whole of this island, North and South. It has been suggested that this might be changed to drop the claim to jurisdiction over Northern Ireland. Would you approve or disapprove of such a change?'

[62] MRBI survey, 15–24 September 1992 (MRBI/4080/92); wording: 'Articles 2&3 of the Constitution which claim jurisdiction over all of Ireland are being discussed by the Irish and British Governments and the Northern Parties. Do you think the claim in Articles 2&3 should be retained, or should the claim be changed to an aspiration?'

[63] IMS survey, 1–8 April 1993 (CMC/1d/j.3S125); wording: 'It has been suggested that Articles 2 and 3 of our Constitution should be amended to confirm our acceptance that there will be no change to the existing status of Northern Ireland except by peaceful means and with the consent of the majority of Northern

amendment had increased by more than 20 per cent: 60 per cent opted for Articles 2 and 3 expressing an aspiration, while only 20 per cent wanted to retain the *de jure* claim.[64]

Compromise

The controversies about recognition in the 1990s differed from the debates of the 1970s and 1980s in an important way. Most opponents shared the repertoire of commonplaces from which the advocates picked their *topoi*. They merely linked the shared repertoire to the issue of recognition in different ways but no longer lived in different lifeworlds. This made it possible for opponents such as Fianna Fáil to compromise on their position in order to escape the mounting costs that the opposition of the newly established majority view entailed.

A small number of defenders of the irredentist claim continued to invoke *topoi* that did not appear in the argumentation of the advocates for constitutional change. John O'Donoghue (FF) cautioned that abandoning the claim would 'alienate' Northern Nationalists and this would cause more rather than less violence.[65] Hugh Conaghan (FF) asserted that only the withdrawal of Britain could lead to unification.[66] Neil Blaney (IFF) fully agreed with this, hailing it as the 'voice of reason'.[67] These arguments, however, still fully based on the colonial episteme and exclusive nationalism, were exceptions. In the Dáil, they were only invoked by Independent Fianna Fáil and Fianna Fáil's radical republican wing.

For the most part, Fianna Fáil and other counter-advocates based their argumentation on the same *topoi* as the advocacy for recognition: the Idea of Europe, inclusive identity, the European territorial status quo norm, and the norm of peaceful resolution of disputes. There was absolutely no question for Fianna Fáil – and there had been none since de Valera banned the IRA – that the IRA's version of Irish nationalism

Ireland. Do you think Articles 2 and 3 should be left as they are, or do you think they should be amended as outlined?'
[64] MRBI survey, 20–22 May 1995 (MRBI/4290/95); wording: 'Should or should not the following provisions be put into the a new or amended constitution? Change of Articles 2 and 3 from a territorial claim on NI to an aspiration of unity?'
[65] John O'Donoghue, *Dáil Éireann Debates* 437, 17 December 1993, col. 1294.
[66] Hugh Conaghan, *Dáil Éireann Debates* 384, 16 November 1988, cols. 906–7; Neil Blaney, *Dáil Éireann Debates* 384, 16 November 1988, col. 912.
[67] Neil Blaney, *Dáil Éireann Debates* 384, 16 November 1988, col. 912.

was to be rejected. When the party was accused of sympathising with the IRA, it reacted with outrage. Fianna Fáil was committed to the norm of peaceful resolution of disputes.[68] Furthermore, Fianna Fáil also fully embraced the Republic's European identity trait and its constituting norms. It was at pains to show that Articles 2 and 3 did not violate the Helsinki Final Act.[69]

The mainstream of Fianna Fáil followed the advocates' comparative and abstract reasoning without, however, linking it to a need to forgo irredentism. Ahern and Reynolds employed in their Dáil speeches inclusive identity representations, including the need for healing, and the respect of Unionist traditions. They spoke about the need to learn the lessons of history and make Irishness more inclusive. They invoked the Idea of Europe and understood the European unification process as a shining example after which the Irish unification process ought to be modelled. To them, however, there was no connection between these lines of reasoning and a withdrawal of the irredentist claim.[70] The *Irish Press* supported Ahern's and Reynolds's stance.[71]

Those actors, such as Ahern and Reynolds, whose repertoire of commonplaces included the *topoi* invoked by the advocates for recognition increasingly bent under the mounting pressure of public opinion. The *Irish Press*, once established by de Valera as the guardian of exclusive nationalism, succumbed to the pressure a year after public opinion had started to favour recognition. It came to endorse recognition. Its justification for doing so is interesting. The *Irish Press* never joined the advocacy. Instead of affirming the advocates' argumentation, the newspaper merely stated that there was 'a sense of urgency to match the public mood'.[72] Thus, the editors were not persuaded by the advocates. They were swayed by the costs of the counter-advocacy.

The pressure of public opinion alone was not sufficient to make Fianna Fáil forgo its opposition. It was not prepared completely to

---

[68] See, for example, the encounter between Brendan McGahon (FG) and Michael O'Kennedy (FF), *Dáil Éireann Debates* 367, 30 May 1986, col. 836.
[69] Albert Reynolds, *Dáil Éireann Debates* 403, 28 November 1990, col. 465.
[70] Bertie Ahern, *Dáil Éireann Debates* 361, 20 November 1985, cols. 2856–63; Albert Reynolds, *Dáil Éireann Debates* 384, 16 November 1988, col. 769.
[71] 'Anglo-Irish Relations', *Irish Press*, 15 March 1990, p. 8; untitled, *Irish Press*, 16 December 1993, p. 8; untitled, *Irish Press*, 18 December 1993, p. 8; untitled, *Irish Press*, 23 February 1995, p. 10; untitled, *Irish Press*, 23 February 1995, p. 10. By 1995, Unionists were seen as friends: untitled, *Irish Press*, 24 February 1995, p. 6.
[72] Untitled editorial, *Irish Press*, 2 April 1993, p. 8.

abandon its stance but sought a compromise. Five years of negotiations for a comprehensive peace agreement for Northern Ireland would eventually provide the opportunity for such a compromise. In December 1993, preliminary peace talks between John Major and Haughey's successor as *Taoiseach*, Albert Reynolds (FF), produced the Downing Street Declaration. More than earlier documents, the Declaration emphasised the need to accommodate all aspirations (i.e. Nationalist and Unionist) on the island, but the Republic did not recognise British sovereignty over Northern Ireland.

Negotiations for a comprehensive peace agreement on Northern Ireland gained further momentum after the IRA and the Combined Loyalist Military Command announced a cessation of military activities in 1994. A year later, John Major and newly elected *Taoiseach* John Bruton (FG) launched the Framework Document. The Fine Gael-led coalition agreed in this agreement to adjust the Constitution to clarify unambiguously that Ireland would only be reunited if this was the wish of the people (i.e. majorities in North and South). The diplomatic formulation clearly aimed at changing the Constitution's irredentist claim into an aspiration for unity.

Given Fine Gael's argumentation on the Irish Question since FitzGerald's constitutional crusade, it was not surprising that the party agreed to change the Constitution in the Framework Document. Yet what would Fianna Fáil do? This issue assumed major relevance when Ahern (FF) replaced Bruton (FG) as *Taoiseach* in June 1997. Fianna Fáil's leadership was prepared to compromise. Reynolds had succeeded in getting Fianna Fáil's approval of the principle of consent in the 1993 Downing Street Declaration. In exchange for the prospect of a major peace agreement including a Council of Ireland for all-Irish affairs, the party was prepared to offer the principle of consent to the United Kingdom and Northern Ireland (Collins, 2000: 254–5). Half a decade later, Ahern and his foreign minister, David Andrews, went a step further. They were prepared to sacrifice the irredentist claim in exchange for such a breakthrough on the Irish Question.

Ahern and Andrews toured the country and tried to convince their party at numerous meetings that a comprehensive peace agreement was not possible without renouncing the claim of legal right to Northern Ireland. The Republic would have to renounce its claim as part of a compromise. In exchange for dropping the irredentist claims, the Council of Ireland would be re-established. This would give the

Republic some say in the affairs of Northern Ireland, and the Council could evolve into the nucleus of Irish unification. Britain would ensure that it would support Irish unity if this was the wish of the majority in Northern Ireland. Furthermore, the Irish–Irish border would lose its significance through the creation of integrative structures, modelled after the European unification process, that would encompass all of the British Isles. Finally, there would be a power-sharing agreement in the North, safeguarding the rights and interests of the Nationalist minority. In short, the agreement would offer a chance for peace in Northern Ireland and the eventual unification of North and South.[73]

Ahern and Andrews succeeded. Given the benefits offered to Ireland and the pressure of public opinion to amend Articles 2 and 3, Fianna Fáil ceased to argue against constitutional change. While in power as *Taoiseach* in 1998, Ahern signed the Good Friday Agreement. The Republic recognised that Northern Ireland is *de jure* part of the United Kingdom. It agreed with the other signing parties 'that Northern Ireland's status as part of the United Kingdom reflects and relies upon that wish; and that it would be wrong to make any change in the status of Northern Ireland save with the consent of a majority of its people'.

Those counter-advocates who did not share the newly dominant repertoire of commonplaces continued to oppose the constitutional amendment. Independent Fianna Fáil approved of the peace process but not of forgoing irredentism. Its new leader Harry Blaney objected that the proposed amendment 'copperfastens the Unionist veto on Irish unity'. Harry Blaney appealed to the *Taoiseach* to conduct two separate referenda, one for the constitutional amendment and one for the Good Friday Agreement, hoping that the amendment would not be carried.[74]

Shortly after the Agreement was signed, however, a referendum was held on the Good Friday Agreement including on the amendment of Articles 2 and 3. Answering an opinion poll question not linking the amendment to the Good Friday Agreement, almost two-thirds of the Republic's populace would have voted in favour of constitutional change in 1995, according to the MRBI survey mentioned above. Combined with the Agreement, a very impressive majority of 94 per cent carried the referendum in 1998.[75]

---

[73] Interview with David Andrews, Dublin, 29 January 2004.
[74] Harry Blaney, *Dáil Éireann Debates* 489, 22 April 1998, cols. 1464–5.
[75] The results of all referenda are available at: http://www.electionsireland.org

The irredentist claim of Article 2 of the *Bunreacht na hÉireann* was replaced by a paragraph on Irish citizenship. According to this stipulation, everybody born on the island of Ireland is entitled to Irish citizenship. Article 3 formulates the aspiration for Irish unity:

> It is the free will of the Irish Nation, in harmony and friendship, to unite all the people who share the territory of the island of Ireland, in all the diversity of their identities and traditions, recognising that a united Ireland shall be brought about only by peaceful means with the consent of the people, democratically expressed, in both jurisdictions of the island.

The enactment of this Article ended the Republic of Ireland's 51-year-old irredentist claim to Northern Ireland.

Despite the severe setbacks during the implementation process of the Good Friday Agreement, the debate about the claim to the North never surfaced again in the Republic after the referendum. The Republic kept its promises but the conflict parties in Northern Ireland failed to reach a consensus on the implementation of crucial aspects of the peace agreement. The decommissioning of weapons was a major problem. Furthermore, many of the institutional arrangements of the Agreement were still pending implementation years after the peace accord was signed. Among these were institutions that made the peace agreement very attractive for the Republic, including the North–South Ministerial Council, the Council of Ireland, and the British–Irish Intergovernmental Council. These difficulties did not trigger a new debate about the Republic's end of the bargain. Not even the former opponents of constitutional change questioned the Republic's commitment to the Good Friday Agreement, including the end of irredentism.[76] The irredentist claim, and even debates about the claim, have remained a thing of the past.

Discussion of findings

The empirical findings lend evidence to the three-stage norm selection mechanism. Figure 6.2 summarises the three ideal-typical stages.

Innovative argumentation characterised the first stage. Environmental change made actors embark on an advocacy in favour of the territorial

---

[76] This consensus is very clear in all major Dáil debates on Northern Ireland since 1998: *Dáil Éireann Debates* 555, 15 October 2002, cols. 403–38; *Dáil Éireann Debates* 558, 26 November 2002, cols. 55–84; *Dáil Éireann Debates* 565, 15 April 2003, cols. 824–45; *Dáil Éireann Debates* 566, 7 May 2003, cols. 71–95.

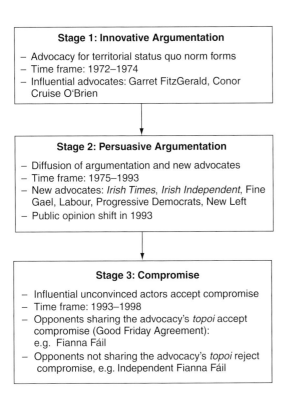

Stage 1: Innovative Argumentation
- Advocacy for territorial status quo norm forms
- Time frame: 1972–1974
- Influential advocates: Garret FitzGerald, Conor Cruise O'Brien

Stage 2: Persuasive Argumentation
- Diffusion of argumentation and new advocates
- Time frame: 1975–1993
- New advocates: *Irish Times*, *Irish Independent*, Fine Gael, Labour, Progressive Democrats, New Left
- Public opinion shift in 1993

Stage 3: Compromise
- Influential unconvinced actors accept compromise
- Time frame: 1993–1998
- Opponents sharing the advocacy's *topoi* accept compromise (Good Friday Agreement): e.g. Fianna Fáil
- Opponents not sharing the advocacy's *topoi* reject compromise, e.g. Independent Fianna Fáil

Figure 6.2 Schematised three-stage selection of territorial status quo norm

status quo norm. The Troubles were the revolutionary event that made it clear to the advocates that the old ways of doing things had become obsolete and the changing repertoire of commonplaces, in particular the change from the colonial episteme to the Idea of Europe and from exclusive to inclusive nationalism, provided the clues for how the new should look.

Persuasive argumentation was the predominant selection mechanism of the second stage. Advocates – especially those who had established a reputation for persistently supporting the *topoi* of their advocacy even outside of the advocacy – succeeded in persuading large segments of the elites and the public by linking the advocated idea of a territorial status quo norm to the newly dominant repertoire of commonplaces. They constructed this linkage through three modes of reasoning that used key aspects of the repertoire as *topoi*. Abstract reasoning related the Idea of Europe and the nation's longing for unification to the advocated

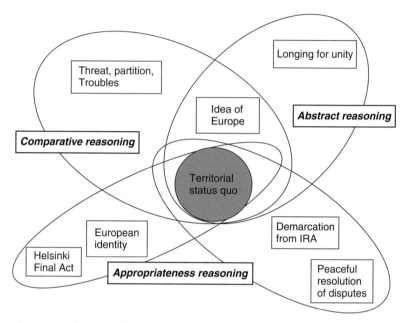

Figure 6.3 Elements of successful argumentation

idea. Comparative reasoning connected the history of partition and violence between Nationalists and Unionists in the North, as seen in the light of the European episteme, to the advocated idea. Appropriateness reasoning linked the established norm of peaceful resolution of disputes, buttressed by juxtaposing Irishness from the IRA, as well as the established norm complex of the Helsinki Final Act as reinforced by the Republic's European identity to the advocated idea of a territorial status quo norm. These components of the successful message, i.e. the three modes of reasoning, the *topoi* employed and the idea advocated, are depicted in figure 6.3.

Compromise was the predominant selection mechanism of the third stage. When the costs of opposing the newly established majority view mounted, those recalcitrant actors who shared the advocates' repertoire of commonplaces compromised on their position, even though the compromise clearly favoured the advocates' position.

As promising as these results are, there is also a caveat. The Irish case reminds us that the three stages are only ideal-types. As useful as they are as a heuristic device, they are not real-types. The decision by the *Irish Press* to cease its support for irredentism, for example, falls in between the persuasion and compromise stages. The editors of the newspaper were not persuaded but they did not seek a compromise either. The newspaper was swayed by public pressure without receiving a concession. Innovative argumentation and persuasive argumentation also overlapped to some extent. The argumentation coined in the early 1970s was vital for persuasive argumentation to be eventually successful. Yet advocates in the early 1990s added the appropriateness mode to the existing abstract and comparative modes.

Despite this caveat, the three-stage norm selection mechanism provides a more compelling account than alternative explanations. Most of the literature follows the division into three contending perspectives on international relations: Realism, Liberalism (its rational choice variant) and Constructivism. Skelly (1997) uses a Realist perspective to explain the Republic's foreign policy. It is not difficult to extrapolate a hypothesis on the resolution of border disputes from this framework. In this reading, the withering away of irredentism was simply a function of the power discrepancy between the Republic and the United Kingdom. Dublin lacked the necessary means to force the United Kingdom into surrendering Northern Ireland. This made the territorial claim futile. This hypothesis cannot explain, however, why Dublin claimed Northern Ireland for over fifty years before withdrawing the claim. The power discrepancy never changed significantly.

Eunan O'Halpin's rational choice framework (1999) provides some important insights into the Republic's domestic politics. Pressure by the electorate influenced recalcitrant elites. Moreover, bargaining theory helps to explain why Fianna Fáil, once under pressure by public opinion, came to end its counter-advocacy. The picture, however, remains incomplete in four ways. First, according to rational choice theory all political actors incurring costs from opposing the newly established majority view should have renounced their irredentist stance. Actors such as Independent Fianna Fáil, however, refused to bend. Second, Rationalist approaches cannot explain why actors, despite the costs this initially inflicted upon them, started an advocacy for overcoming irredentism. At the beginning, the majority of social actors and the public were outraged about the advocates' rejection of Articles 2 and 3 of the Constitution, which inflicted heavy costs on the advocates. Third, it is puzzling from a rational choice perspective that more and more social actors as well as the public became opposed to irredentism years before the Good Friday Agreement offered tangible benefits to the Republic and the Nationalists of Northern Ireland. Fourth, there is no evidence for external inducement. Brussels, for instance, may have induced the Republic to do a number of things but there is no evidence that Brussels linked financial assistance to the withdrawal of the irredentist claim. After the Good Friday Agreement, there has even been a slight decrease in structural and cohesion funds because of the Republic's continuing economic growth.[77]

Existing Constructivist accounts provide an important starting point for analysing the research puzzle. Authors point to the Republic's European world view (MacLaughlin, 2001), to the change from exclusive to inclusive nationalism (Girvin, 1994; Howe, 2000) and allude to the reconstitution of Irishness by European norms (Harris, 2001; MacLaughlin, 2001). Similarly to the rational choice account, these explanations point in the right direction but they are incomplete. The European world view and inclusive nationalism – as important as they were – did not automatically translate into abandoning irredentism. The mechanism linking the change of the environment to the selection of the territorial status quo is missing in these accounts. This study, by contrast, provides evidence that argumentation and compromise provided this mechanism. The norm-based explanations are also incomplete. They do not spell out what European norm made the Republic forgo irredentism. This study, by contrast, shows that the Republic selected the territorial status quo norm. Furthermore, this study has focused on the question of how the territorial status quo norm became an identity-constituting norm. This is a question that other norm-based explanations of the Irish case have neglected so far.

---

[77] The Republic received €11 billion from 1989 to 1999 and €4 billion were earmarked for the period 2000–2006 (National Development Plan, 2005).

Conclusion

This conclusion summarises the main findings, discusses the added value of the theoretical framework, examines the implications of the findings for the study of irredentism and International Relations Theory, and sketches an agenda for future research.

Comparing the two cases

There were a number of important differences between the FRG's and the Republic of Ireland's irredentism. Bonn's claim to the territories east of the Oder–Neiße was connected to the fate of millions of expellees; this factor was absent in the Irish case. The FRG's claim to the GDR was predominantly based on the identification of East Germans as fellow Germans – an identification that East Germans reciprocated; in the Irish case, by contrast, the majority in the North have continuously rejected such a shared national identity. The German Question was firmly embedded in the Cold War; a comparable external conflict dimension was absent in the Irish case. The agreements in which Bonn recognised the territorial status quo in the early 1970s offered very few tangible benefits to the FRG; the Good Friday Agreement, by contrast, included provisions for all-Ireland institutions and a mechanism aimed at safe-guarding the rights of the Nationalist minority in the North. Finally, it took the FRG about twenty years to renounce its territorial claims; Dublin, by contrast, claimed the North for almost seventy years.

These differences notwithstanding, the process through which both states came to renounce irredentism was very similar. Forgoing irredent-ism was not merely a policy change. It was a normative change. The FRG and the Republic of Ireland came to identify with the norm that states ought not to claim territory from other states. Ideal-typically, the process through which the two states came to select the territorial status quo norm can be broken down into three stages: innovative argumentation, persuasive argumentation and compromise. Environmental change – i.e. a shifting repertoire of commonplaces and a revolutionary event – provided the impetus for innovative argumentation. West Germans, jolted out of the old ways of doing things by the Berlin Wall, and Irish Nationalists, equally shocked by the Troubles in Northern Ireland, were searching for new approaches to deal with partition. In both cases, a changing repertoire of commonplaces enabled those actors already embracing the repertoire's novel and more inclusionary aspects to think of radical alternatives that previously had been inconceivable. This new thinking sparked the formation of advocacy networks for the idea of a territorial status quo norm.

Persuasive argumentation did not come easy. In the FRG, it took well over a decade for the territorial status quo advocacy to convince a broad audience. In the Republic of Ireland, the time line was closer to two decades. Despite this small difference, the eventually successful advocacies shared a number of features. Advocates succeeded in making their argumentation resonate with a broad audience by constructing a link between the advocated idea and powerful *topoi*, which they picked from the dominant repertoire of commonplaces (episteme, identity narrative, institutionalised norms). This linkage was constructed through three modes of reasoning: abstract reasoning linked the *topoi* of the Idea of Europe (episteme) and the longing for unification (as ingrained in the identity narrative) to the advocated idea for a territorial status quo norm. The Idea of Europe provided a new vision for attaining the nation's longing for unification. Comparative reasoning revolved around the *topoi* of historical lessons, which were key elements of the identity narrative, and the Idea of Europe. Interpreted through the lens of the Idea of Europe, comparative reasoning constructed a fit between these historical lessons on the one hand – no matter whether that was *Wiedergutmachung* in the FRG or overcoming Unionist fear in the Republic of Ireland – and the advocated normative idea on the other hand. Appropriateness reasoning used already institutionalised norms as well as their justifying underpinnings as *topoi* and linked them to the advocated idea. The norm of peaceful resolution of disputes, for example, featured prominently in both cases. Yet the eventually successful advocacies in the FRG and the Republic of Ireland were not only persuasive because they crafted together compelling messages. They also greatly profited from the reputation of their main advocates. This reputation, similarly to the persuasive power of the message, hinged on the evolution of the repertoire of commonplaces. The main advocates were vilified as traitors when they embraced the novel aspects of the repertoire at a time when they had not become widely accepted. When the novel dimensions assumed the status of a new orthodoxy, however, the audience, seeking for orientation in a changing and uncertain world, looked for guidance from those who had already established a reputation for embracing the novelty. The main protagonists of the advocacies, Brandt in the FRG and FitzGerald in the Republic of Ireland, eventually became almost untouchable for their political opponents, at least as far as debates about forgoing irredentism were concerned.

Compromise was the third step of the process through which the two states selected the territorial status quo norm. The advocacy was enormously successful in both cases. Most importantly, it caused a remarkable public opinion shift from tabooing the recognition of existing borders to fully endorsing it. As successful as the advocacy was, however, some actors remained recalcitrant. In the FRG and the Republic of Ireland, there were two groups of unconvinced actors. There were those whose repertoire of commonplaces did not include the *topoi* invoked by the advocates. Irrespective of the mounting costs of opposing a newly established majority view, these opponents categorically rejected any notion of a compromise. With the advocacy's *topoi* outside of these opponents' repertoire, the advocacy did not make any sense to them and accepting it would have required them to violate their taken-for-granted beliefs. But there was also a group of recalcitrant actors whose repertoire of commonplaces included the *topoi* invoked by the advocates. This made for a less absolute disagreement. With their taken-for-granted beliefs not violated and pressured by the costs of opposing the newly developed majority opinion, they were eager to reach a compromise. In the FRG, this eagerness made them accept the territorial status quo norm with minor adjustments as to how to interpret the norm. In the Republic of Ireland, it made a political party that had initiated and then vehemently defended irredentism for more than seven decades accept the territorial status quo norm in exchange for a comprehensive peace agreement with Belfast and London.

Added value I: why elaborating on argumentation?

The three-stage mechanism adds complexity to existing accounts of norm selection and compliance. It does so in two ways: it elaborates on the argumentation and advocacy literature, and approaches logics of action eclectically. Is this complexity warranted? Or are there other approaches that provide for a more parsimonious and equally plausible explanation of the two cases?[1] This section discusses the complexity arising from elaborating on argumentation while the next section scrutinises the need for eclecticism.

Existing approaches to argumentation and advocacy (Florini, 1996; Finnemore and Sikkink, 1998; Keck and Sikkink, 1998; Risse, Ropp and Sikkink, 1999; Bernstein, 2000; Crawford, 2002; Wiener, 2004) are less complex than the three-stage mechanism presented in this book. When examining the two cases analysed in depth in this study, this literature focuses on the fit that advocates construct between the identity narrative and already selected norms on the one hand and the advocated normative idea on the other. This is, indeed, an important piece of the puzzle. The evolution towards more inclusive identities in the FRG and the Republic of Ireland as well as internalised norms such as the norm of peaceful resolution of disputes served as important anchors for the advocacies.

Yet there are also other important pieces of the puzzle. The literature hints at some of these and remains silent about others. Let me highlight three of them. First, it remains unclear what makes agents engage in an advocacy in the first place. This study has been cautious when trying to answer this question. Over-theorising agency runs the risk of simplistically narrowing the many facets of human agency down to a particular dimension. Rational choice theory, for instance, over-emphasises the detached computation of the individual at the expense of creativity, heuristic devices, collective forms of reasoning, etc. Yet despite this cautious approach, this study has revealed something important about why agents act the way they do. They are embedded in an environment. This environment provides the impetus to act and the clues for what to do. In both cases under scrutiny, a revolutionary event (the Berlin Wall and the Troubles, respectively) made clear that the old ways of doing things could not continue, and new aspects of the repertoire (which made the repertoire more inclusionary) provided agents with an

---

[1] Focusing on the literature dealing specifically with the Federal Republic of Germany's and the Republic of Ireland's foreign policy and irredentist claims, the concluding sections of chapters 4 and 6 discussed rival explanations of the two cases at length. This section discusses alternative explanations on a more theoretical level.

opportunity to put together a new picture about the world that was more intelligible to them than the old one.

Second, the existing literature on argumentation and advocacy does not provide sufficient detail on the construction of the fit between the taken-for-granted and the new. This casts serious doubt over whether the literature can explain the two cases. In the FRG and the Republic of Ireland, norm selection was very contested. Some advocacies tried to make a case that there was a fit between the innovative idea they advocated and the nation's widely taken-for-granted beliefs. Other advocacies vigorously defended the irredentist claim, and they, too, embedded the call for upholding irredentism in the nation's evolving repertoire, including the novel inclusionary aspects. But, in both irre-dentist states, only a particular advocacy for the territorial status quo norm ended up persuading a broad audience. Building on Crawford's modes of reasoning (Crawford, 2002: 14–22) and identifying the *topoi* that make these modes compelling, this study has provided more details as to why an argument persuades. These details were a critical compo-nent of explaining which advocacies succeeded in the FRG and the Republic of Ireland, and which ones failed.

Third, persuasion alone tells only half of the story of winning over an audience. The other half revolves around the repercussions of persua-sive argumentation for self-interested actors. Although some of the advocacy literature hints at this (e.g. Finnemore and Sikkink, 1998), it does not explore this aspect in depth. As successful as the advocacies were in the Federal Republic of Germany and the Republic of Ireland, a number of unconvinced actors remained. Had they all continued their opposition despite the success of persuasive argumentation, neither Bonn nor Dublin would have recognised the territorial status quo. Yet they bent under the pressure of public opinion. Elites managed to persuade large segments of the public, and the public in turn put pressure on recalcitrant elites to compromise. Argumentation and bar-gaining theory help to explain the outcome of the compromise. Bargaining theory reminds us that those actors who are more eager to reach an agreement – in this case the recalcitrant actors who try to rid themselves of the costs associated with arguing against the majority view – compromise more easily on their stance. The compromise, therefore, resembles the original position of the advocates much more closely than the recalcitrant actors' original stance. Argumentation theory – drawing our attention to the repertoire of commonplaces and *topoi* – helps us understand which recalcitrant actors are willing to compromise. Only if the opponents' repertoire of commonplaces includes the *topoi* invoked by the advocates is a compromise conceivable for them. Otherwise, the opponents inhabit a different social lifeworld and such a fundamental disagreement does not allow for a compromise.

Added value II: why be eclectic about logics of action?

The discussion of the advocacy literature above has already provided a glimpse into another issue that generates complexity in the theoretical framework. It is eclectic about logics of action. Albeit weighted differently, there are aspects of the logics of argumentation, consequences, appropriateness and practice in the three-stage norm selection mechanism. Is such eclecticism really necessary or do the existing logics of action provide a plausible answer to the research question on their own?

It is obvious from the discussion in the previous section that the logic of argumentation, while playing a very important role in accounting for the two cases, cannot account for them on its own. The logic of argumentation was paramount in the first two stages of the norm selection mechanism, i.e. innovative argumentation and persuasive argumentation. Actors reasoned, exchanged arguments and persuaded other actors about what to do by constructing linkages between the taken-for-granted and advocated ideas. But argumentation alone was not enough for making the FRG and the Republic of Ireland forgo irredentism. Recalcitrant actors had to bend to the pressure exerted by persuasive argumentation and this bending to the pressure falls predominantly into the realm of the logic of consequences. Eager to rid themselves of the costs of opposition, some recalcitrant actors compromised on their position.

There are also aspects of the logic of appropriateness in my account of the two cases but, again, appropriateness alone did not make the FRG and the Republic of Ireland renounce their irredentist claims. The logic of appropriateness – at least if understood in less all-encompassing fashion as by Müller (2004) – is a logic that revolves around agents acting in accordance with identity-constituting norms. Without reasoning or debating on which norms are applicable to a particular situation and how they ought to be interpreted in a particular situation, actors use these norms as guides for action. Appropriateness thus understood featured in my explanation of the two cases. Appropriateness reasoning, which played a key role in the persuasive argumentation stage of the three-stage mechanism in both cases, is a hybrid between the logics of argumentation and appropriateness. Perhaps more importantly, the analysis of the aftermath of the norm selection process showed that the territorial status quo norm had become an internalised norm guiding political outcomes. The FRG, despite reunification, and the Republic of Ireland, despite Northern Ireland's failures to implement the Good Friday Agreement, did not even consider reviving the irredentist claim. Given the nations' identification with the territorial status quo norm, no longer claiming territory had come to be the natural thing to do for them. Despite these two aspects of appropriateness, however, the process through which the two countries came to forgo irredentism cannot be reduced to appropriateness. Innovative argumentation was about agents assembling an intelligible picture from the clues provided by the evolving repertoire of commonplaces. Persuasive argumentation was not only about appropriateness reasoning – and even this was as much about reasoning and argumentation as it was about appropriateness – but also about comparative and abstract reasoning as well as the reputation of the advocates. Finally, the compromise was about actors serving their own interests – within the parameters set by their repertoire for assembling conceivable lines of reasoning.

There are hints about the logic of practice in my accounts of the two cases but this logic is not sufficient on its own either. Put in very simple terms, the logic of argumentation is about debate and change in the open, whereas the logic of practice is about the production and reproduction of a background so deeply internalised that it does not reach the surface. The background, following Bourdieu (1977 [1972], 1990 [1980]) often conceptualised as habitus, manifests itself in practices but it cannot be uncovered by the analysis of discourse. Neither the FRG's nor the Republic of Ireland's forgoing of irredentism can be explained by the logic of practice alone. This study has demonstrated that actors reasoned, argued, persuaded and nudged unconvinced actors into agreement. Thus, the normative change from tabooing recognition to the selection of the territorial status quo norm occurred not underneath the radar of discourse but was clearly visible on the radar screen. More so, discourse was highly consequential. It mattered how actors composed their messages from the clues available to them, how they conveyed them to their audience, and what impact this made on the audience. Yet this does not mean that the insights generated by the practical turn can be disregarded. Argumentation and compromise are enabled by a background. It is no coincidence, for instance, that I share an interest in the episteme concept as made amenable to the study of practices (Adler, 1991, 2005). Indeed, it has been one of the key findings of this study that the episteme profoundly shaped the chances and limitations of innovative argumentation, persuasive argumentation and compromise. The Idea of Europe made things possible that other epistemes, for example the Republic of Ireland's colonial episteme, would never have made possible. I will further elaborate on the interconnectedness of the logics of argumentation and practice below. It features prominently on my agenda for further research on the theoretical issues arising out of this study.

Let me complete my discussion of logics of action with consequentialism, which continues to dominate the social sciences. Similarly to the other logics of action, consequentialism alone cannot explain why the FRG and the Republic of Ireland renounced their irredentist claims. The logic of consequences captures the key mechanism of the compromise stage but it cannot explain – with the possible exception of those variants that include ideas as constraints (Kiser and Ostrom, 1982; Levi, 1997) – a crucial detail: why were some recalcitrant actors eager to compromise while others categorically rejected a compromise even though they were exposed to the same costs arising from the counteradvocacy? More importantly, consequentialism – no matter what variant – cannot explain how most influential actors and the public came to change their minds about recognition in the first place. Consequentialism does not offer the conceptual tools to understand what happened prior to the compromise.

It is worth dealing with this problem in more depth. Two consequentialist arguments, prominent in the literature on territorial disputes, may be made for the cases at hand, one assuming that selfish agents maximise their own interest (Rothschild, 1981; Gagnon, 1994; Saideman, 1997; Heldt, 1999), and another presuming that agents act according to the preferences of the state (Siverson and Starr, 1991; Goertz and Diehl, 1992; Vanzo, 1999). The assumption of selfish agents trying to safeguard or increase their hold on power cannot explain why agents started an advocacy that was initially very costly for them. When they started their advocacies, Brandt and FitzGerald were branded as traitors, which seriously undermined their chances of political success.

Consequentialism also cannot explain why more and more agents – eventually even the public at large – became persuaded to forgo irredentism. It is unclear what the personal benefits for persuaded elites and masses could have been.

What of the other consequentialist argument? Did elites try to maximise the benefits for the state with the least cost? A simple consequentialist argument would posit that the irredentist states withdrew their claims because of the objective benefits that the agreement with the status quo states entailed. A more complex consequentialist argument would include ideas for understanding preference formation and likelihood estimates (Bates, De Figueiredo and Weingast, 1998). In brief, such an analysis might proceed as follows. Examining the identity narrative tells the researcher about the preferences. Reunification was a key preference for the FRG and for the Republic of Ireland. The episteme provides clues for likelihood estimates. Recognising the territorial status quo makes reunification more likely because it initiates a process of overcoming borders, which may eventually lead to reunification. Recognition, therefore, is a means for reunification.

Neither the simple nor the complex account, however, provides a compelling answer to the research puzzle. The simple one cannot explain why larger and larger segments of elites came to embrace recognition at a time when not even the contours of the agreement with the status quo state were discernible. Furthermore, the FRG hardly received any tangible benefits in its treaties with Moscow, Warsaw and East Berlin. The more complex hypothesis is more promising but ultimately cannot overcome two problems. First, there is a consistency problem. The likelihood estimate should have always been the same across actors sharing the episteme. Yet the FRG's and the Republic of Ireland's withdrawals of irredentist claims show clearly that this was not the case. It took an advocacy to establish the line of reasoning that renouncing irredentism would help overcome the divisiveness of the German–German and Irish–Irish borders in the long run. In rational choice parlance, the likelihood estimates, despite the shared episteme, differed widely in what I label the innovative and persuasive argumentation stages. Even actors sharing the same episteme did not agree on how recognition would affect borders in the long run. Second, there is also the problem that explaining identity formation and likelihood estimates with ideas approximates merely one particular mode of reasoning, namely abstraction. Yet abstract reasoning was not the only mode of reasoning that made the world intelligible to

advocates and audience alike. There were also the comparative and
appropriateness modes. Judging by the empirical evidence, these were
at least as important as the abstract one.

Implications for the study of irredentism
and conflict resolution

It is possible to tailor, in an abductive manner, the major findings of this
research more closely to the study of irredentism and conflict resolution.
The irredentist disputes were resolved by what may be called dejustification. Advocates seized upon the opportunity offered by a changing
ideational environment and brought down the justification on which
the irredentist claim was based – and with it the irredentist claim itself
(Kornprobst, 2007).

The social construction of the nation and its borders is of paramount
importance for the dynamics of irredentist disputes. Two levels of this
construction may be distinguished: deep level and adjustment level. The
former defines where the boundaries of the nation are. These borders
are deeply ingrained in the identity narrative. The nation defines its
ancestral homeland as well as the membership criteria according to
which it distinguishes between those inside and those outside of the
nation. In a very fundamental way, all of this is made conceivable by the
episteme. The very possibility of being able to imagine something like
the nation and the nation-state is due to an episteme that provides the
basic categories for these imaginings.

The adjustment level shapes the nature of the boundary of the nation
and the border of the state. Some nations identify positively with one
another whereas others seek sharp demarcation from one another. The
attachment of meaning to state borders differs in a similar way. Some
nations interpret their state borders in a permeable manner whereas
others see them as impenetrable walls. Again, therefore, identity narrative and episteme feature prominently. The identity narrative constitutes the relationship to another nation within the imaginable space
delineated by the episteme. Yet different aspects of identity narrative
and episteme make up the two levels. The deep level is about the basic
parameters of imagining the nation. It is about the very possibility of
imagining the organisation of human communities into nations and
states (episteme), and about the definition of the borders of the imagined nation (identity narrative). The adjustment level, by contrast, is

about how nations invent and reinvent the quality of their borders within these parameters. It consists of the nuances of the episteme – what different degrees of autonomy and interrelatedness of nations it makes conceivable – and the construction of relationships between nations built on these nuances of the episteme.

There is some good news about settling irredentist disputes. These conflicts would be very difficult to resolve if this necessitated change on the deep level. This level pertains to very fundamental aspects of episteme and identity narrative. They hardly change and, when they do, only over a very long period of time. Yet irredentist disputes can be resolved without a nation changing the definition of its geographical expansion, let alone abandoning the taken-for-granted belief in nationhood as the central organisational principle for communities in world politics. Irredentist disputes can be resolved based on changes on the adjustment level. Neither the FRG nor the Republic of Ireland abandoned irredentism because they stopped regarding the lost territories and populations as part of their nation, and certainly neither of them ceased to take nationhood as a given. Nevertheless, they settled their irredentist disputes. The precondition for settlement was an episteme that, while embracing the fundamental role of nations in world politics, postulated co-operation and integration across them (Idea of Europe), and an identity narrative that, underpinned by the episteme, moved away from enmity towards qualified partnership (FRG) and even friendship (Republic of Ireland) with the status quo states.

Yet in both analysed cases, changes on the adjustment level were merely a necessary condition for an argumentatively induced settlement of irredentism. It took an advocacy to translate the changes of the social context into the end of irredentism. Judging by the two cases, my conceptualisation of argumentation and compromise can be tailored more closely to the study of irredentism. Irredentist nations do not merely assert that a disputed land is theirs and that it has to become theirs again. But, armed with their definition of the nation's spatial boundaries and their interpretation of the nature of national boundaries and state borders, nations justify this assertion. This justification consists of two aspects: the legitimacy aspect explains to a claiming nation why the disputed land is rightfully part of its territory and the visionary aspect elaborates on how the disputed land can actually become part of the nation's territory again. Nations withdraw their irredentist claims if this justification unravels. I refer to this process as dejustification.

Hence, dejustification involves two related processes. First, the pool of taken-for-granted ideas from which the justification is taken changes. The repertoire of commonplaces that used to anchor the justification for irredentism is no longer dominant. Second, an advocacy persuades and sways the nation that there is no longer a match between the reshaped repertoire of commonplaces and the irredentist claim. Thus, the advocacy dislocates the irredentist justification and with it the irredentist claim itself.

Dejustification opens up a new avenue of research on the dynamics of irredentism. Along this way are plenty of new and interesting question marks. Some of them pertain to the social context: what explains change on the deep level? As rarely as this occurs, it has major repercussions for attempts to dejustify irredentism. If the change extends the boundaries of a nation, for instance, dejustification becomes more difficult. Shrinking boundaries, by contrast, provide fertile ground for dejustification efforts. Furthermore, what explains change on the adjustment level? The empirical findings of this study suggest that shifts from an atomistic episteme (e.g. Ireland's colonial episteme) to a communal episteme (e.g. the Idea of Europe) as well as changes from an exclusive identity (e.g. traditional nationalism in Ireland) to an inclusive identity (e.g. inclusive nationalism in Ireland) provided the resources for successful dejustification. Yet more research is needed to explain these changes.

Other questions worth exploring in more depth involve the advocacy itself. To mention only one of them, advocacies sometimes resemble one another. In the case of German and Irish irredentism, domestic advocacies managed to dejustify irredentism. The Irish advocacy, which lagged behind the German one by about two decades, exhibited some resemblances with the advocacy that dejustified irredentism in the FRG. At some stage, there was even an explicit discussion about these similarities among the protagonists of the Irish advocacy and counter-advocacy.[2] What mechanisms explain these similarities?

As promising as the results of this study are, dejustification provides only one possible pathway to the settlement of an irredentist dispute. Elaborating on the scope conditions of dejustification, therefore, is

---

[2] Albert Reynolds, *Dáil Éireann Debates* 403, 28 November 1990, col. 465; John Bruton, *Dáil Éireann Debates* 403, 28 November 1990, cols. 471–2; Peter Barry, *Dáil Éireann Debates* 404, 18 December 1990, col. 71.

another important task for further research. Dejustification provides a compelling explanation for a puzzle within the puzzle. Within the question of why European states, in sharp contrast to the past, have settled their irredentist disputes peacefully since the end of the Second World War, I focused on the question of why the FRG renounced its claims much earlier than Ireland did even though the Cold War context posed an additional hindrance for dispute settlement in the former case that was absent in the latter. Only more empirical research can demonstrate whether dejustification can provide a plausible account of the resolution or persistence of other irredentist disputes in Europe and in other world regions.

Inquiring into scope conditions should not be confined to irredentist disputes. More research can determine to what extent dejustification provides a pathway to the resolution of other types of conflict as well. What kinds of disputes can dejustification explain? Anatol Rapoport's path-breaking research on human conflict may be helpful for answering this question. He contends that there are three modes of conflict: fights, games and debates (Rapoport, 1960). There is some *prima facie* evidence that dejustification does not do very well for conflicts that Rapoport classified as fights. All one can hope for when a fight breaks out is de-escalation and not conflict resolution – especially not an argumentatively induced one. What he categorises as games may be more easily resolved through a redistribution of costs and benefits than through the uncertainties of a usually quite lengthy dejustification process. Yet dejustification may be of major relevance for Rapoport's conflict mode of debates. In current parlance, debates are identity conflicts. Only identity change can resolve them in a sustainable manner. Dejustification provides clues for a particular kind of identity change: the selection of a new identity-constituting norm.

Implications for International Relations Theory

The implications of this study's findings go beyond the study of irredentism and conflict resolution. Its findings provide interesting insights into three issues that are of critical importance for International Relations Theory in general and the study of norm selection mechanisms in particular: argumentation, the nexus of domestic and international politics, and the interplay of logics of action. Pursuing this study's leads on these issues points to an interesting agenda for further research.

My empirical findings highlight three important conceptual issues for the study of international relations. First, reasoning and argumentation matter. The findings suggest that there is often more to agency than social embededness. The agents' environment does not determine their actions but is a resource that enables them to reason and to communicate with one another. The environment is an impetus for actors to try to persuade others, and it is a social context that offers or denies the possibility of this attempt being successful. Hence, the environment is the researcher's analytical starting point, followed by an exploration of how agents, in their quest to make the world intelligible to themselves, collectively come to assemble different aspects of this environment into what is to them a coherent picture. Argumentation theory – and as I emphasised repeatedly there is much more to it than Habermas's ideal-speech situation – provides critical insights into these dynamics.

Second, our explanations of international outcomes cannot afford ruling domestic politics out *a priori*. In both analysed cases, the advocacy started among intellectual and political elites, diffused among elites and the public, and this diffusion eventually changed the distribution of costs and benefits for recalcitrant actors. Bracketing domestic politics means overlooking these internal dynamics, and, ultimately, risks developing a very incomplete understanding of policies and practices pursued by states in the international realm. Although different perspectives in the field have produced very fruitful avenues of research on the domestic–international nexus (Putnam, 1988; Hopf, 2002), this is still a point worth emphasising. Conceptually, the assumption of the state as a unitary actor frequently still slips in through the back door (Gourevitch, 2002: 322). In a similar vein, our methodological choices often truncate research on the domestic–international nexus. Focusing on how to study national identity, I alluded to this problem in chapter 2.

Third, and perhaps most importantly, we need to think of creative ways to link logics of action. Rather than steadfastly following micro-economic accounts of agency (consequentialism) or importing a particular body of social theory to International Relations (logics of appropriateness, argumentation and practices), we should dare to be eclectic. Of course, this is not an easy task. The works of the theorists from whom we borrow these logics of action are partly based on contradictory and non-complementary epistemological and ontological assumptions. But it is an important task. Most phenomena we seek to account for cannot be explained by a particular logic alone. In many circumstances, human beings are not pure norm-followers. They are not perfect cost–benefit calculating machines who operate in a social vacuum. They do not resolve all their differences through argumentation. And there is more to agency than practices emanating from a deep background and feeding back into this deep background.

The three-stage norm selection mechanism and its empirical application in this study contribute to improving our understanding of the above points. But they also highlight the need for further research. In my view, four tasks should be top of the agenda. Two of these pertain to deepening and the remaining two to broadening the research developed in this book. One way of deepening the research calls for closer scrutiny of argumentation. There is a need to examine the communicative power of the three modes of reasoning in more detail. What mode of reasoning is the most persuasive: abstract, comparative or appropriateness? Do some modes of reasoning appeal more to elites and others to masses? There are some hints in my empirical research that abstract reasoning may appeal more to elites and comparative reasoning to broader audiences. But much more research is required on this issue.

Another way of deepening this research pertains to the interplay of argumentation and compromise. As encouraging as the empirical results of this study are and as heuristically useful as the three ideal-typical stages turned out to be, the findings showed that the imposition of ideal-types on a complex social world comes at a price. Argumentation (innovative and persuasive) and compromise fused in more complex ways than the ideal-typical stages suggest. Moving beyond ideal-types may offer the opportunity to capture this fusion more accurately. In my view, argumentation theory is well equipped to deal with this challenge. Argumentation theory, if conceptualised adequately, leaves room for reasoning as defined by rational choice scholars. Argumentation is reasoning. Rational choice is a form of reasoning. But, as Crawford (2002) hints, not every form of reasoning is rational choice.

In addition to these two pathways for deepening research on argumentation as well as on the interplay of argumentation and compromise, there are also two important avenues of research that would shed more light on the broader context in which argumentation and compromise take place. First of all, there is the question of how the repertoire of commonplaces changes. I already emphasised that, given this study's focus on norm selection, the bulk of my research was concerned with a narrowly defined change of the repertoire. I focused in detail on the process through which an idea gets selected as a norm. This selection reconstitutes the repertoire of commonplaces. It is possible to maintain this focus because advocates for a normative idea are not able single-handedly to change rather sticky ideational forces such as an identity-narrative, not to mention an episteme, in order to make the repertoire more supportive of their advocacy. Yet the interesting question remains how something as enduring as an identity narrative and an episteme come to change over time. Since the episteme is of key importance for all three stages of the norm selection mechanism and since it plays a paramount role in the interplay of the repertoire's ingredients, the scrutiny of its evolution seems particularly rewarding. What environment is conducive to epistemic change? What is the mechanism through which an episteme becomes dominant? In all likelihood this avenue of research would revolve around a theory of practice. The episteme – as conceptualised in this study – bears some resemblance to Bourdieu's habitus (Bourdieu, 1977 [1972], 1990 [1980]). It is a deeply internalised social force, shaping and being shaped by human agency. The study of practices has the potential to help understand changes at such a deep layer of the social fabric. Adler's and Pouliot's research is suggestive in this regard (Adler 1991, 2005; Pouliot, 2008).

Finally, there remains the conceptual task of linking the evolution of the repertoire and what agents make of this repertoire into a broader theory of agency. The two pillars of such a theory could be the logics of practice and argumentation. The logic of practice would account for the positioning of actors and their strategies in the political game, and it would be a critical mechanism explaining the evolution of the repertoire of commonplaces. The logic of argumentation – or more precisely a deepened understanding of argumentation and compromise along the lines suggested above – would add to this crucial insights about how actors come to assemble an intelligible picture about the world and how they manage to win over others to adopt this picture. As Luc Boltanski and Laurent Thévenot (2006 [1991]) show, there is room for thinking about such electicism in post-Bourdieuan and post-Habermasian sociology. There is no reason why there should not be room for such electicism in International Relations as well.

Appendix I
Coding procedures

Chapter 1 defines irredentism and gives an overview of irredentist cases in Europe from 1848 to 2000. Appendix I explains my coding procedures.

Filters for the selection of irredentist disputes

I use two filters to identify the population of irredentist disputes:

(1) Filter I: I exclude from my population of cases any positional disputes about the interpretation of where exactly the border between states lies (exact delineation, demarcation). Instead, I exclusively focus on territorial disputes, i.e. disputes where the parties know where the current border is, but disagree about its legitimacy. There are two reasons for this:

   (a) Many of these positional disputes are handled very amicably through the setting up of joint border commissions. The work of these border commissions sometimes takes a very long time despite cordial relations, because the physical demarcation of a border is a time-consuming technical task (the completion of the demarcation of the border between Germany and the Netherlands, for example, took from 1950 to 1960). Territorial disputes, by contrast, tend to be a major irritant in the relations between states.

   (b) Positional and territorial disputes are governed by different sets of international principles. The international order is based on the assumption that states possess an unambiguously identifiable territory. There is an array of principles securing a state's territory. Few principles, however, deal with the possibility that the territory is not unambiguously identifiable. A study that takes international norms seriously, therefore, should always distinguish between positional and territorial disputes.

(2) Filter II: I exclude any claims made during the First World War and the Second World War and in their immediate aftermath. Inter-state relations during these time periods exhibit unique features. Major wars help to solve some claims while they trigger others. Resolving territorial disputes sometimes becomes a necessity during a major war. Survival becomes the absolute priority of virtually all states. If securing survival requires an alliance with a state whose territory was previously claimed, the claim may cease. If securing survival involves hiding, irredentist claims may also cease. Major wars also trigger new territorial disputes. Such wars offer an extraordinary opportunity to gain territory. This applies particularly to the immediate aftermath of such a war. Territorial claims abound because the winners seek to get their share from the losers. Between the end of the First World War and the Versailles Treaty as well as the Treaty of Trianon, for instance, the number of irredentist disputes suddenly peaked and then most claims quickly disappeared.

(3) Filter III: I exclude any territorial claims that are not based on non-selective or persistent definitions of national boundaries. The key difference between irredentist and non-irredentist territorial disputes is the motive for claiming territory. A nation's identity is the main motivational force in irredentist disputes whereas most other types of territorial disputes are underwritten by economic and/or strategic motives. At times, nations claim territory for economic and/or strategic reasons but provide historical justifications for these claims to the international community. Filter III excludes these cases from my population of cases. Chinese and Filipino claims to the Spratly Islands, for instance, are not coded as irredentist. The claimants provide historical justifications but only labelled these islands historical homelands when oil was discovered in the area (no persistent definition of national boundaries). Romania's claim to Ukraine's Serpents Island is not an irredentist dispute either. While Bessarabia remains ingrained in Romanian identity as an ancestral homeland (persistent definition), the claim to Serpents Island has been highly selective. Not the entire historical region has been claimed, but merely a tiny but oil- and gas-rich island. Thus, the dispute has not been motivated by reaching a congruence between the boundaries of the nation and the borders of the state.

Coding of beginning and ending of irredentist disputes

An irredentist dispute is a territorial dispute revolving around identity, and identity dimensions are difficult to measure. I use the following three sets of guidelines to obtain useful data:

(1) Indicators for start of irredentist claim
   A dispute begins when a member of the government of state A, in an official statement, claims part of the territory of state B or the entire territory of state B on the grounds that this piece of territory
   (a) is inhabited by members of the nation that inhabits A, and/or
   (b) is part of A's ancient homeland.
(2) Indicators for end of irredentist dispute
   A dispute ends if
   (a) the governments of the claiming and the defending state agree in a treaty or in an official joint statement to exchange territory, or
   (b) the government of the claiming state recognises the *de jure* sovereignty of the defending state over the disputed territory in a unilateral declaration, a treaty or an official joint statement with the defending state. Note that this does not necessarily mean carving the territorial status quo in stone and excluding the possibility of peaceful territorial change in the future.
(3) Indicators for how a dispute ended
   (a) An irredentist claim is revoked by force if the challenging state withdraws its territorial claim during or in the immediate aftermath of the defending state's threat or actual use of force against the challenger without any transfer of sovereignty over territory occurring from the challenger to the defender.
   (b) An irredentist dispute ends with territorial change by force if a transfer of sovereignty occurs from the defending state to the challenging state of the entire or part of the territory claimed by the challenger, and if this transfer occurs during or in the immediate aftermath of the challenger's threat or actual use of force against the defender.
   (c) An irredentist claim ends with peaceful territorial change if a transfer of sovereignty occurs from the defending state to the challenging state of the entire or part of the territory claimed by the challenger, and if this transfer occurs during or in the immediate aftermath of the challenger's threat or actual use of force against the defender.

(d) An irredentist claim ends with peaceful recognition of the territorial status quo if the challenger withdraws the claim without
being threatened or attacked (3a does not occur) and without
any transfer of sovereignty over territory occurring (3b, 3c do
not occur).

(4) Determining statehood and (threat of) use of force
The Correlates of War (COW) data sets on state system membership (Correlates of War, 2005) and militarised inter-state disputes
(Jones, Bremer and Singer, 1996; Ghosn and Bennett, 2003; Ghosn,
Palmer and Bremer, 2004) proved very useful for determining state
membership (irredentist claims, as I define them, are made by states
against other states) and whether an irredentist dispute ended by
force or the threat to use force (this is important for coding how an
irredentist dispute ended, see 3 above), respectively. Yet creating the
list of irredentist cases required thorough research on the history of
the cases, and when my interpretations acquired in this research
clashed with the COW data, I opted to use my own interpretations
(my codings of Piedmont-Sardinia and Italy as sovereign states, for
instance, deviate from COW).

Sources for compilation of cases

Various sources were used for the compilation of cases. I proceeded as
follows: I started with Paul Huth's and Todd Allee's territorial dispute
data set (2002: 309–39). In the process of adapting the list of cases to my
coding procedures and extending it beyond 1995 and prior to 1914,
I used the following sources:

(1) General sources:
Anderson (2002); Biger (1995); Brecher and Wilkenfeld (1997a);
Brogan (1992); Calvert (2004); Calvocoressi (2001); CIA World
Factbook (2007); Goertz and Diehl (1992); Holsti (1991); Huth
(1996); Institute for the Study of Conflict, Ideology, and Policy
(2002); Kacowicz (1994); Kratochwil, Rohrlich and Mahajan
(1985); Lexis/Nexis (2002); Luard (1986); Open Society Institute
(2002); Smith (1991).

(2) Sources on specific regions and countries:
Abazov (1999); Ahooja-Patel (1974); Albrecht-Carrié (1958);
Anysas (1934); Baumgart (1999); Brownlie (1979); Bugajski

(1993); Centeno (2002); Child (1985); Dávid and Fodor (2000); Dean (1994); Debicki (1963); Dominguez (2003); Drobizheva (1996); Ehteshami (1994); Ferghana Valley Working Group (1999); Geiß (1995); Girot (1994); Grundy-Warr (1994); Gullberg (2000); Hiden and Salmon (1992); Jelavich (1969); Jelavich and Jelavich (1977); Juhász (1979); Karnes (1961); Knippenberg and Markusse (1999); Kornprobst (2002); Landau (1995); Mamatey and Luža (1973); Mandelbaum (2000); Meissner (1990); Müller, (1977); Plaschka and Mack (1970); Rogers (1975); Rothschild (1974); Schofield (1994); Tägil (1999); Taylor (1971); Touval (1972); Trifunovska (1994, 1999); Tunander et al. (1997); Wandruszka and Urbanitsch (1989); Weill (1972); Weinzierl and Skalnik (1983); Widstrand (1969); Zammit (1978); Zentrum für Türkeistudien (1994).

Appendix II
Irredentist cases in Europe and other world regions

This appendix lists the population of irredentist cases, whether they were settled, and, if so, in what way they were settled. Tables A1 to A3 provide an overview of irredentism in Europe from 1848 to 2000. Tables A4 to A7 address irredentist disputes in other world regions from 1946 to 2000.

Year(s)	Challenger	Defender	Disputed area(s)	Settlement of dispute
1908–	Bulgaria	Ottoman Empire	Thrace, Macedonia	– (despite territorial change by force in 1913)
1913–	Bulgaria	Greece	Macedonia	–
1913–	Bulgaria	Serbia	Macedonia	–
1848–	Denmark	Prussia	Schleswig-Holstein	–
1848–1860	France	Piedmont-Sardinia	Nice, Savoy	Peaceful territorial change
1871–	France	Germany	Alsace-Lorraine	–
1843–	Greece	United Kingdom	Ionian Islands (–1846), Cyprus	– (despite peaceful territorial change of Ionian Islands)
1843–	Greece	Ottoman Empire	Thessaly (–1881), Crete and Aegean Islands, Epirus (–1913), Thrace, Macedonia	– (despite territorial changes by force)
1912	Greece	Albania	Northern Epirus	–
1848–	Piedmont-Sardinia	Austria	Lombardy (–1859), Venice (–1866), Istria, south of Brennero	– (despite two territorial changes by force)
1848–1860	Piedmont-Sardinia	Two Sicilies	Two Sicilies	Territorial change by force
1848–1870	Piedmont-Sardinia	Papal States	Umbria, Marches (–1860), Rome	Territorial change by force
1848–	Prussia (German Confederation)	Denmark	Schleswig-Holstein	–
1878–	Romania	Austria-Hungary	Transylvania, Bukovina, Banat	–
1912–	Serbia	Ottoman Empire	Macedonia, Thrace	– (despite territorial change by force)
1908–	Serbia	Austria-Hungary	Bosnia-Herzegovina	–
1878–	Romania	Russia/Soviet Union	Bessarabia	–
1913	Serbia	Bulgaria	Macedonia	Territorial change by force
1713–	Spain	Great Britain	Gibraltar	–
1806–	Sweden	Finland	Åland Islands	–

Table A2 *Irredentism in Europe, 1919–1938*

Year(s)	Challenger	Defender	Disputed area(s)	Settlement of dispute
1919–	Austria	Italy	South Tyrol	–
1919–1924	Czechoslovakia	Poland	Cieszyn, Spiza, Oriva, Jaworzina	Peaceful territorial change
1919–1920	Denmark	Germany	North and Central Schleswig	Peaceful territorial change
1919–	Finland	Soviet Union	East Karelia	–
1933–1939	Germany	Austria	Austria	Territorial change by force
1933	Germany	Czechoslovakia	Sudetenland	Territorial change by force
1922–1936	Germany	France	Rhineland and Saar	Territorial change by force
1933–	Germany	Lithuania	Memelland	–
1933–	Germany	Poland	Danzig and Polish Corridor	–
1919–1923	Greece	Turkey	Epirus, Thrace, Smyrna and offshore islands	Revoked by force
1919–1928	Greece	Italy	Dodecanese Islands	Peaceful recognition
1919–	Greece	United Kingdom	Cyprus	–
1919–1921	Hungary	Austria	Burgenland	Peaceful territorial change
1938–1939	Hungary	Czechoslovakia	Parts of Slovakia, Ruthenia, Subcarpathia	Territorial change by force
1926–	Hungary	Romania	Transylvania	–
1926–	Hungary	Yugoslavia	Banat	–
1922–	Ireland	United Kingdom	Northern Ireland	–
1919–1924	Italy	Yugoslavia	Istrian Peninsula, Fiume, Dalmatian Coastline	Peaceful territorial change
1919–1921	Poland	Soviet Union	Sections of Lithuania, Belarus, and the Ukraine	Territorial change by force
1919–1923	Poland	Lithuania	Vilnius	Territorial change by force
1923–1938	Lithuania	Poland	Vilnius	Revoked by force

1919–1923	Poland	Danzig, East and West Prussia, Upper Silesia	Peaceful territorial change
1919–1924	Poland	Cieszyn, Spiza, Oriva, Jaworzina	Peaceful territorial change
1919–1938	Poland	Cieszyn and parts of Silesia	Territorial change by force
1919–	Romania	Bessarabia	–
1919–1922	Romania	Banat	Peaceful territorial change
1919–	Spain	Gibraltar	–
1919–1921	Sweden	Åland Islands	Peaceful recognition
1919–1924	Yugoslavia	Parts of Istrian Peninsula and Dalmatian Coastline, Fiume	Peaceful territorial change

Table A3 *Irredentism in Europe, 1946–2000*

Year(s)	Challenger	Defender	Disputed area(s)	Settlement of dispute
1949–1969	Austria	Italy	South Tyrol	Peaceful recognition
1949–1973	East Germany	West Germany (France, United Kingdom, United States)	West Berlin	Peaceful recognition
1991–1996	Estonia	Russia	Pechory district	Peaceful recognition
1949–1973	FRG	GDR	GDR	Peaceful recognition
1949–1970	FRG	Poland	Pomerania, Upper Silesia	Peaceful recognition
1949–1970	FRG	Soviet Union	East Prussia	Peaceful recognition
1946–1982	Greece	Cyprus (prior to 1960: United Kingdom)	Cyprus	Peaceful recognition
1946–1985	Greece	Albania	Northern Epirus	Peaceful recognition
1946–1998	Ireland	United Kingdom	Northern Ireland	Peaceful recognition
1946–1975	Italy	Yugoslavia	Trieste	Peaceful recognition
1991–1997	Latvia	Russia	Abrene-Pitalovo district	Peaceful recognition
1946–1947	Romania	Hungary	Transylvania	Peaceful recognition
1991–1995	Serbia	Croatia	Krajina	Revoked by force
1992–1995	Serbia	Bosnia and Herzegovina	Serb-inhabited areas	Revoked by force
1946–	Spain	United Kingdom	Gibraltar	–

Table A4 *Irredentism in Central Asia, Far East and Pacific, 1946–2000*

Year(s)	Challenger	Defender	Disputed area(s)	Settlement of dispute
1947–	Afghanistan	Pakistan	Pathan-inhabited areas	–
1956–1983	Cambodia	Vietnam	Khmer-populated areas	Peaceful recognition
1919–1984	China	United Kingdom	Hong Kong	Peaceful territorial change
1919–1975	China	Portugal	Macau	Peaceful territorial change
1946–1955	China	Soviet Union	Port Arthur	Peaceful territorial change
1950–	China	Taiwan	Taiwan	–
1947–	India	Pakistan	Kashmir, Rann of Kutch	–
1948–1954	India	France	Chandernagor, Pondicherry, Karikal, Mahe, Yanam	Peaceful territorial change
1950–1961	India	Portugal	Goa, Damao, Diu	Territorial change by force
1952–1971	Japan	United States*	Okinawa	Peaceful territorial change
1951–	Japan	Soviet Union/Russia	Kurile Islands	–
1950–	North Korea	South Korea	South Korea	–
1950–	South Korea	North Korea	North Korea	–
1950–	Taiwan	China	China	–
1947–	Pakistan	India	Kashmir, Rann of Kutch	–
1962–	Philippines	Malaysia	Sabah	–
1958–1975	Vietnam	South Vietnam	South Vietnam	Territorial change by force

* The US held residual sovereignty for a specified period of two decades.

Table A5 *Irredentism in the Near East, Middle East and North Africa, 1946–2000*

Year(s)	Challenger	Defender	Disputed area(s)	Settlement of dispute
1991–	Armenia	Azerbaijan	Nagorno-Karabakh	–
1950–1956	Egypt	United Kingdom	Suez Canal Zone	Territorial change by force
1967–1989	Egypt	Israel	Sinai	Peaceful territorial change
1979–	Iraq	Iran	Sunni-populated areas of Khuzestan	–
1932–	Iraq	Kuwait	Kuwait	–
1948–1967	Israel	Jordan	East Jerusalem	Territorial change by force
1960–1975	Mauritania	Spain	Western Sahara	Peaceful territorial change
1956–	Morocco	Spain	Ifni, Tarfaya, Melilla, Ceuta, Western Sahara	–
1957–1970	Morocco	France/Mauritania	Mauritania	Peaceful territorial change
1976–	Morocco	Western Sahara*	Western Sahara	–
1919–1990	North Yemen	South Yemen	South Yemen	Peaceful territorial change
1967–	Syria	Israel	Golan Heights	–
1956–1962	Tunisia	France	Bizerte	Territorial change by force

* It is doubtful whether Western Sahara has become a fully recognised state. Yet since the African Union recognises it as state, I include it in this list.

Table A6 *Irredentism in sub-Saharan Africa, 1946–2000*

Year(s)	Challenger	Defender	Disputed area(s)	Settlement of dispute
1960–1961	Cameroun	United Kingdom	Southern Cameroons	Peaceful territorial change
1961–	Cameroun	Nigeria	Bakassi	–
1975–	Comoros	France	Mayotte	–
1959–1989	Ghana	Ivory Coast	Sanwi District	Peaceful recognition
1966–	Lesotho	South Africa	Parts of Free State, KwaZulu-Natal and Eastern Cape	–
1960–	Somalia	Ethiopia	Haud and Ogaden	–
1960–1981	Somalia	United Kingdom	Somali-inhabited areas	Peaceful recognition
1960–1981	Somalia	Kenya (prior to 1963: United Kingdom)	Somali-inhabited areas	Peaceful recognition
1960–1977	Somalia	France	Djibouti	Peaceful recognition (of Djibouti's independence)
1968–	Swaziland	South Africa	Parts of Mpumalanga and KwaZulu-Natal	–
1960–	Togo	Ghana	Ewe-inhabited areas	–

Table A7 *Irredentism in the Americas, 1946–2000*

Year(s)	Challenger	Defender	Disputed area(s)	Settlement of dispute
1919	Argentina	United Kingdom	Islas Malvinas/Falkland Islands	–
1959–	Cuba	United States	Guantanamo Bay	–
1936–	Guatemala	United Kingdom/Belize	British Honduras/ Belize	–
1950–1977	Panama	United States	Panama Canal Zone	Peaceful territorial change

Appendix III
Analysed parliamentary debates and newspaper editions

Part of the core evidence given in this study stems from a comprehensive analysis of parliamentary debates about the grand issues of foreign policy and the irredentist disputes, as well as the reactions to these debates in the editorials of major newspapers. With the exception of *Die Zeit*, I scrutinised the two newspaper editions following the debate. Daily newspapers usually do not take longer to react to these debates. *Die Zeit* is a weekly newspaper, and I analysed only the first edition following the debate. Table A8 gives an overview of the material analysed for the German case. Table A9 summarises the material for the Irish case.

Table A8 *German parliamentary debates and newspaper editions*

Date of debate	Vol. of report	Brief description of debate	Newspaper editions	
			Die Zeit	Others
20–23 Sept. 1949	1	*Große Regierungserklärung,** Konrad Adenauer	22 and 29 Sept. 1949	21–25 Sept. 1949
15 Nov. 1949	1	*Kleine Regierungserklärung*** on foreign affairs	17 Nov. 1949	16–17 Nov. 1949
20 Nov. 1949	1	*Kleine Regierungserklärung* on foreign affairs	25 Nov. 1949	21–22 Nov. 1949
20 Oct. 1953	2	*Große Regierungserklärung,* Konrad Adenauer	22 Oct. 1953	22–23 Oct. 1953
28 Oct. 1953	2	*Große Regierungserklärung,* Konrad Adenauer (Resumed)	5 Nov. 1953	29–31 Oct. 1953
29 Oct. 1957	3	*Große Regierungserklärung,* Konrad Adenauer	31 Oct. 1957	30–31 Oct. 1957
5 Nov. 1957	3	*Große Regierungserklärung,* Konrad Adenauer (Resumed)	7 Nov. 1957	6–7 Nov. 1957
29 Nov. 1961	4	*Große Regierungserklärung,* Konrad Adenauer	1 Dec. 1961	30 Nov.–31 Dec. 1961
6 Dec. 1961	4	*Große Regierungserklärung,* Konrad Adenauer (Resumed)	8 Dec. 1961	7–8 Dec. 1961
10 Nov. 1965	5	*Große Regierungserklärung,* Ludwig Erhard	12 Nov. 1965	11–12 Nov. 1965

Table A8 (*cont.*)

Date of debate	Vol. of report	Brief description of debate	Newspaper editions	
			Die Zeit	Others
29–30 Nov. 1965	5	*Große Regierungserklärung*, Ludwig Erhard (Resumed)	3 Dec. 1965	1–2 Dec. 1965
25 Mar. 1966	5	*Kleine Regierungserklärung* on renunciation of force (*Friedensnote*)	1 Apr. 1966	26–27 Mar. 1966
13–16 Dec. 1966	5	*Große Regierungserklärung*, Kurt-Georg Kiesinger	16 and 24 Dec. 1966	14–18 Dec. 1966
18 Jan. 1967	5	*Kleine Regierungserklärung* on détente and policy towards Eastern Europe (*Ostpolitik*)	20 Jan. 1967	19–20 Jan. 1967
1 Feb. 1967	5	*Kleine Regierungserklärung* on détente and policy towards Eastern Europe (*Ostpolitik*)	3 Feb. 1967	2–3 Feb. 1967
13 Oct. 1967	5	*Kleine Regierungserklärung* on détente and policy towards Eastern Europe (*Ostpolitik*)	20 Oct. 1967	14–15 Oct. 1967
14 Mar. 1968	5	Report about German partition (*Bericht über die Lage der Nation*)	16 Mar. 1968	15–16 Mar. 1968
18 Oct. 1968	5	*Kleine Regierungserklärung* on détente and policy towards Eastern Europe (*Ostpolitik*)	24 Oct. 1968	19–20 Oct. 1968

Table A8 (*cont.*)

Date of debate	Vol. of report	Brief description of debate	Newspaper editions	
			Die Zeit	Others
28–30 Oct. 1969	6	*Große Regierungserklärung,* Willy Brandt	7 Nov. 1969	29 Oct.–1 Nov. 1969
20 Mar. 1970	6	*Kleine Regierungserklärung* on territorial claims	27 Mar. 1970	21–22 Mar. 1970
15 Apr. 1970	6	*Kleine Regierungserklärung* on territorial claims	16 Apr. 1970	16–17 Apr. 1970
8 May 1970	6	*Kleine Regierungserklärung* about the end of the Second World War	12 May 1970	9–10 May 1970
17 Jun. 1970	6	*Kleine Regierungserklärung* commemorating the 1953 insurrection in East Germany	20 Jun. 1970	18–19 Jun. 1970
18 Jan. 1973	7	*Große Regierungserklärung,* Willy Brandt	22 Jan. 1973	19–20 Jan. 1973
24 Jan. 1973	7	*Kleine Regierungserklärung* on co-operation in Europe	30 Jan. 1973	25–26 Jan. 1973
13 Sept. 1973	7	*Kleine Regierungserklärung* on co-operation in Europe	15 Sept. 1973	14–15 Sept. 1973

* *Große Regierungserklärung* may be translated as Grand Government Declaration. The names in the table indicate who delivered this declaration. When a Chancellor is elected into office, he or she gives an elaborate programmatic speech, which always includes foreign policy. Many deputies address foreign policy issues in the ensuing debate.
** *Kleine Regierungserklärung* means Short Government Declaration. These are more specific and more focused on a particular topic than the *Große Regierungserklärungen*.

Table A9 *Irish parliamentary debates and newspaper editions*

Date of debate	Vol. of report	Title of debate	Newspaper editions
12–13 Jul. 1949	117	Council of Europe	13–15 Jul. 1949
12 Jul. 1950	122	Committee on Finance – External Affairs	13–14 Jul. 1950
24 Apr. 1953	138	Committee on Finance – External Affairs (Resumed)	25–26 Apr. 1953
29 Apr. 1953	138	Committee on Finance – External Affairs	30 Apr.– 2 May 1953
12 Jul. 1955	151	Committee on Finance – External Affairs	13–14 Jul. 1955
3–4 Jul. 1956	159	Committee on Finance – External Affairs	4–6 Jul. 1956
10–11 Jul. 1956	159	Committee on Finance – External Affairs (Resumed)	11–13 Jul. 1956
2 Jul. 1959	176	Committee on Finance – External Affairs	3–4 Jul. 1959
7 Jul. 1959	176	Committee on Finance – External Affairs (Resumed)	8–9 Jul. 1959
8 Jun. 1960	182	Committee on Finance – External Affairs	9–10 Jun. 1960
4–5 Apr. 1962	194	Committee on Finance – External Affairs	5–7 Apr. 1962
3 Apr. 1963	201	Committee on Finance – External Affairs	4–5 Apr. 1963
4–7 Jan. 1966	219	Agreement between the Government of Ireland and the Government of the United Kingdom	5–9 Jan. 1966
3 Mar. 1971	252	Policy on Northern Ireland	4–5 Mar. 1971

Table A9 (*cont.*)

Date of debate	Vol. of report	Title of debate	Newspaper editions
9 Mar. 1971	252	Policy on Northern Ireland (Resumed)	10–11 Mar. 1971
4 Feb. 1972	258	Statements on Northern Ireland situation	5–6 Feb. 1972
26 Feb. 1974	270	British legislation on partition	27–28 Feb. 1974
13 Mar. 1974	271	Sunningdale Agreement	14–15 Mar. 1974
5–6 Nov. 1974	275	Committee on Finance – Foreign Affairs	6–8 Nov. 1974
13 Dec. 1979	317	Committee on Finance – Foreign Affairs	14–15 Nov. 1979
29 May 1980	321	Taoiseach's meeting with British Prime Minister	30–31 May 1980
19–21 Nov. 1985	361	Anglo-Irish Agreement	20–23 Nov. 1985
16 Nov. 1988	384	Review of Anglo-Irish Agreement	17–18 Nov. 1988
1 Apr. 1993	429	Northern Ireland: statements	2–3 Apr. 1993
15 Dec. 1993	437	Joint Declaration on Peace in Northern Ireland	16–17 Dec. 1993
22 Feb. 1995	449	Joint Framework Document on Northern Ireland	23–24 Feb. 1995
28 Mar. 1996	463	White Paper on Foreign Policy	29–30 Mar. 1996
25 Apr. 1996	463	White Paper on Foreign Policy (Resumed)	26–27 Apr. 1996
9 Mar. 1999	501	British–Irish Agreement Bill	10–11 Mar. 1999
2 Dec. 1999	512	British–Irish Agreement	3–4 Dec. 1999

Bibliography

Abazov, Rafis. 1999. *The Formation of Post-Soviet International Politics in Kazakhstan, Kyrgyzstan, and Uzbekistan*. Washington: The Donald W. Treadgold Papers.

Abusch, Alexander. 1996 [1948]. 'Rede auf dem Internationalen Kongreß der Intellektuellen für den Frieden, 28. August 1948', in Helmut Peitsch, ed., *Vom Faschismus zum Kalten Krieg – auch eine deutsche Literaturgeschichte: Literaturverhältnisse, Genres, Themen*. Berlin: Sigma, p. 225.

Acharya, Amitav. 2004. 'How Ideas Spread: Whose Norms Matter?' *International Organization* 58/2, pp. 39–275.

Ackermann, Alice. 1992. *Building Peace with Adversaries: The Case of Postwar Germany*. Ann Arbor: UMI.

Adenauer, Konrad. 1958. 'Protokoll des CDU-Bundesvorstandes', in Günter Buchstab, ed., *Adenauer: Um den Frieden zu gewinnen*. Düsseldorf: Droste, 1994, pp. 44–110.

1963 [1950]. 'Deutschlands Stellung in der Welt: Rede auf dem Parteitag in Goslar, 22 October 1950', in Ossip Flechtheim, ed., *Dokumente zur parteipolitischen Entwicklung in Deutschland seit 1945: Programmatik der deutschen Parteien*, vol. I. Berlin: Dokumenten-Verlag, pp. 76–86.

1965. *Erinnerungen 1945–1953*. Stuttgart: Deutsche Verlags-Anstalt.

1966. *Erinnerungen 1953–1955*. Stuttgart: Deutsche Verlags-Anstalt.

1972a [1949]. 'Erklärung des Bundeskanzlers Dr. Konrad Adenauer vor dem Deutschen Bundestag am 21. Oktober 1949', in Auswärtiges Amt, *Die Auswärtige Politik der Bundesrepublik Deutschland*. Cologne: Verlag Wissenschaft und Politik, pp. 155, 156.

1972b [1951]. 'Rede des Bundeskanzlers Dr. Konrad Adenauer im Chatham-House, London, anläßlich seines offiziellen Besuches in Großbritannien, 6. Dezember 1951', in Auswärtiges Amt, *Die Auswärtige Politik der Bundesrepublik Deutschland*. Cologne: Verlag Wissenschaft und Politik, p. 191.

1972c [1959]. 'Stellungnahme des Bundeskanzlers Dr. Konrad Adenauer vor dem Verein der Ausländischen Presse in Bad Godesberg am 13. Oktober 1959', in Auswärtiges Amt, *Die Auswärtige Politik der Bundesrepublik Deutschland*. Cologne: Verlag Wissenschaft und Politik, p. 413.

1975 [1950] 'Deutschlands Stellung und Aufgabe in der Welt: Rede auf
    dem 1. Bundesparteitag der CDU in Goslar', in Hans-Peter Schwarz, ed.,
    Reden 1917–1967: Eine Auswahl. Stuttgart: Deutsche Verlags-Anstalt,
    pp. 181–93.
1984 [1955]. 'Die Teilung Deutschlands ist abnorm', speech given in
    Moscow, 9 September 1955; in Bernhard Pollmann, ed., *Lesebuch zur
    deutschen Geschichte III.* Dortmund: Chronik Verlag, pp. 234–6.
1989 [1951]. 'Vom Geist menschlicher und religiöser Toleranz', in
    Auswärtiges Amt, *40 Jahre Aussenpolitik der Bundesrepublik
    Deutschland: Eine Dokumentation.* Stuttgart: Bonn Aktuell, pp. 36–7.
Adler, Emanuel. 1991. 'Cognitive Evolution: A Dynamic Approach for the
    Study of International Relations and Their Progress', in Emanuel Adler
    and Beverly Crawford, eds., *Progress in Postwar International Relations.*
    New York: Columbia University Press, pp. 128–73.
    2005. *Communitarian International Relations: The Epistemic Foundations
    of International Relations.* London: Routledge.
Adler, Emanuel and Barnett, Michael. 1998. 'A Framework for the Study of
    Security Communities', in Emanuel Adler and Michael Barnett, eds.,
    Security Communities. Cambridge: Cambridge University Press,
    pp. 29–65.
Adler, Emanuel and Bernstein, Steven. 2005. 'Knowledge in Power: The
    Epistemic Construction of Global Governance', in Michael Barnett and
    Raymond Duvall, eds., *Power in Global Governance.* Cambridge:
    Cambridge University Press, pp. 294–318.
Adler, Emanuel and Haas, Peter. 1992. 'Conclusion: Epistemic Communities,
    World Order, and the Creation of a Reflective Research Program',
    International Organization 46/1, pp. 367–90.
Agnew, John. 1999. 'Mapping Political Power Beyond State Boundaries:
    Territory, Identity, and Movement in World Politics', *Millennium* 28/3,
    pp. 499–522.
Ahooja-Patel, Krishna. 1974. *The Greco-Bulgarian Dispute before the
    League of Nations 1925–1927: An Experiment in Peaceful Settlement.*
    Geneva: University of Geneva.
Albert, Mathias, Jacobson, David and Lapid, Yosef, eds. 2001. *Identities,
    Borders, Orders: Rethinking International Relations Theory.*
    Minneapolis: University of Minnesota Press.
Albrecht-Carrié, René. 1958. *A Diplomatic History of Europe Since the
    Congress of Vienna.* New York: Harper & Brothers.
Alker, Hayward R. 1988. 'The Dialectical Logic of Thucydides' Melian
    Dialogue', *American Political Science Review* 82/3, pp. 805–20.
Altmann, Normen. 1993. *Konrad Adenauer im Kalten Krieg: Wahrnehmungen
    und Politik, 1945–1956.* Mannheim: J. & J. Verlag.

Ambrosio, Thomas. 2001. *Irredentism: Ethnic Conflict and International Politics*. London: Praeger.

Amery, Carl. 1994 [1961]. 'Wegweisung Europa: Eine kritische Reflexion', in Paul Michael Lützeler, ed., *Hoffnung Europa: Deutsche Essays von Novalis bis Enzensberger*. Frankfurt am Main: S. Fischer, pp. 445–66.

Andersch, Alfred. 1994 [1946]. 'Das junge Europa formt sein Gesicht', in Paul Michael Lützeler, ed., *Hoffnung Europa: Deutsche Essays von Novalis bis Enzensberger*. Frankfurt am Main: S. Fischer, pp. 366–71.

Anderson, Ewan W. 2002. *Global Geopolitical Flashpoints: An Atlas of Conflict*. London: The Stationery Office.

Anysas, M. 1934. *Der litauisch-polnische Streit um das Wilnagebiet: Von seinen Anfängen bis zum Gutachten des Ständigen Internationalen Gerichtshofes vom 15. Oktober 1931*. Würzburg: Dissertationsdruckerei Konrad Triltsch.

Arend, Peter. 1975. *Die innerparteiliche Entwicklung der SPD: 1966–1975*. Bonn: Eichholz.

Aristotle. 1989. *Prior Analytics*, ed. and trans. Robin Smith. Indianapolis: Hackett.

   1994. *Posterior Analytics*, ed. and trans. Jonathan Barnes. Oxford: Clarendon Press.

   1995. *Rhetorik*, translated and annotated by Franz G. Sieveke. Munich: Wilhelm Fink.

Arnold, Bruce. 1977. 'Bipartisanship and the Constitution', *Studies*, pp. 1–7.

   1993. *Haughey – His Life and Unlucky Deeds*. London: HarperCollins.

Augstein, Rudolf. 1967. *Meinungen zu Deutschland*. Frankfurt am Main: Suhrkamp.

Baerenz, Horst. 1988 [1971]. 'Ehre sei Brandt in der Höhe!' in Michael Klant, ed., *Der rote Ballon: Die deutsche Sozialdemokratie in der Karikatur*. Hannover: Fackelträger, p. 200.

Bahr, Egon. 1996. *Zu meiner Zeit*. Munich: K. Blessing.

Banchoff, Thomas. 1999. 'German Identity and European Integration', *European Journal of International Relations* 5/3, pp. 259–89.

Barkin, Samuel and Cronin, Bruce. 1994. 'The State and the Nation: Changing Norms and Rules of Sovereignty in International Relations', *International Organization* 48/1, pp. 107–30.

Barnett, Michael N. 1995. 'Sovereignty, Nationalism, and Regional Order in the Arab States System', *International Organization* 49/3, pp. 479–510.

   1999. 'Culture, Strategy and Foreign Policy Change: Israel's Road to Oslo', *European Journal of International Relations* 5/1, pp. 5–36.

Barzel, Rainer. 1998. *Die Tür blieb offen: Mein persönlicher Bericht über Ostverträge–Mißtrauensvotum–Kanzlersturz*. Bonn: Bouvier.

Bates, Robert, Figueiredo, Rui and Weingast, Barry. 1998. 'The Politics of Interpretation: Rationality, Culture, and Transition', *Politics and Society* 26/4, pp. 603–42.

Bates, Robert, Greif, Avner, Levi, Margaret, Rosenthal, Jean-Laurent and Weingast, Barry. 1998. 'Introduction', in Robert Bates *et al.*, *Analytic Narratives*. Princeton: Princeton University Press, pp. 3–22.

Baumgart, Winfried. 1999. *Europäisches Konzert und nationale Bewegung: Internationale Beziehungen 1830–1878*. München: Ferdinand Schöningh.

Belting, Hans. 1999. *Identität im Zweifel: Ansichten der deutschen Kunst*. Cologne: DuMont.

Bender, Peter. 1966. 'Die DDR nicht isolieren', in Theo Sommer, ed., *Denken an Deutschland*. Hamburg: Nannen-Verlag, pp. 121–32.

    1972. *Die Ostpolitik Willy Brandts oder Die Kunst des Selbstverständlichen*. Reinbek: Rowohlt.

Benford, Robert and Snow, David. 2000. 'Framing Processes and Social Movements: An Overview and Assessment', *Annual Review of Sociology* 26, pp. 611–39.

Ben-Israel, Hedva. 1991. 'Irredentism: Nationalism Reexamined', in Naomi Chazan, ed., *Irredentism and International Politics*. Boulder: Lynne Rienner, pp. 23–36.

Benn, Gottfried. 1996 [1953]. 'Brief an F.W. Oelze', in Helmut Peitsch, ed., *Vom Faschismus zum Kalten Krieg – auch eine deutsche Literaturgeschichte: Literaturverhältnisse, Genres, Themen*. Berlin: Sigma, p. 212.

Benoit, William L., Hample, Dale and Benoit, Pamela. 1992. 'Introduction to the Study of Argumentation', in William L. Benoit, Dale Hample and Pamela Benoit, eds., *Readings in Argumentation: Pragmatics and Discourse Analysis*. Berlin: Foris, pp. 3–16.

Bentham. Jeremy. 1974 [1789]. 'Principles of International Law', in M.C. Jacobs, *Peace Projects of the Eighteenth Century*. New York: Garland.

Berger, Peter and Luckmann, Thomas. 1966. *The Social Construction of Reality: A Treatise in the Sociology of Knowledge*. New York: Anchor.

Berger, Thomas. 1996. 'Norms, Identity, and National Security in Germany and Japan', in Peter J. Katzenstein, ed., *The Culture of National Security: Norms and Identity in World Politics*. New York: Columbia University Press, pp. 317–56.

Bernstein, Steven. 2000. 'Ideas, Social Structure and the Compromise of Liberal Environmentalism', *European Journal of International Relations* 6/4, pp. 464–512.

Bernstein, Steven, Lebow, Richard, Stein, Janice and Weber, Steven. 2000. 'God Gave Physics the Easy Problems: Adapting Social Science to an Unpredictable World', *European Journal of International Relations* 6/1, pp. 43–76.

Besson, Waldemar. 1970. *Die Außenpolitik der Bundesrepublik Deutschland: Erfahrungen und Maßstäbe*. Munich: Piper.

Bettinghaus, Erwin and Cody, Michael. 1994. *Persuasion Communication*. Fort Worth: Harcourt Brace.

Bew, Paul. 1980. *C. S. Parnell*. Dublin: Gill.

1994. *Ideology and the Irish Question: Ulster Unionism and Irish Nationalism, 1912–1916*. Oxford: Clarendon Press.

Bially, Janice. 2001. 'The Power Politics of Identity', *European Journal of International Relations* 7/3, pp. 349–98.

Bienek, Horst. 1986 [1975]. *Die erste Polka*. München: Deutscher Taschenbuch-Verlag.

Biger, Gideon. 1995. *The Encyclopedia of International Boundaries*. New York: Facts on File.

Billig, Michael. 1995. *Banal Nationalism*. London: Sage Publications.

Bingen, Dieter. 1998. *Die Polenpolitik, der Bonner Republik von Adenauer bis Kohl, 1949–1991*. Baden-Baden: Nomos Verlagsgesellschaft.

Biswas, Shampa. 2002. 'W(h)ither the Nation-state? National and State Identity in the Face of Fragmentation and Globalization', *Global Society* 16/2, pp. 175–98.

Bjola, Corneliu. 2005. 'Legitimising the Use of Force in International Politics: A Communicative Action Perspective', *European Journal of International Relations* 11/2, pp. 266–303.

Björkdahl, Annika. 2002. 'Norms in International Relations: Some Conceptual and Methodological Reflections', *Cambridge Review of International Affairs* 15/1, pp. 9–23.

Blair, J. Anthony. 1992. 'Everyday Argumentation from an Informal Logic Perspective', in William L. Benoit, Dale Hample and Pamela J. Benoit, eds., *Readings in Argumentation: Pragmatics and Discourse Analysis*. Berlin: Foris, pp. 357–76.

Boehm, Max Hildebert. 1923. *Europa irredenta: Eine Einführung in das Nationalitätenproblem der Gegenwart*. Berlin: Rainer Hobbing.

Böll, Heinrich. 1969. 'An eine deutsche Frau', in Heinrich Böll *et al.*, eds., *Offene Briefe an die Deutschen*. Vienna: Verlag Fritz Molden, pp. 11–56.

1978 [1961]. *Als der Krieg ausbrach*. Munich: Deutscher Taschenbuch Verlag.

Boltanski, Luc and Thévenot, Laurent. 2006 [1991]. *On Justification: Economies of Worth*, trans. Catherine Porter. Princeton: Princeton University Press.

Bostrum, Richard N. 1983. *Persuasion*. Englewood Cliffs: Prentice Hall.

Bourdieu, Pierre. 1977 [1972]. *Outline of a Theory of Practice*. Cambridge: Cambridge University Press.

1990 [1980]. *The Logic of Practice*. Stanford: Stanford University Press.

1998 [1994]. *Practical Reason: On the Theory of Action*. Cambridge: Polity Press.

Bowman, John. 1982. *De Valera and the Ulster Question, 1917–1973*. Oxford: Clarendon Press.

Boyce, D. George. 1995. *Nationalism in Ireland*. New York: Routledge.

1996. *The Making of Modern Irish History: Revisionism and the Revisionist Controversy*. London and New York: Routledge.

Boyce, D. George and O'Day, Alan, eds. 1996. *The Making of Modern Irish History*. London: Routledge.

Boyd, Gavin, ed. 1984. *Regionalism and Global Security*. Lexington: Lexington Books.

Brandt, Willy. 1968. *Friedenspolitik in Europa*. Frankfurt am Main: Fischer.

1976. *Begegnungen und Einsichten*. Hamburg: Hoffmann und Campe.

Brecher, Michael and Wilkenfeld, Jonathan. 1997a. 'The Ethnic Dimension of International Crises', in David Carment and Patrick James, eds., *Wars in the Midst of Peace: The International Politics of Ethnic Conflict*. Pittsburgh: University of Pittsburgh Press, pp. 164–94.

1997b. *A Study of Crisis*. Ann Arbor: University of Michigan Press.

Brenner, Neil. 1999. 'Beyond State-centrism? Space, Territoriality, and Geographical Scale in Globalization Studies', *Theory and Society* 28/1, pp. 39–78.

Breuilly, John. 1993. *Nationalism and the State*. Manchester: Manchester University Press.

Breuning, Marijke. 2003. 'The Role of Analogies and Abstract Reasoning in Decision-making: Evidence from the Debate over Truman's Proposal for Developmental Assistance', *International Studies Quarterly* 47/2, pp. 229–45.

Briand, Aristide. 1929. *The Briand Memorandum*. Leiden Historical University Institute at http://www.let.leidenuniv.nl/history/rtg/res1/briand.htm

Brock, Lothar. 1974. 'Problemlösung und Interessenpolitik: Friendspolitische Funktionen einer gesamteuropäischen Zusammenarbeit', in Vereinigung Deutscher Wissenschaftler, ed., *Durch Kooperation zum Frieden?* Munich: Carl Hanser Verlag, pp. 13–32.

1999. 'Observing Change, Rewriting History: A Critical Overview', *Millennium* 28/3, pp. 483–97.

Brockmann, Stephen. 2002. 'Germany as Occident at the Zero Hour', *German Studies Review* 25/3, pp. 477–96.

Brogan, Patrick. 1992. *World Conflicts: Why and Where They Are Happening*. London: Bloomsbury Publications.

Brown, David. 1999. 'Are There Good and Bad Nationalisms?' *Nations and Nationalism* 5/2, pp. 281–302.

Browne, Vincent. 1996. 'The Rocky Road to Dublin', *Film West* no. 25, at http://www.iol.ie/~galfilm/filmwest/fw25.html

Brownlie, Ian. 1979. *African Boundaries: A Legal and Diplomatic Encyclopaedia*. Berkeley: University of California Press.

Brubaker, Rogers. 1993. 'Social Theory as Habitus', in Craig Calhoun, Edward LiPuma and Moishe Postone, eds., *Bourdieu: Critical Perspectives*. Cambridge: Polity Press, pp. 212–34.

1996. *Nationalism Reframed: Nationhood and the National Question in the New Europe*. Cambridge: Cambridge University Press.

Brubaker, Rogers and Cooper, Frederick. 2000. 'Beyond "Identity"', *Theory and Society* 29/1, pp. 1–47.

Bueno de Mesquita, Bruce. 1985. 'Reply to Stephen Krasner and Robert Jervis', *International Studies Quarterly* 29/2, pp. 151–4.

Bugajski, Janusz. 1993. *Nations in Turmoil: Conflict and Cooperation in Eastern Europe*. Boulder: Westview Press.

Buzan, Barry. 1991. *People, States and Fear: An Agenda for International Security Studies in the Post-Cold War Era*. New York: Harvester Wheatsheaf.

Buzan, Barry and Little, Richard. 1996. 'Reconceptualizing Anarchy: Structural Realism Meets World History', *European Journal of International Relations* 2/4, pp. 403–38.

2000. *International Systems in World History*. Oxford: Oxford University Press.

Cahalan, James M. 1993. *Modern Irish Literature and Culture: A Chronology*. New York: G. K. Hall.

Calhoun, Craig. 1997. *Nationalism*. Minneapolis: University of Minnesota Press.

Calvert, Peter. 2004. *Border and Territorial Disputes of the World*. London: John Harper.

Calvocoressi, Peter. 2001. *World Politics: 1945–2000*. London: Longman.

Cantori, Louis and Spiegel, Steven. 1970. *The International Politics of Regions: A Comparative Approach*. Englewood Cliffs: Prentice Hall.

Carlsnaes, Walter. 1992. 'The Agent–Structure Problem in Foreign Policy', *International Studies Quarterly* 36/3, pp. 245–70.

Carment, David. 1993. 'The International Dimensions of Ethnic Conflict: Concepts, Indicators, and Theory', *Journal of Peace Research* 30, pp. 137–50.

Carment, David and James, Patrick. 1995. 'Internal Constraints and Interstate Ethnic Conflict: Towards a Crisis-based Assessment of Irredentism', *Journal of Conflict Resolution* 39/1, pp. 82–109.

1997. 'Secession and Irredenta in World Politics: The Neglected Interstate Dimension', in David Carment and Patrick James, eds., *Wars in the*

Midst of Peace: The International Politics of Ethnic Conflict. Pittsburgh: University of Pittsburgh Press, pp. 194–231.

2000. 'Explaining Third-party Intervention in Ethnic Conflict: Theory and Evidence', *Nations and Nationalism* 6/2, pp. 173–202.

Centeno, Miguel Angel. 2002. *Blood and Debt: War and the Nation-State in Latin America*. University Park: Pennsylvania University Press.

Cerny, Philip G. 1995. 'Globalization and the Changing Logic of Collective Action', *International Organization* 49/4, pp. 595–625.

Chazan, Naomi. 1991. 'Introduction', in Naomi Chazan, ed., *Irredentism and International Politics*. Boulder: Lynne Rienner, pp. 1–8.

Checkel, Jeffrey. 1997. 'International Norms and Domestic Politics: Bridging the Rationalist–Constructivist Divide', *European Journal of International Relations* 3/4, pp. 473–95.

1999. 'Norms, Institutions, and National Identity in Contemporary Europe', *International Studies Quarterly* 43/1, pp. 83–114.

2001. 'Why Comply? Social Learning and European Identity Change', *International Organization* 55/3, pp. 553–88.

Child, Jack. 1985. *Geopolitics and Conflict in South America*. New York: Praeger.

Choucri, Nazli and North, Robert C. 1979. *Nations in Conflict: National Growth and International Violence*. San Francisco: W. H. Freeman and Company.

Christlich Demokratische Union. 1963 [1961]. 'Kölner Manifest: Das Wahlprogramm zur Bundestagswahl 1961', in Ossip Flechtheim, ed., *Dokumente zur parteipolitischen Entwicklung in Deutschland seit 1945: Programmatik der deutschen Parteien*, vol. I. Berlin: Dokumenten-Verlag, pp. 146–8.

Christlich Soziale Union. 1963 [1957]. 'Grundsatzprogramm 1957', in Ossip Flechtheim, ed., *Dokumente zur parteipolitischen Entwicklung in Deutschland seit 1945: Programmatik der deutschen Parteien*, vol. I. Berlin: Dokumenten-Verlag, pp. 219–24.

Churchill, Winston. 1946. Speech delivered at the University of Zurich, 19 September 1946, at http://stars.coe.fr/a_propos/histoire/zurich_e.htm

Cicero, Marcus Tullius. 1967. *De Oratore*. London: William Heinemann.

2003. *Topica*. Oxford: Oxford University Press.

Citrin, Jack, Haas, Ernst and Reingold, Beth. 1994. 'Is American Nationalism Changing? Implications for Foreign Policy', *International Studies Quarterly* 38/1, pp. 1–31.

Cleary, Joe. 2002. *Literature, Partition and the Nation State: Culture and Conflict in Ireland, Israel and Palestine*. Cambridge: Cambridge University Press.

Clemens, Clay. 1989. *Reluctant Realists: The Christian Democrats and West German Ostpolitik*. Durham: Duke University Press.

Collins, Stephen. 2000. *The Power Game: Fianna Fáil since Lemass*. Dublin: O'Brien Press.

Conner, Walker. 1992. 'The Nation and Its Myth', *International Journal of Comparative Sociology* 23, pp. 48–56.

Cortell, Andrew and Davis, James. 2005. 'When Norms Clash: International Norms, Domestic Practices, and Japan's Internalization of the GATT/WTO', *Review of International Studies* 31/1, pp. 3–25.

Costello, John. 1948. *Dáil-Speech: 24 Nov. 1948*. Dublin: Cahill.

Cottam, Martha L. and Cottam, Richard W. 2001. *Nationalism and Politics: The Political Behaviour of Nation States*. London: Lynne Rienner.

Cozik, Charles P., ed. 1994. *Nationalism and Ethnic Conflict*. San Diego: Greenhaven Press.

Crawford, Neta. 2002. *Argument and Change in World Politics: Ethics, Decolonization, and Humanitarian Intervention*. Cambridge: Cambridge University Press.

Cruz, Consuelo. 2000. 'Identity and Persuasion: How Nations Remember Their Pasts and Make Their Futures', *World Politics* 52/2, pp. 275–312.

Czerwick, Edwin. 1981. *Oppositionstheorien und Außenpolitik: Eine Analyse sozialdemokratischer Deutschlandpolitik 1955–1966*. Königstein: Anton Hain.

Dai, Xinyuan. 2005. 'Why Comply? The Domestic Constituency Mechanism', *International Organization* 59/2, pp. 363–98.

Dávid, Géza and Fodor, Pál, eds. 2000. *Ottomans, Hungarians, and Habsburgs in Central Europe: The Military Confines in the Era of Ottoman Conquest*. Leiden: Brill.

Day, Alan J. 1992. 'The Northern Ireland Question', in John B. Allcock *et al.*, eds., *Border and Territorial Disputes*. Harlow: Longman, pp. 120–41.

Dean, Jonathan. 1994. *Ending Europe's Wars: The Continuing Search for Peace and Security*. New York: Twentieth Century Fund Press.

de Béthune, Maximilian duc de Sully. 2002 [1662]. *L'Europe vue par Henri IV et Sully*, ed. André Puharré. Mon Hélios.

Debicki, Roman. 1963. *Foreign Policy of Poland 1919–1939: From the Rebirth of the Polish Republic to World War II*. London: Pall Mall Press.

de Gaulle, Charles. 1971. *Memoirs of Hope*. London: Weidenfeld and Nicolson.

Deibert, Ronald. 1997. 'Exorcismus Theoriae: Pragmatism, Metaphors and the Return of the Medieval in IR Theory', *European Journal of International Relations* 3/2, pp. 167–92.

de Saint-Pierre, Abbé Charles Irenée Castel. 1986 [1712]. *Project pour rendre la paix perpétuelle en Europe*. Paris: Fayard.

Deudney, Daniel and Ikenberry, John. 1999. 'The Nature and Sources of Liberal International Order', *Review of International Studies* 25/2, pp. 179–96.

Deutsch, Harold. 1990. 'A Pandora's Box of Problems is Open in Europe', *Star Tribune*, 19 January, p. 13.

Deutsch, Karl and Edinger, Lewis. 1959. *Germany Rejoins the Powers: Mass Opinion, Interest Groups, and Elites in Contemporary German Foreign Policy*. Stanford: Stanford University Press.

Deutsch, Karl *et al.* 1957. *Political Community and the North Atlantic Area: International Organization in the Light of Historical Experience*. New York: Greenwood Press.

de Valera, Eamon. 1980a [1920]. 'A Race That Never Ceased To Strive', in Maurice Moynihan, ed., *Speeches and Statements by Eamon de Valera, 1917–1973*. Dublin: Gill and Macmillan, pp. 35–6.

1980b [1920]. 'Ireland's Request', in Maurice Moynihan, ed., *Speeches and Statements by Eamon de Valera, 1917–1973*. Dublin: Gill and Macmillan, pp. 36–46.

1980c [1922]. 'A Stepping Stone?' in Maurice Moynihan, ed., *Speeches and Statements by Eamon de Valera, 1917–1973*. Dublin: Gill and Macmillan, pp. 94–7.

1980d [1933]. 'Ireland Free, Gaelic and United', in Maurice Moynihan, ed., *Speeches and Statements by Eamon de Valera, 1917–1973*. Dublin: Gill and Macmillan, pp. 233–5.

1980e [1949]. 'Taking Stock', in Maurice Moynihan, ed., *Speeches and Statements by Eamon de Valera, 1917–1973*. Dublin: Gill and Macmillan, pp. 522–6.

1980f [1951]. 'Partition', in Maurice Moynihan, ed., *Speeches and Statements by Eamon de Valera, 1917–1973*. Dublin: Gill and Macmillan, pp. 541–4.

Diehl, Paul F. and Goertz, Gary. 1991. 'Interstate Conflict over Exchanges of Homeland Territory: 1816–1980', *Political Geography Quarterly* 10/4, pp. 342–55.

Dilthey, Wilhelm. 1924 [1907]. 'Das Wesen der Philosophie', in Wilhelm Dilthey, *Gesammelte Schriften V*. Leipzig: B. G. Teubner.

1981 [1910]. *Der Aufbau der geschichtlichen Welt in den Geisteswissenschaften*. Frankfurt/Main: Suhrkamp.

Dirks, Walter. 1994 [1946]. 'Europa, Arbeiter, Christen', in Klaus Wagenbach *et al.*, eds., *Deutsche Schriftsteller und ihr Staat seit 1945: Vaterland, Muttersprache*. Berlin: Verlag Klaus Wagenbach, pp. 58–60.

Divo. 1958. *Umfragen: Ereignisse und Probleme der Zeit im Urteil der Bevölkerung, vol. 1*. Frankfurt am Main: Europäische Verlagsanstalt.

1959. *Umfragen: Ereignisse und Probleme der Zeit im Urteil der Bevölkerung, vol. 2.* Frankfurt am Main: Europäische Verlagsanstalt.

1962. *Umfragen: Ereignisse und Probleme der Zeit im Urteil der Bevölkerung, vol. 3.* Frankfurt am Main: Europäische Verlagsanstalt.

Doherty, Róisín. 2002. *Ireland, Neutrality and European Security Integration.* Aldershot: Ashgate.

Dollinger, Hans and Klein, Walther, eds. 1989. *Das waren Zeiten … Achtzehn Karikaturisten sehen vierzig Jahre Bundesrepublik.* Munich: Süddeutscher Verlag.

Dominguez, Jorge I. 2003. *Boundary Disputes in Latin America.* Washington: United States Institute of Peace.

Dönhoff, Marion Gräfin von. 1965. 'Ostpolitik mit de Gaulle', *Die Zeit,* 3 December, p. 1.

1970. *Deutsche Außenpolitik von Adenauer bis Brandt.* Hamburg: Christian Wegner Verlag.

Douglas, Roy, Harte, Liam and O'Hara, Jim. 1998. *Drawing Conclusions: A Cartoon History of Anglo-Irish Relations, 1798–1998.* Belfast: Blackstaff Press.

Downs, George, Rokke, David and Barsoom, Peter. 1996. 'Is the Good News About Compliance Good News about Cooperation?' *International Organization* 50/3, pp. 379–406.

Doyle, Michael. 1986. *Empires.* Ithaca: Cornell University Press.

Drobizheva, Leokadia *et al.* 1996. *Ethnic Conflict in the Post-Soviet World: Case Studies and Analysis.* London: M. E. Sharpe, 1996.

Druckman, Daniel. 1994. 'Nationalism, Patriotism, and Group Loyalty: A Social Psychological Perspective', *Mershon International Studies Review* 38/1, p. 43–68.

Duffy, Gavan, Frederking, Brian and Tucker, Seth. 1998. 'Language Games: Dialogical Analysis of INF Negotiations', *International Studies Quarterly* 42/2, pp. 271–94.

Dwyer, T. Ryle. 1995. *Short Fellow: A Biography of Charles J. Haughey.* Dublin: Marino.

Eagly, Alice H., Wood, Wendy and Chaiken, Shelly. 1978. 'Causal Inferences About Communicators and Their Effects on Opinion Change', *Journal of Personality and Social Psychology* 36/2, pp. 424–35.

Eberlein, Klaus. 1968. *Was die Deutschen möchten: Politische Meinungsumfragen in der Bundesrepublik.* Hamburg: Christian Wegner Verlag.

Eemeren, Frans H. van. 1992. *Argumentation, Communication, and Fallacies: A Pragma-dialectical Perspective.* Hillsdale: Lawrence Erlbaum.

Ehteshami, Anoushiravan, ed. 1994. *From the Gulf to Central Asia: Players in the New Great Game.* Exeter: University of Exeter Press.

Elias, Norbert. *Über den Prozess der Zivilisation: Soziogenetische und psychogenetische Untersuchungen.* Basel: Verlag zum Falken, 1939.

Elster, Jon. 2000. *Ulysses Unbound: Studies in Rationality, Precommitment, and Constraints.* Cambridge: Cambridge University Press.

Emnid. 1948–1973. *Informationen,* vols. 1–25. Bielefeld: Emnid.

Emsley, Clive, Marwick, Arthur and Simpson, Wendy. 1989. *War, Peace and Social Change in Twentieth-Century Europe.* Philadelphia: Open University Press.

Engelmann, Roger. 1993. 'Die Beziehungen zwischen FDP und LDPD: 1956–1966', in Roger Engelmann and Paul Erker, eds., *Annäherung und Abgrenzung: Aspekte deutsch-deutscher Beziehungen 1956–1969.* Munich: Oldenbourg, pp. 13–132.

Erhard, Ludwig. 1965. *The Economics of Success.* London: Thames & Hudson.

European Movement. 1949. *The European Movement and the Council of Europe.* London: Hutchinson.

Fanning, Ronan. 1983. *Independent Ireland.* Dublin: Helicon.

      1990. 'Irish Neutrality', in Bo Huldt and Ati Lejins, eds., *Neutrals in Europe: Ireland.* Stockholm: The Swedish Institute of International Affairs, pp. 1–24.

Fearon, James and Laitin, David. 2000. 'Violence and the Social Construction of Ethnic Identity', *International Organization* 54/4, pp. 845–77.

Feld, Werner and Boyd, Gavin, eds. 1980. *Comparative Regional Systems: West and East Europe, North America, The Middle East, and Developing Countries.* New York: Pergamon Press.

Ferghana Valley Working Group. 1999. *Calming the Ferghana Valley: Development and Dialogue in the Heart of Central Asia.* New York: The Century Foundation Press.

Ferguson, Yale H. and Mansbach, Richard W. 1999. 'Global Politics at the Turn of the Millennium: Changing Bases of "Us" and "Them"', *International Studies Review* 1/2, pp. 78–107.

Fichte, Johann Gottlieb. 1978 [1808]. *Reden an die deutsche Nation.* Hamburg: Meiner.

Finnemore, Martha. 1996. *National Interests in International Society.* Ithaca: Cornell University Press.

Finnemore, Martha and Sikkink, Kathryn. 1998. 'International Norm Dynamics and Political Change', *International Organization* 52/4, pp. 887–917.

FitzGerald, Garret. 1972. *Towards a New Ireland.* London: Charles Knight.

      1991a. 'The Impact of European Community Membership on Political Opinion in Britain and Ireland', *Working Papers on European Economic and Public Affairs,* no. 3. Dublin: Centre for European Economic and Public Affairs.

1991b. *All in a Life*. Dublin: Gill and Macmillan.

Fitzpatrick, David. 1977. *Politics and Irish Life 1913–1921*. Dublin: Gill and Macmillan

Florini, Ann. 1996. 'The Evolution of International Norms', *International Studies Quarterly* 40/3, pp. 363–89.

Foerster, Rolf Hellmut. 1967. *Europa: Geschichte einer politischen Idee.* Munich: Nymphenburger Verlagsbuchhandlung.

Foley, K. and Enright, F. 1977. *The Nineteenth Century: New Syllabus Intermediate History*. Dublin: School and College Services.

Fontaine, Pascal. 2000. *A New Idea for Europe: The Schuman Declaration, 1950–2000*. Luxembourg: Office for Official Publications of the European Communities.

Forsberg, Tuomas. 1995. 'Theories on Territorial Disputes', in Tuomas Forsberg, ed., *Contested Territory: Border Disputes at the Edge of the Former Soviet Empire*. Alderhot: Edward Elgar, pp. 23–41.

Foster, Roy. 1986. 'We Are All Revisionists Now', *The Irish Review* 1, pp. 1–5.
  1998. *Modern Ireland: 1600–1972*. London: Penguin.

Foucault, Michel. 1970 [1966]. *The Order of Things: An Archeology of the Human Sciences*. New York: Random House.
  1989a [1966]. *The Order of Things*. London: Routledge.
  1989b [1969]. *The Archaeology of Knowledge*. London: Routledge.

Franklin, Daniel. 1992. 'International Boundaries: Ex-Soviet Union and Eastern Europe', *The World Today* 48, pp. 38–40.

Freeman, John. 1991. *Security and the CSCE Process: The Stockholm Conference and Beyond*. London: Macmillan.

Freie Demokratische Partei. 1963 [1952]. 'Grundsatzentschließung für eine freiheitliche und rechtsstaatliche, nationale und europäische, christlich-abendländische und soziale Haltung', in Ossip Flechtheim, ed., *Dokumente zur parteipolitischen Entwicklung in Deutschland seit 1945: Programmatik der deutschen Parteien*, vol. I. Berlin: Dokumenten-Verlag, pp. 325–6.
  1976 [1957]. 'Das Berliner Programm der Freien Demokratischen Partei', in Heino Kaack, ed., *Zur Geschichte und Programmatik der Freien Demokratischen Partei: Grundriß und Materialien*. Meisenheim am Glan: Verlag Anton Hain, pp. 84–91.

Friedrichs, Jörg. 2003. 'The Meaning of New Medievalism', *European Journal of International Relations* 7/4, pp. 475–501.

Fritz, Walter Helmut. 1979. 'Das Wort Friede', in Karl H. Van D'Elden, ed., *West German Poets on Society and Politics*. Detroit: Wayne State University Press.

Gagnon, V. P. 1994. 'Ethnic Nationalism and International Conflict: The Case of Serbia', *International Security* 19/3, pp. 130–66.

Gallagher, Frank. 1957. *The Indivisible Island: The History of the Partition of Ireland*. Westport, CT: Greenwood Press.

Gallagher, Michael. 1982. *The Irish Labour Party in Transition: 1957–1982*. Manchester: Manchester University Press.

1985. *Political Parties in the Republic of Ireland*. Manchester: Manchester University Press.

Gamson, William. 1992. *Talking Politics*. Cambridge: Cambridge University Press.

Garratt, Robert F. 1989. *Modern Irish Poetry: Traditions and Continuity from Yeats to Heaney*. Berkeley: University of California Press.

Garton Ash, Timothy. 1993. *In Europe's Name: Germany and the Divided Continent*. London: Jonathan Cape.

Geiß, Paul Georg. 1995. *Nationenwerdung in Mittelasien*. Frankfurt am Main: Peter Lang.

Gibbons, Luke. 1996. *Transformations in Irish Culture*. Cork: Cork University Press, 1996.

Gibson, Ralph. 1994. 'The Intensification of National Consciousness in Modern Europe', in Claus Bjørn, Alexander Grant and Keith Stringer, eds., *Nations, Nationalism and Patriotism in the European Past*. Copenhagen: Academic Press.

Gieseke, Frank and Markert, Albert. 1996. *Flieger, Filz und Vaterland: Eine erweiterte Beuys Biographie*. Berlin: Elefanten Press.

Gilland, Karin. 2000. 'Ireland and European Integration', in John Hutchison and Anthony Smith, eds., *Nationalism: Critical Concepts in Political Science II*. London: Routledge.

Gilpin, Robert. 1983. *War and Change in World Politics*. Princeton: Princeton University Press.

Girot, Pascal, ed. 1994. *The Americas*. London: Routledge.

Girvin, Brian. 1994. 'Constitutional Nationalism and Northern Ireland', in Brian Barton and Patrick J. Roche, eds., *The Northern Ireland Question: Perspectives and Policies*. Aldershot: Avebury, pp. 5–52.

1999. 'The Making of Irish Nationalism: Between Integration and Independence', in Patrick J. Roche and Brian Barton, eds., *The Northern Ireland Question: Nationalism, Unionism, and Partition*. Aldershot: Ashgate, pp. 1–29.

Glaab, Manuela. 1999. *Deutschlandpolitik in der öffentlichen Meinung: Einstellungen und Regierungspolitik in der Bundesrepublik Deutschland 1949 bis 1990*. Opladen: Leske & Budrich.

2000. 'Die Deutschland- und Ostpolitik Willy Brandts in der öffentlichen Meinung', in Carsten Tessmer, ed., *Das Willy-Brandt-Bild in Deutschland und Polen*. Berlin: Druckerei Hermann Schlesener, pp. 41–51.

Goertz, Gary and Diehl, Paul. 1992. *Territorial Changes and International Conflict*. London: Routledge.

Goffman, Erving. 1974. *Frame Analysis: An Essay on the Organization of Experience*. New York: Harper & Row.

Goldman, Kjell. 2002. 'Internationalisation and the Nation-state: Four Issues and Three Non-issues', *European Journal of Political Research* 41/3, pp. 281–305.

Goldstein, Judith and Keohane, Robert O. 1993. 'Ideas and Foreign Policy: An Analytical Framework', in Judith Goldstein and Robert O. Keohane, eds., *Ideas and Foreign Policy: Beliefs, Institutions, and Political Change*. Ithaca: Cornell University Press, pp. 3–30.

Goodman, James. 1996. *Nationalism and Transnationalism: The National Conflict in Ireland and European Union Integration*. Aldershot: Ashgate.

Görtemaker, Manfred. 1998. 'Die Ursprünge der "neuen Ostpolitik" Willy Brandts', in Arnd Bauerkämper, Martin Sabrow and Bernd Stöver, eds., *Doppelte Zeitgeschichte: Deutsch-deutsche Beziehungen 1945–1990*. Bonn: J. H. W. Dietz, pp. 44–57.

Gottmann, Jean. 1973. *The Significance of Territory*. Charlottesville: University Press of Virginia.

Gourevitch, Peter. 2002. 'Domestic Politics and International Relations', in Walter Carlsnaes, Thomas Risse and Beth A. Simmons, eds., *Handbook of International Relations*. London: Sage, pp. 309–28.

Grass, Günter. 1986 [1959]. *Die Blechtrommel*. Munich: Deutscher Taschenbuch-Verlag.

Greenfeld, Liah. 1992. *Nationalism: Five Roads to Modernity*. Cambridge, MA: Harvard University Press.

Greenfeld, Liah and Chirot, Daniel. 1994. 'Nationalism and Aggression', *Theory and Society* 23/1, pp. 79–130.

Griffith, William E. 1982. *The Ostpolitik of the Federal Republic of Germany*. Cambridge, MA: MIT Press.

Griffiths, Stephen Iwan. 1993. *Nationalism and Ethnic Conflict: Threats to European Security*. Oxford: Oxford University Press.

Gronbeck, Bruce E. 1992. 'From Argument to Argumentation: Fifteen Years of Identity Crisis', in William L. Benoit, Dale Hample and Pamela J. Benoit, eds., *Readings in Argumentation: Pragmatics and Discourse Analysis*. Berlin: Foris, pp. 17–31.

Grundy-Warr, Carl. 1994. *Eurasia*. London: Routledge.

Gullberg, Tom. 2000. *State, Territory and Identity: The Principle of Self-Determination, the Question of Territorial Sovereignty in Carinthia and other Post Habsburg Territories after the First World War*. Åbo: Åbo University Press.

Gutmann, Emanuel. 1991. 'Concealed or Conjured Irredentism: The Case of Alsace', in Naomi Chazan, ed., *Irredentism and International Politics*. Boulder: Lynne Rienner, pp. 37–49.

Guzzini, Stefano. 2000. 'A Reconstruction of Constructivism in International Relations', *European Journal of International Relations* 6/2, pp. 147–82.

Haas, Ernst B. 1999. 'The Late Flowering and Early Fading of German Nationalism', in John S. Brady, Beverly Crawford and Sarah Elise Wiliarty, eds., *The Postwar Transformation of Germany: Democracy, Prosperity, and Nationhood*. Ann Arbor: University of Michigan Press, pp. 286–338.

2000. *Nationalism, Liberalism, and Progress: The Dismal Fate of New Nations*. Ithaca: Cornell University Press.

Habermas, Jürgen. 1995a [1981]. *Theorie des kommunikativen Handelns I: Handlungsrationalität und gesellschaftliche Rationalisierung*. Frankfurt am Main: Suhrkamp.

1995b [1981]. *Theorie des kommunikativen Handelns II: Zur Kritik der funktionalistischen Vernunft*. Frankfurt am Main: Suhrkamp.

1998a [1992]. *Faktizität und Geltung: Beiträge zur Diskurstheorie des Rechts und des demokratischen Rechtsstaats*. Frankfurt am Main: Suhrkamp.

1998b. *Die postnationale Konstellation: Politische Essays*. Frankfurt am Main: Suhrkamp.

Hacke, Christian. 1975. *Die Ost- und Deutschlandpolitik der CDU/CSU: Wege und Irrwege der Opposition seit 1969*. Cologne: Verlag Wissenschaft und Politik.

1988. *Weltmacht wider Willen: Die Außenpolitik der Bundesrepublik Deutschland*. Stuttgart: Klett-Cotta.

1997. *Die Außenpolitik der Bundesrepublik Deutschland: Weltmacht wider Willen?* Frankfurt am Main: Propyläen.

Haffner, Sebastian. 1985. *Im Schatten der Geschichte: Historisch-politische Variationen aus zwanzig Jahren*. Stuttgart: Deutsche Verlags-Anstalt.

Haftendorn, Helga. 1985. *Security and Détente: Conflicting Priorities in German Foreign Policy*. New York: Praeger.

2001. *Deutsche Außenpolitik zwischen Selbstbeschränkung und Selbstbehauptung*. Stuttgart: Deutsche Verlags-Anstalt.

Hajer, Maarten. 1993. 'Discourse Coalitions and the Institutionalization of Practice: The Case of Acid Rain in Great Britain', in Frank Fischer and John Forester, eds, *The Argumentative Turn in Policy Analysis and Planning*. Durham: Duke University Press, pp. 43–76.

Hall, Patrick. 1998. *The Social Construction of Nationalism: Sweden as an Example*. Lund: Lund University Press.

Hall, Peter. 1986. *Governing the Economy: The Politics of State Intervention in Britain and France*. New York: Oxford University Press, 1986.

Hall, Rodney Bruce. 1999. *National Collective Identity: Social Constructs and International Systems*. New York: Columbia University Press.

Hallstein, Walter. 1969. *Der unvollendete Bundesstaat: Europäische Erfahrungen und Erkenntnisse*. Vienna: Econ.

Hanafin, Patrick. 2001. *Constituting Identity: Political Identity Formation and the Constitution in Post-independence Ireland*. Aldershot: Ashgate.

Harris, Clodagh. 2001. 'Anglo-Irish Elite Cooperation and the Peace Process: The Impact of the EEC/EU', *Irish Studies in International Affairs* 12, pp. 203–14.

Hastings, Adrian. 1997. *The Construction of Nationhood: Ethnicity, Religion and Nationalism*. Cambridge: Cambridge University Press.

Haughey, Charles J. 1986a [1980]. 'Presidential Address at the 49th Fianna Fáil Ard-Fheis', in Martin Mansergh, ed., *The Spirit of the Nation: The Speeches and Statements of Charles Haughey (1957–1986)*. Cork: Mercier, pp. 327–38.

1986b [1983]. 'Presidential Address at the 51st Fianna Fáil Ard-Fheis', in Martin Mansergh, ed., *The Spirit of the Nation: The Speeches and Statements of Charles Haughey (1957–1986)*. Cork: Mercier, pp. 733–42.

1986c [1980]. 'Downing Street Talks', in Martin Mansergh, ed., *The Spirit of the Nation: The Speeches and Statements of Charles Haughey (1957–1986)*. Cork: Mercier, pp. 362–70.

1986d [1980]. 'Ireland's Place Among the Nations of Europe: An Historic Opportunity', in Martin Mansergh, ed., *The Spirit of the Nation: The Speeches and Statements of Charles Haughey (1957–1986)*. Cork: Mercier, pp. 161–4.

1986e [1980]. 'Ireland's Place in a Troubled World', in Martin Mansergh, ed., *The Spirit of the Nation: The Speeches and Statements of Charles Haughey (1957–1986)*. Cork: Mercier, pp. 346–50.

1986f [1980]. 'Ireland's Membership of the EEC: A Re-appraisal', in Martin Mansergh, ed., *The Spirit of the Nation: The Speeches and Statements of Charles Haughey (1957–1986)*. Cork: Mercier, pp. 964–78.

1986g [1980]. 'The Anglo-Irish Summit in Dublin Castle', in Martin Mansergh, ed., *The Spirit of the Nation: The Speeches and Statements of Charles Haughey (1957–1986)*. Cork: Mercier, pp. 406–15.

Hayes, Carleton. 1960. *Nationalism: A Religion*. New York: Macmillan.

Hegel, Georg Wilhelm Friedrich. 1969 [1830]. *Enzyklopädie der philosophischen Wissenschaften im Grundrisse*. Hamburg: Meiner.

Heinemann, Horst. 2004. 'Argumente für und gegen Adenauers "Politik der Stärke"', in *Vorwärts online*, 28 January 2004 at http://www.vorwaerts.de/allother.php/iAid/6339

Heldt, Birger. 1999. 'Domestic Politics, Absolute Deprivation, and the Use of Armed Force in Interstate Territorial Disputes: 1950–1990', *Journal of Conflict Resolution* 43/4, pp. 451–78.

Hensel, Paul R. 2001. 'Contentious Issues and World Politics: The Management of Territorial Claims in the Americas, 1816–1992', *International Studies Quarterly* 45/1, pp. 81–109.

Herman, Robert G. 1996. 'Identity, Norms, and National Security: The Soviet Foreign Policy Revolution and the End of the Cold War', in Peter J. Katzenstein, ed., *The Culture of National Security: Norms and Identity in World Politics*. New York: Columbia University Press, pp. 271–316.

Hermand, Jost. 1991. 'Freiheit im Kalten Krieg: Zum Siegeszug der abstrakten Malerei in Westdeutschland', in Hans Boger, Ekkehard Mai and Stephan Waetzoldt, eds., *'45 und die Folgen: Kunstgeschichte eines Wiederbeginns*. Cologne: Böhlau, pp. 135–62.

Herz, Dietmar. 1989. *Frieden und Stabilität: Die Nordirland-Politik der Republik Irland, 1969–1987*. Bochum: Studienverlag Dr. N. Brockmeyer.

Herz, Thomas A. 1979. *Europa in der öffentlichen Meinung: Zur politischen Mobilisierung in Deutschland und Frankreich zwischen 1962 und 1977*. Bonn: Europa Union Verlag.

Hiden, John and Salmon, Patrick. 1992. *The Baltic Nations and Europe: Estonia, Latvia and Lithuania in the Twentieth Century*. London: Longman.

Hilferding, Rudolf. 1955 [1910]. *Das Finanzkapital. Eine Studie über die jüngste Entwicklung des Kapitalismus*. Berlin: Dietz.

Hobden, Stephen. 1999. 'Theorising the International System: Perspectives from Historical Sociology', *Review of International Studies* 25/2, pp. 257–71.

Hobsbawm, Eric J. 1990. *Nations and Nationalism Since 1780: Programme, Myth, Reality*. Cambridge: Cambridge University Press.

Hobson, J.A. 1938 [1902]. *Imperialism: A Study*. London: Allen & Unwin.

Höfig, Willi. 1980. 'Der deutsche Heimatfilm', in Manfred Brauneck, ed., *Film und Fernschen*. Bamberg: C. C. Buchners, pp. 368–92.

Holmes, Michael, Rees, Nicholas and Whelan, Bernadette. 1993. *The Poor Relation: Irish Foreign Policy and the Third World*. Dublin: Gill and Macmillan.

Holsti, Kalevi J. 1991. *Peace and War: Armed Conflicts and International Order, 1648–1989*. Cambridge: Cambridge University Press.

Holzinger, Katharina. 2001. 'Kommunikationsmodi und Handlungstypen in den Internationalen Beziehungen: Anmerkungen zu einigen irreführenden Dichotomien', *Zeitschrift für Internationale Beziehungen* 8/2, pp. 243–86.

Homer-Dixon, Thomas and Karapin, Roger. 1989. 'Graphical Argument Analysis: A New Approach to Understanding Arguments, Applied to a Debate about the Window of Vulnerability', *International Studies Quarterly* 33/4, pp. 389–410.

Hooson, David, ed. 1994. *Geography and National Identity*. Oxford: Blackwell.

Hopf, Ted. 2002. *Social Construction of International Politics: Identities and Foreign Policies, Moscow, 1955 and 1999*. Ithaca: Cornell University Press.

Horowitz, Donald L. 1985. *Ethnic Groups in Conflict*. Berkeley: University of California Press.

1991. 'Irredentas and Secessions: Adjacent Phenomena, Neglected Connections', in Naomi Chazan, ed., *Irredentism and International Politics*. Boulder: Lynne Rienner, pp. 9–22.

Howe, Stephen. 2000. *Ireland and Empire: Colonial Legacies in Irish History and Culture*. Oxford: Oxford University Press.

Hughes, Michael. 1994. *Ireland Divided: The Roots of the Modern Irish Problem*. Cardiff: University of Wales Press.

Husserl, Edmund. 1954 [1937]. *Die Krisis der europäischen Wissenschaften und die transzendentale Phänomenologie*. Haag: Martinus Nijhoff.

Hussey, Gemma. 1994. *Ireland Today: Anatomy of a Changing State*. London: Viking Press.

Huth, Paul H. 1998. *Standing Your Ground: Territorial Disputes and International Conflict*. Ann Arbor: University of Michigan Press.

Huth, Paul H. and Allee, Todd L. 2002. *The Democratic Peace and Territorial Conflict in the Twentieth Century*. Cambridge: Cambridge University Press.

Hyde, Douglas. 1910 [1890]. *Beside The Fire: A Collection of Irish-Gaelic Folk Stories*. London: David Nutt.

1986 [1892]. 'On the Necessity of De-Anglicising Ireland', in Breandán Ó Conaire, ed., *Douglas Hyde: Language, Lore, and Lyrics*. Dublin: Irish Academic Press, pp. 153–70.

Ikenberry, John and Kupchan, Charles. 1990. 'Socialisation and Hegemonic Power', *International Organization* 44/3, pp. 283–315.

Infas. 1974. *Resonanz der innerdeutschen Beziehungen: Ergebnisse einer Repräsentativerhebung*. Bonn: Bad Godesberg.

Institut für Auslandsbeziehungen. 1989. *Karikaturen aus der Bundesrepublik Deutschland*. Stuttgart: Dr. Cantz'sche Druckerei.

Isensee, Josef. 1993. 'Europa – die politische Erfindung eines Erdteils', in Josef Isensee, ed., *Europa als politsche Idee und rechtliche Form*. Berlin: Duncker und Humblot, pp. 103–20.

Ivory, Gareth. 1999. 'Revisions in Nationalist Discourse Among Irish Political Parties', *Irish Political Studies* 14/1, pp. 84–103.

Iyob, Ruth. 2000. 'The Ethiopian–Eritrean Conflict: Diasporic versus Hegemonic States in the Horn of Africa, 1991–2000', *Journal of Modern African Studies* 38/4, pp. 659–82.

Jachtenfuchs, Markus. 2002. *Die Konstruktion Europas: Verfassungsideen und institutionelle Entwicklung*. Baden-Baden: Nomos.

Jackson, Robert and Rosberg, Carl. 1986. 'Sovereignty and Underdevelopment: Juridical Statehood in the African Crisis', *Journal of Modern African Studies* 24/1, pp. 1–31.

Jackson, Sally. 1992. 'The Arguer in Interpersonal Argument: Pros and Cons of Individual-Level Analysis', in William L. Benoit, Dale Hample and Pamela J. Benoit, eds., *Readings in Argumentation*. Foris: Berlin, pp. 513–22.

Jacobsen, Hans-Adolf and Tomala, Mieczyslaw, eds. 1992. *Bonn–Warschau 1945–1991: Die deutsch-polnischen Beziehungen*. Cologne: Verlag Wissenschaft und Politik.

Jahn, Hans Edgar. 1985. *Die deutsche Frage von 1945 bis heute: Der Weg der Parteien und Regierungen*. Mainz: V. Hase & Koehler.

Jänicke, Martin. 1966. 'Die DDR konföderationsfähig machen', in Theo Sommer, ed., *Denken an Deutschland*. Hamburg: Nannen-Verlag, pp. 133–40.

Jaspers, Karl. 1969a [1960]. 'Freiheit und Wiedervereinigung', in Hans Saner, ed., *Provokationen*. Munich: Piper, pp. 169–76.

    1969b [1962]. 'Wie Erinnerung an das Erlebte zur Auffassung der Gegenwart führt', in Hans Saner, ed., *Provokationen*. Munich: Piper, pp. 147–68.

Jelavich, Barbara. 1969. *The Habsburg Empire in European Affairs: 1814–1918*. Chicago: Rand McNally.

Jelavich, Charles and Jelavich, Barbara. 1977. *The Establishment of the Balkan National States: 1804–1920*. Seattle: University of Washington Press.

Jenkins, Richard. 2002. *Pierre Bourdieu*. London: Routledge.

Jepperson, Ronald L., Wendt, Alexander and Katzenstein, Peter J. 1996. 'Norms, Identity, and Culture in National Security', in Peter J. Katzenstein, ed., *The Culture of National Security: Norms and Identity in World Politics*. New York: Columbia University Press, pp. 33–75.

Jervis, Robert. 1991. 'The Future of World Politics: Will It Resemble the Past?' *International Security* 16/1, pp. 39–73.

Joffe, Josef. 1973. 'Westverträge, Ostverträge und die Kontinuität der deutschen Außenpolitik', *Europa-Archiv* 4, pp. 111–24.

Johnson, Paul. 1988. 'Irredentist Perils in Faltering Soviet Empire', *Wall Street Journal*, 23 August, p. 1.

Johnson, Rulph H. 2000. *Manifest Rationality: A Pragmatic Theory of Argument*. Mahwah: Lawrence Erlbaum.

Johnston, Alastair I. 2001. 'Treating International Institutions as Social Environments', *International Studies Quarterly* 45/4, pp. 487–515.

Johnston, Ronald. 1995. 'Territoriality and the State', in Georges B. Benko and Ulf Strohmayer, eds., *Geography, History and Social Sciences*. Dordrecht: Kluwer Academic Publishers, pp. 213–26.

Johnstone, Ian. 2003. 'Security Council Deliberations: The Power of the Better Argument', *European Journal of International Law* 14/3, pp. 437–80.

Jordan, Anthony J. 2003. *W. B. Yeats: Vain, Glorious, Lout – A Maker of Modern Ireland*. Dublin: Westport Books.

Jordan, Neil. dir. 1992. *The Crying Game*. Produced by Palace Pictures. United Kingdom.

Judt, Tony. 2002. 'The Past is Another Country: Myth and Memory in Post-war Europe', in Jan-Werner Müller, ed., *Memory and Power in Post-war Europe*. Cambridge: Cambridge University Press, pp. 157–83.

Juhász, Gyula. 1979. *Hungarian Foreign Policy: 1919–1945*. Budapest: Adadémiai Kiadó.

Jünger, Ernst. 1994 [1945]. 'Der Friede', in Paul Michael Lützeler, ed., *Hoffnung Europa: Deutsche Essays von Novalis bis Enzensberger*. Frankfurt am Main: S. Fischer, pp. 328–65.

Jungk, Robert. 1994 [1959]. 'Die Treue zur Menschheit', in Klaus Wagenbach *et al.*, eds., *Deutsche Schriftsteller und ihr Staat seit 1945: Vaterland, Muttersprache*. Berlin: Verlag Klaus Wagenbach, pp. 154, 155.

Kacowicz, Arie. 1994. *Peaceful Territorial Change*. Columbia: University of South Carolina Press.

Kant, Immanuel. 1871 [1791]. 'Idee zu einer allgemeinen Geschichte in weltbürgerlicher Absicht', in Immanuel Kant, *Kleinere Schriften*. Leipzig: Philosophische Bibliothek.

1995 [1795]. *Zum ewigen Frieden: Ein philosophischer Entwurf*. Stuttgart: Reclam.

Kapil, Ravi L. 1966. 'On the Conflict Potential of Inherited Boundaries in Africa', *World Politics* 18/4, pp. 656–73.

Karnes, Thomas L. 1961. *The Failure of Union: Central America, 1824–1960*. Chapel Hill: University of North Carolina Press.

Katzenstein, Peter. 1996. 'Introduction: Alternative Perspectives on National Security', in Peter Katzenstein, ed., *The Culture of National Security: Norms and Identity in World Politics*. New York: Columbia University Press, pp. 1–32.

1997. 'United Germany in an Integrating Europe', in Peter Katzenstein, ed., *Tamed Power: Germany in Europe*. Ithaca: Cornell University Press, 1997, pp. 1–48.

Kearney, Richard. 1988. 'Introduction: Thinking Otherwise', in Richard Kearney, ed., *Across the Frontiers: Ireland in the 1990s*. Dublin: Wolfhound Press, pp. 7–28.

1997. *Postnationalist Ireland: Politics, Culture*, Philosophy. London: Routledge.

Keatinge, Patrick. 1978. *A Place Among the Nations: Issues of Irish Foreign Policy*. Dublin: Institute of Public Administration.

Keck, Margaret and Sikkink, Kathryn. 1998. *Activists beyond Borders: Advocacy Networks in International Politics*. Ithaca: Cornell University Press.

Keck, Otto. 1995. 'Rationales kommunikatives Handeln in den internationalen Beziehungen: Ist eine Verbindung von Rational-Choice-Theorie und Habermas' Theorie des kommunikativen Handelns möglich?' *Zeitschrift für internationale Beziehungen* 2/1, pp. 5–48.

Kedourie, Eli. 1960. *Nationalism*. Oxford: Blackwell.

Keenan, Joe. 2006. 'Garret FitzGerald's Pack of Misbegotten Lies', *Irish Political Review* at http://www.atholbooks.org/review/garrett.php

Kelemen, R. Daniel and Sibbitt, Eric C. 2004. 'The Globalization of American Law', *International Organization* 58/1, pp. 103–36.

Kennedy, Dennis. 1999. 'Politics of North–South Relations in Post-partition Ireland', in Patrick J. Roche and Brian Barton, eds., *The Northern Ireland Question: Nationalism, Unionism, and Partition*. Aldershot: Ashgate, pp. 71–96.

Kennedy, Liam. 1996. *Colonialism, Religion and Nationalism in Ireland*. Belfast: Institute of Irish Studies.

Kennedy, Michael and Skelly, Joseph Morrison. 2000. 'The Study of Irish Foreign Policy from Independence to Internationalism', in Michael Kennedy and Joseph Morrison Skelly, eds., *Irish Foreign Policy: 1919–66*. Dublin: Four Courts Press, pp. 13–24.

Keogh, Dermot. 1995. *Twentieth-Century Ireland: Nation and State*. New York: St. Martin's Press.

2000. 'Irish Neutrality and the First Application for Membership of the EEC: 1961–3', in Michael Kennedy and Joseph Morrison Skelly, eds., *Irish Foreign Policy: 1919–66*. Dublin: Four Courts Press, pp. 265–85.

Keohane, Robert and Martin, Lisa. 1995. 'The Promise of Institutionalist Theory', *International Security* 20/1, pp. 39–51.

Khagram, Sanjeev, Riker, James and Sikkink, Kathryn. 2002. 'From Santiago to Seattle: Transnational Advocacy Groups Restructuring World Politics', in Sanjeev Khagram, James Riker and Kathryn Sikkink, eds., *Restructuring World Politics: Transnational Social Movements, Networks, and Norms*. Minneapolis: University of Minnesota Press, pp. 1–58.

Khrushchev, Nikita S. 1956. *The Report of the Central Committee of the Communist Party of the Soviet Union to the 20th Party Congress.* Ottawa: Press Office of the USSR Embassy in Canada.

Kiefer, Markus. 1993. *Auf der Suche nach nationaler Identität und Wegen zur deutschen Einheit: Die deutsche Frage in der überregionalen Tages- und Wochenpresse der Bundesrepublik 1949–1955.* Frankfurt am Main: Peter Lang.

King, Charles and Melvin, Neil. 1999. 'Diaspora Politics: Ethnic Linkages, Foreign Policy, and Security in Eurasia', *International Security* 24/3, pp. 108–38.

King, Gary, Keohane, Robert and Verba, Sidney. 1994. *Designing Social Inquiry: Scientific Inference in Qualitative Research.* Princeton: Princeton University Press.

Kiser, Larry L. and Ostrom, Elinor. 1982. 'The Three Worlds of Action: A Metatheoretical Synthesis of Institutional Approaches', in Elinor Ostrom, ed., *Strategies of Political Inquiry.* Beverly Hills: Sage, pp. 179–222.

Kissinger, Henry. 1979. *White House Years.* Toronto: Little, Brown and Company.

Kistler, Helmut. 1982. *Die Ostpolitik der Bundesrepublik Deutschland: 1966–1973.* Bonn: Bundeszentrale für politische Bildung.

Klant, Michael. 1988. *Der rote Ballon: Die deutsche Sozialdemokratie in der Karikatur.* Hannover: Fackelträger Verlag.

Klotz, Audie. 1995a. 'Norms Reconstituting Interests: Global Racial Equality and US Sanctions Against South Africa', *International Organization* 49/3, pp. 451–78.

1995b. *Protesting Prejudice: Apartheid and the Politics of Norms in International Relations.* Ithaca: Cornell University Press.

Knight, David B. 1994. 'People Together, Yet Apart: Rethinking Territory, Sovereignty and Identities', in George J. Demko and William B. Wood, eds., *Reordering the World: Geopolitical Perspectives on the 21st Century.* Boulder: Westview Press, pp. 209–26.

Knippenberg, Hans and Markusse, Jan. 1999. *Nationalising and Denationalising European Border Regions 1800–2000: Views from Geography and History.* Dordrecht: Kluwer Academic Publishers.

Knopp, Guido. 2001. *Die große Flucht: Das Schicksal der Vertriebenen.* Munich: Econ.

Kohn, Hans. 1962. *Die Idee des Nationalismus.* Frankfurt am Main: Fischer Verlag.

Kommunistische Partei Deutschlands. 1963 [1945]. 'Aufruf des Zentralkommitees der Kommunistischen Partei Deutschlands (KPD) vom 11. Juni 1945', in Ossip Flechtheim, ed., *Dokumente zur parteipolitischen*

Entwicklung in Deutschland seit 1945: Programmatik der deutschen Parteien, vol. II. Berlin: Dokumenten-Verlag, pp. 313–18.

Koppel, Thomas Paul. 1972. *Sources of Change in West German Ostpolitik: The Grand Coalition, 1966–1969*. Ann Arbor: University Microfilms.

Kornprobst, Markus. 2002. 'The Management of Border Disputes in African Regional Sub-systems: Comparing West Africa and the Horn of Africa', *Journal of Modern African Studies* 40/3, pp. 369–93.

⎯⎯ 2005. 'Episteme, Nation-builders, and National Identity: The Re-construction of Irishness', *Nations and Nationalism* 11/3, pp. 403–21.

⎯⎯ 2007. 'Dejustification and Dispute Settlement: Irredentism in European Politics', *European Journal of International Relations* 13/4, pp. 459–87.

Koschyk, Hartmut. 1989. *Das ganze Deutschland soll es sein: Perspektiven einer europäischen Friedensordnung*. Asendorf: Mut-Verlag.

Kowert, Paul and Legro, Jeffrey. 1996. 'Norms, Identity, and Their Limits: A Theoretical Reprise', in Peter Katzenstein, ed., *The Culture of National Security: Norms and Identity in World Politics*. New York: Columbia University Press, pp. 451–97.

Krämer, Martin. 1996. *Der Volksaufstand vom 17. Juni 1953 und sein politisches Echo in der Bundesrepublik Deutschland*. Bochum: Universitätsverlag Dr. N. Brockmeyer.

Kratochwil, Friedrich. 1989. *Rules, Norms and Decisions: On the Conditions of Practical and Legal Reasoning in International Relations and Domestic Affairs*. Cambridge: Cambridge University Press.

Kratochwil, Friedrich and Ruggie, John. 1986. 'International Organization: A State of the Art on an Art of the State', *International Organization* 40/4, pp. 753–75.

Kratochwil, Friedrich, Rohrlich, Paul and Mahajan, Harpreet. 1985. *Peace and Disputed Sovereignty: Reflections on Conflict over Territory*. Boston: University Press of America.

Kubal, Timothy. 1998. 'The Presentation of Political Self: Cultural Resonance and the Construction of Collective Action Frames', *Sociological Quarterly* 39/4, pp. 539–54.

Kuenheim, Haug von. 2003. 'Die Preußin', *Süddeutsche Zeitung*, 28 April.

Kuhn, Thomas. 1996 [1962]. *The Structure of Scientific Revolutions*. Chicago: University of Chicago Press.

Kulski, W. W. 1976. *Germany and Poland: From War to Peaceful Relations*. Syracuse: Syracuse University Press.

Laffey, Mark and Weldes, Jutta. 1997. 'Beyond Belief: Ideas and Symbolic Technologies in the Study of International Relations', *European Journal of International Relations* 3/2, pp. 193–237.

Landau, Jacob M. 1991. 'The Ups and Downs of Irredentism: The Case of Turkey', in Naomi Chazan, ed., *Irredentism and International Politics*. Boulder: Lynne Rienner, pp. 81–96.

1995. *Pan-Turkism, From Irredentism to Cooperation*. London: Hurst and Company.

Langlois, Catherine and Langlois, Jean-Pierre. 2004. 'Provisions for Noncompliance and Treaty Value: A Game Theoretic Perspective', *International Studies Quarterly* 48/2, pp. 383–408.

Lapid, Yosef. 2001. 'Introduction', in Mathias Albert *et al.*, eds., *Identities, Borders, Orders: Rethinking International Relations Theory*. Minneapolis: University of Minnesota Press, pp. 1–20.

Lee, J.J. 1989. *Ireland, 1912–1985: Politics and Society*. Cambridge: Cambridge University Press.

Leggewie, Claus. 2001. 'Gibt es eine transnationale Bürgergesellschaft?' *Internationale Politik und Gesellschaft* 2, pp. 154–64.

Legro, Jeffrey. 1997. 'Which Norms Matter? Revisiting the "Failure" of Internationalism', *International Organization* 51/1, pp. 31–63.

2000. 'Whence American Internationalism', *International Organization* 52/4, pp. 253–89.

Leitch, Maurice. 1969. *Poor Lazarus*. London: MacGibbon & Kee.

Lemass, Seán. 1959. *One Nation: A Speech Delivered at a Meeting of the Oxford Union Society*. Dublin: Stationery Office.

Lemke, Michael. 1992. *CDU/CSU und die Vertragspolitik der Bundesrepublik Deutschland in den Jahren 1969–1975*. Saarbrücken: Dadder.

Lenin, Vladimir I. 1975 [1917]. 'Imperialism, the Highest Stage of Capitalism', in Robert C. Tucker, ed., *The Lenin Anthology*. New York: W. W. Norton & Company, pp. 204–74.

Lennon, Peter. dir. 1968. *The Rocky Road to Dublin*. Produced by Victor Herbert. Ireland.

Lenz, Siegfried. 1986 [1978]. *Heimatmuseum*. Munich: Deutscher Taschenbuch-Verlag.

1997 [1960]. 'Eine Grabrede auf Henry Smolka', in Siegfried Lenz, *Erzählungen 2: 1956–1962*. Hamburg: Hoffmann und Campe, 1997.

Levi, Margaret. 1997. 'A Model, a Method, and Map: Rational Choice in Comparative and Historical Analysis', in Mark I. Lichbach and Alan S. Zuckerman, eds., *Comparative Politics: Rationality, Culture, and Structure*. Cambridge: Cambridge University Press, pp. 19–41.

Linden, Ronald. 2000. 'Putting on Their Sunday Best: Romania, Hungary, and the Puzzle of Peace', *International Studies Quarterly* 44/1, pp. 121–45.

Lingard, Joan. 1995. *Across the Barricades*. London: Puffin Books.

Lipinsky-Gottersdorf, Hans. 1982 [1961]. *Wenn es Herbst wird.* Munich: Herbig.

Lipschutz, Ronnie D. 1999. 'Members Only? Citizenship and Civic Virtue in a Time of Globalization', *International Politics* 36/2, pp. 203–33.

Luard, Evan. 1986. *War in International Society.* London: I. B. Tauris and Company.

Luckmann, Thomas. 1991. *Die unsichtbare Religion.* Frankfurt am Main: Suhrkamp.

Lynch, Jack. 1972. *Irish Unity, Northern Ireland, Anglo-Irish Relations: August 1969–October 1971.* Dublin: Government Information Bureau.

Lyons, F.S.L. 1977. *Charles Stewart Parnell.* London: Collins.

MacDonagh, Oliver. 1983. *States of Mind: A Study of Anglo-Irish Conflict 1780–1980.* London: George Allen & Unwin.

Machiavelli, Niccolò. 1979 [1532]. *The Prince.* New York: Penguin Books.

MacLaughlin, Jim. 2001. *Reimagining the Nation-state: The Contested Terrains of Nation-building.* London: Pluto.

MacLaverty, Bernard. 1983. *Cal.* London: Jonathan Cape.

Mair, Peter. 1987. 'Breaking the Nationalist Mould: The Irish Republic and the Anglo-Irish Agreement', in Paul Teague, ed., *Beyond the Rhetoric: Politics, the Economy, and Social Policy in Ireland.* London: Lawrence & Wishart, pp. 81–110.

Mamatey, Victor S. and Luža, Radomír, eds. 1973. *A History of the Czechoslovak Republic: 1918–1948.* Princeton: Princeton University Press.

Mandelbaum, Michael, ed. 2000. *The New European Diasporas: National Minorities and Conflict in Eastern Europe.* New York: Council on Foreign Relations Press.

Mann, Golo. 1963 [1958]. *Deutsche Geschichte des neunzehnten und zwanzigsten Jahrhunderts.* Frankfurt am Main: S. Fischer Verlag.

Mann, Michael. 1997. 'Has Globalization Ended the Rise and Rise of the Nation-state?' *Review of International Political Economy* 4/3, pp. 472–96.

Mansfield, Edward and Snyder, Jack. 1995. 'Democratization and the Danger of War', *International Security* 20/1, pp. 5–38.

March, James and Olsen, Johan. 1989. *Rediscovering Institutions: The Organizational Basis of Politics.* New York: Free Press.

Marcussen, Martin, Risse, Thomas, Engelmann-Martin, Daniela, Knopf, Hans-Joachim and Roscher, Klaus. 2001. 'Constructing Europe? The Evolution of Nation-State Identities', in Thomas Christiansen, Knud Erik Jørgensen and Antje Wiener, eds., *The Social Construction of Europe.* London: Sage, pp. 101–20.

Marienfeld, Wolfgang. 1990. *Die Geschichte des Deutschlandproblems im Spiegel der politischen Karikatur.* Hameln: Verlag C. W. Niemeyer.

Markovits, Andrei S. and Reich, Simon. 1999. 'The Contemporary Power of Memory: The Dilemmas for German Foreign Policy', in John S. Brady, Beverly Crawford and Sarah Elise Wiliarty, eds., *The Postwar Transformation of Germany: Democracy, Prosperity, and Nationhood*. Ann Arbor: University of Michigan Press, pp. 439–72.

Marzian, Herbert. 1968. *Zeittafel und Dokumente zur Oder-Neisse-Linie*, vol. XVI. Würzburg: Holzner.

   1969. *Zeittafel und Dokumente zur Oder-Neisse-Linie*, vol. XVII. Würzburg: Holzner.

Mayall, James and Simpson, Mark. 1992. 'Ethnicity is Not Enough: Reflections on Protracted Secessionism in the Third World', *International Journal of Comparative Sociology* 33/1, pp. 5–25.

Mayer von Achenbach, Richard. 1986. *Gedanken über eine konstruktive deutsche Ostpolitik*. Frankfurt am Main: Athenäum.

McGuirk, Cathleen Knowles. 2000. Speech Delivered at the Grave of Theobald Wolfe Tone. At http://www.iol.ie/~saoirse/video/boden00.htm

McLoone, Martin. 2000. *Irish Film: The Emergence of a Contemporary Cinema*. London: British Film Institute.

Mearsheimer, John. 1990. 'Back to the Future: Instability in Europe after the Cold War', *International Security* 15/1, pp. 5–56.

   1994. 'The False Promise of International Institutions', *International Security* 19/3, pp. 5–49.

Meehan, Elisabeth. 2000. 'Bringing in Europe: The Peace Process and the Europeanisation of the Irish Question', *Irish Studies in International Affairs* 11/2, pp. 179–91.

Meier, Charles. 1999. 'The End of Longing? (Notes toward a History of Postwar German National Longing)', in John S. Brady, Beverly Crawford and Sarah Elise Wiliarty, eds., *The Postwar Transformation of Germany: Democracy, Prosperity, and Nationhood*. Ann Arbor: University of Michigan Press, pp. 271–85.

Meissner, Boris. 1970. *Die deutsche Ostpolitik 1961–1970: Kontinuität und Wandel*. Cologne: Verlag Wissenschaft und Politik.

   1990. *Die Baltischen Nationen: Estland, Lettland, Litauen*. Cologne: Markus.

Mercer, Jonathan. 1995. 'Anarchy and Identity', *International Organization* 49/2, pp. 229–52.

Meyer, Christoph. 1997. *Die deutschlandpolitische Doppelstrategie: Wilhelm Wolfgang Schütz und das Kuratorium Unteilbares Deutschland*. Landsberg am Lech: Olzog.

Mitrany, David. 1966 [1943]. *A Working Peace System*. Chicago: Quadrangle Books.

Mitzen, Jennifer. 2005. 'Reading Habermas in Anarchy: Multilateral Diplomacy and Global Public Spheres', *American Political Science Review* 99/3, pp. 401–17.

Mommsen, Wolfgang J. 1990. *Nation und Geschichte: Über die Deutschen und die deutsche Frage*. Munich: Piper.

Moore, Thomas. 1823 [1821]. *Irish Melodies*. London: William Clowes.

Moravcsik, Andrew. 1998. *The Choice for Europe: Social Purpose and State Power from Messina to Maastricht*. London: UCL Press.

1999. 'Is Something Rotten in the State of Denmark? Constructivism and European Integration', *Journal of European Public Policy* 6/4, pp. 669–81.

Morrison, George. dir. 1969. *Mise Éire*. Produced by Seán Ó Riada. Ireland.

1971. *Soirise?* Produced by Seán Ó Riada. Ireland.

Morrow, Raymond. 1994. *Critical Theory and Methodology*. London: Sage.

Most, Benjamin A. and Starr, Harvey. 1989. *Inquiry, Logic, and International Politics*. Columbia: University of South Carolina Press.

Müller, Adolf. 1977. *Die Tschechoslowakei auf der Suche nach Sicherheit*. Berlin: Berlin Verlag.

Müller, Harald. 1994. 'Internationale Beziehungen als kommunikatives Handeln: Zur Kritik der utilitaristischen Handlungstheorien', *Zeitschrift für internationale Beziehungen* 1/1, pp. 15–44.

1995. 'Spielen hilft nicht immer: Die Grenzen des Rational-Choice-Ansatzes und der Platz der Theorie kommunikativen Handelns in der Analyse der internationalen Beziehungen', *Zeitschrift für internationale Beziehungen* 2/3, pp. 371–91.

2004. 'Arguing, Bargaining and All That: Communicative Action, Rationalist Theory, and the Logic of Appropriateness in International Relations', *European Journal of International Relations* 10/3, pp. 395–435.

Müller, Helmut. 1990. *Schlaglichter der deutschen Geschichte*. Mannheim: Bibliographisches Institut & F. A. Brockhaus.

Münkel, Daniela. 2000. 'Zwischen Diffamierung und Verehrung: Das Bild Willy Brandts in der bundesdeutschen Öffentlichkeit', in Carsten Tessmer, ed., *Das Willy-Brandt-Bild in Deutschland und Polen*. Berlin: Druckerei Hermann Schlesener, pp. 23–40.

Murphy, Alexander. 1990. 'Historical Justification for Territorial Claims', *Annals of the Association of American Geographers* 80/4, pp. 531–48.

Murphy, Gary. 2000. 'A Wider Perspective: Ireland's View of Western Europe in the 1950s', in Michael Kennedy and Joseph Morrison Skelly, eds., *Irish Foreign Policy: 1919–66*. Dublin: Four Courts Press, pp. 247–64.

Mushaben, Joyce Marie. 1998. *From Post-War to Post-Wall Generations: Changing Attitudes toward the National Question and NATO in the Federal Republic of Germany*. Boulder: Westview Press.

Mutimer, David. 2007 'Waging Wars in Iraq: The Metaphoric Constitution of Wars and Enemies', in Markus Kornprobst, Vincent Pouliot, Nisha Sha and Ruben Zaiotti, eds., *Metaphors of Globalization: Mirrors, Magicians, and Mutinies*. Basingstoke: Palgrave Macmillan, pp. 114–29.

National Development Plan. 2005. *Ireland and the EU Structural Funds* at http://www.csfinfo.com/htm/overview/structural_funds.htm

Neuberger, Benyamin. 1991. 'Irredentism and Politics in Africa', in Naomi Chazan, ed., *Irredentism and International Politics*. Boulder: Lynne Rienner, pp. 97–108.

Neumann, Iver. 1996. 'Self and Other in International Relations', *European Journal of International Relations* 2/2, pp. 139–74.

Newman, David and Paasi, Anssi. 1997. 'Fences and Neighbours in a Postmodern World: Rethinking Boundaries in Political Geography', *Progress in Human Geography* 22/2, pp. 186–207.

Nierop, Tom. 1994. *Systems and Regions in Global Politics: An Empirical Study of Diplomacy, International Organization and Trade, 1950–1991*. Toronto: John Wiley & Sons.

Nölle, Elisabeth and Neumann, Erich Peter, eds. 1956. *Jahrbuch der öffentlichen Meinung: 1947–1955*. Allensbach: Verlag für Demoskopie.

1957. *Jahrbuch der öffentlichen Meinung: 1957*. Allensbach: Verlag für Demoskopie.

1965. *Jahrbuch der öffentlichen Meinung: 1958–1964*. Allensbach: Verlag für Demoskopie.

1967. *Jahrbuch der öffentlichen Meinung: 1965–1967*. Allensbach: Verlag für Demoskopie.

1974. *Jahrbuch der öffentlichen Meinung: 1968–1973*. Allensbach: Verlag für Demoskopie.

Nölle-Neumann, Elisabeth, ed. 1981. *The Germans: Public Opinion Polls, 1967–1980*. London: Greenwood.

Noonan, S. 1976. *Assignments in New Syllabus Intermediate History: The Modern World*. Dublin: School and College Services.

O'Brien, Conor Cruise. 1972. *States of Ireland*. London: Hutchinson.

1999. *Memoir: My Life and Themes*. Dublin: Poolbeg.

O'Clery, Conor. 1999. *Ireland in Quotes*. Dublin: The O'Brien Press.

O'Cuinneagain, Micheal. 1986. *Partition: From Michael Collins to Bobby Sands*. Donegal: Tantallon.

Odell, John. 1982. *US International Monetary Policy: Markets, Power, and Ideas as Sources of Change*. Princeton: Princeton University Press.

O'Donnell, Rory. 1999. 'Fixing the Institutions', in Robin Wilson, ed., *No Frontier: North–South Integration in Ireland*. Belfast: Blackstaff Press, pp. 773–88.

O'Grady, Standish. 1919a [1892]. *The Coming of Cuculain.* Dublin: Talbot.
1919b [1896]. *Ulrick, the Ready.* Dublin: Talbot.
1919c [1901]. *In the Gates of the North.* Dublin: Talbot.
1923 [1920]. *The Triumph and Passing of Cuculain.* Dublin: Talbot.
O'Halpin, Eunan. 1999. *Defending Ireland: The Irish State and Its Enemies Since 1922.* Oxford: Oxford University Press.
Öhlschläger, Günther. 1977. 'Über das Argumentieren', in Michael Schecker, ed., *Theorie der Argumentation.* Tübingen: Niemayer, pp. 11–25.
O'Leary, Desmond. 1996. *History Revision Notes for Leaving Certificate.* Dublin: Gill and Macmillan.
O'Mahony, Patrick and Delanty, Gerard. 1998. *Rethinking Irish History: Nationalism, Identity and Ideology.* Basingstoke: Palgrave Macmillan.
O'Malley, Desmond. 2001. 'Redefining Southern Nationalism: A Political Perspective', *Working Papers in British-Irish Studies*, no. 1. Dublin: Institute for British-Irish Studies, University College Dublin, pp. 1–3.
Onuf, Nicholas. 1989. *World of Our Making: Rules and Rule in Social Theory and International Relations.* Columbia: University of South Carolina Press.
Paasi, Anssi. 1995. 'Constructing Territories, Boundaries and Regional Identities', in Tuomas Forsberg, ed., *Contested Territory: Border Disputes at the Edge of the Former Soviet Empire.* Aldershot: Elgar, pp. 42–61.
1996. *Territories, Boundaries and Consciousness: The Changing Geographies of the Finnish–Russian Border.* New York: John Wiley.
Papandreou, Georges. 2002. Speech Given at the Opening Ceremony of the Academic Year 2000–2001, at http://www.coleurop.be/about/speeches2.htm
Parsons, Craig. 2002. 'Showing Ideas as Causes: The Origins of the European Union', *International Organization* 56/1, pp. 47–84.
Patterson, Glenn. 1988. *Burning Your Own.* London: Chatto & Windus.
Payne, Rodger A. 2001. 'Persuasion, Frames and Norm Construction', *European Journal of International Relations* 7/1, pp. 37–61.
Pearse, Pádraic. 1916. *Collected Works.* Dublin: Phoenix Public.
Peitsch, Helmut. 1996. *Vom Faschismus zum Kalten Krieg – auch eine deutsche Literaturgeschichte: Literaturverhältnisse, Genres, Themen.* Berlin: Sigma.
Perelman, Chaïm and Olbrechts-Tyteca, Lucie. 1958. *Traité de l'argumentation.* Paris: Presses Universitaire de France.
Perloff, Richard. 1993. *The Dynamics of Persuasion.* Hillsdale: Lawrence Erlbaum.
Pflaum, Hans Günther. 1990. 'Auf der Suche nach Heimat', in Heinz Müller, ed., *Film in der BRD.* Berlin: Henschelverlag.

Plaschka, Richard Georg and Mack, Karlheinz, eds. 1970. *Die Auflösung des Habsburgerreiches. Zusammenbruch und Neuorientierung im Donauraum*. Munich: Oldenbourg.

Poppinga, Anneliese. 1975. *Konrad Adenauer: Geschichtsverständnis, Weltanschauung und politische Praxis*. Stuttgart: Deutsche Verlags-Anstalt.

Pötzsch, Horst. 1997. *Deutsche Geschichte nach 1945 im Spiegel der Karikatur*. Munich: Olzog.

Pouliot, Vincent. 2008. 'The Logic of Practicality: A Theory of Practice of Security Communities', *International Organization* 62/1.

Prange, Heiko. 2003. 'Rethinking the Impact of Globalisation on the Nation-state: The Case of Science and Technology Policies in Germany', *German Politics* 12/1, pp. 23–42.

Pridham, Geoffrey. 1975. 'The Ostpolitik and the Opposition in West Germany', in Roger Telford, ed., *The Ostpolitik and Political Change in Germany*. Westmead: Saxon House, pp. 45–93.

Prittwitz, Volker von. 1996. 'Verständigung über die Verständigung: Anmerkungen und Ergänzungen zur Debatte über Rationalität und Kommunikation in den Internationalen Beziehungen', *Zeitschrift für internationale Beziehungen* 1/1, pp. 133–47.

Putnam, Robert D. 1988. 'Diplomacy and Domestic Politics: The Logic of Two-Level Games', *International Organization* 42/3, pp. 427–60.

Quigley, Patrick. 1994. *Borderland*. Dingle: Brandon.

Quinn, Bob. dir. 1983. *Atlantean*. De Facto Films. Ireland.

1987. *Budawanny*. De Facto Films. Ireland.

1994. *The Bishop's Story*. De Facto Films. Ireland.

Quintilian. 1953. *Institutio Oratoria*, trans. H. E. Butler. Cambridge, MA: Harvard University Press, 1953.

Radan, Peter. 2002. *The Break-up of Yugoslavia in International Law*. London: Routledge.

Rapoport, Anatol. 1960. *Fights, Games and Debates*. Ann Arbor: University of Michigan Press.

Rasmussen, Mikkel Vedby. 2003. 'The History of a Lesson: Versailles, Munich and the Social Construction of the Past', *Review of International Studies* 29/3, pp. 499–519.

Reichman, Shalom and Golan, Arnon. 1991. 'Irredentism and Boundary Adjustments in Post-World War I Europe', in Naomi Chazan, ed., *Irredentism and International Politics*. Boulder: Lynne Rienner, pp. 51–68.

Reus Smit, Christian. 1999. *The Moral Purpose of the State: Culture, Social Identity, and Institutional Rationality in International Relations*. Princeton: Princeton University Press.

Richter, Hans-Werner. 1996 [1948]. 'Deutsche Opposition', in Helmut Peitsch, ed., *Vom Faschismus zum Kalten Krieg – auch eine deutsche Literaturgeschichte: Literaturverhältnisse, Genres, Themen*. Berlin: Sigma, p. 180.

Riha, Karl and Seel, Peter. 1996. *Europa in der deutschen Karikatur*. Siegen: Hausdruckerei Universität Siegen.

Risse, Thomas. 1999. 'To Euro or Not to Euro? The EMU and Identity Politics in the European Union', *European Journal of International Relations* 5/2, pp. 147–87.

    2000. 'Let's Argue! Communicative Action in World Politics', *International Organization* 54/1, pp. 1–39.

    2001. 'A European Identity? Europeanization and the Evolution of Nation-state Identities', in Maria Green Cowles *et al.*, eds., *Transforming Europe: Europeanization and Domestic Change*. Ithaca: Cornell University Press, pp. 198–216.

Risse, Thomas, Ropp, Stephen and Sikkink, Kathryn, eds. 1999. *The Power of Human Rights: International Norms and Domestic Change*. Cambridge: Cambridge University Press.

Robinson, William I. 2003. 'Remapping the Development in Light of Globalisation: From a Territorial to a Social Cartography', *Third World Quarterly* 23/6, pp. 1047–71.

Rogers, Hugh I. 1975. *A Study in Baltic Diplomacy: 1912–1934*. Hamden: Archon Books.

Rohlinger, Rudolf. 1969. 'Anmerkungen zur NPD', in Günter Gaus, ed., *Zur Wahl gestellt*. Hamburg: Rowohlt, pp. 99–107.

Rösel, Jakob. 1995. 'Ethnic Nationalism and Ethnic Conflict', *Internationale Politik und Gesellschaft* 2, pp. 117–30.

Rotfeld, Daniel and Karp, Regina. 1993. 'Preface', in Stephen Iwan Griffiths, *Nationalism and Ethnic Conflict: Threats to European Security*. Oxford: Oxford University Press.

Roth, Florian. 1995. *Die Idee der Nation im politischen Diskurs*. Baden-Baden: Nomos-Verlagsgesellschaft.

Rothe, Hans, ed. 1992. *Die Historische Wirkung der östlichen Regionen des Reiches*. Weimar: Böhler Verlag.

Rothschild, Joseph. 1974. *East Central Europe between the Two World Wars*. Seattle: University of Washington Press.

    1981. *Ethnopolitics: A Conceptual Framework*. New York: Columbia University Press.

Ruggie, John. 1975. 'International Responses to Technology: Concepts and Trends', *International Organization* 29/3, pp. 557–83.

    1993. 'Territoriality and Beyond: Problematizing Modernity in International Relations', *International Organization* 46/1, pp. 139–74.

1995. 'The False Premise of Realism', *International Security* 20/1, pp. 62–70.

1998. *Constructing the World Polity: Essays in International Institutionalization*. New York: Routledge.

Rühl, Marco. 2002. *Arguing and Communicative Asymmetry: The Analysis of the Interactive Process of Arguing in Non-ideal Situations*. Frankfurt am Main: Peter Lang.

Russett, Bruce. 1967. *International Regions and the International System: A Study in Political Ecology*. Chicago: Rand McNally & Company.

Sack, Robert. 1986. *Territoriality: Its Theory and History*. Cambridge: Cambridge University Press.

Saideman, Stephen M. 1997. 'Explaining the International Relations of Secessionist Conflicts: Vulnerability Versus Ethnic Ties', *International Organization* 51/4, pp. 721–53.

1998. 'Inconsistent Irredentism? Political Competition, Ethnic Ties, and the Foreign Policies of Somalia and Serbia', *Security Studies* 7/1, pp. 51–93.

Saideman, Stephen M. and Ayres, R. William. 2000. 'Determining the Causes of Irredentism: Logit Analyses of Minorities at Risk Data from the 1980s and 1990s', *Journal of Politics* 62/4, pp. 1126–44.

Sander, Martin. 1989. *Der andere Blick – Deutsche Schriftsteller aus polnischer Sicht 1945–1986*. Saarbrücken: Breitenbach.

Scheuner, Ulrich. 1970. 'Die Oder-Neiße-Grenze and die Normalisierung der Beziehungen zum Osten', *Europa-Archiv* 11, pp. 377–86.

Schieder, Theodor. 1991. *Nationalismus und Nationalstaat: Studien zum nationalen Problem im modernen Europa*. Göttingen: Vandenhoeck & Ruprecht.

Schimmelfennig, Frank. 2003. *The EU, NATO and the Integration of Europe: Rules and Rhetoric*. Cambridge: Cambridge University Press.

Schirmer, André. 1988. *Die Deutschlandpolitik der SPD in der Phase des Übergangs vom Kalten Krieg zur Entspannungspolitik, 1955–1970*. Münster: Lit.

Schlichte, Klaus. 1998. 'La Françafrique – Postkolonialer Habitus und Klientilismus in der französischen Afrikapolitik', *Zeitschrift für internationale Beziehungen* 5/2, pp. 309–43.

Schmalz-Bruns, Rainer. 1995. 'Die Theorie kommunikativen Handelns – eine Flaschenpost? Anmerkungen zur jüngsten Theoriedebatte in den Internationalen Beziehungen', *Zeitschrift für internationale Beziehungen* 2/3, pp. 347–70.

Schmidt, Michael. 1995. *Die FDP und die deutsche Frage: 1949–1990*. Hamburg: Lit.

Schmied, Wieland. 1995. 'Ausgangspunkt und Verwandlung', in Christos M. Joachimides, Norman Rosenthal and Wieland Schmied, eds., *Deutsche*

Kunst im 20. Jahrhundert: Malerei und Plastik 1905–1985. Munich: Prestel-Verlag, pp. 63–71.

Schneider, Peter. 1994. 'Plädoyer für eine Kultur des Zweifels', in Paul Michael Lützeler, ed., *Hoffnung Europa: Deutsche Essays von Novalis bis Enzensberger*. Frankfurt am Main: S. Fischer, pp. 488–99.

Schneider, Reinhold. 1994 [1957]. 'Europa als Lebensform', in Paul Michael Lützeler, ed., *Hoffnung Europa: Deutsche Essays von Novalis bis Enzensberger*. Frankfurt am Main: S. Fischer, pp. 406–27.

Schnurre, Wolfdietrich. 1994 [1967]. 'Was von uns hätte verhindert werden müssen', in Klaus Wagenbach *et al.*, eds., *Deutsche Schriftsteller und ihr Staat seit 1945: Vaterland, Muttersprache*. Berlin: Verlag Klaus Wagenbach, pp. 159–61.

Schofield, Clive. 1994. *The Middle East and North Africa*. London: Routledge.

Schütz, Alfred. 1974 [1932]. *Der sinnhafte Aufbau der sozialen Welt*. Frankfurt am Main: Suhrkamp.

Schütz, Alfred and Luckmann, Thomas. 1975. *Strukturen der Lebenswelt*. Neuwied: Luchterhand.

Searle, John. 1983. *Intentionality: An Essay in the Philosophy of Mind*. Cambridge: Cambridge University Press.

1995. *The Construction of Social Reality*. New York: Free Press.

Seiter, John and Gass, Robert. 2004. 'Embracing Divergence: A Definitional Analysis of Pure and Borderline Cases of Persuasion', in John Seiter and Robert Gass, eds., *Perspectives on Persuasion, Social Influence, and Compliance Gaining*. Boston: Pearson, pp. 13–29.

Sending, Ole Jacob. 2002. 'Constitution, Choice and Change: Problems with the "Logic of Appropriateness" and Its Use in Constructivist Theory', *European Journal of International Relations* 8/4, pp. 443–70.

Sethe, Paul. 1966. *Öffnung nach Osten: Weltpolitische Realitäten zwischen Moskau, Paris und Bonn*. Frankfurt am Main: Verlag Heinrich Scheffler.

Shain, Yossi and Sherman, Martin. 1998. 'Dynamics of Disintegration: Diaspora, Secession and the Paradox of Nation-states', *Nations and Nationalism* 4/3, pp. 321–46.

Shaw, Jo. 2001. 'Postnational Constitutionalism in the European Union', in Thomas Christiansen *et al.*, eds., *The Social Construction of Europe*. London: Sage, pp. 66–84.

Simmons, Beth. 2000. 'International Law and State Behavior: Commitment and Compliance in International Monetary Affairs', *American Political Science Review* 94/4, pp. 819–35.

Singer, Alex. 1993. *Nationalstaat und Souveranität: Zum Wandel des europäischen Staatensystems*. Frankfurt am Main: Peter Lang.

Siverson, Randolph and Starr, Harvey. 1991. *The Diffusion of War: A Study of Opportunity and Willingness*. Ann Arbor: University of Michigan Press.

Skelly, Joseph Morrison. 1997. *Irish Diplomacy at the United Nations, 1945–1965: National Interests and the International Order*. Dublin: Irish Academic Press.

Smelser, Neil J. 2003. 'Pressures for Continuity in the Context of Globalisation', *Current Sociology* 51/2, pp. 101–12.

Smith, Anthony D. 1979. *Nationalism in the Twentieth Century*. Oxford: Martin Robertson.

———. 1993. 'The Ethnic Sources of Nationalism', *Survival* 35/1, pp. 48–62.

Smith, Paul, ed. 1991. *Ethnic Groups in International Relations: Comparative Studies on Governments and Non-dominant Ethnic Groups in Europe, 1850–1940*. New York: New York University Press.

Smith, P. Christopher. 1998. *The Hermeneutics of Original Argument: Demonstration, Dialectic, Rhetoric*. Evanston: Northwestern University Press.

Snow, David A. *et al.*, 'Frame Alignment Processes: Micromobilization and Movement Participation', *American Sociological Review* 51/4, pp. 464–81.

Snow, David and Benford, Robert. 1988. 'Ideology, Frame Resonance, and Participant Mobilization', in Bert Klandermans, Hanspeter Kriesi and Sidney Tarrow, eds., *From Structure to Action: Social Movement Participation Across Cultures*. Greenwich: JAI Press, pp. 197–217.

Somers, Margaret R. 1994. 'A Narrative Constitution of Identity: A Relational and Network Approach', *Theory and Society* 23/5, pp. 605–49.

Sommer, Theo. 1966. *Denken an Deutschland: Zum Problem der Wiedervereinigung – Ansichten und Einsichten*. Hamburg: Nannen-Verlag.

Sowinski, Oliver. 1998. *Die deutsche Reichspartei 1950–1965: Organisation und Ideologie einer rechtsradikalen Partei*. Frankfurt am Main: Peter Lang.

Sozialdemokratische Partei Deutschlands. 1963 [1952]. 'Aktionsprogramm von 1952 mit den Erweiterungen vom Berliner Parteitag 1954', in Ossip Flechtheim, ed., *Dokumente zur parteipolitischen Entwicklung in Deutschland seit 1945: Programmatik der deutschen Parteien*, vol. II. Berlin: Dokumenten-Verlag, pp. 93–122.

———. 1968. *Parteitag der Sozialdemokratischen Partei Deutschlands vom 17. Februar bis 1. März 1968 in Nürnberg: Protokoll der Verhandlungen*. Bonn: Neuer Vorwärts Verlag.

Spencer, Philip and Wollmann, Howard. 1998. 'Good and Bad Nationalism: A Critique of Dualism', *Journal of Political Ideologies* 3/2, pp. 255–74.

Steffens, Meggy. 1989. *Die deutsche Ostpolitik im Spiegel publizistischer Stellungnahmen in den USA: 1969–1973*. Frankfurt am Main: Verlag Peter Lang.

Suhrke, Astri and Noble, Lela Garner, eds. 1977. *Ethnic Conflict in International Relations*. New York: Praeger Publishers.

Sweringen, Bryan T. van. 1989. *Kabarettist an der Front des Kalten Krieges: Günter Neumann und das politische Kabarett in der Programmgestaltung des Radios im amerikanischen Sektor Berlins (RIAS)*. Passau: Wissenschaftsverlag Richard Rothe.

Swidler, Ann. 1986. 'Culture in Action: Symbols and Strategies', *American Sociological Review* 51/2, pp. 273–86.

Tägil, Sven, ed. 1999. *Regions in Central Europe: The Legacy of History*. London: Hurst.

Taylor, A.J.P. 1971. *The Struggle for the Mastery of Europe*. Oxford: Oxford University Press.

Taylor, Charles. 1986. 'Interpretation and the Sciences of Man', in Fred R. Dallmayr and Thomas A. McCarthy, eds., *Understanding and Social Inquiry*. Notre Dame: University of Notre Dame Press, pp. 101–31.

Throgmorton, J.A. 1993. 'Survey Research as Rhetorical Trope: Electric Power Planning Arguments in Chicago', in Frank Fischer and John Forester, eds., *The Argumentative Turn in Policy Analysis and Planning*. Durham: Duke University Press, pp. 117–44.

Tiggemann, Anselm. 1998. *CDU/CSU und die Ost- und Deutschlandpolitik: 1969–1972*. Frankfurt: Peter Lang.

Tondra, Ben. 1999. 'The Europeanisation of Irish Foreign Affairs', *Irish Studies in International Affairs* 10, pp. 149–65.

Tonge, Jonathan. 1998. 'Irish Pan-nationalism: Myth or Reality?' *Working Papers in Contemporary History and Politics*, no. 16. Dublin: European Studies Research Institute.

Toulmin, Stephen. 1958. *The Uses of Argument*. Cambridge: Cambridge University Press.

1990. *Cosmopolis: The Hidden Agenda of Modernity*. Chicago: University of Chicago Press.

Touval, Saadia. 1972. *The Boundary Politics of Independent Africa*. Cambridge, MA: Harvard University Press.

Trifunovska, Snežana, ed. 1994. *Yugoslavia Through Documents: From Its Creation to Its Dissolution*. Dordrecht: Martinus Nijhoff.

1999. *Yugoslavia Through Documents: From Its Dissolution to the Peace Settlement*. Dordrecht: Martinus Nijhoff.

Trumbore, Peter F. 1998. 'Public Opinion as a Domestic Constraint in International Negotiations: Two-Level Games in the Anglo-Irish Peace Process', *International Studies Quarterly* 42/3, pp. 545–65.

Tunander, Ola, Baev, Pavel and Nagel, Victoria. 1997. *Geopolitics in Post-Wall Europe: Security, Territory and Identity*. London: Sage.

Ungeheuer, Gerold. 1974. 'Kommunikationsemantik: Skizze eines Problemfeldes', *Zeitschrift für germanistische Linguistik* 2/1, pp. 1–24.

Urban, Jan. 1992. 'Europe's Darkest Vision: An Unsentimental Reading of the Past Invokes a Grim Scenario for the Continent's Future', *Washington Post*, 11 October, p. 1.

Van D'Elden, Karl W. 1979. *West German Poets on Society and Politics*. Detroit: Wayne State University Press.

Van Evera, Stephen. 1994. 'Hypotheses on Nationalism and War', *International Security* 19/1, pp. 5–39.

Vanzo, John P. 1999. 'Border Configuration and Conflict: Geographical Compactness as a Territorial Ambition of States', in Paul F. Diehl, ed., *A Road Map to War: Territorial Dimensions of International Conflict*. Nashville, Vanderbilt University Press, 1999, pp. 73–112.

Vasquez, Paul. 1993. *The War Puzzle*. Cambridge: Cambridge University Press.

Vogtmeier, Andreas. 1996. *Egon Bahr und die deutsche Frage: Zur Entwicklung der sozialdemokratis chen Ost- und Deutschlandpolitik vom Kriegsende bis zur Vereinigung*. Bonn: Dietz.

Voigt, Klaus. 1988. *Friedenssicherung und europäische Einigung: Ideen des deutschen Exils, 1939–1945*. Frankfurt am Main: Fischer.

Wæver, Ole. 1995. 'Identity, Integration and Security: Solving the Sovereignty Puzzle in EU Studies', *Journal of International Affairs* 48/2, pp. 389–431.

    1996. 'European Security Identities', *Journal of Common Market Studies* 34/1, pp. 103–32.

Walby, Sarah. 2003. 'The Myth of the Nation-state: Theorising Society and Polities in a Global Era', *Sociology* 37/3, pp. 529–46.

Wallace, William. 1999. 'Europe after the Cold War: Interstate Order or Post-sovereign Regional System?' in Michael Cox, Ken Booth and Tim Dunne, eds., *The Interregnum: Controversies in World Politics 1989–1999*. Cambridge: Cambridge University Press, pp. 201–24.

Walser, Martin. 1990 [1988]. *Über Deutschland reden*. Frankfurt am Main: Suhrkamp.

Walsh, Dick. 1986. *The Party: Inside Fianna Fáil*. Dublin: Gill and Macmillan.

Wandruszka, Adam and Urbanitsch, Peter. 1989. *Die Habsburgermonarchie im System der internationalen Beziehungen*. Vienna: Verlag der österreichischen Akademie der Wissenschaften.

Weill, Herman N., ed. 1972. *European Diplomatic History: Documents and Interpretations*. New York: Exposition Press.

Weiner, Myron. 1971. 'The Macedonian Syndrome: An Historical Model of International Relations and Political Development', *World Politics* 23/4, pp. 665–83.

Weinzierl, Erika and Skalnik, Kurt. 1983. *Österreich 1918–1938: Geschichte der Ersten Republik*. Graz: Styria.

Wells, Samuel F. and Smith, Paula Bailey. 1996. *New European Orders: 1919 and 1991*. Princeton: Woodrow Wilson Center Press.

Wendt, Alexander. 1992. 'Anarchy is What States Make of It: The Social Construction of Power Politics', *International Organization* 69/2, pp. 391–425.

    1995. 'Constructing International Politics', *International Security* 20/1, pp. 71–81.

    1999. *Social Theory of International Politics*. Cambridge: Cambridge University Press.

Wendt, Alexander and Friedhelm, Daniel. 1995. 'Hierarchy under Anarchy: Informal Empire and the East German State', *International Organization* 49/4, pp. 689–722.

Weyrauch, Wolfgang. 1963. 'Das Vaterland', in Wolfgang Weyrauch, *Die Spur*. Freiburg: Walter.

Whetten, Lawrence L. 1971. *Germany's Ostpolitik: Relations between the Federal Republic and the Warsaw Pact Countries*. Oxford: Oxford University Press.

Widstrand, Carl. ed. 1969. *African Boundary Problems*. Uppsala: Almquist & Wiksells.

Wiener, Antje. 2004. 'Contested Compliance: Interventions on the Normative Structure of World Politics', *European Journal of International Relations* 10/2, pp. 189–234.

Willard, Charles Arthur. 1989. *A Theory of Argumentation*. Tuscaloosa: University of Alabama Press.

Williams, Rhys and Kubal, Timothy. 1999. 'Movement Frames and the Cultural Environment: Resonance, Failure, and the Boundaries of the Legitimate', *Research in Social Movements, Conflicts and Change* 21, pp. 225–48.

Wolf, Martin. 2001. 'Will the Nation-state Survive Globalisation?' *Foreign Affairs* 80/1, pp. 178–90.

Wolff, Stefan. 2002. 'The Politics of Homeland: Irredentism and Reconciliation in the External Minority Policies of German Federal Governments and Expellee Organisations', *German Politics* 11/2, pp. 105–27.

Yeats, William Butler. 1990 [1929]. *A Vision*. London: Arena.

Zacher, Mark W. 2001. 'The Territorial Integrity Norm: International Boundaries and the Use of Force', *International Organization* 55/2, pp. 215–50.

Zammit, Ann. 1978. *The Belize Issue*. London: Latin American Bureau.

Zehfuss, Maja. 2002. *Constructivism in International Relations: The Politics of Reality*. Cambridge: Cambridge University Press.

Zentrum für Türkeistudien, ed. 1994. *Aktuelle Situation in den Turkrepubliken: Innenpolitik, Sicherheitspolitik, Wirtschaft, Umwelt, Bevölkerung*. Essen: Önel-Verlag.

Zürn, Michael, Walter, Gregor, Dreher, Sabine and Beisheim, Marianne. 2000. 'Postnationale Politik? Über den politischen Umgang mit den Denationalisierungs-Herausforderungen Internet, Klimawandel und Migration', *Zeitschrift für internationale Beziehungen* 7/2, pp. 297–329.

Government documents

Anglo-Irish Agreement. 1985. At http://cain.ulst.ac.uk/events/aia/aiadoc.htm

Auswärtiges Amt. 1972. *Die Auswärtige Politik der Bundesrepublik Deutschland*. Cologne: Verlag Wissenschaft und Politik.

Bunreacht na hÉireann. At http://www.maths.tcd.ie.local/JUNK/Constitution/Preamble.html

Christopher McGimpsey and Michael McGimpsey, Plaintiffs, versus Ireland, An Taoiseach and Others, Defendants [S.C. No. 314 of 1988], The Irish Reports, 1989.

Dáil Éireann Debates. At http://www.oireachtas-debates.gov.ie

Freie und Hansestadt Hamburg. 1960. *Richtlinien für die Erziehung und den Unterricht in den Klassen 7 bis 9 der Volksschule*. Bonn: Archiv der Kultusministerkonferenz.

Government of Ireland. 1985. *New Ireland Forum Report*. Dublin: Stationery Office.

1996. *Challenges and Opportunities Abroad: White Paper on Foreign Policy*. Dublin: Department of Foreign Affairs.

Kevin Boland, Plaintiff, v. An Taoiseach and Others, Defendants [1973 No. 3289 P.], The Irish Reports, 1974.

New Ireland Forum Report. 1984. Dublin: Stationery Office.

Niedersächsische Landesregierung. 1964. *Richtlinien für die Volksschulen des Landes Niedersachsen*. Bonn: Archiv der Kultusministerkonferenz.

Protokolle des deutschen Bundestages: Stenographische Berichte. Bonn, Bundesanzeiger Verlagsgesellschaft.

Sunningdale Agreement. 1973. At http://ireland.com/special/peace/troubles/sunning.htm

Newspapers

Die Welt. Newspaper Archives. Bayerische Staatsbibliothek, Munich.

Die Zeit. Newspaper Archives. Bayerische Staatsbibliothek, Munich.

Frankfurter Allgemeine Zeitung. Newspaper Archives. Bayerische Staats-
    bibliothek, Munich.
Irish Independent. Newspaper Archives. National Library of Ireland, Dublin.
Irish Press. Newspaper Archives. National Library of Ireland, Dublin.
Irish Times. Newspaper Archives. National Library of Ireland, Dublin.
Süddeutsche Zeitung. Newspaper Archives. Bayerische Staatsbibliothek,
    Munich.

Electronic data sets

CIA World Factbook. Accessed 2007. Online: www.odci.gov.cia/publications
Correlates of War Project. 2005. *State System Membership List, v2004.1.*
    Online: http://correlatesofwar.org
Ghosn, Faten and Bennett, Scott. 2003. *Codebook for the Dyadic Militarized
    Interstate Incident Data, Version 3.0.* Online: http://cow2.la.psu.edu
Ghosn, Faten, Palmer, Glenn and Bremer, Stuart. 2004. 'The MID3 Data Set,
    1993–2001: Procedures, Coding Rules, and Description', *Conflict
    Management and Peace Science* 21, pp. 133–54.
Institute for the Study of Conflict, Ideology, and Policy. Accessed 2002.
    Online: www.by.edu/iscip/database.html
Irish Marketing Surveys (IMS), in Irish Opinion Poll Archive. Accessed 2005.
    Online: www.tcd.ie/Political_Science/cgi/File.htm
Jones, Daniel M., Bremer, Stuart and Singer, J. David. 1996. 'Militarized
    Interstate Disputes, 1816–1992: Rationale, Coding Rules, and Empirical
    Patterns', *Conflict Management and Peace Science* 15/2, pp. 163–213.
Lexis/Nexis. Accessed 2002. Online: www.lexisnexis.com
Market Research Bureau of Ireland (MRBI), in Irish Opinion Poll Archive.
    Accessed 2005. Online: www.tcd.ie/Political_Science/cgi/File.htm
Open Society Institute. Accessed 2002. Online: www.eurasianet.org

Index